John Gorham Palfrey
and the
New England Conscience

John Gorham Palfrey
and the
New England Conscience

FRANK OTTO GATELL

HARVARD UNIVERSITY PRESS

Cambridge, Massachusetts

1963

Distributed in Great Britain by Oxford University Press, London

Publication of this work has been aided by a grant from
the Ford Foundation

Library of Congress Catalog Card Number 63-17200

Printed in the United States of America

FOR
KAY AND
SUSAN VALERIE

Preface

WHEN eighty-five-year-old John Gorham Palfrey died in his Cambridge study in 1881, the literary, social, and hereditary aristocracy of New England mourned the event. A man of moral substance, a man who represented, as much as any single individual could, the victory of New England Conscience, had closed a blameless and exemplary life. Palfrey's career was a monument to the Puritan ideal of rectitude, and his survivors could take pride in themselves as part of the same stock. Such was the feeling of the time, and Palfrey's family, his daughters in particular, had no desire to disturb the bland consensus of eulogy, however much it distorted the reality of their father's life.

Could he have registered an opinion, Palfrey would have admitted candidly that he had been anything but a success. He had desired too many unattainable things. But the New England of 1881 saw only the myth of the "Good Doctor Palfrey," forgetting the disappointments of previous decades, and declared with certainty that Palfrey's memory would live forever—if nothing else, his massive and definitive *History of New England* would never allow generations that followed to forget this kindly, honest, and representative New Englander.

But the eulogists proved poor prophets. Charles Sumner and Charles Francis Adams, Palfrey's political colleagues, acquired fame and lasting reputation; and unlike another friend, Richard Henry Dana, Jr., Palfrey did not write a classic of American literature to keep his name current. His colonial history was no best-seller, and sprightlier accounts came along in time to supersede it. Palfrey, the historian, became one of a type; historiographers labeled him a filiopietist, bent on justifying the ways of the Puritans, and grudgingly allotted him a page or less in their histories of historians.

Palfrey was not indifferent to the judgment of history. Yet few Americans have heard of him. This is not an indictment. I do not intend to pose as the angry biographer of a "neglected" figure, and imply that in telling my long-postponed story the whole picture of an age will emerge. Late in life Palfrey wrote a frank autobiography (still in manuscript), intended for posthumous publication, proof that he thought a critical account of his life worth telling. He was right, and the significance of his life may be examined on several levels. First, as a Bay State morality play (for such was the way he chose to live); or as a record of achievement within a limited but important sphere; and, finally, and equally significant, in terms of the man as part of an American ruling group buffeted by forces which, in Palfrey's case, were barely understood. Despite an early colonial lineage, he had to work hard to enter the New England aristocracy. His "arrival" coincided with the upheavals of economy and society whch severely challenged and often bested the elements of established power. Palfrey was a loser in this struggle, despite a rise to prominence, though never predominance, in religious, literary, and political circles. Thus his retreat to the New England past late in life.

In reconstructing this experience one goes beyond what Palfrey called his "personal tragi-comedy," into the larger problem of the traditionalist engulfed by the acceleration of history. Like his brilliant young friend, Henry Adams, Palfrey found himself and the times out of joint. *His* "Education" came half a century earlier.

*　　　*　　　*

Among the pleasant debts I have incurred while on Palfrey's trail, I owe a particular one to Dr. and Mrs. James B. Ayer, of Milton, Massachusetts. The late Mrs. Ayer (née

Hannah Palfrey), was my subject's granddaughter, and if all biographers are treated half as well as I have been by "the descendants," they will be fortunate indeed. Mrs. Ayer's encouragement and unflagging curiosity were of immense value to me. I cannot adequately express my thanks for her interest and support.

To John Gorham Palfrey (the fourth to bear that name), formerly of Columbia College, New York, and now a member of the Atomic Energy Commission, go my thanks for his cooperation and permission to examine and use the Palfrey Family Manuscripts at Harvard University.

I benefited greatly from criticism of my draft chapters by several able and very busy scholars who gave me much of their precious time: David Donald, The Johns Hopkins University; Louis Filler, Antioch College; Frank Freidel, Harvard University, under whose direction this study first took shape, and to whom I shall always be grateful for the kindness he has shown me from the day I presented myself in his seminar; Samuel Shapiro, Michigan State University, Oakland; and Conrad Wright, Harvard Divinity School.

My thanks go as well to Miss Marcia Buehler, University of Maryland; Lyman H. Butterfield, The Adams Papers; George M. Elsey, American National Red Cross; Tilden Edelstein, Simmons College; Al Fein, Long Island University; the Reverend Dan Huntington Fenn; Frederick Merk, Harvard University; Mrs. Grace Overmyer, New York, N.Y.; Miss Marcelle Schertz, Louisiana State University Library; Richard H. Sewell, Northern Illinois University; Mrs. Catherine Stepanek, Syracuse, N.Y.; D. H. Stiel, Franklin, La.; Mrs. Fay Tapper, Bronx, N.Y.; Roger E. Willson, Cambridge, Mass.; and Mrs. Margaret Palfrey Woodrow, Schenectady, N.Y.

Many library staff members aided me, particularly William Bond and Miss Carolyn Jakeman, of Harvard's Houghton Library; and at the Massachusetts Historical Society, Stephen

T. Riley, Director, Warren Weaver, and that most *simpática* of all librarians, Miss Winifred Collins.

Chapter VIII and parts of Chapter X have appeared in the *New England Quarterly*. Parts of Chapters X and XI have appeared in *The Historian*. My thanks to the editors for per-permission to reproduce the material, as well as to the Adams Manuscript Trust for permission to cite and quote from the Diary and Papers of Charles Francis Adams.

FRANK OTTO GATELL

University of Maryland
College Park, Maryland

Contents

Illustrations

following page 50

John Gorham Palfrey
and the
New England Conscience

I

The Child

THE dollar bill was secure in young Gorham Palfrey's pocket. It had remained there for the incredibly long span of several days—incredibly long for a boy of nine to deny himself pleasures that so much money could easily bring in the city of Boston. A few days before, he had said goodbye to his father, John Palfrey, who was returning to his business in New Orleans; and now in that summer of 1805 Gorham was alone again, his mother dead two years, his father sailing away an immense distance, never to return to his native Boston. The frayed bill was Gorham's only tangible connection with his surviving parent, and he knew that it would not stay in his pocket forever. As the boy trudged to the school where he studied too much and was loved too little, he found it hard to keep back the tears. But there was no restraining them that night when his head touched the pillow.[1]

*   *   *

"Mary is confined with a Son. He is a very weakly child. I suppose he will not live many days." In this apprehensive and unappreciative fashion Susan Palfrey Lee greeted the birth of a nephew, John Gorham Palfrey, on May 2, 1796.[2] Boston was his birthplace, and that city and nearby Cambridge remained his residence for nearly all the eighty-five years of life that lay before the frail infant.

Like so many New Englanders, Palfrey showed a great interest in his family's genealogy. He wrote proudly of the fact that he came from "three good Calvinistic stocks": early Plymouth, early Massachusetts Bay, and Huguenot.[3] But these

New World antecedents did not satisfy Palfrey's thirst for information about his ancestors. Whenever he traveled in England he sought, with limited success, to trace his family origins. On one occasion, his close friend Jared Sparks reported from London that Palfrey's notion that he was of Welsh descent was incorrect, and that Vitalis Palfrey, one of William the Conqueror's men and baron of Foxton, was his actual progenitor.[4] Palfrey, delighted with this genealogical gem, unabashedly recorded this "fact" when writing his autobiography.

Palfrey's early New England ancestors were respectable though undistinguished. Among those few Englishmen who settled at Salem prior to the arrival of Governor John Endicott in 1628 was one Peter Palfrey. He had come there two years before with the Dorchester Company settlers led by Roger Conant, and is mentioned as one of the "three prudent men" whose advice Conant sought.[5] After Peter Palfrey's death there is a gap in the family record until the appearance of two Williams, father and son, sailmakers and owners of brick houses in eighteenth-century Boston.[6] The younger William Palfrey died in 1766. His grandson, William Palfrey III, born in 1741, became the first Palfrey to attain any prominence.

William Palfrey, a Boston merchant, who sometimes sailed as supercargo on voyages to the West Indies or to the southern colonies, came of age during the struggle between the American colonies and the mother country. Young Palfrey was as ardently anti-British as anyone in Boston; his business connections with John Hancock doubtless helped arouse his enthusiasm for the American cause.[7] When the colonials formed the Sons of Liberty, Palfrey took the job of secretary. One of his tasks was to write letters of encouragement to John Wilkes in England, while that erratic champion of American liberty was confined in King's Bench Prison.[8] During the Revolutionary War Palfrey attained the rank of colonel. He was on General Washington's staff, and his chief later named him paymaster general of the Continental Army. For some years the Palfrey family played with the notion that the colonel was the scribe who wrote the final copy of the Declaration of Independence, but an examination of his papers revealed that he was in New York during the summer of 1776. Consequently the Palfreys deemed the penmanship of the Declaration not handsome enough.[9] No military smugness marred the colonel's character, recalled Harrison Gray Otis: "He wore a blue uniform, was called Col. Palfrey, and walked —not strutted— . . . his image is before me as that of a gentleman of the old school—polite, manly & elegant." Joseph Nourse added: "The public Records are evidence of the regularity of Col. W. Palfrey's Accounts." [10] Palfrey became consul general to France in 1780, but he never reached Europe; his Bordeaux-bound ship went down at sea without a trace.[11]

The death of William Palfrey left his widow in financial difficulty, and she had to take in boarders. All thoughts of sending her sons, William and John, to college evaporated when no word came about the missing ship. Of her three children, John Palfrey was the youngest. Like his father he became a merchant. In 1789 he sailed for Demerara (now British Guiana) where he remained for three years. In 1792 he took advantage of a three-month visit to Boston to propose marriage to Mary Sturgis Gorham, whom he had known since school days. The proposal accepted, Palfrey lost no time in returning to Demerara to seek the fortune needed for the proper establishment of a household. He purchased some slaves and was on the point of switching from commerce to planting when unstable conditions in the sugar market, the result of war in Europe, prompted him to abandon the South American coast. In August 1794 he returned to Boston, pleased to find that his sister Susan had married William Lee, a wealthy merchant.[12]

Despite his failure to make a fortune in Demerara, Palfrey decided to go ahead with his marriage. For three years his

fiancée Mary Gorham had been motherless, and thus already
mistress of a household. When her father died in 1795 there
was no reason to postpone matters further. The marriage took
place on May 3, two months after her father's death. John
Palfrey established hs bride in a house on Sea Street, Boston,
and rented a store on Long Wharf. Because his business failed
within a few months, Palfrey sailed early in 1796 as supercargo
on a vessel bound for South Carolina and the Baltic, leaving
behind his pregnant wife.[13]

"I had been born in his absence," John Gorham Palfrey
wrote many years later. Throughout his childhood he suffered
sharply from a feeling of paternal neglect, a feeling which
grew within him from his earliest recollections.[14] John Palfrey
did not see his son Gorham until the middle of October. His
stay in Boston was, as usual, short. Throughout the years of
Gorham's early childhood, his father alternated one year at
sea with one at home.[15] These long absences were naturally
disagreeable to Gorham's mother. Delighted by her baby's
prattle, she wrote of him as her only remaining comfort.
Gorham's exclusive claim on his mother's love came to an
end when he was two years old. In 1798 his brother Henry
was born, and the births of two more boys, Edward and
William, followed in successive years.[16] A measure of economic stability came to the household in the winter of 1798
when John Palfrey became an employee of Thomas H.
Perkins, one of Boston's richest merchants. There was no
fundamental change in family life, however, for the father's
next voyage came too soon afterward, and lasted over a year.

A reliable means of livelihood that did not demand long
voyages had thus far escaped John Palfrey. He had little to
show for his years of business activity. But if success proved
elusive, the responsibilities of a husband with a large family
were ever present. Once more he tried his luck on land. In
January 1801 the partnership of Bradford & Palfrey, ship
chandlers, was formed. The agreement with Gamaliel Brad-

ford was to run for three years.[17] Bradford was the more active partner, and during one of his trips he reported the difficulties of selling to the frugal merchants Down East:

> The first I applied to was a great merchant. When I told him we kept a *Ship Chandler's store* he did not know what I meant, & asked me what I sold. I explained myself by mentioning lanterns, compasses, speaking trumpets, &c. Why says he your Boston vessels I suppose have these things, but we do very well without—a lobster shell answers very well for lantern, and we can track a vessel to the W. I. by the shingles and chips that fall over, and as for the speaking trumpets . . . our vessells always avoid speaking with others lest they want any thing.[18]

Gorham's childhood, if lonelier than some, was unexceptional, at least while both his parents were alive. With countless other boys, he bore the nickname "little boy blue," and was bribed with sweets not to call his mother "ma." One of his earliest recollections was that of watching the funeral pageant for President Washington in December 1799. After his family moved to Middlecot (now Bowdoin) Street he was a constant admirer of the Parkman boys' proficiency at marbles, and Joseph Coolidge's house gave him his first ideas of magnificence. More important was his early love for books. Even before he could read, he loved to inspect the English volumes his father had bought at auction in Lisbon.[19] In 1801 Gorham began his first formal schooling. Madam English's Hawkins Street establishment imparted the rudiments of reading and spelling.

Two additions to the Palfrey household were more than balanced by the greatest loss of Gorham's life. First, his mother's half-sister, Charlotte Gorham, arrived. She was ten years older than Gorham and played the role of a loving big sister with enthusiasm.[20] Charlotte was the idol of all the children. She also was able to relieve the none-too-robust Mary Palfrey of many of her household duties. In October 1802 Mary gave birth to her fifth son, George. Her family had had more than its share of tuberculosis in its medical history, and the strain of this pregnancy proved too much for her. She never left her bed; by mid-December her friends had given her up, and John Palfrey had but the faintest hope for her recovery.[21] She lingered on until January 31, 1803.

The death of his mother was a traumatic experience for six-year-old Gorham. The day she died he and his brothers had been sent to a friend's house. The family servant came in and blurted out the news. Gorham sprang up from the dinner table screaming. That night he hurried home through the snow, and next day he was allowed to see the body. "Then came the funeral—all so new to me & so full of awe. The black pall impressed me as something sublimely sad." She had been the parent to whom he could turn for affection and understanding. Gorham had always sensed that his parents had not had a happy marriage. There was no doubt in his mind where the fault lay. John Palfrey as husband and father was short-tempered, brusque, and capricious. Gorham would ever strive to do his duty toward his father, but the love that gives meaning to the father-son relationship was lacking.[22] The scenes associated with Mary Palfrey's death never left Gorham's consciousness for long; he often returned to the room where she had died. Sixty-eight years later all the events came back to him as vividly as if they had just occurred.[23]

Frail as she was, Mary Palfrey had given the family whatever cohesiveness it possessed. After his wife's death, John Palfrey made no attempt to maintain his household. He sold the house and sent his four oldest boys to board with Miss Margaret Howe in Milton. Palfrey left for Baltimore, where he had in mind a new business connection with his wife's uncle, William Taylor, a Baltimore merchant of good repute and abundant capital.[24] The partnership with Bradford was not renewed at its expiration on December 31, 1803; the dissolution suggests that the Boston enterprise did not prosper.

When the Palfrey brothers arrived at Miss Howe's they were the only boarders. Much to their delight, however, the children of James Lovell arrived soon after. Miss Howe had kept school herself, but Gorham got his education from male teachers in the vicinity. He was fairly well adjusted to the new life, since Miss Howe was kindly and cared for him and his brothers well. In addition he became friendly with the family of a butcher who lived next door, and visited them frequently. Not so pleasant were the visits to Dr. Holbrook: "My father had set his heart on my having a good set of teeth, & as one way to this, he had given orders for some of my first set of teeth to be extracted before they loosened. Accordingly I used to visit the doctor on this cheerful errand." [25] The visits certainly did nothing to dispel the feelings of antagonism he felt toward his father, which mixed with and tempered the natural affectionate yearnings of a lonely boy. Gorham spent over a year at Miss Howe's with his brothers. His father advised: "As you are the oldest [how many times Gorham heard that phrase!], let me request of you to continue the same good Boy I have ever known & a fair example for your Brothers to copy by; tho' at the same time you must consider them fully your equal in everything except a trifling difference in age." [26]

Although Gorham's education was not being neglected, John Palfrey considered it inadequate for the future he had planned for his eldest son. Eventually he wanted Gorham to go to Baltimore, to William Taylor's counting-house. In the spring of 1804 he instructed one of his Boston friends, probably his ex-partner Bradford, to take Gorham to see William Payne, proprietor of the Berry Street Academy. A few months later, the boy entered Payne's school. Payne, a former Long Island schoolmaster, had come to Boston in 1799, and in a building near Faneuil Hall he set up his school. He was a strong Unitarian and an ardent follower of William Ellery Channing, whose parsonage was also on Berry Street. Undoubtedly the contacts between the teacher and the minister were frequent, and the proximity of so forceful a personality as Channing must have influenced Gorham's later religious views.[27]

Schoolmaster Payne was delighted with his new charge. A month after Gorham's arrival he wrote that the child was superior not only in "talents, which he possesses to an extraordinary degree, but, as much in respect of *habits* and *disposition*, which are of the most favourable & fortunate kind." The only cause for concern was the lad's delicate health. Payne promised to do what he could to rectify this,[28] but when someone suggested that Gorham spend the summer of 1805 in the country, the master remonstrated strongly. Ebenezer Gay, who succeeded Bradford in the role of unofficial guardian of the Palfrey children, vainly sought to free Gorham temporarily from the Berry Street regimen. Despite the fact that a doctor recommended the move, Payne would not hear of it. Gorham was never in better health, he contended, and, speaking more frankly, he would not "be reconciled to the Idea that the fruit of my Labours should pass to the Credit of others who have had no share in producing it." Gay decided not to press the issue, leaving it to be settled during John Palfrey's expected visit to Boston that summer.[29]

John Palfrey was pleased with his son's new location. Since June 1804 he had been in New Orleans, where he went into business with a young Virginian, R. D. Shepherd. The Baltimore connection was not completely severed, however, for Palfrey, Shepherd & Co. enjoyed the support of silent partner William Taylor.[30] Thinking of Gorham's chances for advancement with William Taylor in Baltimore, he counseled his son in Boston to pay close attention to his studies: "You have the good fortune to be under the direction of a Gentleman who is unrivald in his profession, of course a great deal will be expected from you." When his brother-in-law William Lee, then American consul at Bordeaux, proposed that he send his own brother in exchange for the services of Gorham, John Palfrey declined, explaining that in Baltimore, Taylor eagerly awaited the arrival of the young prodigy.[31]

Mr. Payne's academy may have been adequate for the development of Gorham's mind, but it was not the place for a love-starved boy. Mrs. Payne was an invalid, and the other members of the family gave Gorham little attention. His clothes became ragged, no one cared if he bathed or not, and on one occasion his hair became infested with lice. He slept in a small attic room with two other persons. There was little to do but study, and when he tried to do this in the comfort of the sitting room the Paynes banished him to the uninviting schoolroom. Gorham's uncle, William Palfrey, a clerk in the Boston Custom House, made it plain that he did not relish visits from his nephew, so Gorham's only escape was the monthly visit to his brothers in Milton. When his last "natural protector," Charlotte Gorham, left Boston for Baltimore in February 1806, Gorham felt completely abandoned, and it did little good to read of John Palfrey's regret over the necessity of living so far from his children.[32]

Gorham's one consolation was his friendship—adulation, rather—for John Howard Payne. Young Payne, later famous as the author of "Home Sweet Home," was being groomed by his father for a counting-house, but he had other ideas. Declamation was an important part of the Berry Street curriculum, with theatricals in the schoolroom, which had a small stage, curtain, and pit. John Howard excelled in these and made no secret of his desire to become an actor, while Gorham was perfectly content to play the second part to his hero and receive a small portion of the applause. He was heartbroken when Payne sent John Howard to New York to begin commercial training, and he gladly performed errands in Boston for his absent friend.[33]

With the departure of John Howard, life at the Paynes' lost what little zest it had to offer. There was a boy of Gorham's age in the house, Thatcher Payne, but he was stronger than Gorham and bullied him.[34] Fortunately, a new subject of instruction, French, occupied his time. As with all his studies, Gorham showed remarkable ability in grasping the language. He began to write letters in French to his father, who was obliged to aswer in English, assuring Gorham that his letters in the opinion of qualified judges in New Orleans were perfectly correct.[35] New responsibilities came to Gorham. John Palfrey sent him drafts in large amounts with instructions on how to distribute the money to his creditors. Gorham did as he was told. All seemed serene: "Gorham in especial manner is everything a fond parent could wish in a child."[36] No one seemed concerned about the wishes of the unhappy child.

In 1807 John Palfrey decided to marry again. The new Mrs. Palfrey, the former Hannah Cushing Phillips of Middletown, Connecticut, had come to New Orleans as her sister-in-law's traveling companion. Although the marriage took place in March, Gorham did not learn about it until July. There would be no lessening of fatherly affection, wrote John Palfrey, and he assured Gorham that their new mother frequently thought of him and his brothers.[37] Palfrey purchased a half interest in a sugar plantation about thirty miles from New Orleans, which became his residence. He managed the entire enterprise although the other half belonged to his brother-in-law, George Phillips. Palfrey's active role indicates he came into the agreement with little capital.

Everyone agreed that John Palfrey had made a judicious marital choice, and the family's hopes were high. Aunt Charlotte reminded Gorham that he might now look forward to a mother's love.[38] But the new stepmother never became a real person for the boys. Hannah Palfrey died in September 1808, eight days after the birth of a daughter who died almost immediately. Gorham never exchanged letters with his stepmother. His feminine guidance since 1803 had come from Charlotte Gorham exclusively. Now his stepmother's sister-in-law, a widow named Emily Phillips, took a strong interest in him. Her husband's early death in Louisiana left Emily Phillips childless and financially insecure. She returned to

Connecticut and visited Boston frequently. Perhaps she reached out to Gorham because she had also been an orphan; perhaps he was the child she had never borne.[39] The Phillips connection also brought him to the attention of the family of United States Supreme Court Justice William Cushing. These contacts helped to make life in Boston more pleasant for Gorham.[40]

John Palfrey soon found himself in difficulties which had unpleasant repercussions for Gorham. A month after his second wife's death Palfrey dissolved his business connection with Shepherd and the silent partner William Taylor. He seemed content with life on the plantation, but sudden failure shattered this rustic withdrawal. These difficulties produced a pile of unpaid bills at Payne's Academy. William Payne was understanding but firm. During one of Charlotte Gorham's visits to Boston, he suggested that Gorham take on the duties of assistant in the school in return for continued tutoring, board, lodging, and clothing. Since prospects of a prompt remittance from New Orleans were slim, she accepted for the boy. Misfortunes crowded in on top of each other. Reports of John Palfrey's bad luck and ill-health were matched by the sad condition of William Payne and his school. The only cause for jubilation was the return from New York of John Howard Payne. Young Payne worked for a Boston newspaper in an effort to shore up his family's crumbling finances. At night Payne and Palfrey avidly practiced their elocution lessons.[41]

At this juncture, when John Palfrey seemed to have renounced all responsibility for his children, it was fortunate indeed for Gorham that he had acquired a friend in Mrs. Phillips. Although she lived in Connecticut, she often visited Boston, and Gorham had made a favorable impression on her. When it became obvious that William Payne could not maintain his school, she assumed the responsibility of guiding Gorham's future.[42] There was some talk of Gorham's accompanying the Paynes to New York, where the schoolmaster planned to open another, larger academy. Mrs. Phillips would not hear of it. Her principal objection was to John Howard Payne's passion for the theater: "For Gorham to . . . live in the same house with a *stage player* would be the height of impropriety." She enlisted the aid of a friend, Boston merchant Mark Pickard, and had Gorham taken from the Payne household. Mrs. Phillips' plans for the boy did not include the life of a counting-house clerk. She tried to convince John Palfrey that Gorham should have a college education: "Is it probable that when he is fitted for college with so little expense to you—you will be able to carry him through? He has powerful friends here, he is so much beloved by all who know him, that every exertion will be made for him." [43] Among the "powerful friends" referred to by Mrs. Phillips were William Ellery Channing, Joseph S. Buckminster, minister of the influential Brattle Street Church, and William Sullivan, a prominent banker. Channing agreed to devote an hour each afternoon to preparing Gorham for Exeter Academy, and Buckminster, whose father was an Exeter trustee, took care of arrangements at the school. Buckminster found that Exeter would admit Gorham free of tuition and that board would amount to two dollars per week. Naturally it would be best for his father to provide this amount, but in any case many persons had evinced an interest in the boy and a willingness to assume whatever expenses arose. [44]

William Payne had little objection now to severing his connection with the Palfreys. The balance of Gorham's account up to October 1808, when he became an assistant, was $260. [45] And Gorham's were not the only bills that remained unpaid. In Milton, the long-suffering Miss Howe claimed that her patience was exhausted. For six months she had received no money and was about to withdraw the Palfrey brothers from Milton Academy. Mrs. Phillips' friend, Pickard, feared that they would be dumped at his doorstep, and he persuaded Gorham to ride out to Milton to plead with Miss Howe. She agreed to a stay of three months after she was promised a dollar a week more for her forbearance.

Aunt Charlotte had no faith in John Palfrey as a provider, despite his promise to Gorham that "every exertion in my power shall be made for your collegiate Education." She urged Gorham to give up all plans for college and enter business. Even if his father gave some assistance, his education would only cause dissension in the family. All his brothers would expect the same treatment, and this was out of the question. But Mrs. Phillips and her Boston friends had already decided.[46]

Gorham must have been elated by this change in his prospects. The counting-house held no attractions for him. He was now the object of attentions only dreamed of in the Berry Street Academy years. In a few months he would be pursuing his career in the only world that had ever given him security, the world of books and learning. In the meantime he must prepare for the Exeter adventure. Instruction in Latin and Greek began immediately at Channing's home.[47]

II 〜

The Student

O N THE evening of September 6, 1809, Gorham Palfrey assembled his belongings and went to the home
of Thomas H. Perkins to spend the night. Perkins' son was
to return to Exeter the next morning and to see that Master
Palfrey got to the academy. Early the next day the boys, and
several other returning Exeter students, crowded into a coach.
The trip was not a pleasant one for Palfrey; the Newburyport
Turnpike made no concessions to geography. Each new hill
seemed steeper than the last, and Gorham was constantly
jostled by his rowdy and drunken companions.

It was a tired and dusty scholar who presented himself to
the principal, Dr. Benjamin Abbot, for an interview that
evening. After a brief and instructive visit with Dr. Abbot,
Gorham went to Captain Halliburton's boarding-house where
the charity scholars lived. He was one of eight scholars whose
board was paid for by the academy. In 1789, John Phillips,
Exeter's founder, had set up a fund for the aid of indigent
students of superior scholastic abilities.[1] Palfrey never got
over the humiliation of having the word "charity" put after
his name in the official enrollment book. It seemed gratuitous
cruelty to thus label the boys: "It was not only humiliating
and mortifying, but seriously & permanently injurious." [2]

As a charity scholar, Gorham's accommodations were aus-
tere. Halliburton was a retired sea captain who had, according
to student gossip, married an Exeter widow for her money.
He made no attempt to coddle his charges, and was generally
disliked, though Palfrey had to admit he was a "rough but
intelligent" freethinker. The amount of money Halliburton

received from the academy for the care of charity scholars was not great; consequently the boys were left to fend pretty much for themselves. The captain gave the phrase "bare minimum" its precise meaning. The eight boys slept four to a room, with only half as many beds as there were occupants.[3]

One of Palfrey's fellow charity scholars at Halliburton's was to become a life-long friend. The morning after his arrival Gorham met Jared Sparks, a penniless Connecticut youth. Sparks had been unable to afford a coach ride to the academy, and had been walking for four days. Sparks later recalled in detail the outfit Palfrey was wearing that morning; the condition of Sparks's clothes after so many days on the road must have made Palfrey's look like those of a dandy.[4] Palfrey immediately sought out Sparks's friendship. The latter was twenty years old at the time—seven years older than Palfrey— and the relationship established was not one of complete equality, though Sparks was kind to this desperately lonely child. Intellectually, however, Palfrey could hold his own with his new friend, and Sparks gratefully accepted French lessons from him.[5]

When John Gorham Palfrey arrived, Phillips Exeter Academy, though founded but a quarter-century before, already bore the indelible stamp of Dr. Benjamin Abbot. A Harvard honor graduate of 1788, Abbot had become preceptor at Exeter in that same year, and two years later he became the school's principal, a position he held for nearly half a century.[6] Abbot was a strict disciplinarian. Most of the students feared him; all respected him. When a boy went to Dr. Abbot's library for discipline, his schoolmates trembled for their chum. Abbot did not abuse the rod, however; such was his power over the boys that a reprimand of the order to sweep out the recitation room was usually sufficient. Abbot, Palfrey recalled, "would somehow find out almost everything that was going on." On one occasion Gorham received the dread command to await the doctor in the library, but after some anxious minutes the real offender was caught and Gorham, who was as well-behaved as he was studious, fled happily from the room.[7]

Preparation for college was the prime function of the academy. The work day began every morning at half past seven with prayers in Dr. Abbot's room. Study until noon, then three hours for dinner and recreation, and more study from three to six in the afternoon. Students were expected to be in their boarding-houses by seven and in bed by nine o'clock. Palfrey studied a curriculum heavily weighted with Latin and Greek. He read all the poems of Virgil, and mastered liberal amounts of Sallust, Livy, Ovid, and Terence. Greek selections were brought together in two well-known collections: the *Graeca Minora* and the *Graeca Majora*. One of Palfrey's first Exeter bills covers the purchase of copies of the *Graeca Minora* and Cicero's orations.[8]

Palfrey found that the training he received at Payne's enabled him to do well at Exeter, and he made rapid progress in his studies. On one occasion when he wrote to his benefactor, Pickard, and made two requests for money for books and for a trip to Boston, he had the good sense to sandwich a favorable scholarship report in between. He was sorry to have appeared neglectful of his Boston friends, but:

> When I have in *propia persona* informed you how my time has been appropriated, I trust you will acknowledge [your complaints] are ungrounded. Suffice it at present to say that during this term, I have been put forward two classes in Latin and one in Greek—among scholars who have been studying here three years or more.[9]

A few days after reaching Exeter, Palfrey had learned that his father, unpredictable as ever, had sent a remittance to Milton that more than covered all of Miss Howe's outstanding bills. He had taken little notice of Pickard's previous letters about Gorham's departure for Exeter, but did muse about the possibility of bringing his younger sons to Louisiana. There was some talk of trying to get William into Exeter

Academy, but that came to nothing.[10] John Palfrey's indifference was offset by Emily Phillips' regular admonitions: "You have now attained the heights of your wishes," she pompously informed her young friend. "Improve then each fleeting moment, and in the sweet season of youth lay up a store of useful knowledge."[11] As they came in Mrs. Phillips relayed good scholastic reports to John Palfrey. She reminded him of the fact that Gorham's stay at Exeter was costing him practically nothing, and that this schooling should be a prelude to college training.[12]

Mrs. Phillips failed to interest John Palfrey in the blessings of higher education. Early in 1810 Palfrey obtained a favorable court decree on a mortgage claim, and although he was not entirely happy with the sum realized from the later sale of his plantation, he was at least solvent. Free of all debt, and with $4,500 at his disposal, Palfrey set about to find another plantation. Failure as a merchant had turned John Palfrey into a physiocrat; he urged Gorham to join him in his agricultural life, "the most rational & happy in the world," whenever he felt so inclined.[13] The plantation that John Palfrey purchased in 1810 was at Attakapas, near St. Martinville, Louisiana. It was nearly a wilderness. He renamed it "Forlorn Hope," despite his physiocratic happiness, and it remained his home for the rest of his life.[14]

Ironically, John Palfrey's move into the interior brought closer ties with most of his children. In August 1810 Pickard suggested that the interest of all parties would be served if Henry and Edward joined their father. Palfrey needed help on his plantation, and the boys had received as much education as they required: "What they are deficient in you can supply. . . . They are stout healthy Boys & may be of much service to you & lessen the expense here. . . . Fortunes are more rapidly made in the South than North."[15] The boys sailed from Boston on November 15. Before they left, Henry wrote a touching letter to Gorham in which he hoped that his older

and more-favored brother might "go through College and be
a worthy member of society." Before he had been in New
Orleans a few weeks, Henry showed his New England up-
bringing by voicing disapproval of the easy-going Creoles and
their Sabbath-breaking society.[16] Gorham might have gone
with his brothers if John Palfrey's wishes had been put into
effect. The father requested that Gorham be sent to him, but
the reaction of those in Boston interested in the boy's education quickly changed his mind. For Gorham, this reversal was
"a very happy circumstance." [17]

With John Palfrey established at Attakapas, Pickard made
a direct request that Palfrey support his son through college.
The estimates made of the expense of Gorham's Harvard
education were based on the assumption that he would enter
the sophomore class directly from Exeter. Yearly expenses for
tuition, board, and clothing were about $200. Financial aid
("on the foundation," as Pickard put it), meant a saving of
$70 a year. After the Exeter experience, Gorham made it clear
that he preferred to be on the same footing with the other
paying scholars. "You can do nothing better with him,"
Pickard told Palfrey, "he is too slender to Bustle for a living
& as a scholar he will be a honour to you." Gorham added his
own plea for support, but his figures—expenses of $120, finan-
cial aid of $80—were considerably lower than Pickard's. John
Palfrey's answer was negative. He claimed that relative poverty made such aid impossible, and as for Gorham's health,
what better way to restore it than to send him to the salubrious
climate of Louisiana? Professional careers were not for men of
delicate constitution; the best he would promise, should it be
decided that Gorham continue, was to help "at a future
time." [18]

Whether or not young Palfrey's friends expected this refusal, they lost no time in enlisting the aid of those interested
in his future. Pickard went to see Channing, who informed
him that there was nothing to fear. He had already made

inquiries and received firm promises that Gorham would be supported through Harvard. In addition, Buckminster thought a three-year college program might prove too much for Palfrey's health, and he recommended to Abbot that the boy enter with the freshman class. Mrs. Phillips was the fundraiser in this case. She obtained pledges of $450 which would cover expenses if Gorham were awarded "what is termed a *waitership*, but which is only nominally such, and is a situation much sought after by those who are not in the most eligible circumstances. . . . Mr. Buckminster & Mr. Channing have conversed with the President & engaged a place for him." [19]

What of Palfrey the student, the lad Charles Folsom called "the little boy with the green coat," in his second and final year at Exeter? Mrs. Phillips was certainly exaggerating when she informed John Palfrey that Gorham was running away with all the prizes, although he did win the Latin versifying and penmanship awards in both years.[20] Gorham was a heartless taskmaster if he accomplished all that he included in his lists of things to be done. "It is my intention if practicable during the ensuing week, besides getting my regular lessons, to . . ."; here followed a long list of books to be read, letters to be written, and selections to be copied.

One of Gorham's chief delights was to receive mail from his brothers in New Orleans. In the spring of 1811, Henry wrote that he was preparing to enter a counting-house, after a short spell in a French boarding-school, and that Edward was to accompany his father to the plantation. Edward reported some grisly details about the punishment meted out after a slave rebellion. After the offending Negroes were hanged, their heads were impaled on sticks and exhibited. This was the first mention of Negro slavery in the brothers' corespondence; later there would be occasion for many more references.[21] Later that summer, Gorham heard of his father's purchase of twenty-one slaves and of his plans to expand his landholdings. But for him there were only second-hand coats sent by Pickard, who wrote that John Palfrey had not yet fulfilled his promise of sending money for Gorham's support. Gorham knew he was alone.[22]

In August, Exeter Academy celebrated its week of exhibitions. Principal Abbot took charge of every detail, for it was customary that all trustees be present. In view of his high scholastic standing, Palfrey received one of the best parts, an oration from Sallust. Buckminster was in the audience, and when the ceremonies ended, the young orator had the honor of riding to Boston in Buckminster's chaise. Next day he went to Cambridge for his college examinations. One of Palfrey's classmates was so sure that Palfrey would be admitted to Harvard that he swore to pay him $100 should he fail, and one cent if he succeeded. When made, the payment was for the smaller amount.[23]

"Gorham has entered college with uncommon applause," gushed Mrs. Phillips, "my heart throbs with pride & pleasure at the brilliant entree he has made." Palfrey obtained the highest grades in the entrance examination, and to cap his triumph, John Lowell, "an enthusiastic admirer of genius," invited him to spend a week at his country house.[24] Palfrey realized that whatever prestige and social standing he acquired would come from his outstanding scholarship, a realization which spurred him on throughout his Harvard days.

The Harvard College of Palfrey's student years was to a great extent the preserve of one man. This was not a new situation to Palfrey: at Exeter the leading spirit had been Benjamin Abbot; at Harvard it was John Thornton Kirkland. In office but one year, Kirkland had already taken complete charge of the institution. His eighteen-year tenure became Harvard's most remarkable presidency until the advent of Charles W. Eliot later in the century.

The new president was a Federalist and a Unitarian, and Harvard followed him in both religion and politics. During his ministry at Boston's South Church he delivered many "logical, intelligent, and sugar-coated" sermons which, as Professor Morison aptly puts it, "led the parish into Unitarianism before they realized whither they were bound." [25] And if Kirkland had little trouble in winning over a congregation, is it any wonder that Gorham Palfrey, after his exposure to such strong Unitarian minds as Payne's, Channing's, and Abbot's, emerged from Harvard shorn of the asperities of Calvinism, a believer in liberal theology? But such sectarian problems lay ahead; first came years of scholastic work.

Palfrey's joy at his successful college entrance was diminished by a rebuff suffered at the hands of his friend Sparks. Palfrey had set his heart on rooming with Sparks, but the latter declined. He told Palfrey that he was too inclined toward sociability, and that there would be little or no studying done in their room. Instead Sparks chose John B. Davis, who was even younger than Palfrey. "I took it something as a rejected suitor might have done. I had fed my imagination with the thought of the steady & friendly diligence with which we should pursue our studies together." [26] Even if Sparks had agreed to room with Palfrey, the two would have seen relatively little of each other because Sparks had to leave the college frequently to augment his scholarship income. He taught school that first winter, and in the spring of 1812 went to Maryland as a tutor.

Palfrey, always conscious of the debt he owed his benefactors, was determined to prove that their confidence had not been misplaced. Not mere gratitude, but a strong feeling of self-interest, the best possible guarantee of success, possessed him: "My ambition was high. Independently of the consideration that success in scholarship was my only chance for success in life, I intensely coveted a literary reputation & literary attainments for their own sake." The college had granted him $90 a year, and his friends, some of them anonymous, established a reserve fund for his needs. [27] Not knowing who his benefactors were made Gorham impatient. While at

Exeter he had vainly implored Emily Phillips to supply him with their names, and at Harvard he complained that his only unhappiness was his ignorance in this respect. Gorham was, of course, grateful for the aid given him, but his over-long explanation of his attitude toward the college grant shows that he was not comfortable in the role of deserving but needy scholar:

> My situation is so far from being unpleasant that while others, who do not receive so much, have troublesome and . . . humiliating tasks to perform, it is not even a public thing that I receive this; not that I ever attempted to conceal it; by no means, for I do not think it disgraceful . . . ; all my intimate friends here know it, but it is no more my business to trumpet it abroad, than it is to keep it secret when asked the question.

As far as Harvard College was concerned, Gorham Palfrey was but one of many boys who needed help, and President Kirkland, who felt the problem very keenly, devised several ways to help those students, including odd jobs on the campus and extra time off in winter for schoolteaching.[28]

Palfrey came to regard his studies as enemies to be mastered. When his logic teacher demanded solid memorization, and Palfrey, unprepared, fell behind in rank, he got up an hour earlier each morning and forced whole pages into his brain. With the air of a martyr he observed that all the outstanding Harvard scholars of previous years had had their health impaired.[29] In his sophomore year he had the temerity to enter the Bowdoin Prize competition with an essay "On the Moral Uses of History," and won a second prize. This achievement awed his classmates, and he began to be mentioned as a candidate for first scholar.[30]

Palfrey described his room as the "smallest and worst in college," with the walls a mass of nails for hanging up clothing. His roommate was not a congenial companion, and when Sparks departed for Maryland, Palfrey moved into Hollis Hall with young Davis.[31] Upperclassman Charles Folsom suggested

the arrangement. The older Folsom noted Palfrey's studious-
ness approvingly and charged Palfrey repeatedly to consider
how responsible he was "for John [Davis]'s character. I believe they will do very well together." This prediction was
borne out by the performances of the two scholars. They had
persevered in their studies, especially mathematics, and were
"almost thro' with Surds." But success had made them reluctant to accept Folsom's control.[32] Palfrey was very much the
sophomore by then. He complained of the insufferable inso-
lence of the freshmen who presumed to mix with their betters
outside chapel. Even those above him were not spared. When
Harvard's brightest star, Edward Everett, read a poem before
Phi Beta Kappa, Palfrey informed Sparks that it was more
calculated to tickle the ears of the audience than to stand the
criticism of the "knowing ones." [33]

Palfrey's correspondence with Sparks, who was tutoring
at Havre de Grace, near Baltimore, was a sporadic affair. The
letters were full of the usual college gossip (Palfrey) and
pompous comments on literature (Sparks). Two events had
occurred, claimed Palfrey, which suppressed his never-too-
strong inclinations to write. These were the deaths of Joseph
S. Buckminster and Mrs. Pickard, who had opened her home
to him and whom he had loved. Buckminster's death, at the
age of twenty-eight, in addition to being a loss to Palfrey,
deprived the Unitarian movement of a leader who might
have surpassed even Channing in influence had he lived.[34]

From the beginning of Palfrey's school days Mrs. Phillips
had been a regular correspondent. She confined herself, for
the most part, to moral homilies and practical advice. In
December 1811, however, she penned the first of a long
series of warnings on the dangers of Unitarianism, or as she
insisted on calling it, Socinianism: "I pray to God that you
may not [be contaminated]—always bear in mind that you
belong to the Episcopal Church," though there is no evidence
of Gorham's membership in that church. A note of despera-

tion fills these appeals for orthodoxy. Surely the woman knew that an education at Abbot's Exeter and Kirkland's Harvard was not the ideal road to episcopacy. Buckminster and Channing were Palfrey's idols, and the testy epistles from Connecticut were less than useless.[35] In replying Gorham made no mention of these strictures. Though the Unitarian "heresy" was taking hold of him, he thought it wiser to avoid an argument at this stage.

Gorham had not heard from his father for nearly two years. "If you have any regard for your son," the boy implored, "pray write me the very day you receive this letter. If only to say 'I am well & love you as dearly as ever' these few words would give me more joy, than you have any conception of." [36] John Palfrey, as usual, was in trouble financially. He no longer felt able to keep his two youngest sons in Boston. Credit was not available, and he resorted to selling his pistols and candlesticks.[37] He had become more and more of a recluse at his Attakapas plantation. Gorham's plea for news went unheeded. Despite John Palfrey's refusal in December 1810 to aid his son's education, he had later promised $500. But characteristically he did not keep the promise, and Pickard found he had advanced over $300 with little prospect of repayment.[38]

Throughout his junior and senior years at Harvard, Palfrey maintained his fine academic record. Although formal grades were not given then, his high standing is borne out by the fact that he was always assigned a prominent part in college exhibitions. This was no small matter to the students. The assignment of parts was a prime object of speculation in the schoolboy correspondence of the day.[39] Palfrey's friends feared his work schedule would ruin his health, and his brother in New Orleans heard that he was operating on only two hours of sleep a day.[40] Although Palfrey was too modest to brag about his achievements, they were, of course, no secret to the college administration, which had recognized his merits in a very concrete manner—the continution of his financial aid.[41] The aroused members of his class put Palfrey's literary talents to use in drafting a protest to the college authorities on a perennial subject. An increase in board fees had done nothing to improve conditions in the dining halls:

The vessels in which our food has been served up (particularly the mugs in which our drink has been set before us) have frequently been filthy and offensive. Our sugar has often been shamefully dirty. In the more substantial part of our food we have still more serious grounds of complaint. Besides the attempt which has lately been made to limit the small variety of its choice which we have heretofore enjoyed, a great portion of our puddings are composed of the most coarse and unpalatable materials, & our meals, besides the careless & often uncleanly manner in which it [sic] has been prepared, has frequently been notoriously nauseous, putrid & unwholesome. . . .[42]

College life, then as now, was not all study. John Gorham Palfrey at the age of seventy might have believed that the Harvard clubs were of no use to him,[43] but as a student Palfrey acted quite differently. At Harvard in that age only those boys "invincibly unsocial in temperament and tastes" remained unclubbed, and financial and social position were not all-important.[44] The two most important organizations were Porcellian and Phi Beta Kappa, with Hasty Pudding a stepping-stone to the latter. Although Palfrey joined several of the clubs, his ultimate aim was election to Phi Beta Kappa. At the end of his junior year it seemed that he would achieve his goal, but he was caught in the toils of student politics. Palfrey was a close friend of Virginian Theodorick T. Randolph, nephew of the brilliant and eccentric John Randolph of Roanoke. Like his uncle, young Randolph was skilled in the art of making enemies, a good many of whom were in the senior class. Palfrey's friendship with Randolph was well known. At the time of the Phi Beta Kappa elections the seniors who controlled the admission of new members elected only three juniors, one of whom was Sparks.[45] Palfrey wrote bravely to the absent Sparks about the despicable seniors:

"Their praise is censure, & their censure praise." But he coveted the election desperately, and his later attempt at matter-of-factness ("the Phi Beta have elected no more members") fooled no one, least of all himself.[46] Classmates who thought his election a certainty reacted with disgust to this display of spitefulness. Charles Bruce informed Sparks:

> I rely with perfect confidence upon you, & [Convers] Francis to defeat the unprovoked attempt to rob our friend of his reputation, & rights. I never felt more indignant than when I passed Palfrey in the procession ØBK day. I was conscious that he had as perfect a claim as I or any one else to share in the privileges of the occasion, & that nothing but envy, & caprice excluded him. He had no reason to blush, however, except for the degeneracy of the club, or rather, for those who managed its concerns.[47]

It was more than a disappointment for Palfrey; it was a tragedy. He had staked everything on his studies, or as he called it, his "literary reputation," as the pathway to success. The snub shattered what little self-confidence he had and made him prey to all manner of gloomy predictions about his future. So insulted was he, that when offered membership in the society a year later, he refused it.[48]

Palfrey's college years coincided with the second war with England. In religion Harvard may have been liberal and Unitarian, but in politics it was conservative and Federalist. The college administration shared the general New England feeling toward the War of 1812, but the Harvard boys showed more patriotism than their mentors. They organized a military corps, and never seemed to tire of drills and parades—activities as much attributable to youthful spirits as to martial ardor. There is no indication that Gorham joined in these excursions. On the contrary, one of his junior dissertations was an attack on war as a vestige of barbarism. He attended the religious festival in Boston in June 1814, held to celebrate the victory of the Allies over Napoleon, where Channing delivered "the most eloquent sermon that ever was read from a pulpit." [49] Yet he could not conceal his pride when the *Constitution* was victorious over H.M.S. *Java*. In the summer of 1814 there was considerable apprehension over the possibility of an attack on Boston, and one of the city's banks prudently moved its specie to Worcester.[50]

The War of 1812 meant more to Palfrey than to most New Englanders because of his family in Louisiana. With the conflict depressing the foreign cotton market, John Palfrey's customary bad situation had grown worse, and he attempted to alleviate it by manufacturing salt. "There is news to-day of the capture of N. Orleans," wrote Gorham early in 1815, "but it is not much relied upon. I have two brothers there, so I am extremely anxious." [51] Sixteen-year-old Henry Palfrey was a member of the New Orleans militia and fought in several skirmishes as well as in the Battle of New Orleans itself. Father and son might have fought there if John Palfrey, bent on joining a volunteer company, had reached the city in time.[52] But all the glory went to young Henry, who wrote proudly of his participation in four pitched battles, and manfully of the horrors he had seen. Shortly after the signing of the Treaty of Ghent, William and George left Boston to join their father and Edward at the Attakapas plantation. Henry remained in New Orleans where he proved himself extremely capable in the business world.[53]

In the winter of his senior year Gorham put some of the knowledge he had acquired to profitable use. For three months he tutored the five children of Cornelius Coolidge of Roxbury. His pay was ample, thirty dollars a month and board, and the young pedagogue luxuriated in two rooms of his own at a nearby farmhouse.[54] He spent his evenings among Boston society as a "recognized member of the young *beau monde*." The young ladies of Boston did not escape Palfrey's admiring glances. The only drawback involved was the necessity of taking a readmission examination when he returned to college, but the income and pleasures the interlude afforded made this more than bearable.[55]

Despite his employment as a teacher, financial worries were

always present. Palfrey received some anonymous contributions, but they were not nearly enough to cover outstanding debts. The largest amount owed was $320 to Henry Rice, his father's cousin. Rice, a Boston storekeeper, had loaned the money in 1813, and he agreed then that payment might be deferred until six months after Palfrey's graduation.[56] In mid-June 1815 Gorham took charge of an elementary school in Cambridge for several weeks. He taught eight hours a day, but still managed to keep up with his college work.[57]

Commencement Day fell on August 30. With all due pomp and ceremony Harvard observed the greatest day in its scholastic calendar. The Boston Hussars, in full dress uniform, escorted the day's distinguished guests across the Charles, and one Boston newspaper reported:

> The audience was unusually numerous and respectable. The extensive galleries were literally filled with the beauty, elegance, taste and fashion of the capital and state; and there appeared to be a general assembly of the literati of New England. . . . The entertainments were numerous and splendid.

Palfrey contributed number eighteen, an oration in English entitled: "On republican institutions, as affecting private character." [58] "It gives me great pleasure to say he is all a father could wish," wrote Henry Rice. "He leaves Colledge with the highest honours the Govournment can bestow." [59] As to the future, Palfrey was not certain of what course to pursue, but he told inquirers that his "talents and inclination" made him favor theology.

III ✒

Liberal Theology

ALL signs pointed to the ministry: "The Church was then the great opening for aspiring young men," recalled the son of a Unitarian minister of that era. "Theology was the most tempting study. The ministry was the chosen profession. . . . Advancement was through this calling. Literature clustered about it. The community honored it." [1] Palfrey first began to think of a ministerial career in November 1814. He told Pickard of his intention, and was pleased when his unofficial guardian supported the idea. But Palfrey was not yet certain that he had chosen rightly. When Pickard prodded him a few days after Commencement, he replied that there were two things troubling him: he felt he might lack the necessary piety, and as a minister his talents would go relatively unrewarded financially. [2]

Palfrey's doubts found echoes in the remarks of his friends. Sparks, then teaching at a country school, heard of Palfrey's intentions, and wrote a blistering letter which his friend did not answer for two months. Sparks reminded Palfrey of the unenthusiastic statements he had made about the ministry while at college, and warned him not to be swayed by thoughts of a fashionable Boston parish. Only religious ardor and pious devotion to his calling could be the bases for such a step. The Harvard seniors retailed rumors that Palfrey coveted the vacant pulpit of Boston's Brattle Street Church,[3] and was rushing headlong into the ministry to block off potential rivals. Sparks concluded:

If the *prospect* of a parish in Boston has any more influence in deciding you, than a *positive* assurance that you must, if you become a divine, spend your life in a country parish at 600 a year, I beseech you not to think of it.[4]

Despite these doubts, Palfrey went ahead. A week after Commencement he conferred with Channing, seeking specific information about the requirements necessary for the ministry. Channing, whom he considered the "best of all men qualified to judge," outlined qualifications he thought he possessed; Palfrey could then proceed confidently. The only other person he saw was John Lowell, one of his benefactors. Palfrey consulted only these two because he was aware that such decisions were best made by the individual himself, and that too much advice on the matter would be a hindrance. Shortly thereafter, Palfrey made his decision in favor of the ministry.[5] This met with general approval. Henry Rice, a prominent Brattle Street member, urged him to stop teaching at his Cambridge school and begin his new studies at once.[6]

In a manner which revealed a talent for diplomacy, Palfrey informed those persons closest to him of his plans. Though he observed the formality of appearing to ask his father's consent, there was no doubt that he was not seeking the elder Palfrey's advice. Another sort of letter went to Connecticut, addressed to Mrs. Phillips, the staunch Episcopalian. Palfrey admitted that a "heretical spirit" prevailed at Harvard, but he promised to keep his mind open. Palfrey was not being completely candid. Not every Harvard student became a Unitarian, but the fact remains that the Palfrey of 1815 was much more of a "heretic" than he would admit to the orthodox Mrs. Phillips. In his long-delayed reply to Sparks, Palfrey explained that when he learned that his motives were being questioned by people of influence, he was contemptuous. But if he wanted to be respected in his profession, he had to protect his reputation. Palfrey denied that he had ever seriously considered any other career, and as for the Brattle Church, he knew only two pewholders there. He reaffirmed his plan to give up his teaching, and he made his theological intentions visible when he had his blue coat dyed black.[7]

With the end of the year came peace, and Sparks playfully proposed a trip to Germany: "Nobody ought to preach in these enlightened days till he has slept over a course of musty lectures at Göttingen." [8] However attractive a trip to Europe seemed to them, neither Sparks nor Palfrey could afford it. Palfrey decided to confine his traveling to his own country. Before plunging into his studies he would see the South his father and brothers had been praising for so long. Also, Henry Rice, who would pay part of the expenses of the trip, had asked to have George Palfrey sent to him to work in his Boston store, and Gorham was to bring his younger brother back with him. Besides, thought Palfrey, the trip would show that he was not entering the ministry with indecent haste.[9]

* * *

On February 2, 1816, the brig *Mexican* set sail from Boston's India Wharf, bound for New Orleans. While at sea Palfrey made his pulpit debut. He delivered a sermon and conducted a service on the quarter deck for the crew whom he found "sincere & apparently interested." The ship reached the mouth of the Mississippi at the end of February. After viewing the plantations on the banks of the river, Palfrey observed that they all exhibited the "miserable appearance of sloth peculiar . . . to a slave-trading country." There was as yet no moral indictment of slavery in Palfrey's mind.[10]

The visitor's initial reaction to New Orleans was a mixture of satisfaction and condescension. For him the presence of several "respectable & intelligent American families" compensated for the large numbers of Negroes and foreigners.[11] While in the city he stayed with his Aunt Charlotte, by then the wife of Thomas Harman, a local merchant. The reunion of the five Palfrey brothers took place at the Harmans' and made Gorham's stay memorable for him.

Although John Palfrey's plantation was only about one hundred miles from New Orleans, it was all but inaccessible. It took Gorham a week to reach the town of St. Martinville, where his father was waiting for him, and the next day they proceeded to Forlorn Hope. John Palfrey lived primitively in a plantation house made of logs. But Gorham enjoyed what were for him the new pleasures of hunting, fishing, and loafing. It was at Forlorn Hope that he first came into close contact with Negro slaves. When he left the plantation he said good-bye and gave presents to each of them. Gorham returned to New Orleans at the end of March, and a month later he was back in Boston.

Palfrey was no longer the retiring scholar, and Boston society opened its door to him. A friend noted that he was in great demand "as a Beau." [12] One day's itinerary consisted of twenty-four calls and ended with a large party at the Amorys'. But he interrupted his socializing long enough to enter the Bowdoin Prize competition. As a sophomore he had won a second prize; this time he wanted the highest honor, and he devoted eighteen days to the essay. The same diligence and perseverance he had displayed as a young man about town were again put to use. In July, President Kirkland announced that "The Reciprocal Influence of Literature and Morals" had won first prize. A copy of the work began to circulate, and Palfrey was happy to learn the opinion of John Lowell, "there there was no young man in the country, except Everett, that could have equalled it." [13]

Palfrey's trip to Louisiana merely whetted his appetite for further travel. Well-supplied with letters of recommendation he visited New York, Philadelphia, and Baltimore. In Washington, a classmate, Benjamin Tayloe, acted as his guide. It was here that he rode out to see a Methodist camp meeting, "a scene not at all agreeable, nor consistent with the spirit of devotion." [14] The return trip included a voyage up the Hudson by steamboat. After this trip Palfrey felt ready to take up the serious study of liberal theology.

*   *   *

"Unitarianism," wrote Channing, "is a rational and amiable

system." [15] But there was little amiability in the antagonisms that existed between Unitarians and orthodox Congregationalists. Palfrey began his theological training a year after the full-scale eruption of the Unitarian controversy. In Palfrey's graduation year, 1815, Jedidiah Morse, editor of the conservative religious magazine, *The Panoplist*, printed a chapter of Thomas Belsham's biography of Theophilus Lindsey which had appeared in London three years before. The chapter consisted of letters written by certain American ministers and showed them in an extreme latitudinarian light. Morse called his republication *American Unitarianism*, and from then on what had previously been a half-waged, shadowy warfare between liberal and orthodox Congregationalists became an open and bitter struggle.[16]

The roots of American Unitarianism can be traced to the beginnings of New England history. Recent scholarship has shown that it was an indigenous product, growing independently out of New England Congregationalism. It drew no sustenance from continental Socinianism, and very little from English Unitarianism. In fact, the journey from the asperities of strict Calvinism to the benevolence of full-blown Unitarianism began among the Puritan settlers of New England themselves. That "pure" Calvinism did not emigrate to New England is well known. The covenant or federal theology of the Puritans was a significant modification of a theological system, the logical implications of which even those doughty believers hesitated to embrace. The covenant of grace did not reduce the power and majesty of the Almighty, but it did give man a status a cut above that of a sinning worm. God had made terms for salvation—of his own volition, it is true—but he had made terms.[17]

This theological *tour de force* was a compromise, a precarious balance between what colonial New England considered the polar heresies of Antinomianism and Arminianism, or to put it simply, salvation through faith, or through works. Antinomianism was never a serious threat to the New England way, but Arminianism, with its appealing doctrine of man as an active instrument of his own salvation, became the main current in the Unitarian stream.

Unitarianism, the anti-Trinitarian Arian heresy, was not an important element in the process of religious liberalization until late in the eighteenth century. Arminianism paved the way, and it was against Arminianism that the orthodox mounted their sharpest attacks. If the covenant theology of the seventeenth century seemed well suited to the society which adopted it, Arminianism seemed better suited to the New England of the Age of Reason. The intense fires of Puritan theology had of necessity cooled, and Arminianism was a new compromise, a compromise between orthodoxy and infidelity.[18]

The Great Awakening of the mid-eighteenth century helped to sharpen the doctrinal differences between Calvinism and Arminianism, and for the next fifty years sniping warfare ensued and increased in intensity. The original Congregational church covenants reflected the homogeneity of New England society, but in the post-Awakening period orthodox congregations sought to protect themselves by demanding doctrinal declarations of their ministers before ordination. Arminianism grew in strength, however, and received indispensable aid from the New England church polity itself. Congregationalism was a poor foundation on which to build a unified orthodox belief—or any unified point of view, for that matter. Orthodox efforts to establish a form of centralization called consociation had been defeated in Massachusetts in the first decade of the eighteenth century. With each congregation virtually its own master, the Arminians could avoid a frontal assault on New England orthodoxy. Small victories in scattered townships, when added up, meant significant gains.

The doctrinal controversies of the rival groups abated during the War for Independence, when political issues dominated men's thinking. Such men as Jonathan Mayhew, an outspoken anti-Trinitarian from Boston, might have forced the controversy into the open a generation earlier had not energies been diverted into the struggle against England. The restoration of peace brought a resumption of hostilities to the New England churches. In 1785 James Freeman, a liberal Congregationalist, assumed charge of King's Chapel, which had been one of Boston's three Episcopalian churches. He was ordained by his congregation four years later, after they had agreed to abandon the old doctrines. By 1800 the Arminian-Unitarian position was solidly entrenched in eastern Massachusetts, and of the ten Congregational churches in Boston, only the Old South clung to orthodoxy.[19]

Prior to the publication of the Belsham chapter on American Unitarianism in 1815, Harvard College was the scene of the sharpest battle. David Tappan, Harvard's Hollis Professor of Divinity, died in 1803. Tappan was a mild Calvinist who eschewed controversy and would have been pained to witness the rancor which attended his succession. For two years orthodox and liberals were at odds, and when liberal Henry Ware obtained the chair in 1805, the orthodox cried that the citadel of learning had fallen to the heretics. The orthodox reply, the founding of Andover Theological Seminary, was three years in the making.[20]

For their part the "liberal Christians" (they still were extremely wary of using the name "Unitarians") were willing to remain on friendly terms with the orthodox ministers of their denomination. Only in retrospect does any real sharpness appear along doctrinal lines. Channing was not yet fully committed. But the Belsham incident severed the frayed cords which remained between the two groups. Channing wrote the reply to Morse's charges of Socinianism (the denial of Christ's divinity) and disassociated himself from Belsham's brand of English Unitarianism. Pulpits were no longer exchanged, and in 1816 the Unitarians organized the Society for the Promotion of Theological Education to support the training of liberal ministers at Harvard.[21]

*   *   *

When Palfrey began his graduate studies, the program of the Harvard Divinity School was getting under way. Before 1816 provisions for theological education at the college were scanty. Students were under the very general supervision of Professor Henry Ware, and there was but one weekly exercise and no examinations. In October of that year President Kirkland announced a "new order of studies" which called for more courses designed specifically for the theologians.[22]

Palfrey was one of twelve of the class of 1815 who were in residence as graduates at Cambridge. Soon after he began his studies Bowdoin College offered him a tutorship, but on Kirkland's advice he declined it.[23] Palfrey carefully read the Bible, annotating the passages which he wished to go over again, and compiled a two-hundred-page abstract of Old Testament history, presaging his biblical scholarship of later years. In addition to self-instruction in a variety of languages, Palfrey received Hebrew lessons from Professor Willard, and Palfrey's fellow students came to think he knew as much as his instructor.[24]

Although Palfrey stayed on the Cambridge side of the Charles most of the time he had made many Boston friends. Even so, he did not lack companionship at the college. Fraternization with the undergraduates was out of the question, but faculty members and the other resident graduates provided the basis for a select circle of friends, including Edward T. Channing, Jonathan Wainwright, and Andrews Norton. The group spent many fine evenings, feet propped up before a log fire, with a plentiful supply of cheese, crackers, wine, "segars," and good talk.[25] At one of these gatherings Andrews Norton, whom Carlyle later dubbed the "Unitarian Pope," told the current John Adams anecdote. At a Boston dinner party, the ex-president listened as long as he could to a minister praising General Washington's administration to the disadvantage of Adams', and when his patience was at an end he exploded: "General Washington, sir, was a block of wood!" Young Palfrey, properly shocked, made a memorandum of the story that evening.[26]

In his second year of residence Palfrey became a proctor, and was put in charge of Massachusetts Hall, where he lived. The duties of a disciplinarian were not pleasant to this slight, studious young man, but the yearly salary of $250 was too attractive to be turned down. His brother Edward warned him to take care not to have his head broken in by his rebellious charges.[27] Proctor Palfrey was fairly popular with the students, but in December 1817 he imposed a fine on an unruly student and the college buzzed with rumors of retaliation. Palfrey heard that he might be assaulted in his room, and he went to bed that night with two loaded pistols under his pillow. When the expected attack came around midnight, the pistols became entangled in the bedding. Palfrey could make out two figures in the moonlight, before pieces of firewood began to fly past his head. One struck him on the mouth and split his upper lip. Next day, after an investigation, the culprits confessed and were expelled.[28]

In 1817 Jared Sparks returned to Cambridge to become a Harvard tutor. Despite the rebuffs that Palfrey had suffered and imagined at Sparks's hands, he was eager to maintain as close a friendship as Sparks would allow. When Sparks became editor of the two-year-old *North American Review*, Palfrey let himself believe that the new editor would share the job with him. He had been interested in the *North American* from its beginning, and Sparks, without committing himself, dropped hints of making his friend an assistant editor.[29]

Palfrey thought the matter settled, and did what he could to increase the *North American*'s circulation, but once again Sparks disappointed him.[30]

*   *   *

The question of Palfrey's Unitarianism remained unsettled—or so thought Mrs. Phillips. In April 1817 he tried to reassure her (put her off, rather) by writing that although his reading, at her request, of Episcopalian literature had not suggested any new reasons why he should believe in the Trinity, no one could yet call him a "Unitarian at heart." He claimed that he spent much of the end of that year reading the literature of Trinitarian controversy: "My excellent friend, Mrs. Phillips, found it a very hard thing to give up the hope of my being a priest, and she flattered herself that if I could only be made to read Bishop Potter on Episcopacy, all would be right." [31] Mrs. Phillips' illusions were finally shattered when Palfrey openly embraced the full Unitarian position. Though he apologized for the pain he was causing her, he wrote frankly that he believed Trinitarianism to be unscriptural and that it struck at the roots of all religion, natural and revealed. Mrs. Phillips' reading suggestions had had no effect. Palfrey refuted Potter on church government point by point, and Jones, another authority, was so unacceptable that Gorham thought Unitarians might use the book for missionary purposes. Some praise of the Episcopal church came much too late to heal his aunt's wounds, but Palfrey implored:

> God knows whether I have been sincere. He knows that I have not found my opinions without thought, study, and care. . . . I do hope that you will never look upon me with any sentiment more unkind than pity.

When Mrs. Phillips found heart to answer a few months later, she devoted most of her attention to other topics, although she did promise to pray for his eventual enlightenment.[32]

Despite Kirkland's reforms of 1816, Harvard divinity students were still pretty much on their own. This informality left Palfrey with a sense of inadequacy. He had had little practice in preparing sermons, and even less in "pulpit eloquence." [33] But however apprehensive he might be, his professional debut could not be postponed. In January 1818 the Boston ministers heard him deliver a sermon, and within a week he was approved as a minister. The next Sunday he and Sparks drove to Brookline for Palfrey's first sermon before a full congregation. On successive Sundays he preached at the Federal Street and First churches in Boston.[34]

Several members of the Brattle Street Society attended these services. Long before Palfrey completed his religious training, there had been talk of him as a candidate for the Brattle Street pulpit. Since Edward Everett's tenure as pastor had been so short, the Brattle church had had no regular leadership since the death of Buckminster in 1812. Sparks, too, was mentioned as a possible successor, but by 1817 there seemed to be a tacit agreement that when Palfrey was ready, he would be selected.[35] Henry Rice wrote solicitously that after Palfrey's Brookline sermon a prominent Brattle Street member complained that his delivery was "cold and uninteresting." Rice urged Palfrey, who had been hired to preach for four weeks at Brattle Street, to shun "Cambridge oratory" and to put his heart as well as his mind into his sermons.[36]

Rice's words apparently had some effect, for Palfrey's first appearance at Brattle Street on February 14 was a success.[37] When the four-week trial engagement ended, Deacon Peter O. Thacher informed Palfrey confidentially that he was certain of being asked to continue his preaching on probation. This was a preliminary to a formal offer of the pastorate. On April 26 one of Boston foremost churches invited the twenty-one-year-old divine to take charge.[38]

IV

Brattle Street

I N 1818 the world of Boston and its environs looked good to Palfrey. The Brattle Street pulpit assured him of a comfortable niche in this world. If Harvard's purpose was to produce proper Bostonians,[1] Palfrey was a Cambridge graduate eager to assume that role. Geographically and socially Boston still looked backward to the certainties of the colonial era. The city was practically an island, and the old landmarks served to reassure the conservative of the permanence of his way of life. Of Boston's forty thousand inhabitants only two thousand were of foreign birth, and these were mostly Irish servants who were no threat to the established social order.

The general tone of society was as important to Palfrey as the homogeneity and compactness of Boston life, and was thought by him to be a result of these qualities. "Society in Boston at that time," Palfrey mused many years later, "was eminently virtuous, enlightened, cultivated & elegant." There were wealthy men, but few millionaires, and such men as the Appletons and the Lawrences, the later textile kings, were small retailers in Washington Street. Every young man was expected to take up a trade or profession, and the man of leisure was regarded with suspicion.

Clergymen were among the chief beneficiaries of this genteel society. There was a deep interest in religion which gave the ministers considerable standing in the community. Influential families were active in church affairs. At dinner parties, a host's minister sat at a place of honor. Academic distinction at Harvard also meant a cordial welcome in Boston society: "A young man who did well at College had made his fortune. . . . Strange as it may now seem, the young scholars, not the young heirs, were the young aristocracy." [2]

Although the Unitarians controlled less than half of Boston's twenty-two Protestant churches, they were the dominant religious force. The extent of their power has been aptly, if somewhat unctuously, described by Palfrey:

> The Unitarian influence dominated, without rivalry, the society & the general sentiment of Boston. It was not in the slightest degree intolerant; indeed, toleration if it had not been its principle, would have been its interest & its necessity; but its friends were of that weight in character & that prominence in position, that every thing not involving a controversial issue, naturally yielded itself to their management, & in politics, literature, beenvolent efforts . . . they took the undisputed lead.[3]

Among the original Congregational churches only the Old South held firmly to orthodoxy, although this solitary stronghold had been reinforced in 1809 with the organization of the Park Street Church. Charles Lowell's West Church had more members than the other Unitarian churches, but since many of the members were poor, and families shared pews, leadership fell naturally to the second largest congregation, Brattle Street.

The Brattle Street Church[4] had not always been a pillar of respectability. It was founded in 1699, amid a controversy that earned it the title of "The Manifesto Church." Before the first service, the members issued a declaration of principles which included some significant modifications of the old Puritan order. The organizers of the new church disclaimed any intention of subverting established religion, but to the orthodox such practices as unrestricted baptism, an option on publicly relating religious experiences, and participation by women in the selection of ministers could be viewed in no other light. "Manifesto Church" remained a term of derision for many decades. By the nineteenth century, however, the church had put its outcast origins far behind. No congregation in Boston had so many members of high standing. John Adams went to the heart of the matter when he called it "the politest Congregation in Boston." [5]

The offer made Palfrey by Brattle Street was everything he could hope for. In addition to the use of the vestry, which would be kept in repair and supplied with as much firewood as needed, Palfrey was to receive thirty dollars a week. Nor was this all. "From a tender regard to the health and permanent usefulness of Mr. Palfrey," and to enable him to continue his studies, the society assumed the expense of hiring a substitute minister every fourth Sunday for five years. Palfrey noted with elation: "This is the greatest *encouragement* wh[ich] has ever been given in N[ew] England." [6] The unanimity of the call was also gratifying. Palfrey tried to discount this, and pointed out that the church had long been without a regular pastor, but he must have been pleased with the show of confidence. The church pressed for an early answer. Deacon Alden Bradford sent a "friendly hint" that allowed for no further postponement. On May 5 Palfrey accepted, though that under the circumstances he should have been hesitant does not speak well for his decisiveness. [7]

"In the good providence of God, we have been led . . . to the choice of Mr. John G. Palfrey, to be our religious Teacher and Pastor." The ordination ceremonies were scheduled for June 17. Palfrey had hoped that William Ellery Channing would deliver the ordination sermon, but Channing was not able to attend the service because of illness. [8] Another disappointment came from Mrs. Phillips. Even though he offered to go to Hartford and escort her to Boston, she begged off. Never at a loss when it came to giving advice, she counseled him to be watchful against malevolent detractors (she undoubtedly thought the prevalence of this type greatest in Unitarian congregations) and to try to achieve Christian dignity while avoiding "Puritan stiffness." She wrote in a friendly tone, but her beliefs would not allow her to witness Gorham's fall into the "dreadful heresy" of Socinianism. [9]

The ordination of a new minister at a church as important at Brattle Street was a notable event. All the eminent men of Boston would be there. Unfortunately everything did not go smoothly. An "unpleasant difficulty" occurred on the morning of the ordination, when pastors and delegates from twenty churches met at the courthouse. They called upon Palfrey to express his views of the Christian religion, and Huntington of the Old South challenged his doctrine. Huntington was the only member of the ordaining council who voted against Palfrey's acceptance.[10]

The statement of Christian principle which Palfrey read to the ministers was a concise exposition of the early Unitarian point of view. He wrote the first draft in forty minutes. Although he made corrections and additions, he left the original basically unchanged, showing how well ordered the Unitarian tenets were in his mind. There was but one God, who exercised a close watch over the affairs of men, and interposed his power in these affairs through direct revelations. Palfrey accepted the Old and New Testaments in their entirety. Christ came to spread the Father's commandments and lived without sin:

> I rest my faith in the truth of the divine authority of Jesus on various proofs which seem to me irrefragable; on those of miracle & prophecy; of miracles which I believe none but God or one acting under his commission could have wrought. . . . Secondarily on . . . the pure morality which he taught [and] the rapid progress of his religion.

Each man had the right to interpret the Bible for himself, and to act on his individual responsibility. Only an understanding of the Scripture could fortify a man in a life of affliction, deter him from sin, or fit him for heaven. As a Christian minister, Palfrey would try to contribute to this understanding.[11]

Doctrinal matters attended to, Palfrey turned to more mundane affairs. The Brattle Street parsonage was in nearby Court Street, and was in keeping with the affluence of the church. A gift to the society from John Hancock's aunt in 1778, the three-story brick building was the most stylish parsonage in

Boston. Since it was far too large for occupancy by a bachelor, Buckminster had shared the house with a family. George Sullivan suggested to Palfrey that Deacon Thacher would be willing to make a similar arrangement. Palfrey signed an agreement under which he was to have the library and the nearest bedroom and would eat at Thacher's table. In return for the use of the rest of the house, Thacher would supply domestic service.[12]

Palfrey soon settled down to the routine of a minister's life, although inexperience caused him some difficulty. His primary problem was the preparation of effective sermons. He came to his profession with very few sermons ready or even drafted in rough form, so that by the second Sunday after his ordination he had exhausted hs small stock. Palfrey often made the situation worse by waiting for Saturday afternoon or evening before beginning to write the two sermons needed for the next day's services. Sometimes there seemed nothing for him to say, and fretful procrastination was the result. Fortunately the leaders of the congregation were willing to put up with his initial deficiencies.[13]

Although Palfrey knew that his sermons would be only as good as the amount of effort he put into them, their uneven quality continued. At a Watertown ordination he gave the right hand of fellowship in an address acclaimed as a model of its kind, but soon after, a parishioner called on him to suggest that he alter his style of preaching.[14] Improvement in the pulpit came with time. He assumed "the mien, voice, & dignity of manhood." On Sundays the good people of Brattle Street had no idea how many battles their pastor had fought with himself the day before.[15]

Palfrey was a believer in the usefulness of resolutions, schedules, and peremptory memoranda of things to be done. He invariably overcalculated his capabilities, however, and the result was a caustic self-criticism at the end of the week, accompanied by a pledge of future devotion to duty. The duties in question were those as a pastor, including calls on his parishioners at least once a year, and frequent visits to sickbeds. At first he found calls on the sick and on families in mourning embarrassing,[16] but after a little experience he "could converse & pray naturally, copiously & profitably, because I did it feelingly." He also achieved a practical result. Such participation in family intimacies earned for him the confidence that would not have come from merely presiding over church services. Another of his duties was to visit the poor of the parish and distribute food and money supplied by the church's relief fund. In 1822 Palfrey joined two other Unitarian ministers who began holding Sunday evening services for Boston's unchurched poor. This led later to the establishment of Joseph Tuckerman's Ministry at Large to the Boston Poor.[17]

The concern which the church society had shown for Palfrey's health when he was hired did not diminish with time. After six months of service Palfrey claimed that he was working harder than he ever had, and his friends at the church suggested that he slow down. There was no specific illness, just a general weakness which all attributed to overwork. Whenever Palfrey looked run down he was allowed to take a leave of absence. One such leave lasted several months. The Brattle Street people certainly could not be accused of lacking understanding or sympathy for their pastor's problems. Sparks, who had just entered the ministry, also complained of overwork. Palfrey gave him some advice which he apparently meant to follow himself: "Write one sermon each week & preach an old one. About one in ten will be discovered by somebody, who will say that they are good enough to preach four times instead of two." [18]

*   *   *

In 1818 Sparks had become the minister of a small Unitarian society in Baltimore. His ordination in May 1819 was a significant event in the history of American Unitarianism. The

New England Unitarians sensed that this was to be no ordinary ceremony, and they sent a large delegation from four states. Open controversy with the orthodox had drawn liberals closer together, and they could see no reason why Unitarianism should not now branch out and become a national religion. Boston had given America political liberty. Surely the gift of religious liberty would not be refused.

Palfrey, as a close friend of Sparks, was naturally included in the delegation from Boston. His parishioners paid for all his traveling expenses. The high spot of the ordination was the sermon delivered by William Ellery Channing, "a very eloquent and able exposition and defence of the principles of rational Christians." Channing spoke with a boldness that surprised and delighted his hearers. The sermon received a large printing and remains unsurpassed as the classic statement of nineteenth-century Unitarian belief. Palfrey's contribution to the ordination service was to extend the right hand of fellowship to his friend. He remained for a short while in Baltimore and preached several times. He and Channing later spoke in New York to enthusiastic audiences.[19]

Palfrey's Baltimore remarks had created a "sort of sensation," and were to be published with Channing's sermon. In New York, Palfrey went over the piece with Channing and decided that it could not appear without extensive alterations. Certain phrases, he felt, showed that his "zeal had got the start of my wisdom." To publish an expurgated version would be dishonest; therefore, he wanted no publication at all. Sparks told of his congregation's desire to publish all the ordination addresses. When Palfrey proved adamant, Sparks commented acidly: "You seem to think that everything, like sermon writing, may be put off till Saturday night. . . . I am sorry if you are determined to confine all you have to say in this world, to a pulpit in Boston." [20]

The short-lived period of Unitarian expansion was under way. Soon after Sparks had established himself, Samuel Gilman set up a Unitarian church in Charleston, South Carolina, and following the visit of Channing and Palfrey to New York, Unitarians founded a church there as well. A year before the Baltimore ordination, Palfrey and other Unitarian ministers of the Boston area had gathered at Channing's Berry Street vestry to argue the merits of caution versus outspoken proselytism. The activists, lead by Channing and Aaron Bancroft of Worcester, carried the day. This unofficial conference was the forerunner of the annual Berry Street Conference of Unitarian ministers which began in 1820.[21]

The chief vehicle of this new doctrinal militancy was to be a rejuvenated magazine, the *Christian Disciple*. Noah Worcester, its editor, had resigned to devote all his time to pacifism, and Henry Ware, Jr., became head of a new board of editors. As a member of the board Palfrey was given the task of explaining to the public the "altered plan" of the magazine. When subscriptions increased the new editors were able to publish Unitarian tracts as well, to counteract the supposedly nonsectarian tracts of the orthodox New England Tract Society. Andrews Norton, who had lately become Harvard's Professor of Sacred Literature, was the most outspoken activist. He would give no quarter: "Orthodoxy must be broken down, our motto must be Babylon est delenda." [22]

Palfrey found his connection with the *Disciple* boring. Some of the editorial advisors did not favor the activist policy. To the disgust of Palfrey and others who did, they illogically contended that the success of the magazine warranted a return to less controversy. Palfrey left one meeting "after having listened to two hours of prose from Br. Channing," with the certainty that, as usual, the meeting had accomplished nothing. When Norton, the Unitarian Cato, heard of these waverings he dispatched letters of encouragement to his friends. Palfrey considered Channing a waverer, but he thought the inane vacillations of the worst waverers had had the good effect of fortifying Channing's resolve.[23]

Almost as soon as it began, the Unitarian penetration of the South ceased. The Baltimore and Charleston churches, instead of becoming bridgeheads for a general advance, became isolated outposts. Gilman's ordination at Charleston was not attended by the New England ministers. Sparks lectured his New England friends incessantly, telling them that strong-lunged preachers, not books and tracts, would convert the South. He began his own militant magazine, the *Unitarian Miscellany*, and when Boston greeted it coolly as too polemical, this clearly exposed the gap between what was imagined in Boston and what was actually needed to influence the rest of the country. Although Palfrey and a few other Unitarians did preach in Baltimore, there was no rush southward. Palfrey contributed to the *Miscellany*, but he was almost alone. "Little things are great to little men" who could not be expected to write twenty pages for the *Miscellany* without much prior thought.[24] The final blow for Sparks came in 1822 when he became chaplain of the United States House of Representatives. The invitations he sent to his installation were declined by the New Englanders. Palfrey did not come, claiming that he was writing a reply to an orthodox pamphlet, a task he never completed. Sparks was beyond anger when he learned that many Unitarians had attended an unimportant ordination in Burlington, Vermont, which took place at the same time as his installation. When he thought of what a stimulus to Unitarian expansion a strong delegation at Washington would have been, he exploded to Palfrey: "Our friends are traversing a nutshell, while they fancy themselves circumnavigating the globe." However, Sparks's condescending attitude toward the South shows that he himself was enamored of the nutshell. When rumors reached him that Andrews Norton might resign his professorship at Harvard, he asked Palfrey to speak for him.[25] Sparks was not the true adventurer; he did not burn his boats.

*   *   *

If Palfrey was traversing a nutshell, he was not aware of it. A bachelor's salary more than covered his normal expenses. He found living with the Thachers extremely pleasant, and the church society thought highly enough of him to authorize the expenditure of two thousand dollars for repairs on the church and vestry.[26] The rewards of his position were not exclusively material. For the first year of his ministry, 1818, Palfrey was a person of influence in Boston society. Three months after his ordination, Andrews Norton had asked him to do what he could to help him obtain a Harvard appointment. The following year Palfrey was chosen chaplain of the Massachusetts Senate.[27]

In 1820 a convention met to amend the Massachusetts constitution. Article III of the Declaration of Rights provided for use of public funds to support religion. A coalition of the antireligious and the orthodox "Andoverians" sought to eliminate the article. The Calvinists put themselves in this position in order to cut off public support of Unitarian churches. Palfrey conferred with Daniel Webster about the preparation of a defense of the threatened article, but this became unnecessary when Chief Justice Isaac Parker published a pamphlet which effectively covered the same question.[28]

The convention's activities gave Palfrey an opportunity to express his conservative political views. While keeping his brother William informed of the progress of the Massachusetts constitution makers, he remarked: "The sovereign people, in the plenitude of their power and folly, have rejected some of the most important amendments." [29] The height of Palfrey's Federalism came in an anonymous broadside published on New Year's Day, 1822, as the "Carrier's Address" of the *Boston Daily Advertiser*. Anonymity allowed Palfrey to launch attacks in all directions. Times did improve, for even General Jackson,

> The State Department's cautious protege,
> Chief Justice commandant of Florida,

> By pleading pity feels his bowels wrung,
> Content to banish whom of old he hung.

But Palfrey saw no hope for Secretary of State John Quincy Adams, whom he attacked via Adams' Report on Weights and Measures:

> Oh! thou, (whatever title suit thine ear,)
> Senator, mechanist, or pamphleteer,
> Minister, rhetorician, secretary,
> Thou, of our land ascendant luminary,
> Big northern bear! New England's spotted sun!
> Great Jack of many trades, and good at none,
> Aid though a simple carrier to express
> The "weight and measure" of thy fam'd address.
>
> *   *   *   *   *   *   *   *   *   *   *   *
>
> Yet say, thy "fictive" figures hadst thou learn'd
> Ere, thriftless garb, thy Federal coat was turned.
> Or hast thou found, in balancing the state,
> A *scruple's* lighter than a *penny-weight?*

Palfrey's later friendship with the Adams family caused him to regret this "production of the days of my folly," and he never revealed his authorship.[30]

Although Palfrey claimed he was being overworked, his journal indicates otherwise. He took many short vacations and trips, and belonged to a variety of societies and associations, which, whatever their stated aims, also served social purposes. Palfrey loved to make social calls on his numerous friends, many of whom he encountered at meetings of the several social clubs to which he belonged. At one of these, the literary elite of Boston would often meet to exchange ghost stories![31]

The early years of Palfrey's ministry were marred by only one major controversy. This involved Henry Rice, Palfrey's former benefactor and a prominent member of his congregation. When Palfrey decided to share his parsonage with Thacher, Rice charged that Thacher, whom he hated, was unfit to be a member of the church. Much to Palfrey's sorrow,

Palfrey at 30, as minister
of the Brattle Street Church, Boston

Palfrey at 52, as a member of Congress

Thacher moved from the parish house, so as not to compromise Palfrey, who feared that an open break with Rice could
not be postponed for long. After Thacher's departure, Palfrey
made a similar arrangement with another parishioner.[32] But
nothing would please Rice. He accused Palfrey of having had
his brother George copy sermons while he worked at Rice's
shop. George left Rice's shop and returned to Louisiana. Rice
asked to be formally dismissed from the church and this was
done, although he was not given a certificate of recommendation to other churches. However justified Palfrey may have
been, he was greatly upset by this affair, since Rice had been
such a help to him in his final student years. He made a generous estimate of what he owed Rice and offered him $1,200
to cover all obligations, financial and moral. Rice would not
accept the money, so Palfrey used it to establish an anonymous
scholarship fund at Harvard.[33] Palfrey's act was an exhibition
of the strong sense of rectitude which was later to handicap
him in his political career. The acrimony of the Rice incident
was an anomaly in a generally peaceful picture, however. If
the minister's life was what Palfrey wanted, he had it under
circumstances that many of his colleagues might envy.

* * *

As an eligible young bachelor, Palfrey had to contend with
frequent rumors of romantic attachments. While a divinity
student, he began denying reports of his engagement. His
father and brothers in Louisiana were eager for him to be
married. Their letters often referred to the "choice lamb"
Gorham was bound to find.[34]

Twice, in the years before he met his future wife, he thought
the lamb had been found. While a college senior he briefly
imagined himself in love with Esther Sargeant. There was no
doubt, however, about his next attachment, Charlotte Brooks.
She was the daughter of Peter Chardon Brooks, Boston's first
millionaire. Palfrey never had the courage to propose to her,

although his attachment was obvious to his friends. In 1821, Edward Everett bluntly asked him if he "had any aspirations to Miss Brooks." Soon after Palfrey indicated that he had no such aspirations, Everett and Miss Brooks were engaged. Palfrey had assumed that Mr. Brooks would consider him an unsuitable choice for Charlotte because of his relative poverty. Yet another of Brooks's daughters married Nathaniel L. Frothingham, minister of the First Church, and Brooks gave financial aid to both Frothingham and Everett after their marriages. Either Palfrey's timidity was more of an obstacle than his poverty, or he did not tell all about the matter. He was not so distraught that he could not write flirtatious letters to other young ladies,[35] but he felt his failure with Charlotte Brooks very deeply. He did not get over it until he fell in love with Mary Ann Hammond.

Mary Ann was four years younger than Palfrey and the daughter of Samuel Hammond, a Brattle Street parishioner. Hammond was a businessman with a comfortable income derived from trade and real estate. If Palfrey really believed he was barred from marrying into the richest families, the Hammonds fitted his requirements exactly. While Charlotte Brooks was on his mind, no mention of Mary Ann was made in his journal. He could not help noticing her, however, since he often visited the Hammond home.[36]

In July 1821 Palfrey made a "clumsy and abrupt" proposal to Miss Hammond, "the good and lovely lady who has been the great blessing of my life." She made him wait six months for an answer. The delay can be attributed to Samuel Hammond's hesitancy. A week after Palfrey thought he had been accepted, he had to give Hammond a detailed explanation of his financial condition. He admitted that as a bachelor he had not saved anything from his salary, but promised that his extravagance would cease after marriage. As he saw it, his income of $2,000, with fixed expenses of $1,300, would provide for a wife with no difficulty. A long conference with

Hammond concluded matters. The Brattle Street Society did
their part by agreeing to repair Palfrey's house.[37]

The period of courtship lasted a little over a year. Palfrey's
friends were not entirely sure that he had made the best choice,
but "he was doubtless pleased himself—and that is saying a
good deal in these days of terrible calculations and management." The courtship might have been longer if Mary Ann
had had her way. She asked Palfrey to postpone the marriage
until he had accumulated four or five thousand dollars, pointing to her father's apprehensions about her welfare.[38] How
Palfrey got by this obstacle is not clear. The wedding date
was not put off, though he certainly did not acquire that much
money.

There is a lack of warmth on Palfrey's part that leads one
to believe that his relationship with Mary Ann was, at this
point, more of the head than of the heart. During the engagement, the couple saw each other often and exchanged many
notes. The formality of some of these is not remarkable for
that age, but Palfrey's reticence when writing to friends, or in
his journal, is. His journal merely records the fact of his
marriage, and gives a list of the wedding guests. And his autobiography, written thirty-odd years later, devotes an inordi-
nate amount of space to his unrequited loves. The marriage,
which took place on March 11, 1823, was a modest affair. The
couple moved in with the Hammonds so that the Court Street
parsonage could be renovated.[39]

The responsibilities of marriage were not long in coming.
Palfrey's estimate of expenses had been for two people. On
December 11 their first child, Sarah, was born. Another
daughter, Hannah (later known as Anna), was born in 1825.
The financial burden of supporting a family forced Palfrey
to borrow from his friends. If he ever longed for the lost
extravagances of bachelor days he kept such thoughts to himself. Now he had the love of a woman who could write with
complete sincerity: "I hope I shall be growing more worthy

to be associated with you." Marriage was a tonic for him. To his amazement, he was able to finish a sermon on a Wednesday.[40]

Repairs on the Brattle Street Church and its enlargement were the occasion of Palfrey's first venture into the field of history. He spent several afternoons of research at the Massachusetts Historical Society library and delivered two sermons on the history of the church that were published with extensive and careful annotations. Although his election to membership in the society coincided with the appearance of the printed sermons, this honor came as a result of his social standing. No one could have predicted then that he would earn recognition as a historian.[41]

Despite his rejection by Sparks in 1817, Palfrey maintained during these years a close interest in the *North American Review*. In 1819, his interest became a financial one when he paid $160 to become one of seven associates in the enterprise. When Edward T. Channing stepped down from the editorship, Palfrey and Andrews Norton blocked Richard Henry Dana's bid for the job. Dana had affronted Boston's conservative literati with a review of Hazlitt that was too "modern." Sparks, not yet secure in Baltimore, had his eye on the *North American*, and warned Palfrey: "If it goes into the hands of [Dana] it can never be recovered." [42]

Palfrey supported Edward Everett for the vacant editorship, but he soon had cause for regret. From its inception the *North American*'s editor had been *primus inter pares*. Everett wanted to change that. He saw himself as editor-in-chief, which to him meant sole editor. There was continued friction between Everett and his associates. In 1820 he tried to persuade Palfrey to sell him his share. Palfrey replied smoothly: "I should be more than ever unwilling to resign it, now that under your direction it promises to do so much credit to all." A year later Everett made another attempt to obtain the magazine. It could not be well managed by a "club." One

individual had to assume responsibility, "any *one* person."
Everett had the support of one other owner, and he put great
pressure on Palfrey for his vote, but things continued as before.[43]

The meetings of the directors soon became open quarrels.
Every disagreement became a dispute, and Palfrey and Everett
were on the verge of an exchange of angry letters. The idea
of a single editor was not distasteful in itself. Everett was the
problem; his colleagues did not trust him. He was accused of
hurting the *North American* by metaphysical "Germanizing"
in its pages and using it as a means of support for two of his
brothers. Sparks offered a solution to this impasse when he
decided to quit his Baltimore church. He wanted to edit the
North American in Philadelphia, but gave up the idea when
it got no support. Palfrey acted as Sparks's agent in the final
acrimonious sessions with Everett, who insisted on protecting
his brother Oliver's position as distributing agent. Everett made
the transfer to Sparks in September 1823.[44]

The *North American* was not the only magazine to which
Palfrey devoted his time. He was an assistant editor of, and
made frequent contributions to, the *Christian Disciple*. Henry
Ware, Jr., the chief editor, tired of the job in 1822, deciding
that too much of his time was being taken up by a magazine
which did not even pay its own way. Sparks urged Palfrey
to take over the magazine, and offered to help out as soon as
he could leave Baltimore. Palfrey, who did not think highly
of Ware as an editor, was willing, but only if Sparks made
good his promise. Sparks was more interested in a general
review such as the *North American*, but Palfrey decided to
go ahead alone. His hesitation nearly cost him the editorship,
for two other Unitarian ministers were asked to edit the
Disciple before he was.[45]

Palfrey's first act as editor was to change the *Disciple*'s
name to the *Christian Examiner*. In addition to a desire to
make a fresh start, he may have changed the name for mone-

tary reasons. A good source of income was the sale of complete runs of the *Disciple*. There was to be no fundamental change in the magazine, though Palfrey did promise not to belabor old doctrinal controversies. His editorship lasted a year and a half and was not distinguished.[46]

*   *   *

In the spring of 1825 Palfrey began to consider taking a European tour. His congregation's concern for his health was as strong as ever, and his doctor suggested a complete change of scene for at least a year. What was the reason for such a drastic recommendation? Palfrey was not sure. He referred to a "dyspeptic habit," and thought that "the seat of my disorder is the stomach, though my lungs have been lately a little affected. I am by no means sick." Palfrey joined the stream of Unitarian clergy who then went to Europe on "missions of health." He applied for a year's leave of absence, and the Brattle Street committee consented. A friend confided that no one had made any objection, and that Palfrey could depart with the assurance of his church's complete support.[47]

Support came in tangible form as well. Since the expense of supplying the Brattle Street pulpit was Palfrey's responsibility, his parishioners knew he could not travel extensively on the remainder of his salary. Small and large gifts came in. One joint donation from Harrison Gray Otis, Amos and Abbott Lawrence, and others amounted to $370. Since the total expense of the trip was to come to $2,500 Samuel Hammond probably made a sizable contribution. Mary Ann was to stay with her parents. Palfrey waited for the birth of his second daughter in June, and two weeks later he left for New York. The ship on which he sailed was bound for Liverpool. He entertained himself by reading Cervantes, and claimed to have learned Spanish in nineteen days—as long as it had taken Jefferson when he sailed for France in 1784.[48] Instead of going directly to England, Palfrey debarked at Cork for a short tour of Ireland.

The two months Palfrey spent in Britain were busily un-eventful. He followed the well-worn paths of other New England travelers, saw the accustomed sights ("the witchery of these cathedrals is indescribable"), made pilgrimages to the home of Wordsworth ("the self-gratified poet, who enter-tained me for about two hours with very striking talk about himself & his works"), and of Southey ("he was none of your moping, sickly, daffadowillidy sort of person, as one might imagine"). In Leeds, he visited a textile factory which em-ployed more than "500 pairs of hands." Unlike Melville, Pal-frey made no comment on the youth of some of these, or the horrors of the early Industrial Revolution.[49]

Palfrey's impressions of England did not crystallize until he crossed the Channel. In France his high opinion of every-thing English disappeared. Especially shocking to his clergy-man's sense of propriety was the lack of discipline in church services. Open house seemed the rule. Reservation cards on pews were ignored, and church ushers were not beyond taking bribes for choice seats. In France a change in the attitude of the people was immediately noticeable: "The French are . . . civil, kind & gay, as much as the English are self-sufficient, & morose." The difference between defiant looks and talkative friendliness made him glad he had gone first to England. One thing had been gained, however. In talks with English Uni-tarians he became convinced that Milton had been a Unitarian of the Arian school. "The third great name of England is ours." [50]

In Paris, La Fayette greeted Palfrey with special cordiality and referred to Brattle Street as "our church." He invited Palfrey to spend a few days at his estate, La Grange, in November. Palfrey readily accepted, and after several days there he went on to Geneva where he was pleased to note that in the city of Calvin most of the churches were anti-Trinitarian and anti-Calvinistic.[51]

This break in the routine of his profession was what Palfrey needed for his psychological well-being. A few months of traveling had banished all thoughts of dyspepsia. He teased his wife with hints of an early return to Boston. Was he being entirely honest when he wrote: "I have occasionally [had] indications that my health is not quite sufficiently matured to try a voyage in the autumn, & a N[ew] England winter," or was he contemplating the pleasures of a winter in Italy? Mary Ann dutifully replied that he should take as much time as he needed.[52]

It was fortunate that Palfrey decided to go to Italy, for it was there that he became for the first time the enchanted traveler. His New England reserve disappeared momentarily in the Mediterranean sun. He gave himself completely to the charms of Rome:

> Of every other city I have been weary before I left it, but it is impossible to tire of Rome. . . . Apart from the amazing interest of its antiquities, I am satisfied now, like the rest of the world, that there is nothing so magnificent. One lives a little age of thought the first time one sees its great church.

There was so much to be seen that he found himself losing precious time in delightful indecision—the *dolce far niente* of the Italians. Even the beauties of Florence suffered because he had seen Rome first. He lingered on in Italy as long as possible ("The Tuscans are the most . . . respectable of the Italians"), then returned to London via Switzerland and the Rhine. His fellow Bostonians' conception of Germany may have been one of poets and universities, but Palfrey saw nothing but bayonets and drums.[53]

Back in London in June 1826, Palfrey found the city still unimpressive. The best thing he saw there was an "Infant School," employing Joseph Lancaster's monitorial system of teaching. An older pupil led the children in recitations with many animated gestures. This was "capital play," reported Palfrey enthusiastically, and "at the same time that it teaches them, gratifies a childish passion for exercise & noise."[54]

Palfrey returned home in August 1826, the limited purpose

of his trip accomplished. To say that Palfrey had been "sick of his work" is too strong. But the lack of any real physical ailment and his unbroken good health while in Europe leave little doubt that he had had a bad case of *Wanderlust*.

*   *   *

In his improved frame of mind, Palfrey returned to work and family with pleasure. He was very much the serious parent. While still abroad he had suggested that Mary Ann begin teaching Sarah prayers, but not the Lord's Prayer, which could not be wholly understood by her. And Sarah was never to recite her prayers for the amusement of adults. One day after his return a domestic crisis arose when Sarah swallowed a large chunk of beef. Palfrey hurriedly scrawled a note summoning the doctor, and added a hopeful postscript: "The meat was tender." In 1827 a son and namesake was born. Mounting famliy expenses were met through the generosity of Samuel Hammond, or sometimes other parishioners.[55]

The second half of Palfrey's twelve-year Brattle Street ministry was a period of intense activity. "I both performed diligently the regular duties belonging to my place, & abounded in professional services of a less definite kind." These included direct participation in most of the committees then existing in Boston. In 1825 he had helped found the American Unitarian Association. In addition to belonging to societies for the promotion of missionary work in India, religious charities, and aid for the Greeks, Palfrey made his first venture into reform. This was an attack on intemperance. He spent considerable time in amassing facts against Demon Rum, and published two sermons on the subject. In "Mother and Her Child," Palfrey warned against giving babies paregoric because it tended to produce "infant sots." [56] No teetotaler himself, he was fond of a glass of Madeira.

Palfrey's most distinct contribution to his church, other than conducting regular services, was the enormous amount of time he gave to instructing the young people. He wrote and published two prayer books for children, and began a special program of Sunday school classes before going to Europe, but it was after his return that the program was fully developed. Children of ages six through seventeen were eligible to attend. Palfrey divided the pupils into small groups. There is no indication that he used the Lancastrian method that had so impressed him in England. But if he did, we can be sure that the playful gesticulations were absent. Religion was serious business to Palfrey, as the formidable outline of courses taught at the Brattle Street Sunday Schools bears out. There was no nonsense, wrote Edward Everett Hale, who recalled learning most of his Bible history at Brattle Street: "There you were expected to learn something, and you did." [57]

However time-consuming his parish duties may have been, Palfrey kept himself well informed on political events. His Federalism was soon to become Whiggism. When one of his brothers became a "rank Jacksonite" in 1827, Palfrey was properly downcast. When William, an anti-Jacksonian, apologized for including some news of politics in his letters, Palfrey assured him that

> I, for one, will never allow that my profession deprives me of any particle of my right to busy myself in matters of this sort. . . . I go regularly to the polls as men in other walks, & express my sentiments as freely. . . . It is a strange infatuation who prevails about the General [Jackson], but we have strong confidence here that he will be defeated. [58]

Palfrey's interest in magazine work continued. The European tour had forced him to give up editing the *Christian Examiner*, but his close connection with the *North American* did not end. On the contrary, editor Sparks had begun his career of historical research, and on two occasions Palfrey became temporary editor. This prelude to Palfrey's full control of the *North American* a decade later tells us little about him as an editor since it lasted only a few months. Palfrey cautiously and regularly communicated with Sparks, although the latter seemed to have more confidence in Palfrey than Palfrey had in himself. Palfrey displayed his caution when he received a pamphlet on an indelicate subject for review. The author condemned the marriage of a widower and his sister-in-law as incestuous. "We can hardly do it here," Palfrey wrote to Sparks, "whatever side you may take, some of our most respectable friends would be horrified to learn that any one thinks they have been guilty of incest." [59]

Palfrey served Sparks in a variety of ways. Sparks, who was aware that many of his friends thought that his work on Washington's papers was a waste of time, instructed Palfrey to enlighten Boston on this point. When Sparks's work took him to Europe, he made Palfrey the recipient and guardian of the manuscripts he sent home. Palfrey also tried very hard to obtain the Harvard presidency for his friend. President Kirkland resigned under fire in 1828. Palfrey and Samuel A. Eliot did everything possible to influence the Harvard Corporation in Sparks's behalf. There were many candidates—as usual, Edward Everett was pushing the candidacy of one of his brothers—and the choice of Josiah Quincy caused many disappointments. Even after Quincy's nomination Palfrey tried to block final approval.[60]

* * *

As a prominent Unitarian minister Palfrey was, of course, interested in the Harvard Divinity School. He had followed with optimism the development of a program of theological studies from its inception in 1816, the first year of his graduate residence:

As was natural to my age, & appropriate to the existing state of the controversy, I had taken a strong interest in the propagation of Unitarian opinions, & entertained a sanguine hope of their rapid & wide spread. I had been earnest for that object in the pulpit, through the press, & by all agencies that seemed fit & promising.

Early in 1825, the directors of the Society for the Promotion of Theological Education issued an appeal to the Unitarian clergy, suggesting that meetings of "the influential members of your society" be called to solicit support for the construction of a new Divinity Hall. The fund-raising languished until March 6, when Palfrey preached two sermons on the subject. When the afternoon service was over he asked the congregation to remain and raised $2,000. Palfrey's boast that he "saved the movement from utter failure" was no idle one. Contemporaries readily agreed that Palfrey had infused new life into the project. The published sermons were widely distributed, and the following year he proudly helped dedicate the new building.[61] Much later, when he was accused of having deserted the Divinity School, Palfrey pointed to his role in launching it as a separate institution.

Palfrey formalized his ties with the Divinity School in 1827. The theological education society still directed the activities of the school, and in that year Palfrey became its secretary. This gave him a direct voice in the school's management. He had acquired the reputation of a Biblical scholar on the basis of several of his sermons. When Andrews Norton went abroad in 1828, Palfrey took over some of the duties of Professor of Sacred Literature. This involved a weekly lecture on the Old Testament over a seven-month period. He continued in this temporary capacity until 1830. His penchant for drawing up plans and schedules appeared again when he prepared an elaborate scheme for reorganizing studies and enlarging the faculty of the school.[62]

The most important part of the proposed enlargement was the creation of a new professorship of Pulpit Eloquence and Pastoral Care. Palfrey did what he could to "extract from the pockets of our Creosuses" enough to support Henry Ware, Jr., for the place. He became exasperated with the delays and obstacles that the board of directors of the theological education society put in Ware's way: "They are undoubtedly the most slippery gentlemen with whom it has been my fortune to deal." But persistence wore down the procrastinators. Early in 1829 Ware got the appointment.[63]

A year after this strengthening of the Divinity School faculty, Andrews Norton resigned his professorship. When Palfrey first heard of Norton's intentions he tried unsuccessfully to persuade him to make his retirement a partial one, suggesting that Norton could lecture three times weekly without danger to his health. As secretary of the board, Palfrey was one of the men who had to select Norton's successor.[64]

Palfrey was genuinely surprised to learn that he himself was under consideration for the vacancy. He was unhappy about the fact that his name was being used without his consent and sent a note to Henry Ware, the Hollis Professor, disclaiming any foreknowledge of the proposed nomination. He wished to avoid having anyone think he was trying to undermine the newly acquired influence of Henry Ware, Jr. The elder Ware replied in the friendliest terms, urging Palfrey to take the appointment.[65]

In the negotiations that followed, Palfrey proved himself a sharp bargainer. Agreement in principle had been reached, so that with the renewal of his temporary status in September 1830 all knew that this would last only until the college Corporation met. Palfrey found two points objectionable in the offer when it came. A salary of $1,500 a year was unacceptable because it was considerably less than what he earned at Brattle Street. The stipulation that he conduct the prayers at the chapel every day also had to be modified. A compromise on the chapel meetings was easily obtained, but the question of salary proved more difficult. In 1827 a financial crisis at Harvard had forced the Corporation to decrease professors' salaries by $200 to $1,500. To give Palfrey more would mean running the risk of arousing faculty jealousy. But with a large family Palfrey could not be expected to agree to a decrease of six or seven hundred dollars in yearly income.

He knew how good his case was and pressed President Quincy for an early decision, citing the fact that the Brattle Street congregation knew of the negotiations. Quincy finally agreed that in addition to a regular professor's salary he would receive an extra five hundred dollars from the Society for the Promotion of Theological Education.[66]

The Brattle Street members were not happy about the arrangement. They were at first confident that the low salary would keep Palfrey where he was. George Bond expressed the feelings of many: "Our society must necessarily suffer. . . . In regard to the children and youth the injury will be greatest. It requires years to get their confidence." Informal delegations of parishioners called and tried to dissuade Palfrey; he replied that he must "go forward in the peace of a good conscience." [67] On December 12, 1830, the church reluctantly agreed to the separation.

According to Palfrey his last years at Brattle Street were particularly happy ones. Why then did he accept the professorship? He gives two reasons: his successful lecturing as Norton's substitute, and the advice of Justice Joseph Story, who spoke in terms of duty—at Harvard, Palfrey could do more to aid "the spread of pure religion." [68] Palfrey's ambition was another factor. Despite the fact that the professorship meant some financial loss, it would put him in a better position to achieve the "literary reputation" he had wanted since college days. However hard he worked on the Sunday school program at Brattle Street, the horizons there were not wide enough for him. When the new position opened up unexpectedly, he seized it eagerly. His ministry, Palfrey felt,

was not an eminent success. I did not preach very well. But, in the later years especially, I was a pains-taking, zealous, and faithful pastor, and I allow myself to believe that my labors were not unfruitful of some good results.[69]

V

Dean Palfrey

"I, John Gorham Palfrey, elected Professor of Sacred Literature, believe in the Christian religion, and have a firm persuasion of its truth. . . . I will not only labour to advance the knowledge of the department committed to my charge, but . . . will in every other Subject consult the prosperity of this University." With these words, Palfrey, as professor and dean, took charge in 1831 of a Divinity School badly in need of reorganization. In his last report as secretary of the Theological Education Society board of directors, Palfrey noted that "some systematick discipline" must be introduced.[1]

The first order of reform was the elimination of the Society for the Promotion of Theological Education as a power in Divinity School affairs. Although this change occurred before Palfrey took charge of the school, he helped bring it about. He opposed the role of the society's board and used his position of influence at Harvard (he had been elected an overseer in 1828) to help change it. In 1824 the society had acquired a large measure of control over the faculty and finances of the Divinity School, a move stemming in part from the college Corporation's indecision as to whether it was going to take responsibility for the school. Two years later, when the college Corporation would not agree to separate incorporation for the society, the two governing bodies were at odds. There were no doctrinal differences between most of the men of both groups, but it was clear that a system of dual authority would not do. No one knew precisely where the Corporation left off and where the powers of the society began. In November 1830, as part of the general reform of the Divinity School and assumption by the college of full powers, the society disbanded and transferred its funds to Harvard College.[2]

Palfrey held two Harvard posts. As professor of Biblical literature, he was to give instruction in the New Testament to all three grades of divinity students and to teach the Old Testament to the middle and senior classes. In addition he would teach Hebrew if the college authorities requested it. Palfrey's second job was that of dean of the faculty. This newly created office made him executive head of the Divinity School. He was to have charge of the building, call faculty meetings, and attend to disciplinary problems.[3]

The question of discipline required immediate attention. Remembering his own schoolmasters, Abbot and Kirkland, Palfrey tried to emulate them by blending courtesy and firmness. On the eve of his inauguration Palfrey read the new set of rules he had drawn up, and explained to the students the "reasons and spirit" of the regulations.[4] "Palfrey's Code" was anything but harsh, and it serves to illustrate how lax the discipline of the school had become. Unknown candidates for admission were to be college graduates, or else had to pass an entrance examination. Candidates for admission with advanced standing had to show proof of previous work. Within a year all students would live in Divinity Hall. The regulation most resented by the students was the prohibition against preaching outside the school prior to graduation, which eliminated a source of extra income. As a curb on this practice Professor Henry Ware, Jr., recommended postponement of instruction in sermon composition until the senior year, but Palfrey would not compromise. Breaking the rule meant expulsion. When a skeptical student tested Palfrey's resolve, he was expelled and there was "restiffness and discontent" among the students. Though Palfrey later relented in this case, he had made his point. The fledgling preachers gave him no more trouble. A further tightening came when the assignment of dormitory rooms was taken over by the faculty, and with the institution of a strict system of monitoring unauthorized absences.[5]

Palfrey also reorganized the curriculum. He had the lecture schedule arranged so that most instruction came in the afternoon, thus giving the students the whole morning for preparation. He had the lectures spread out evenly over the week, and there was to be no classroom work on Saturdays. For all practical purposes the school was Unitarian. There were five main fields of study: natural religion and evidences of revealed religion, Hebrew, Biblical criticism, ecclesiastical history, and pastoral theology. Palfrey's courses were in the second and third fields. Students came to him totally unprepared in Hebrew, which had to be learned for critical analysis of Biblical texts. Palfrey believed greatly in the importance of Biblical interpretation.[6]

The faculty consisted of three men—Dean Palfrey and the Henry Wares, father and son. For a short while Charles Follen gave courses in ethics and ecclesiastical history, but these stopped because the $500 Follen had been receiving was transferred to Palfrey's salary. President Quincy was also a nominal member of the divinity faculty.[7]

As dean of the faculty, Palfrey was in an awkward position. The fact that his salary was $500 greater than that of his colleagues was unsettling enough; and "something was to be apprehended from assigning the principal place to the youngest and the latest comer." Henry Ware, Sr., had been Palfrey's teacher, and his son had held a Divinity School professorship while Palfrey was still a parish minister. The dean's position of superiority "occasioned some feeling." Several arguments over policy with Henry Ware, Jr., may have had their origin in this resentment. It was the younger Ware's job to train preachers, and he was aware of the acute shortage of trained liberal ministers. Thus he was inclined to be lenient with the students who wished to preach outside before graduation. A more important difference arose over admissions. Palfrey had tightened up requirements, and his policy was too rigid and demanding for Ware. The latter did on one occasion make a protest on the subject of salaries, but with no result. Palfrey

charitably ascribed the younger Ware's irritability to poor
health. On the other hand, Ware's father was even more of a
problem. Although it was Palfrey's duty to conduct faculty
meetings, he wisely deferred to Ware's age and experience by
allowing him to preside. Ware, Sr., was unhappy about not
being paid to conduct chapel services and complained to President Quincy in a letter which contained clear signs of dis-
satisfaction with the state of Divinity School finances.[8]

The attempt to go over Palfrey's head and appeal directly
to the college authorities proved unsuccessful. Palfrey had
already asked the president for a clarification of his position.
Quincy was reluctant to express any opinion, and wished "that
the immediate faculty should endeavour to settle all such
questions, among themselves." The net effect of this hesitancy
was to affirm the autonomy of the Divinity School:

> The policy of the President & the Corporation . . . was to ignore
> the Divinity School as much as possible, & keep it from attracting
> public notice. But, what was the main thing, they were in general quite
> willing to let me have my own way in respect to its internal adminis-
> tration, & even to allow that my way was the best, & to sustain me in it.

Once Palfrey's authority had been established beyond question, there was no more trouble. When the first class of Palfrey's tenure graduated in 1833, Henry Ware, Jr., wrote that
his duties were growing "more and more delightful" to him,
and that the school's prospects had never seemed brighter.[9]

*   *   *

The change from a Boston minister to a Cambridge professor naturally had a great effect on Palfrey's family life. An
obvious change was the move from Court Street. For a few
months Palfrey lived in Divinity Hall. He then bought twelve
acres of land north of the college from Edward Everett and
built a house, called Hazelwood, with money loaned by
Samuel Hammond.[10] The family moved into the house in
October 1831, four months after the birth of Palfrey's second

son, Francis. The Palfreys were now eight strong (including two servants), but tragedy soon darkened the new home. Scarlet fever struck the three youngest children, and Gorham, Jr., weakened by loss of blood from leeches and excessive bleedings, died in January 1832. "Mary Ann," wrote Palfrey proudly, "sustains herself as angels would, if they could know trouble." [11]

No sooner had Palfrey settled himself in Cambridge, than the Brattle Street Church asked him to return. Even after he left the church, Palfrey made frequent appearances in the Brattle pulpit. This brought him extra income and did not demand too much of his time, since most of the sermons he delivered were revisions of old ones. He even continued to pay occasional parish calls. The church had not been able to find a satisfactory successor to Palfrey, and this prompted Abbott Lawrence to suggest that Palfrey give up the professorship. Palfrey conferred with Lawrence but told him that "honor & good conscience" made such a step unthinkable.[12]

Nothing more was said for a year and a half. In the interim the church had divided over the candidacies of Chandler Robbins and William H. Channing. The members felt that only the return of the old pastor would restore harmony. This time the entire congregation asked Palfrey to come back, and the request carried the signatures of a formidable roster of Boston's great men, including Daniel Webster, Harrison Gray Otis, and Abbott Lawrence. Many of the members wrote to Palfrey, and there was much discussion of where duty lay and the relative importance of the Divinity School and Brattle Street. When the divinity students heard of the offer they reacted immediately. They organized a protest meeting, stating their hope that the published reports of his imminent departure from the school were unfounded.[13]

Although Palfrey was tempted, he gave the Brattle Street people no reason to think he could be swayed. They begged him not to answer hastily: "as to salary & other encouragements I might have almost *carte blanche*." The economic pressure was enormous. Palfrey was only too aware of the advantages of moving back to Boston, and Mrs. Palfrey made it plain "with delicate forbearance" that she wished to return to her family and friends. Mr. Hammond wanted them back, and was prepared to make it profitable for them. But Palfrey would not be convinced. It was a matter of "judgement and conscience" and he was sure that to leave the Divinity School would be desertion. The decision to remain was a brave one. Another son was born in 1833, and in addition to the large amount owed his father-in-law, Palfrey's income was to fall when the Brattle church hired a permanent pastor and his temporary services were no longer needed.

He had to find a way to earn more money. In 1835 Palfrey hit upon the scheme of adding the Hancock Professorship of Oriental Languages to his titles and five hundred dollars to his income: "I have not a livelihood," he told the Corporation, "I left an income of $2,500 in Boston. . . . Servants' wages have all along been a heavier tax to us than in town, where there is a greater competition for places." He proposed to give courses in Hebrew, Arabic, and "Aramaean." "They are useful in the illustration of Scripture. They are attractive, some of them particularly so, to the general student," he claimed disingenuously. The college Corporation made no comment about the attractiveness of the languages, but it did deny Palfrey's request. Another salary increase, however much work were attached to it, would be bad policy. Palfrey would then be earning more than President Quincy![14] This refusal led Palfrey to consider the *North American Review* as a possible source of income, and he purchased the journal in 1835.[15]

Despite his financial problems, Palfrey's social activities continued, including his dabbling in reform societies. He was interested in temperance, which to him meant abstinence from hard liquor. His speech, given before a meeting of the Cambridge Temperance Society, did much to get that group started and was remembered long afterward. More important for Palfrey's future career was his first involvement with an organized antislavery group. Henry Ware, Jr., had become president of the newly formed Cambridge Anti-Slavery Society, and Palfrey attended a few meetings. Previously, he had not shown any pronounced feeling on the subject of slavery. He did make a speech in 1822 on the slave trade, which he certainly opposed, but there was nothing else in his past to foreshadow his coming abolitionism. His letters to John Palfrey contained off-hand references to "my friends of the sable complexion," or "my sooty friends," with not a word of criticism of the slave system.[16]

Palfrey's first antislavery commitment ended as quickly as it began. When notices of the Cambridge society's activities and controversy over them at the Divinity School appeared in the Boston papers, he told Ware and Follen that he must withdraw from the society. He did this despite the fact that the Cambridge group had drawn a clear line between themselves and the Garrisonian abolitionists. Ware was no extremist. He declined to invite Samuel J. May to speak before the society, saying: "We feel our way amongst ourselves at first." Even this respectable antislavery position was too much for the Palfrey of 1834. His withdrawal was final, and the group dissolved a year later.[17]

The issue of slavery was not to be avoided so easily. Henry Palfrey reported from New Orleans that one of his slaves had been "kidnapped" by Philadelphia abolitionists while traveling with Henry's wife. He went to Philadelphia and learned that his slave, Lucinda, had escaped to Canada. Four years before, John Palfrey had boasted that his slaves were "as happy as any of their color in the State & as conscious of it." Lucinda had been particularly well treated as a house servant. Palfrey knew that his brother was no tyrant. Happiness, to "the sooty people," was obviously not just a matter of good or bad treatment.[18]

*   *   *

In 1835 Palfrey decided to visit Louisiana. President Quincy was displeased about losing Palfrey for several months, but he reluctantly consented. A brilliant young man, Theodore Parker, was put in charge of Palfrey's courses. A justification for the journey, which was to be entirely overland, was that Palfrey would arouse interest and increase subscriptions to the *North American Review*. He stopped in the principal cities along the Atlantic coast for that purpose. In Philadelphia, Nicholas Biddle, president of the Bank of the United States, was "vastly civil," and Professor Francis Lieber equally attentive when he reached South Carolina. Palfrey arrived at the Attakapas plantation in February 1836 and found his father prospering "according to the standard of his caste." The slaves greeted him as "young marssa" and used his arrival as an excuse for an impromptu celebration. After a late tea with his father, "we went to bed, with his dogs and two negro boys sleeping by the fire in the room between us." [19]

A falling-out between Palfrey and one of his former students, James Freeman Clarke, marred the trip. Clarke was the pastor of the Unitarian church in Louisville. When Palfrey returned to the East by way of the Mississippi and Ohio rivers, and did not preach to the Unitarians of the Mississippi Valley, Clarke's *Western Messenger* criticized him sharply. His reproaches were the same that Sparks had made from Baltimore a decade earlier: "What we wanted," wrote Clarke with more patience, "was not an eloquent discourse—it was a word of sympathy—it was to see the face of a friend—it was to be told that there were thoughts for us in other places—that we were not alone." Clarke later apologized for the tone of his published remarks.[20]

As a teacher Palfrey was even more conscientious than he

had been in the last year of his ministry. At the Harvard bi-centennial in 1836, he spoke of the unity of learning and religion. His work at the Divinity School was an attempt to strengthen that union. Some of his teaching emanated from the chapel pulpit, where his sermons ("animated without being impassioned"), were listened to with respect.[21]

But it was in the classroom that Palfrey did his most effective work. He expanded the scope of the courses in Hebrew, and made the study of other Eastern languages optional for seniors. He taught these languages for no antiquarian purpose:

> Syriac was more interesting still than [Chaldee], as giving the use of the best & perhaps the oldest translation of the New Testament, & enabling the student to read the discourses of Jesus in substantially the same language, in which they were originally pronounced.

This was indicative of Palfrey's attitude toward instruction in Biblical interpretation. His predecessor, Andrews Norton, had been so positive in the classroom that most discussion and all dissent had been crushed out. Palfrey, on the other hand, led his students to the sources, stated his views, and waited for and welcomed dissent. Often, when a good discussion was under-way, the class would continue beyond its scheduled time. The method was wearing:

> To reply at the moment to the variety of questions which ingenious, generally conscientious, moderately, or even little informed, sometimes whimsical, & sometimes even cavilling young men could present, was a great exertion of the mind to be kept up for a stretch of two hours.

Palfrey sometimes wished he were teaching mathematics, with its precise proofs. His cardinal rule of teaching was never to interfere with the students' free judgment. An ill-phrased or even silly question must not be treated with contempt. His role was to help the student shape his thoughts into a coherent system. Whatever fatigue he brought upon himself by avoid-ing the dogmatic approach was more than compensated for by the affectionate admiration of his students. "How hard it must be," mused one of them about Palfrey, "for a man of so sensitive intellectuality—physically & morally—quick to perceive every glimpse of Truth, & susceptible to every shadow of feeling . . . to be in the eye of the superficial world, consistently. But he has a character—deep though it be." [22]

*   *   *

Amid all this serenity came a formidable challenge. The most famous day in the history of the Harvard Divinity School was July 15, 1838. At the invitation of the senior students, Ralph Waldo Emerson lectured in the chapel of Divinity Hall. Since that time the popular impression of Palfrey's Divinity School has been fixed: students searching for truth and being spoon-fed "pale negations" and "corpse-coldness" instead; moth-eaten professors of theology looking backward with the tenacity native to dull minds. So much for impressions.

Prior to July 1838 Palfrey's contacts with Emerson had been infrequent but friendly. On one or two occasions, while Emerson was still a minister at Boston's Second Church, they had exchanged pulpits. Palfrey had loaned Emerson's brother, Edward, some money, and after Edward's death Emerson attempted to pay, but Palfrey declined. His loan was to have been repaid only if Edward had been successful as a lawyer. This was the extent of their personal contacts, but when Palfrey read Emerson's *Nature* he wrote: "Emerson has sent forth a Carlisle-like book. . . . Some parts of it strike me as beautiful; several, as unintelligible; some . . . as noxious." Palfrey agreed with his friends who found Emerson's views "very attractive & delightful as matters of poetry—but quite unsatisfactory as realities—they can't pass the ordeal of common sense." [23]

Dean Palfrey was one of many persons who crowded into the chapel to hear Emerson's address. Emerson's introductory material was thoroughly innocuous—"matters of poetry." But when he launched into the explanation of the gross errors into which the Christian churches had fallen, Palfrey stiffened in his seat. "The word Miracle, as pronounced by Christian churches, gives a false impression; it is a Monster." Emerson could not stomach the "noxious exaggeration about the *person of Jesus.*" As for the church itself, it "seems to totter to its fall, almost all life extinct," consumed by spiritual famine. Then came an attack on the soulless preacher who defrauds the worshiper.[24] Redemption was to be found within the soul, not through the church.[25]

The audience heard the address with "profound attention," records the divinity students' history. "Emerson preached odiously," was Palfrey's reaction, and he later told Long-fellow that what was not folly in the address was impiety. That night at Palfrey's home, Emerson was the sole topic of con-versation. Young Edward Everett Hale followed the crowd to the house, and noted the "brilliant aurora" of agitated Unitarians who had gathered there. The following evening brought more conferences on the same subject at the Norton and Ware homes.[26] Palfrey never made a public reply to Emerson. We can be sure, however, that he took an active part in the strategy consultations which followed.

It was essential that the Divinity School disassociate itself from Emerson's position. Orthodox Congregationalists had never stopped contending that Unitarianism was but a way sta-tion on the road to infidelity. Emerson's address shook the Unitarians' view that their system tended more than others to Christian piety. Thus the reaction to Emerson was defensive on two fronts.[27] Andrews Norton sent a blistering letter to the *Boston Advertiser* expressing the "disgust and strong dis-approbation" of the Divinity School officers, and published his *Discourse on the Latest Form of Infidelity*, an attack on Emerson.[28]

Four years after he left the Divinity School Palfrey looked back at the address:

The prospect that even the small number of pupils were to be reared up to be useful servants of the church, was lessened by the introduc-

tion among them, to some extent, of infidel opinions. Mr. Emerson's
Address . . . with the indications accompanying it, has been a bad
blow to our hopes.[29]

No Christian divinity school would have pleased Emerson, and
Palfrey had no reason to be defensive about his record. The
school had risen greatly in stature since his arrival in 1831.
The methods of instruction had improved and the scope of
courses broadened. Palfrey took his work seriously, and the
standards, if not the content, of his Biblical criticism (the
*Academical Lectures on the Jewish Scriptures and Antiqui-
ties*), are still admired.[30] The roster of distinguished graduates
of the Divinity School of the 1830's—Clarke, Peabody, Hedge,
Eliot, W. H. Channing, Bellow—attest to the fact that all was
not dust and cobwebs at Divinity Hall. Perhaps the best
tribute to Palfrey's work was a farewell letter from the same
senior class that had invited Emerson. Though stilted as such
letters invariably are, a few of its phrases break through the
crust of polite language: "Now that we are about to lose the
advantages of your instruction . . . we are moved with love
towards those who have guided us in our inquiries, & communicated to us the fruits of their toils." [31]

*   *   *

In the year following the Emerson affair, Palfrey concluded
that he could not continue as a full-time professor at the
Divinity School. The *North American Review* demanded so
much of his time that he felt only a reduction in teaching
duties would allow him to keep up the quality of his work.
The proposal Palfrey made in this respect led unwittingly to
his separation from the school. He suggested that his course in
Biblical interpretation be limited to one term, and that he be
relieved of teaching Hebrew and of chapel preaching. The
college Corporation was agreeable, except that it insisted on
five appearances in the chapel pulpit each year. But this decision had been made at a poorly attended meeting. Justices
Joseph Story and Lemuel Shaw, who were absent, later

opposed Palfrey's request, and it was evident that a full meeting would have refused Palfrey. President Quincy informed Palfrey of the "decided character" of the opposition.[32]

For Palfrey there was only one thing to do. His letter of resignation, dated April 5, 1839, suggested the next Commencement as an appropriate time for his retirement. President Quincy, who felt partially responsible for Palfrey's decision since he had told him of the dissension within the Corporation, tried unsuccessfully to dissuade him. In August, Palfrey turned over the papers of the Divinity School—the written records of eight years of work—complete and in order.[33]

Palfrey had deeper reasons for leaving the Divinity School.[34] The immediate cause was the nature of the opposition to his proposal, which he took as a personal affront. More important was the conviction that the Divinity School was not as important on the Harvard scene as it had once been. When Palfrey's young friend, Charles Sumner, sent a list of books that ought to be purchased for the divinity library, Palfrey replied that funds would probably not be appropriated: "The theological department had its day of favor formerly. Others have it now." Although he later felt that the "unchristianizing of the unitarian denomination" had undone most of his work, Palfrey could, and did, look back with pride on his professorial years. The very liberal nature of Unitarianism—the relative lack of doctrinal explicitness or denominational cohesion—had set in motion a new religious current that eventually superseded the Unitarianism of Palfrey's generation. The challenge came almost as soon as the first Unitarians had established themselves. Historical acceleration had scarcely allowed them time to emerge from their negative stage.[35]

Once again Palfrey had resigned a position of influence in his community, but this time he was not moving into a waiting situation. The "literary reputation" was as elusive as ever; it must be approached directly. Longfellow noted: "[Palfrey] will now go to Boston, and give himself up to literature."[36]

VI

The North American

SEVERAL years before his resignation, Palfrey realized that the Divinity School did not offer sufficient stimulation or challenge. Like the Brattle Street ministry, he found the Cambridge deanship wanting. In March 1835 Edward Everett, who had repurchased it from Sparks, offered to sell Palfrey the *North American Review*, an offer which Palfrey found attractive. Everett had been in politics for a decade, and was considered Daniel Webster's understudy in Massachusetts politics. In 1830 he had turned over the editorship, but not the ownership, of the *North American* to his brother Alexander. The latter's tenure has been called the high point of the *North American*'s first fifty years, but whatever the quality of content, the magazine was in danger financially, and for several years the Everetts discussed the possibility of selling the *North American*.[1]

Edward Everett thought first of leaving Congress to resume the editorship himself, but decided instead to get rid of the journal.[2] Sparks suggested that Everett approach Palfrey, and at the same time warned his friend Palfrey not to make any purchase without scrutinizing the magazine's accounts. Everett admitted that receipts had decreased during the two previous years, but asserted blandly: "the vital power of the Establishment is Unimpaired." At the time Palfrey was in the middle of his unsuccessful negotiations for the Hancock professorship of Oriental languages, and he put Everett off for several months. Though Everett tried to interest Longfellow and several other persons in the review, he was still its reluctant owner when Palfrey asked to have negotiations resumed.

The two men quickly came to terms. Everett was willing to

sell his three-quarter share for $10,000 (it had cost him $15,000 in 1830). Palfrey was to pay $1,000 at once, and the balance in six yearly installments. He could then purchase the remaining one-quarter share from F. C. Gray.[3]

Generous as these terms appeared, Palfrey had to turn to friends for the money. His appeal to Amos Lawrence phrased the issue in terms of public policy:

> I believe you will agree with me that it is a matter of some general interest, what principles the work in question should maintain, & I venture to flatter myself that you give me some credit for attachment to sound principles in morals, politics, & literature. . . . It is important to have it go into hands, such as . . . will prevent it from becoming the instrument of any hurtful influence.[4]

Convinced of the new editor's "soundness," Lawrence advanced Palfrey $2,000, and George Bond supplied an additional $1,000. There was much opposition to the arrangement, however. Lawrence himself tried to dissuade Palfrey, and when he told Samuel Hammond of the loan, the latter rushed to see his son-in-law. Hammond, a hardheaded businessman, had no use for literary foolishness. He considered the *North American*, sound political organ or no, a questionable investment and offered to advance the Palfreys a portion of Mary Ann's inheritance if the plan were forgotten.

Once more Palfrey's overbearing sense of rectitude took over. He had gone too far to withdraw honorably, or so he told Hammond. After a brief hesitation, "by the blessing of a kind Providence . . . things cleared away, & made my duty plain." He summoned Everett and signed the contract. Palfrey's awareness of the dangers of the venture did not dampen his enthusiasm or expectations.[5]

Palfrey's optimism soon underwent several sharp tests. A week after the purchase, a warehouse fire destroyed a large part of the stock of back issues, and nearly all of the October number, then ready for distribution. Also, Everett had sold the review to Palfrey while a third party held a mortgage on his share. When Palfrey confronted him with this, Everett hastily borrowed money to clear the title. "The transaction," according to Palfrey, "was no untrue symptom of E. Everett's character, whether in public or in private life." [6]

*   *   *

The new editor's first task was to insure a sufficiently large number of contributors—preferably contributors who were already known to the reading public. Although the *Review's* subject matter was not geographically restricted, most of the contributions came from men living in or near Boston. Palfrey paid authors one dollar per page, but the trouble he had recruiting reluctant writers proves that the payment was not much of an inducement. But he was persistent. When Edward Everett, who at the time of the sale had promised to contribute regularly, at first claimed that he could not review the de Tocqueville adequately, only Palfrey's insistence prevailed upon Everett to write the piece. Caleb Cushing, Whig Congressman from Newburyport, had made similar promises: "I have you booked for the Mackerel Fishery [piece]," reminded Palfrey.[7]

During his first editorial years Palfrey had to write many of the articles himself and sometimes published two of his own articles in the same number. In his eight years he wrote twenty-two major articles. The choice of topics ranged from shipwrecked sailors in Polynesia to the theory of federal government, and from health conventions to relations with England. Five of the articles were historical, and none theological, an indication of the shift in his interests.

Palfrey's greatest assistance came from Cornelius C. Felton, the young classical scholar who later became president of Harvard College. He wrote a score of articles on an equally wide variety of subjects, and was also helpful in regularly contributing short reviews.

There were other steady contributors. Edward Everett kept

his word and aided Palfrey with articles in the early years, but later, when he found his duties as governor of Massachusetts too time-consuming, Everett's contributions ceased. Henry Wadsworth Longfellow was one of the first persons Palfrey sought to interest in the *Review*. Longfellow responded favorably, and although he did not write often, his literary essays were of high quality. William H. Prescott complained of lack of time, but found enough to spare to write eight articles. Francis Bowen and Charles Francis Adams contributed frequently during the latter part of Palfrey's editorship. Despite all the help Palfrey had given Sparks and the *North American* during the 1820's, Sparks wrote only two articles.

Not all the pages of the *North American* were filled by resident New Englanders. There were occasional articles by Governor Lewis Cass of Michigan, Henry Rowe Schoolcraft on the American Indian, and others. But despite Palfrey's attempts to achieve a wider geographical appeal by eliciting contributions from the South and Southwest, a glance at the index leaves no doubt that Boston was the place of publication.[8]

The *North American*'s New England insularity and assumption of superiority did not endear it to literary men in other parts of the country. Perhaps the fiercest hater of New England literary circles was Edgar Allan Poe. While literary editor of *Graham's Magazine* in Philadelphia, Poe wrote two series of essays which used the signatures of literary figures as the point of departure for judgments of the individuals. His appraisal of Palfrey went far beyond permissible literary grievance:

Professor Palfrey is known to the public principally through his editorship of the "North American Review." He has a reputation for scholarship; and many of the articles which are attributed to his pen evince that this reputation is well based, so far as the common notion of scholarship extends. For the rest, he seems to dwell altogether within the narrow world of his *own* conceptions; imprisoning them by the very barrier which he has erected against the conceptions of others. His manuscript shows a total deficiency in the sense of the beautiful. It has great pretension, great straining after effect, but is altogether one of the most miserable manuscripts in the world—forceless, graceless, tawdry, vacillating, and unpicturesque. The signature conveys but a faint idea of its extravagance. However much we may admire the mere knowledge of the man who writes thus, it will not do to place any dependence upon his wisdom or upon his taste.[9]

*   *   *

During his editorship Palfrey came into contact with several men who were to be his political allies in later years. Samuel Gridley Howe wrote an article on his favorite reform cause, instruction for the blind, and Charles Sumner reviewed Francis J. Grund's *The Americans*. Charles Francis Adams was a regular contributor. In typical Adams fashion, he claimed never to be satisfied with what he wrote.[10]

George Bancroft, historian and politician, was the cause of Palfrey's worst moments as an editor. Already the author of several volumes of his *History of the United States*, he had alienated conservative Boston by joining the Massachusetts Democracy, but in 1835 Palfrey sought to enlist him as a *North American* reviewer. He spoke flatteringly of Bancroft's work, adding assurances that party politics would have no place in his *North American*. Bancroft was receptive: "You do right in excluding party politics. . . . I hope to see in your journal free discussion, bold examination of principles, a reverence for humanity." Palfrey, however, could never completely overcome his political prejudice against the Democrat Bancroft.[11]

Three years after Palfrey's original inquiry Bancroft submitted an article on American historians requesting Palfrey to send him final proofs for inspection. He found that Palfrey had made a significant deletion. After the phrase: "during the Administration of General Jackson," Palfrey struck out the words "whose fame is closely blended with the history of his country." Furious, Bancroft demanded that Palfrey and the printers hold up the issue. Palfrey tried to placate his irate contributor, promising to restore the elision. The statement itself was not objectionable, explained the editor; he had deleted it merely because he thought it was out of place. Palfrey's subsequent attempt to remedy the situation worsened matters. In addition to restoring the disputed phrase, he added some praise of Bancroft's *History*. Since the identity of the *North American*'s authors was well known, it now appeared that Bancroft had lauded himself. Bancroft exploded, and intermediaries soon appeared. Prescott suggested an explanation was in order; Palfrey published a disclaimer in the next number. Sparks tried to play the peacemaker with Bancroft, since Palfrey had gone to Washington on business, but his success was limited.[12]

From this point on, the unhappy Palfrey combined private contrition with public truculence. Prescott saw him in New York "melancholy as a cat, wending his way South." When he returned, the correspondence with Bancroft degenerated into a series of short, sharp notes. When Palfrey refused to open Bancroft's letters, Bancroft published them in the Democratic *Boston Post*. Palfrey's friends supported him, denouncing Bancroft's act as Loco-Foco churlishness and a breach of the sanctity of private correspondence, and the *Boston Daily Advertiser* made a party issue of it. But Palfrey had been wrong from the beginning, compounding party prejudice with ineptitude. His rigid sense of rectitude should have told him that he had broken his promise to let Bancroft see exactly what was to appear in print. But he stubbornly refused to admit any such thing. When James Freeman Clarke's *Western Messenger* mentioned the unwritten agreement, Palfrey angrily denied it. His irascibility throughout the affair was the measure of his shaky position. This was not Palfrey's finest hour.[13]

*   *   *

Editor Palfrey was conscientious but unimaginative. "Dull and hoary," was the reputation the *North American* had acquired, and Palfrey's tenure did little to change it. The magazine's pervading tone was conservative. The "bold examination of principles" which Bancroft had called for never materialized. Literary men (and an occasional woman) filled its pages with decorous discussion of topics that would interest respectable ladies and gentlemen. Palfrey's *North American* was not a Unitarian review as has been claimed, but it certainly was a Whig review. Boston conservatives considered the mazagine their ideological and political property.[14] Nor was this all. The Transcendentalists, such "inane and insane" persons as Orestes Brownson or Henry Thoreau, were not to be found in its pages. Emerson's two *North American* articles had appeared before the Divinity School Address scandalized Whig-Unitarian Boston.

Palfrey, in the judgment of one historian, devoted too much space to history and tried to avoid politics.[15] An examination of the *Review* index from 1836 to 1843 does not substantiate the first charge. The major articles display a wide range of subject matter, with many on literature and travel, and not a few on such diverse topics as music, fashions, common schools, penology, and beet-sugar production. On the second count Palfrey is guilty, with an explanation. When assigning a review on Aaron Burr to Charles Francis Adams, he included the reminder: "the North American is, as far as the frailty of nature permits, a neutral in respect of party politics." [16] Yet Palfrey was not himself politically neutral, nor was the *North American*. It represented a defined point of view, clearly aligned with one of two major political parties, the Whigs. What Palfrey meant by neutrality was the absence of political invective and the barring of immediate party squabbles from the magazine's pages. The *North American* did not endorse tickets; it electioneered quietly behind the soothing protection of accepted major premises.

This form of political "neutrality" was but a part of Palfrey's desire to keep the publication out of unnecessary arguments.

He tried to exclude material critical of living persons or their sensitive descendants that might "embroil me with the sufferers," and he feared offending Boston authors by publishing negative or lukewarm reviews. Andrews Norton, incensed over some pamphlets of Transcendentalist George Ripley, and the viewpoint of the *Dial*, called on Palfrey to mount a "triumphant resistance to this great evil." Palfrey declined to joust with Ripley, however. Perhaps he felt he would get the worst of it; more probably he was simply sick of controversy. His conservative independence reached its high point when he rejected a manuscript by ex-President John Quincy Adams defending the moral position of the British during the Opium War. Palfrey's Federalist dislike for Adams had long since vanished. He now regarded the old man deferentially, and was painfully reluctant to offend, but

> However badly the Chinese have behaved to the "outside barbarians" . . . I canot see, till I have had opportunity to know the President's reasons,—that this behaviour was justifiable cause for a war of invasion. No living man's opinion on that point is worth more than Mr. Adams', & no man can produce stronger reasons for it. But I own I want to see those reasons when I pledge the *Review* to the correctness of the conclusion.[17]

The 1830's witnessed the growth of a militant abolitionist movement, but this development cannot be traced in the pages of the *North American*. Palfrey's distaste for controversy meant exclusion of the abolitionist point of view. The anti-Garrisonian Cambridge Anti-Slavery Society had been too much for him in 1834. As editor of an ostensibly national publication, Palfrey felt that he must bar whatever tended to irritate sectional antagonism. The magazine had traditionally favored African colonization of Negroes as a solution to the slavery problem, an evasive formula which still had much appeal in conservative circles, although it made no significant reduction in the American Negro population. When Lydia Maria Child sent Palfrey a copy of her *Evils of Slavery*, she thought it best to apologize for any possible offense due to the book's subject matter. Abolitionist Edmund Quincy tried in vain to have a book extolling West Indian emancipation reviewed in the *North American*. Even a staunch conservative like Charles Francis Adams found Palfrey a timid and at times frightened editor, who often toned down passages in Adams' articles. On one occasion Adams agreed to do a review but only if he might probe at the plague spot of the American social system, whatever the reaction of southern readers. Palfrey demurred, and next day asked Adams to forget about the piece.[18]

Although many of the reviews, then as now, were thinly disguised essays which bore little relation to the volume supposedly under discussion, Palfrey insisted on preserving custom. Each contribution had one or more books or articles listed in a headnote. The only change that Palfrey made in the format was the introduction of a section of "Critical Notices." These were short reviews of single books. Palfrey wrote most of them, but he had help from his friends, especially Felton. He also received substantial aid from Charles Folsom, whom he had known since Harvard days, and who was then in the publishing business. Palfrey shared many of the details of editorial work with him, letting Folsom take charge when he was absent. Folsom, who did much more work than Palfrey could pay for, relished commenting with gusto and good critical sense on the literary merits of the manuscripts he inspected. Palfrey was not shy about demanding contributions from his friends. He had no qualms about asking Longfellow to meet publication deadlines in a half-joking, half-peremptory manner which he dared not use with his other contributors.[19]

*   *   *

Palfrey took the *North American* with an eye to increasing his income. The years of his editorship present a tangled financial picture. Initially the magazine made a good profit. After two years Palfrey was more than happy with the returns—so happy in fact, that he was fearful that the financial honeymoon could not last. Everything was going too well. Subscriptions had increased, and even after interest payments of $600, the *Review* was earning well over $1,000 a year.

This happy condition ended soon after America's first real depression, following the Panic of 1837. By the end of that year circulation declined appreciably, and in July of 1838 came the "truly appalling intelligence" of the loss of over two hundred subscriptions. To cut expenses Palfrey transferred his printing to a new Boston firm which offered cheaper rates, but gross profits dropped to $200 in 1839, and to only $15 in 1840. This did not include the fixed interest charges! Palfrey felt that the new printers were somehow responsible for the catastrophe, but it is difficult to see how this could have been so.[20]

At this critical point some aid came from Louisiana. Henry Palfrey, dealing shrewdly on the New Orleans market, was on his way to making a fortune despite the depression. Several times he suggested that Palfrey come to Louisiana. Finally Henry offered to build a church for Gorham at a cost of $40,000 and give his brother a salary of $5,000 a year. In addition, Henry was willing to pay expenses incurred in moving from Massachusetts. Henry found his brother's reasons for declining convincing, and dropped the idea. A financial windfall came to Palfrey following the death of Thomas L. Harman, the New Orleans merchant who had married his aunt Charlotte. Harman set aside some money for Charlotte's relatives, and the Palfrey brothers received $1,000 each. This was not enough to meet all of Palfrey's needs, and he asked Henry for a loan. When Henry complied promptly Palfrey dedicated the first volume of his *Academical Lectures* to his generous brother.[21]

As the condition of the *North American* worsened, Palfrey had to seek another loan, this time from his father. John Pal-

frey was willing to put up $1,000 a year, depending on the
return on his crop. He told Gorham to consider the arrangement an advance of his portion of his patrimony, rather than a
loan. When Palfrey sent a promissory note for the money
loaned, John Palfrey returned it.[22]

In 1838 Palfrey's father-in-law, Samuel Hammond, died
suddenly. Instead of bringing an immediate increase in family
income through Mary Ann's inheritance, the death put an
added strain on Palfrey's purse. Hammond's money was in
trust, and while the Palfreys were to receive a yearly income
of $2,000 they owed the estate $10,000, the money borrowed
to build Hazelwood. This forced Palfrey to appeal to his
family and friends for additional loans.[23]

Some relief came in an appointment as Lowell lecturer.
John Lowell, Jr., who died in 1836, left a quarter of a million
dollars to support a series of public lectures in Boston. Palfrey
was to receive $1,000 for a series of eight lectures on the
Evidences of Christianity, in the winter of 1840, which were
to be repeated the following year for another $1,000. Palfrey
accepted at once. Although there was a heavy demand for
tickets at first and considerable discussion of the lectures, both
demand and discussion soon died down. Charles Folsom had
counseled Palfrey that he ought to "select weapons, & in going
forth follow tactics suited to the day," but the Boston community did not find the subject of evidences absorbing. The
second series was still more poorly attended. Even Palfrey's
friend Charles Francis Adams found the lectures disappoint-
ingly thin in research and reasoning.[24]

In 1840 Harvard asked Palfrey to lecture at the Divinity
School. Both the scope of the lectures and the compensation
corresponded to Palfrey's Hancock professorship plan, the
rejection of which had brought about his resignation. As his
sheaf of unpaid bills multiplied, Palfrey reflected morosely
upon the fact that he might have retained this source of income
had he not been so ready to take offense.

Palfrey's hopes for the *North American* as a vehicle for literary and financial advancement could not survive examinations of quarterly statements and the dwindling subscription list. In June 1840 he recorded: "Received this morning $262 from the N. A. R. the first I have received these fifteen months. Obviously, he could not go on without outside help. Palfrey decided to mortgage part of his holding. Five of his friends loaned him $1,000 each, against Palfrey's pledge of a portion of the *Review*'s income. Considering the amount of past income, the loans were more in the nature of friendly accommodation than practical investment.

There was another possible avenue of relief. The *North American* had not been so valuable a piece of property when he purchased it as Edward Everett had made it out to be. Palfrey claimed that he had been able to collect only one quarter of the amount Everett had asserted was owed him; furthermore, Everett had given him an incorrect circulation figure. F. C. Gray, who had held part of the magazine's stock in 1835, agreed to reduce Palfrey's indebtedness, but Everett would make no adjustment. Justice Joseph Story advised that Palfrey might refuse to honor the final note, because of Everett's misrepresentations. Everett would not budge. Palfrey did not press further since the note was in the hands of Everett's father-in-law, Peter C. Brooks: "I would not, for the value of the note, hazard a disturbance of the agreeable relations I have so many years sustained with Mr. Brooks." [25]

It was clear that the *North American* was not to prosper under Palfrey. He had even tried to act as his own publisher, succeeding in increasing profits slightly. But before long he was back to his accustomed position: "I am tempted with Gen. Jackson to say, that my sufferings is intolerable." It was galling to have friends, such as Charles Francis Adams, offer to forgo payment for contributions.

Despite the variety of methods employed to remain solvent and the loans from family and friends, Palfrey knew he would have to give up the *Review*. "Thank God! Thank God! In consequence of a conversation this morning . . . I have a prospect of relief from my pecuniary annoyances." This frantically elated journal entry referred to negotiations between Palfrey and J. L. Stackpole. In this case Palfrey's happiness was short-lived, for Stackpole offered him only $4,000, an offer he could not accept. Another purchaser had to be found since the *North American* was closer to bankruptcy each day. Publicly Palfrey's friends tried to bolster him, but in private they agreed with Charles Sumner, who asked: "Would it not be far preferable to let the *Review* drop down into oblivion rather than be forced to this perpetual rally?" [26]

In December 1842 Palfrey sold the *North American* to Francis Bowen. This was an act of desperation, for he described Bowen's offer as "discouraging." Palfrey received very little money at once; instead he had to take long-term notes. On the night of the sale Palfrey went to bed anticipating a good night's sleep for the first time in many years. Thus ended the bleakest episode of Palfrey's life. He had taken over the *North American* for the purpose of making money. By his own criterion his editorship was a complete failure. At the age of forty-six he was "loose on the world again, just as when, twenty-five years ago, I was embarking in the ministry. Pastor, professor, & editor meanwhile, & now—nothing. . . ." [27]

VII

The State House

Long before he succeeded in unburdening himself of the *North American*, Palfrey allowed his thoughts to wander to new occupations. Whatever the setbacks or failures of his life, he felt compelled to push ahead and find a niche suited to his talents and position. No man more thoroughly conscious and desirous of the approval of his peers than Palfrey ever lived. A man who aspired to acceptance by the best of Boston society could not survive socially on his wife's $2,000 a year.[1] But this was not solely a matter of self-respect. From a financial point of view the continuance of the Palfrey family's high standard of living made immediate and unavoidable demands. It was natural that Palfrey should seek some new road to success. The road he chose, politics, was to bring him his greatest disappointments as well as his greatest moments of personal satisfaction; eventually it was to bring an end to the genteel poverty which had plagued him since his departure from the Harvard Divinity School—but this happier turn lay many years ahead.

In selecting politics Palfrey looked with envy upon the career of Edward Everett. Despite his low opinion of the man, Palfrey could not deny that Everett's position in Massachusetts was one of considerable importance. Why not follow? Both men were outstanding scholars and professors at Harvard; both had been pastors of the Brattle Street church; both editors of the *North American*. Palfrey felt no less talented when he compared himself to Everett, the governor of the Commonwealth. As for integrity, there was no question in his mind as to who possessed more of that vital quality. Musings on the subject led him to dream of the possibilities of "public life." [2]

Palfrey had always shown an interest in political events. During his ministry he had defended his right to hold and express political opinions. Yet all this had been more in the realm of political speculation than action. Palfrey, who had prided himself on his youthful Federalism, naturally gravitated into the Whig party of his conservative friends. The Loco-Foco enthusiasm of the Jacksonians did not appeal to his temperament, nor did it coincide with his interests.

During the presidential election campaign of 1840—the Log Cabin campaign of General William Henry Harrison's managers—Palfrey's interest in political events increased markedly. He attended the immense Whig celebration of September 10 in Boston, and later that same day listened to the Whig speechmakers extol the virtues of hard cider well into the night. His sons, Frank and John, were caught up in the Log Cabin fever. Palfrey allowed them to attend the political parades, though he himself was not so pleased by the Whig expropriation of Loco-Foco enthusiasm. His daughter Sarah echoed her father's words when she wrote that it scarcely seemed possible that the sedate people of Boston could be raised to such a state of excitement. She admitted enjoying all the agitation, but the perspicacious youngster added candidly: "I do not think I should approve the plan of operations so decidedly if the Democrats should turn it against us, at the next election." [3]

*   *   *

In 1841, when Palfrey had been living in Boston for two years, he was elected one of the thirty-five Whig representatives to the General Court (the state legislature) from the city. There is no record of whether Palfrey solicited a place on the ticket or whether the idea originated with someone else. In any case Palfrey's friends intimated that he would be watched closely by the political powers of the Whig party and that "something" was expected of him as a legislator. When he entered the State House, for the first time in an official capacity, on January 5, 1842, Palfrey had these expectations uppermost in his mind.[4]

The Whigs of Massachusetts controlled both houses of the General Court. In the House of Representatives, where Palfrey was one of 323 members, there were nearly 200 Whigs. They had no difficulty in electing a Whig to the speakership of the House on the first ballot. Speaker Thomas H. Kinnicutt sounded the Whig keynote when he spoke of the economy which the people of the Commonwealth expected and hoped that the session would not be a prolonged one. Palfrey was one of many newcomers, noted fellow member Charles Francis Adams, in an early appraisal of the composition of the legislature: "The number of new faces is prodigiously augmented. It is a little remarkable to notice the revolution that has taken place within a year. Almost all of the ambitious young men have been swept out and a fresh race have come in who as yet show no distinct complexion." [5]

Because of his previous educational experience Palfrey received the chairmanship of the House Standing Committee on Education. There were six other members of the committee, all representatives from small towns and not prominent House members.[6] Although the education committee was not the most important of the House committees, it was an active group and gave Palfrey an opportunity to make himself well known at the State House. Chairman Palfrey called the committee together on January 15, for the first of a series of frequent meetings. Horace Mann, the secretary of the State Board of Education, maintained close contact with the legislative committees on education, conferring with Palfrey several times a week.[7]

Palfrey's industriousness soon became evident. Four days after the first committee meeting he presented a report to the

House calling for stronger legislation to compel parents to send their children to school. A few days later came a carefully drafted report on a trivial matter: the circulation of engraved maps of Massachusetts. Palfrey had apparently forgotten the admonitions of Speaker Kinnicutt on the need for economy, for he called for a wide distribution outside the state.[8]

With nearly a quarter-century of preaching and lecturing behind him, Palfrey might have expected that his first words on the floor of the House would come during a formal debate and thereby fortify his reputation for scholarship in his maiden effort. Such was not the case, for his speaking debut came about accidentally. On January 27, during a debate on the incorporation of a company in Nantucket ("a small affair enough, but one which became important by being made the battle ground of party," wrote Adams), Palfrey attacked the view that no corporate charters shoud be given to purely private enterprises. Although he felt the necessity of explaining to his audience that fifteen minutes before he rose he had no idea of speaking, Adams recorded that Palfrey had done very well for a beginner.[9]

Encouraged by his initial success, Palfrey rose twice again on educational matters to make pleas for a liberality of outlook on the part of the legislature's economizers. Certainly the distribution of state maps involved expense, conceded Palfrey one Monday morning, but why had they been printed if not for distribution: " 'Where there are no oxen, the crib is clean,' says the good book which you gentlemen were all reading yesterday. Where there is no instruction, the cost is light." Another bill, this one giving financial aid to Williams College, gave Palfrey an opportunity to defend higher education. A rural representative did not wish to promote the "ingenuity and cunning, and sharpen the wits of gentlemen educated at this institution," and suggested putting the money in common school education exclusively. Palfrey replied at length in what may be termed his first full-dress speech. Colleges existed for the poor as well as the rich, he asserted with conviction. Their destruction would mean the end of all higher education for the sons of poor men since the rich would simply send their sons abroad. He reminded his ungrateful colleague of the patriotic role played by the men of Harvard College in the Revolution.[10]

Early in the session the House requested its committee on education to prepare a report defining the powers and duties of local school committees. Palfrey responded with a report which went to the heart of the problem: to function effectively, school committees needed strong powers, including the right to dismiss incompetent teachers, refuse admittance to pupils less than four or more than twenty-one years old, and order the construction of schoolhouses in negligent districts. These were all powers that Horace Mann was then fighting for, and doubtless much of the report originated during Palfrey's conferences with Mann.[11]

Slavery, the issue which was to be the chief concern of Palfrey's political career, was not a key issue of the legislative session of 1842. Nevertheless, several incidents foreshadowed the political travail of coming sessions. Abolitionists presented two petitions to Charles Francis Adams asking for the use of a meeting hall in the State House. "Here is a difficult path to tread," mused Adams, "in which I shall need all the support which my judgment can give." He presented the petitions to the appropriate committee, which in turn reported unfavorably. Henry Wilson of Natick, who was to become one of the leaders of the Massachusetts political antislavery movement, moved for a recommitment. The ensuing debate clearly showed the beginnings of the party rifts on the slavery issue. On a compromise amendment to allow the meeting but frown upon its object, the 27 Boston representatives present (all Whigs) split 14 to 13. How Palfrey voted on the issue is not recorded, but on another point he took the "anti-slavery line." Massachusetts law prohibited marriage between Negroes and Caucasians. The introduction of a repeal bill drew the fire of many Boston conservatives; Nathan Hale blasted the bill in his *Daily Advertiser:* "Mixed races . . . are proverbially the most vicious of all." Adams was prominent in speaking against the old prohibition, and Palfrey followed his friend's lead in the voting. But the repeal bill did not pass.[12]

Palfrey's most significant act in the legislature of 1842 came during the last days of the session. On March 2, he reported resolves from his committee calling for continued support to normal, or teachers', schools, and for the establishment of a library in each school district. The sums requested seem pitifully small ($6,000 yearly for three years for the normal schools, and $15 for each district library!), but obtaining even these amounts proved difficult, despite support from the Boston press.[13] Next day Palfrey was about to explain and defend the resolves, when several friends dissuaded him, pointing to the press of business on what was scheduled to be the last day of the session. Palfrey agreed to remain silent, but with misgivings, for he voted against his own resolves on the second reading (three readings, or votes, were necessary before legislation went to the governor), so that he then might be able to move a reconsideration. As Palfrey feared, the vote went against the resolves. He then made his motion, and spoke at length with "very satisfactory results." On the next vote the House performed a complete about-face, voting approval handily. There was no trouble in the Senate, and the resolves went to Governor John Davis for his signature.[14]

The friends of public education were jubilant. From Connecticut, Henry Barnard rushed his congratulations. Not only had Palfrey made a distinguished start in his legislative career, but it was "impossible to over estimate the results, immediate and remote, of the legislation of those two pithy resolves." Barnard confessed that he had considered the passage of such legislation little more than a dream. His hopes for "old Connecticut" were now revived; the splendid example of a neighbor could not be ignored. Horace Mann was pleasantly surprised. "Never was a triumph more complete," he crowed, and the victory seemed even greater when one considered the fact that a body of politicians had acted in such a far-sighted manner.[15] Mann was quick to give Palfrey credit for what had been done. Palfrey replied modestly and correctly that Mann had for years been doing the spadework, and that he had come in at the eleventh hour "for scarcely as much labour in the vineyard as might soil a white glove." Nevertheless, Palfrey was to recall that if there was one day in his life in which he did better service to a great cause of "truth & righteousness" than the third of March, 1842, he was not aware of it.[16]

The legislature adjourned a few minutes after the Senate approved the school resolves. The members waited for their pay, and then "left the scenes of their glory." Palfrey had diligently attended every session. He professed to be glad to have had two months "a little diversified." The life of a legislator was pleasant enough, and pursuing such a career seemed inviting, were it not for the troublesome necessity of earning a living. A few months of legislator's *per diem* did not go far in that direction.[17]

A month after the end of the legislative session Palfrey decided to visit New York and Washington. The sale of the *North American* was still six months away, and he had business to transact relating to the *Review*. A letter received a few months later from Whig Congressman Leverett Saltonstall indicates that Palfrey was seeking a federal appointment. He was disappointed in his search.[18]

* * *

The question of representation was a recurrent problem in Massachusetts politics. The growth of urban centers, with no corresponding changes in the makeup of the legislature, had produced a situation clearly favoring the small towns. Much was said, but nothing done, until 1840, when Democratic Governor Marcus Morton succeeded in getting a reapportionment bill through the Whig-controlled legislature.[19] By virtue of the law, representation came closer to reflecting the population shifts, but by no means completely.

Closely allied to this problem was the issue of changes in Congressional districts made necessary by the same population shifts. A special session of the legislature was to meet in September 1842 to arrange the redistricting. Throughout the summer Palfrey devoted much time to the preparation of a redistricting plan. He displayed a flair for thorough research, going so far as to compare the population figures easily obtainable with manuscript census returns.[20] It is not clear at whose suggestion Palfrey embarked on such an ambitious and time-consuming task, but the fact that he conferred with many prominent Whigs indicates that he was not acting independently of party leadership.[21] The Massachusetts Whigs had not agreed on how far the redistricting ought to be carried, however. Adams feared that any bill embodying significant changes would be scuttled by the party whose principles he had never fully accepted. After all, the Whigs had lost but one state election, and the natural tendency was to walk on well-worn and successful paths. A Whig caucus on the evening before the special session could agree on nothing.[22]

During the ten-day special session Palfrey had a lesson in political disappointment and the acceptance of party solidarity. He introduced his bill on September 8. It was based on near-equality of population; he had brought each district to within two thousand inhabitants of each other. Despite all the work it cost him, and the high hopes he nourished, a Whig caucus voted down the plan. That Palfrey was hurt was evident from the terseness of his journal entry: "It was thrown out, & the business of districting harmoniously planned." When the caucus compromise plan came up for debate, Palfrey spoke in its behalf, calling it "honest and liberal" and a needed protection for minority rights. He claimed, with little conviction, that he had changed his mind on nearly equal representation. Palfrey's plan was objectionable in that it ignored county lines. Its author now admitted that such old voting units ought to be preserved.[23]

With regard to national politics, 1842 was a year of turmoil for the Massachusetts Whigs. The great Log Cabin victory of 1840 had been all but nullified by the accession to the presidency of John Tyler one month after General Harrison's inaugural. Tyler, a Virginia state rights conservative, had been put on the Whig ticket to attract anti-Jacksonian Democrats. In 1841, he infuriated the Whigs, first by following an independent course, and then by vetoing two Whig bank bills. Even before the return of the first veto message Massachusetts Whigs waited apprehensively. Abbott Lawrence, tired of Virginia politicians, felt "that the time has come to take a stand against the follies of the South." Professing unconcern, Charles Francis Adams predicted the destruction of the party as the result of "incongruity in the materials of which the Whig party is made"; Tyler's actions might hasten its demise, but it was all a matter of time.[24] All the members of Tyler's cabinet, with the exception of Massachusetts' leading Whig, Daniel Webster, resigned. Webster wished to complete the negotiation of a treaty with Great Britain before he stepped down. This brought sharp criticism from his own party, criticism which came to a head in the fall of 1842.

During that same fall Palfrey campaigned actively for the first time. As one of four signers of a party convention call, he denounced Tyler for "treachery and apostasy," and summoned the agitated Whigs of the Bay State to Faneuil Hall on September 14. For a man of such short political experience, Palfrey's name was surprisingly prominent in party affairs. He was a member of the committee which welcomed the Massachusetts Congressional Whigs on their return from Washington and applauded their anti-Tyler position.[25] Palfrey visited Abbott Lawrence regularly for long political discussions. Who influenced whom is not known, but Lawrence had been feuding with Webster over the latter's remaining in the cabinet, and at the Whig convention Palfrey made a speech lauding Webster's rival, Henry Clay, as the next Whig presidential candidate. Boston's *Atlas* reported that the address had a great effect on the audience, and that it was punctuated with many "facetious hits." [26] Here, Palfrey once again revealed his fear of criticism. A few days after the speech he overheard a chance remark to the effect that he had referred to a Clay-Webster antagonism. "Utterly a mistake," he assured a friend, explaining that his reference had been to the Clay-Calhoun fight, and implying that he wanted the explanation circulated among the Webster men. The Whig convention had called for a "full and final separation" from the Tyler administration, making Webster's position seemingly untenable. Palfrey was in the audience that heard Webster defend himself in the famed Faneuil Hall address of September 30. Although he discussed Webster with his Whig friends that evening, he did not indicate whether or not he was one of the many who were propitiated by the god-like Daniel's oratory.[27]

As November approached Palfrey undertook a formidable speech-making schedule. He appeared in over a dozen towns, but his work went unrewarded. For the second time since its organization, Massachusetts Whiggery lost a state election. Democrat Marcus Morton had more votes than Whig John Davis, but was 5,000 votes short of the necessary majority. The abolitionist Liberty party, running in its third election, polled over 6,000 votes and prevented a decision on election day, thus revealing the pattern of Massachusetts politics for years to come: the election of a governor went into the hands of the state legislature.[28]

*   *   *

The session of 1843 opened amid charges and counter-charges of electoral fraud by both Whigs and Democrats. In nearly one hundred towns two elections were necessary to obtain majorities for representatives, and the result of these second trials was a near-deadlock in the House, with the Whigs finally obtaining control of that chamber. Democrats controlled the Senate, however. Under the Massachusetts constitution, the House selected two names from the list of gubernatorial candidates and sent them to the Senate for the choice.[29] A few days before Morton's election, Palfrey tried to rally a party caucus to oppose acceptance of the Democratic leader as one of the two candidates, despite the fact that Morton had obtained the largest individual vote. When the Whigs declined to bargain with the five Liberty party representatives, the upper chamber elected Marcus Morton governor.[30]

Palfrey had no trouble winning re-election to the legislature. Boston ignored the Democratic surge of 1842. Once again a solid Whig delegation of thirty-five men represented the capital city. Palfrey was reappointed chairman of the education committee; only one member of the previous year's committee returned, so that Palfrey's position of leadership in his bailiwick remained unchallenged. But his low opinion of Governor Morton very nearly cost him support for an educational bill. During debate on renewal of appropriations for libraries, Palfrey launched into an attack on the governor. Adams recorded drily that however correct the criticism of Morton may have been, it was hardly a judicious move on Palfrey's part: "As a consequence . . . his bill floundered heavily for two or three hours until one or two of the democratic party had the magnanimity to set it upon its legs again." [31]

During the election campaign, Massachusetts Democrats had promised to follow a policy of economy should they gain control of the State House. One way of accomplishing this was to reduce the salaries of state officials. Palfrey was among those Whigs who wished to exclude judges' salaries from the retrenchment, but an amendment to that effect was lost. The economy bill passed easily, despite the solid opposition of the Boston delegation. The rural representatives of both parties were strong for economy. The Whig conservatives protested formally in the house, and Palfrey later suggested that the state judiciary receive their reduced pay under protest against the "nefarious law which is to place law in Massachusetts under the hoof of the demagogue of the day." [32]

Palfrey had a perfect opportunity to show his anti-Democratic bias during the affair of "General Jackson's fine." Since neither major party controlled both houses of the legislature, the session of 1843 was largely given over to political sniping. Senate Democrats passed a resolve requesting the state's Congessmen to vote to refund $1,000 to Andrew Jackson, whose cavalier attitude toward New Orleans courts and judges in 1815 had brought on the fine. Adams, who declined the job, had Palfrey put on a joint "Fine Committee." [33] Palfrey leaped into the fray with gusto. Here was a chance to combine his belief in the importance of an independent judiciary with his distaste for the "barbarism" of Andrew Jackson. He put all his oratorical abilities into a two-hour effort which even the mordantly critical Adams had to admire. The *Advertiser* reported that he had gone "over the whole historical ground and all the legal and equitable argument with much soundness and tact." As might be expected this was not a matter in which logic or well-marshaled facts played an important part. Several Whigs were absent on voting day, and Palfrey's anti-Jackson minority report was tabled by a party-line vote.[34] In this minor incident Palfrey was carried away by his commitment to his concept of justice. The issue, which no doubt brought smiles to the faces of the professional politicians at the State House, was to Palfrey a major crusade. His inability to place political incidents in their proper place, and to prevent the injection of righteousness into even the trivia of party jousting—an inability, in short, to relax—already marked Palfrey the politician.

Palfrey made no noteworthy legislative contribution during

his second year in the House. Most of his committee reports concerned routine educational matters. The novelty of the legislature had worn off: "Worn out & disgusted this evening with the day's work." Shortly before the session's end he spoke for the last time as a House member. The speech was part of a successful attack on one of Governor Morton's "popularity hunting schemes," the secret ballot! When the Whig legislators scattered on March 25, they were determined to wipe off the stain of "Mortonism" at the next election.[35]

*   *   *

The summer of 1843 found Palfrey at loose ends once again. The *North American* had been disposed of in January, and he tried to divert his "anxious hours with some desultory reading" in history.[36] The anxiety he spoke of resulted from his financial condition. Palfrey found it impossible to keep up his style of life without some new source of income. In Boston the Palfreys enjoyed the city's full social life, but they had to do their share of entertaining.[37] By 1843 a move to Cambridge had become mandatory. A heavy bout with his accounts made Palfrey ill one morning, and he did not leave the house for the rest of the day. Hazelwood, the Palfrey house in Cambridge, stood vacant, its tenant of three years having just moved out. Palfrey sold the theological section of his library at auction as an emergency measure, and he had to pay "roundly," as he put it, for breaking the lease on his Boston house. Even more vexing was the strain in family relations caused by the move. Mary Ann reacted petulantly at the thought of returning to Cambridge. The Hammond family offered to pay the rent on the Boston house if Palfrey could be persuaded to remain. Naturally, he refused. By mid-November the Palfreys were back at Hazelwood.[38]

Several employment opportunities opened up, and closed just as quickly. Palfrey had discussed the problem in general terms with his friend Samuel A. Eliot, and a few weeks later several persons suggested that he consider taking the pulpit at King's Chapel. Palfrey replied negatively, and explained self-righteously: "What it would have come to, had I encouraged it, I cannot say. But I did not. I revolted from the thought of resuming the ministry under the influence of pecuniary distress." [39] Another possibility was Palfrey's own idea: the establishment of a newspaper. A few inquiries revealed that no capital was available, and he abandoned the plan.[40]

In July 1843 Palfrey called on his Harvard classmate and friend, John P. Bigelow, to discuss a state office. Bigelow had been secretary of state of Massachusetts before the Democratic victory of the previous November. Should the Whigs recapture the state government (they acted as if such a victory were certain), the office would again belong to a deserving Whig. Bigelow did not want the job again; instead he promised to support Palfrey's bid.[41] When the Whigs succeeded in electing George N. Briggs to the first of seven consecutive terms as governor, and carried both houses of the legislature, Palfrey sought further aid. Ex-Speaker Kinnicutt was delighted to know that "that responsible office" would be "so worthily filled," and that the Democratic incumbent (John A. Bolles, whom Palfrey considered "an improper person"), would soon be displaced.[42]

Bigelow kept his promise. At the Whig caucus of January 4, 1844, he declined the nomination, and two thirds of the Whigs accepted Palfrey. Palfrey's last-minute canvassing in Boston was unnecessary, for a few days later the Whig-controlled legislature eased in their candidates. The process of restoration was complete. Bolles, the "improper person," cordially informed Palfrey "as one friend & neighbor to another" of his election.[43]

Palfrey was painfully aware that the office of secretary was regarded by many, particularly himself, as a step downward for a man who had held offices of greater importance. This fall in status was unfortunately matched by a decrease in the secretary's salary. The economy drive of the previous session had reduced the amount to $1,600 per year, a $400 reduction. Palfrey's self-consciousness and oversensitiveness were now working furiously. To expressions of compassion for his descent, he replied bravely: "Every man's first point of honor should be to pay his way & educate his children."[44]

* * *

A less-conscientious man might have regarded the post of secretary a sinecure, and left actual operations to his clerks. Palfrey proceeded on the opposite assumption. Always self-conscious to a fault, he thought all Boston was watching his performance as secretary. Palfrey's object then was to increase the importance of the office by a scrupulous attention to detail. Early in his tenure Massachusetts Whigs sought to elevate Palfrey by issuing reports critical of his Democratic predecessor's one-year tenure, and expressing their relief at having a new and competent secretary.[45]

Palfrey's duties were varied but usually of a routine nature. He had a staff of two permanent clerks, and several part-time clerks whose combined labor amounted to the equivalent of three more permanent clerkships. The secretary's salary from 1844 to 1847 remained $1,600, but the clerks received increases nearly every year, until by 1847 Palfrey was receiving only $400 more than his chief clerk. The work consisted mainly of preparing reports and transmitting documents.

The aspect of his job that Palfrey enjoyed most was the ceremonial. Not only did the secretary open and prorogue the legislature, but he was expected to accompany the governor on many official trips, duties Palfrey took very seriously. Being secretary hardly made Palfrey political boss of the state— a power he would not have known what to do with had he possessed it—but he did control a few clerkships and his many contacts with Governor Briggs enabled him to urge successfully the appointment of some important officials.[46]

Palfrey best displayed his conscientiousness in the compila-
tion of statistical tables. These included reports on many
subjects, including vital statistics, insurance companies, banks,
and conditions in state prisons. The yearly reports on vital
statistics were particularly well done. Not only were the
tables carefully compiled, but Palfrey added extended analyses
of the material. He went far beyond the legal requirements,
and the performances of predecessors, in using European
statistics for purposes of comparison, and supplying many
additional columns of averages and recapitulations. He did
this so well that in 1848 his successor made virtually no changes
in the report's form, though he declined to enter into as much
analysis as Palfrey. He also supervised a massive project on the
records of the Revolutionary War. Pension claims had got
out of hand, and service rolls badly needed indexing and binding. Two years of such labor led Palfrey to rejoice that justice
would now be done to many Revolutionary widows, and news
of his good work spread to Connecticut where Palfrey's
counterpart asked for information on the subject.[47]

The office housed about 14,000 volumes and 40,000 pamphlets, mainly state and federal documents. Palfrey found the
state records in poor condition with regard to accessibility. A
haphazard topical arrangement was in use, which could not
be conveniently abandoned. Instead Palfrey launched into the
preparation of a massive chronological index which took
several years to complete. With no abatement of his zeal,
Secretary Palfrey noted that the Massachusetts Historical Society had among its manuscript prizes three volumes of Governor Hutchinson's papers. Palfrey requested that this Commonwealth property be returned at once; the society maintained
a dignified silence.[48] He had better luck in another manuscript
project, obtaining transcripts of material pertaining to Massachusetts from foreign archives. Sparks had suggested that
Benjamin P. Poore be hired for the purpose, and Palfrey
passed the word on to Adams: "Say a word to the Governor

who (I tremble while I say it) has perhaps no very distinct notions of the matter, but will incline to take advice." Poore got the job, and valuable transcripts came from England and France. Palfrey kept close watch on the matter, even taking a paternal interest in seeing that Poore received fair pay for his work.[49]

During Palfrey's first year as secretary, learning the requirements of the job occupied a good deal of his time. He served throughout the year, although the early months of the year, during which the legislature met, were the busiest. In addition to regular reports, his office had to supply legislators with information on few days' notice. The secretary's office was enlarged in 1847, but by then Palfrey had so arranged the routine and drilled his clerks that he found he had much free time for reading and writing at home.[50] Palfrey was soon to be the object of intensive political attack. The best possible testimony to his honesty and efficiency as secretary was his enemies' silence on that phase of his career.

VIII ⟿

A Practicing Abolitionist

PALFREY's father was a boy of eight, playing in the narrow streets of Boston, when the Declaration of Independence was signed in 1776. As he approached his seventieth year John Palfrey could look back on a relatively uneventful life as a Louisiana planter, isolated by geography and by choice. He nursed himself through his many illnesses, illnesses which came more frequently as he grew older. His sons knew that the end would not be too long in coming. In 1838, Henry Palfrey first mentioned to his brother Gorham the question of a division of property when their father died.

According to Louisiana law, the estate was to be equally divided among the three surviving sons, John Gorham, Henry, and William. Henry estimated that if sold, the plantation would bring from thirty to forty thousand dollars, and that if operated by the brothers, each could expect to net about two thousand dollars yearly. The rub in this case was that slaves represented two thirds of the value. Would Gorham be willing to sign for the sale of "this species of property" and receive the proceeds of such a transaction? Henry realized the difficulties of such an action for someone living in New England. "You might incur the risk," he told Gorham "of some busy abolitionist taking particular pains to report that Revd. Dr. P. had been selling human flesh &c &c or living on the income of slave labor." Nevertheless, Henry emphasized that any other course would not only reduce Gorham's share by two thirds, but work a corresponding hardship on himself and William: "No one could then have a legal title to any of [the

slaves] . . . By our Laws Slaves are Real Estate & not transfer-
able by Delivery but by Notarial Act."

Gorham found the subject so delicate that he delayed
answering for several weeks, and even then refrained from
expressing opinions for fear that they might be misunderstood
by his brothers. Better to wait for a chance to talk the matter
out in person. To set his brothers' minds at rest, however,
he pointed out that whatever his decision, their property rights
were protected. They might obtain title to their share of all
the property by means of an amicable suit. Ever the scholar,
Palfrey cited the pertinent chapters of the civil code of
Louisiana.[1] Nothing more was said about the matter.

*   *   *

As Palfrey's interest and participation in politics deepened,
so too did his interest in slavery. The issue had grown in
importance during his two years in the legislature, and "both
parties were playing fast & loose with it, for both wanted to
keep up their connection with their southern wing, while
both were afraid of outraging the rising Anti-Slavery feeling
of Massachusetts." [2] Palfrey attended the riotous Faneuil Hall
meeting of October 30, 1842, held to protest the attempted
abduction of fugitive slave George Latimer. He was one of
four thousand persons, proslavery and antislavery, who
jammed the hall and the street outside to shout in each other's
ears, and perhaps to hear Wendell Phillips curse the Constitution. Before the year was out, Palfrey had studied the fugitive
slave law of 1793 and the cases arising from it, to be in a better
position to support petitions which in the legislative session of
1843 led to Massachusetts' first personal liberty law.[3]

Palfrey continued reading the literature of slavery. The
excoriation of slaveholders must have upset him as he thought
of his father and brothers. However neglectful John Palfrey
may have been—and the bitter memories of a lonely childhood
had not been wiped out—Palfrey nurtured a strong affection

for his father. His relations with his brothers had generally been good. Infrequent as their meetings were, a cordial fraternity marked these occasions, and all remembered them with pleasure. It is ironic that a time when Palfrey was to adopt a point of view (and act upon it in private and political life) which could have no other effect than to tear the family apart, he decided to visit Louisiana, "to perform, probably for the last time, a filial duty." [4]

The trip in 1843 was a two-month affair, involving travel by nearly all the means then available, coach, railroad, and river boats (with steam and without). Palfrey took his daughter Sarah with him. She had been undergoing hydrotherapy for a curvature of the spine, and the trip was her reward for being a good patient. Sarah was nonplused by the carnival atmosphere which swept the plantation once the slaves spotted them approaching, to say nothing of hearing her father called "Marse Gorham." They spent eight days at Attakapas and followed this with a short stay at William's plantation. Palfrey was impressed, doubly so considering his own troubles: "William lives in very handsome style, but a kind of style somewhat different from our own, & one which a person must visit this country to appreciate;—great plenty of servants & horses, plenty to eat & drink, & a very free hospitality with very little parade." [5] The return trip gave Palfrey a chance to see some new sights, including Chicago and the other port cities of the Great Lakes.

*   *   *

Six months after his return to Boston, Palfrey received news of his father's death. The old man succumbed during an attack of influenza. [6] Palfrey's brothers pressed for immediate action in the settlement of the estate, hoping to terminate the matter before their brother could formulate any definite plans with regard to the slaves. William blandly offered a plan which he knew Gorham would not accept: "I see no obstacle in the way of settling the estate in a manner that will be satisfactory to you, namely, by having the land & implements allotted to you by consent of all concerned." During his visit that spring, Gorham had brought up the question of the estate, and William promised to discuss the "plan we in part matured" with John Palfrey. But a favorable moment never arose. Henry joined his brother in requesting speed. The sale of all the property before January 15 was imperative since at that time labor would be most in demand for the new planting season. Henry asked for a power of attorney, and assured Gorham that none of the slaves would be sold to strangers.[7]

There was no doubt in Palfrey's mind as to where his duty lay. No sooner had he received a copy of his father's will than he returned to his study of the Civil Code of Louisiana. Any arrangement involving his holding or profiting from slave property was out of the question: "I hope, & I believe, that there never was a time, after I came to an age for any thought & judgment, when I could have thought for a moment of holding or selling a slave." After discussing the matter with his lawyer friends, Georgs S. Hillard and Charles Sumner, and Supreme Court Justice Joseph Story, Palfrey proceeded with his plans, cautiously adding a codicil to his will:

Whereas, by the death of my father, I have acquired . . . an interest in his estate, which included certain slaves . . . ; & whereas I regard the claim of property in human beings (however the same may be sanctioned by human laws) as utterly null & void before God, I have accordingly renounced all property in said slaves, & am proceeding to take . . . the needful steps to divest myself of my legal relation to said slaves, & to grant them their unconditional emancipation.[8]

The first of the "needful steps" was to find a trustworthy representative in Louisiana. This role fell to Adam Giffen of New Orleans.[9] In his initial letter of instructions, Palfrey made it clear that he insisted on one third of all the divisions of property. John Palfrey's will stipulated that the slaves' family ties were to be respected as much as possible; to this Palfrey, of course, made no objection. Once the three-way division was made, he wanted the lot which contained the largest number of persons, preferably those who would most likely be able to support themselves. Giffen was to hire out the slaves until Palfrey completed his arrangements. It was apparent "that these directions have a view to their emancipation; but this I state to you in confidence." Giffen was not to mention these plans, except to Henry and William, until they were ready to put into execution. Giffen replied punctually and enthusiastically: "Rest assured that your accompanying Letter of Instructions shall be in the Letter and Spirit strictly complied with . . . and most particularly in regard to that part of them relative to the completion of your noble and humane views." [10]

Giffen lost no time in visiting the plantation. The slaves appeared to be in good health and at work under John Palfrey's overseer. With an excellent crop expected that year, William, who lived in neighboring St. Mary's parish, had taken charge and decided that it would be best for all if the plantation were operated for another year. Giffen advised acceptance of this plan, citing a depressed market for land and the large stock of provisions at the plantation. If sold then, land and improvements might bring only $5,000. Early in January 1844 he had a conference with Henry and William in New Orleans. Henry, upon learning of Gorham's intention, remonstrated calmly but firmly with his brother. The emancipation plan would not only injure all the heirs, he contended, but would be a form of cruelty prepetrated on the hapless Negroes. They were not capable of supporting themselves off the plantation, and Louisiana law required their removal from the state. Gorham refused to accept money for slave property, but did he realize how much expense and trouble the transportation of his Negroes to the North involved? The suggestion that Giffen hire out the slaves was not realistic, since no planter would take the risk of having Negroes who knew they were to be free living with his own slaves. Henry hid his annoyance, although both he and William were furious with their Yankee brother. William, who did not write to Gorham, told Giffen that unless he could operate the plantation as usual for a year, he would sue "amicably" to protect his interests.[11] Palfrey was determined that his portion of the slaves be converted to wage laborers during the transition period before emancipation. If William wished to continue operations for a year, why not simply leave the Negroes undisturbed and pay them "as high wages to remain there as are ever paid the labor of persons of their sex & age. A disposition to exert themselves for my benefit would perhaps be a motive for some of them . . . to come into the scheme. Their having family ties on our plantation & the adjoining one would be a stronger inducement." When he heard of his brothers' anger, Palfrey still hoped that they could be persuaded to accept his notion of paying wages. If not, he would accede to William's wishes in any way that did not block his ultimate aim.[12] William was adamant on one point: under no circumstances could the Negroes remain on the plantation with his and Henry's slaves if told of their coming freedom. Knowing the antipathy that existed in Louisiana against increasing the number of free Negroes, Giffen suggested that Palfrey bring them to Boston at once, and then send them on to Liberia. Lacking specific instuctions, he agreed to William's condition.[13]

In March a division of the slaves occurred, and Giffen carried out his instructions as nearly as possible. Of the fifty-two slaves, Giffen succeeded in getting a lot of twenty persons, twelve of whom were females. "I considered that your views would be best carried out," he explained, "by taking women whose progeny will of course be free & more fully extend the philanthropy of Emancipation. I have also taken the old servants of your father as a matter of Conscience & Justice." The ages of the slaves ranged from sixty-five for an old house servant to an unnamed newborn child.

Palfrey's brothers each received lots of sixteen Negroes, and for bookkeeping purposes they agreed to value all lots at $6,666.66. Thus twenty "black souls" were to remain ignorant of their imminent journey to the land of free men. Giffen extracted one concession from William: the house servants could be freed at any time Gorham thought expedient.[14]

Despite Giffen's warning, Palfrey still had plans for emancipation in Louisiana. Yet even if he could get the necessary approval, fourteen of his Negroes could not be manumitted without special permission. According to state law a slave had to be at least thirty years old before he could be freed. Palfrey petitioned the state legislature to waive the requirement. Otherwise, freedom would mean removal from the state in which "as the place of their past residence from birth, or for many years, it would . . . be materially for their advantage to be at liberty to remain." At the same time that he sent the petition off, Palfrey retained an Attakapas lawyer and Harvard graduate, Isaac E. Morse, who was then a state senator. Palfrey requested him to present his petition in the Louisiana Senate, with the reminder that such an act implied no support of the petition itself.[15] On March 11 the Louisiana legislature voted unanimously to table the petition. News of the legislative veto appeared in the New Orleans papers, and Henry and William became incensed by the fact that they had not been told of the attempt in advance. Henry stormed into Giffen's office waving a copy of the New Orleans *Courier*, shouting that the emancipation scheme had become a public affair, and that it would reach the "Ears of the People on the Plantation, and make them restless & unhappy." [16]

His brothers' anger caused Palfrey genuine concern, for he had imposed a dual mission upon himself: to free his slaves, and to keep the family from falling apart over the issue. When Giffen decided to charge him interest on the earlier loan from John Palfrey, Gorham readily assented, vowing that in a matter of dollars and cents, his brothers would never have any cause to complain of him.[17]

In view of all these difficulties, Palfrey decided to go to Louisiana. Giffen had already urged him to journey south, if only for a few days to clear up matters. His duties as Massachusetts secretary of state obliged him to wait until the adjournment of the legislature in mid-April 1844. Palfrey told his wife of his intentions for the first time, and left for New Orleans apprehensively invoking a special blessing of Providence that he might be allowed to see his family again.[18]

During his journey Palfrey stopped to see two abolitionists. In both cases he desired information about placing the freedmen in homes once they arrived in the North. In New York, Lydia Maria Child welcomed him enthusiastically: "I have lately heard of you from the Legislature of Louisiana, and felt joy at your public recognition of the brotherhood of man." Mrs. Child, who had once apologized for sending editor Palfrey a book on slavery, now confided that she had helped one of Henry Palfrey's slaves escape to Canada some years before, but asked him not to advertise the fact in Louisiana. She agreed to take charge of five or six of the Negroes should Palfrey decide to send them north immediately.[19] At Lexington, Kentucky, Palfrey consulted with Cassius M. Clay on the same subject, but with no apparent result.[20]

Despite his apprehensions about his personal safety, Palfrey received a cordial reception in New Orleans. Instead of the expected "annoyances" due to the nature of his mission, he found many calling cards and invitations from "gentlemen of mark, on whom I had no sort of claim, & have had many more invitations than I could accept." Later that year he told abolitionist Edmund Quincy of the "marked attention and civility" with which the New Orleans gentlemen and the upriver planters greeted him. The memory of this southern hospitality did not survive the trials of coming antislavery years and Civil War. Palfrey's autobiography contains a melodramatic account of two perilous days spent among the planters of Attakapas, "many of whom were coarse & passion-

ate people, much excited by what they heard of my plans."
He proceeded with his task bravely—in his memoirs, at least—
before the "passions of my neighbors should have time to boil
too high." [21]

Palfrey had already made up his mind that he would allow
the men, but not the women, to choose freely whether or not
to go north for freedom. The women by remaining behind
condemned their children, born and unborn, to bondage. He
had a short private talk with each adult slave. Only one
objected, but Palfrey soon convinced him that he ought to go
with the others. All the slaves joined in requesting that they
be allowed to delay their departure until the end of the planting
season, so that they could get in "their own little produce."
Palfrey agreed; the slaves were to remain as wage laborers for
his account. William's threat that under no conditions would
he allow "freedom-conscious" slaves to mix with his own was
not carried out, for the plantation continued in operation as
before. Palfrey returned to Massachusetts greatly relieved to
have made an arrangement "so satisfactory to my judgment
& my conscience." [22]

*   *   *

From Cambridge, Palfrey maintained a close interest in the
welfare of his slaves. In fact, as the time for their departure
approached, his solicitousness increased. Should any slave
change his mind and request to leave earlier, Giffen was to
provide passage at once. When a sailing date of March 1845
was finally established, Palfrey made sure that the Negroes
would have comfortable quarters in New Orleans and aboard
ship.[23] Giffen assured him that the captain and the mate had
personally promised to treat the Negroes with consideration.
Palfrey was also concerned about the question of what wage
to pay for their labor throughout 1844. The plantation was
sold in January 1845, and Palfrey thought the new owner
ought to pay his people two months' wages. Giffen suggested

fifty dollars as fair compensation for a year's work; the new owner at Attakapas declined to enter into any philanthropic arrangement. On March 21, 1845, the bark *Bashaw* weighed anchor at New Orleans, while on the levee Henry and William Palfrey waved farewell to their father's former chattels who must have looked back at the receding shore with mingled regret and jubilation.[24]

Not all of Palfrey's slaves were aboard the *Bashaw*. Giffen had advised that it would not be too difficult to obtain freedom locally for the old house servants. Two of these were included in Palfrey's lot. Giffen filed a petition for permission to emancipate four slaves (all more than fifty years old) with the St. Martin's Parish Police Jury. After an initial rejection, which he attributed to a "general Excitement against Abolition and Emancipation," Giffen bribed several members of the jury and got the permission without further delay.[25]

When the sixteen Negroes landed at Boston a month later they were, of course, no longer slaves. Slavery was prohibited in Massachusetts by the terms of the constitution of 1780, which declared "all men are born free and equal." Nevertheless, Palfrey arranged a religious ceremony at King's Chapel to formalize the emancipation. An eyewitness recalled how awkward the red-turbaned colored women appeared as they curtseyed in the church doorway, and the diffidence the former slaves displayed while they listened to the few words that declared them free.[26]

With the question of emancipation settled to Palfrey's satisfaction, he faced a real problem in placing the freedmen in suitable homes as servants. Palfrey tried fruitlessly to place a boy in the Hopedale Community, but he had better luck in his other attempts. Mrs. Child, true to her word, helped place a Negro woman, Anna, and her four children with a Quaker family named Hathaway near Canandaigua, New York. This group had been Palfrey's greatest worry, since Anna was in bad health and her children were too young to work for their

keep. Palfrey escorted them to their new home, where Hathaway and his Quaker neighbors brought up the children "most
kindly and judiciously." The other Negroes remained in Massachusetts as servants, and were able to support themselves
with relatively little trouble. In the 1860's, Palfrey observed
that it had been many years since he had to bear any expense
for them, beyond an occasional present.[27]

Palfrey's act of emancipation put him publicly and irrev-
ocably in the antislavery camp. Even before the slaves arrived, Massachusetts abolitionists requested details of his experiences in the South for publication, but Palfrey put them
off with a plea that they wait until he concluded the affair.
Palfrey later met Edmund Quincy, a Garrisonian abolitionist,
on the Worcester railroad and had a long conversation with
him about abolitionism. Quincy asserted that Palfrey was just
as entitled to run for president as James G. Birney, the
Alabama slaveholder turned abolitionist, who was then the
Liberty party candidate.[28]

If it had been Palfrey's intention to play the role of an
anonymous emancipator, he was soon to be disappointed. Ellis
Gray Loring insisted that abolitionist newspapers could not
let the incident go unnoticed. It was desirable, he added, that
Palfrey be named specifically, because his course in the matter
had deeply interested many persons. Cornelius Felton, Palfrey's former assistant on the *North American*, was proud
that Palfrey had done more than any man in Boston for the
great cause of antislavery: "I have often thought of it with
admiration and reverence. It is a great act, the memory of
which must be a joy and happiness to you as long as you live."
Finally, Palfrey's philanthropy became the subject of a political address, during a last-ditch attempt to block the admission of Texas into the Union. Charles Sumner, ignoring his
friend's request for silence on the issue, and pointing to the
"beauty of the example," called on Massachusetts to do as a

state what Palfrey had done as an individual—to reject any accession of slave property.[29]

Palfrey's course was an expensive one, at a time when he could ill afford such charity. Aside from the question of the Negroes as valuable slave property (a value Palfrey never acknowledged), there was still the expense of transportation from Attakapas to Boston and beyond. Palfrey kept the amount of these expenses to himself, nor did he ever mention them in his correspondence, but they were nevertheless deducted from the approximately $2,800 he received from the sale of the plantation land and buildings.[30]

Whatever the cost, there were compensations which could not be reduced to dollars and cents, such as a report from Clara, one of the emancipated slaves who had remained in Louisiana:

I have much to thank you for and it would be hard if both Amos and myself should ever forget that we owe you so much, for ourselves personally, and so very much for the kindness you have shown in taking upon yourself the care and education and support of our little boy. I only write to express to you how thankful we feel for all you have done for us. We are living here and managing to make ourselves comfortable, and trying to be respectable in the eyes of the old friends of our Master, and I hope we are succeeding pretty well in preserving a good character.[31]

A southern historian has upbraided Palfrey for not preaching against the sin of slavery to his father while John Palfrey was alive.[32] Palfrey wisely refrained from expressing his feelings. Self-righteous letters would not have freed a single slave, and would only have antagonized the old man and infuriated William and Henry Palfrey. Palfrey had long harbored the idea of emancipation, and his increasing interest in slavery and its political implications—an interest which became intense over what Palfrey considered to be the aggression of the "Slave Power" in forcing the annexation of Texas—stiffened his resolve. While John Palfrey lived agitation was pointless. After 1843, emancipation could be put into effect, and this Palfrey did, promptly and honorably.

Palfrey never sought any reward for his act. But in 1863 he received news from a friend in New York that gave him all the compensation he needed.[33] Anna's youngest son, William Woodlin, a child of two during the emancipation, and now a respected member of his community, had just enlisted and was off to fight for the Union.

IX

Conscience and Judgment

THE annexation of Texas produced reactions of fundamental importance in the political history of Massachusetts. The movement for annexation had begun soon after the establishment of the Lone Star Republic in 1836, and Bay State antislavery men quickly responded to this threat of one or more new slave states. Abolitionist sentiment was predictably emotional. Texas must be kept out of the Union, warned John Greenleaf Whittier—"it is a life and death matter with us." Conservatives shared the concern, although at a more restrained level. Edward Everett saw nothing but folly in the position of southern annexationists and predicted dissolution of the Union on the annexation rock—an eventuality he was not then prepared to struggle against.[1]

After the initial alarm, the Texas issue remained quiescent for several years, until the presidential election of 1844 pushed it once again into national prominence. The Massachusetts Whigs, fresh from triumph in the state election of the previous year and united as they were never to be again, presented a solid front on Texas. With President Tyler pressing for immediate annexation through a treaty with the Texas republic, Whig members of the Massachusetts Congressional delegation urged that the state react to the imminent danger. When Secretary of State John C. Calhoun, himself a convert to annexation after initial opposition, presented a Texas treaty to the Senate, Daniel Webster exploded: "Never did I see such reprehensible sentiments and unsurpassed nonsense unite." He was astonished that Calhoun could suppose that Massachusetts would adopt the sentiments of the South Carolinian.[2]

Webster need not have worried about his state's conversion to Calhounism. Too slowly to suit some, the Whig press nevertheless began to air the Texas question, and even before the presentation of the treaty a group of anxious Whigs met at Abbott Lawrence's home to voice apprehension, but not, it developed, to advance any plan of action. Editorials and legislative resolutions would have to suffice. The Whig presidential nomination of Henry Clay on an antiannexation platform gave the Bay State Whigs justification for a policy of quietism. Furthermore, the Democratic nominee, Tenneseee's James K. Polk, ran on an openly expansionist platform. Clay's position was "on the whole satisfactory" to Palfrey, but early Whig confidence soon disappeared when it became clear that Clay had guessed wrongly on Texas. His antiannexation Raleigh Letter made him unpopular among the expansionists, and frantic attempts to salvage the election by straddling the issue merely accentuated the original error and alienated a portion of his northern supporters.[3] In 1844 Henry Clay was neither right nor President.

Despite reservations about Clay, Palfrey worked hard for a Whig victory in 1844. He joined the local Clay Club, and spoke at many Whig meetings in western Massachusetts. The Whigs feared the growing strength of the abolitionist Liberty party which had declared a plague on both major political parties. To combine hatred of slavery and political impracticality was self-defeating, Palfrey reminded them. He thought every sincere antislavery man should support Clay as the only hope of keeping Texan slavery out of the Union. The Whigs held their firm hold on the state government and carried Massachusetts for Clay, but when Palfrey cast his ballot on November 11 it appeared that New York, and the election, had already gone for Polk. With defeat many Whigs came to believe that only a man of "negative qualities" could win; Clay, and other party leaders, would have to be shelved.[4]

*   *   *

Annexation was sure to come with the new administration. John Tyler, preparing to leave the White House, had determined to hasten the process by presidential intercession and devoted every effort to bringing Texas in during his expiring term of office. He signed a joint resolution of annexation on March 1, 1845, three days before Polk's inauguration.

But before this consummation, Massachusetts blood was stirred up. Webster moaned: "I feel sick at heart, to see the depths of our disgrace. This free Country, this model Republic, disturbing its own peace, and perhaps the peace of the world, by its greediness for more slave territory, and for the greater increase of Slavery!" He urged circulation of the previous year's anti-Texas resolutions, and reluctantly agreed to the calling of a "non-partisan" convention at Faneuil Hall at the end of January 1845. Webster's choler never conquered his political prudence, however. To organize the meeting he designated Whigs Stephen C. Phillips and Charles Allen, thinking that these future Free Soilers would act "with all becoming temperance and moderation," and would "say nothing which might displease or embarrass our Southern friends." [5]

Palfrey, chosen a Cambridge delegate, attended the sessions, but was not aware of his election, since notification reached him after adjournment. Webster, who knew the public demanded something strong, wrote a forceful and impressive convention address denouncing annexation. At the convention the Whigs labored primarily to keep down the Garrisonian abolitionists and defeat disunion resolutions. Garrison himself led the extremists' assault, but the Whigs tethered him without much difficulty. For many, the convention provided needed emotional stimulus; yet the Whigs were not completely united in their appraisal of its effectiveness. Abbott and Amos Lawrence, Nathan Appleton, Levi Lincoln, and Leverett Saltonstall and other prominent Whigs did not participate, nor did they believe anything had been accomplished by the meeting. The absence of these men reflected the struggle between the

Webster and Lawrence factions for control of Massachusetts Whiggery, a division which had been apparent since 1842.[6]

The activists of the Faneuil Hall convention intensified efforts to arouse public opinion, even after the joint resolution for annexation passed both houses of Congress. At the convention they established a Texas committee, but when Phillips called the first meeting attendance was light. Nevertheless Adams, with some assistance from Phillips, prepared Texas resolutions which Palfrey thought marked out the true course of Massachusetts policy. Asked for his opinion, Palfrey suggested an additional resolve, calling for the end of the internal slave trade. The resolutions were too strong for Governor Briggs, who refused to support them, but the legislature approved them easily. The committee activists, Phillips, Allen, and Adams, wrote a circular letter outlining the "Crime of Texas" in militant terms. There was still time to act, they asserted. Congress had not yet voted on the financial aspects of annexation. The writers called for advice on the proper course of action and proposed yet another convention. Those who had shied away from activism reacted negatively.[7]

During this agitation on the Texas issue Palfrey established an intimate friendship with Charles Francis Adams. The two had known each other since Palfrey's years with the *North American* and in the Massachusetts legislature, but "anti-Texasizing" made them close friends. When Palfrey first met Adams "the reserve and want of geniality (at least of demonstrativeness) of his manner," had prevented any personal attraction. The Adams ice melted a little in the legislature, so that by 1845 Palfrey and Adams consulted together "trustfully and cordially." The Texas issue also brought closer relations with Charles Sumner, although Palfrey's critical remarks on Sumner's antiwar Boston Fourth of July Oration of 1845 threatened to end the friendship almost as soon as it began.[8]

Anti-Texas conventions followed each other in rapid succession throughout 1845. Party regulars might decry the lack of real issues between the two major parties, but the Texas activists thought otherwise. Their course forced Robert C. Winthrop to try to recoup lost ground by speaking more forcefully on Texas at the Whig state convention, but his lukewarm reception left no doubt that Massachusetts Whiggery was entering a stormy period.

Palfrey and his friends met with the disjointed and warring abolitionist factions of Massachusetts at Concord on September 22 for a day of anti-Texas oratory. The Whigs who attended shifted uncomfortably in the company of those who damned the Constitution and preached disunion. But they agreed to continue a wary and loose association with the abolitionists.[9]

Palfrey's main contribution at this time was the preparation of a circular letter to the nation's clergymen, protesting the admission of Texas and asking the ministers to devote one Sunday's sermon to the alleged outrage. His militancy had increased since the timid days of the Cambridge Anti-Slavery Society and the *North American;* the sharp increase in non-abolitionist antislavery activity made it easier to be militant. Early in November the Texas Committee met at Faneuil Hall for the usual protests, but this time a subcommittee of Palfrey, Sumner, and Adams emerged charged to solicit signatures for a petition to Congress and financial aid from Boston's well-to-do. "Our operations," recalled Palfrey, "and our applications . . . brought refusals and resentments and defined the position of these gentlemen."

The gentlemen in question were the principal Whig textile lords, Abbott Lawrence and Nathan Appleton. Adams appealed to Lawrence to back up his anti-Texas words at the state convention and to help keep the petition primarily a Whig venture. Lawrence would have none of it, however, and Appleton soon joined him. "I consider the question settled," said Appleton; "I cannot think it good policy to waste our energies in hopeless efforts upon the impossible." When approached by the committee, Winthrop demurred, fearing any association with abolitionists, but also showing very clearly that he was sick of the Texas issue. On the conclusive nature of the refusals, Adams commented: "Well, we must bear it with dignity—and pursue our course."[10]

This pursuit involved more speechmaking and the publication of a small-sized, short-lived newspaper, *The Free State Rally and Texan Chain-Breaker*. Abolitionist Elizur Wright christened the sheet and the abolitionist faction of the committee controlled it. Among Palfrey's many appearances was one at Lowell, where he presented resolutions declaring that annexation was not a closed issue, that the free-state majority in the House of Representatives might block Texas admission. Whatever profligacy prevailed in the rest of the nation, New Englanders must stand firm as the descendants of the Puritans and never "cast foul shame on our lineage." Palfrey often "anti-Texasized" with Adams, who thought highly of his speaking ability. Palfrey, the dispassionate orator—as befitted his Unitarian minister's background—appealed to his audience to follow the flow of his argument, rather than trying to dazzle with rhetorical flourishes. Political harangues were out of the question for Palfrey. A Democratic listener thought Palfrey a "rambling and fanatical speaker," but this was a partisan judgment on the content of these antislavery speeches, not on the mode of delivery.[11]

Inevitably the meetings and speeches led to personal antagonism between the Whig activists and quietists. The activists decided to publish the Lawrence and Appleton refusals, with appropriate comments, a proceeding which all agreed was an "extremely delicate operation." Further trouble came from extremist remarks published in the *Chain-Breaker* attacking the conservative Whigs. Nathan Hale, editor of Boston's *Daily Advertiser*, equated the Texas Committee with the *Chain-Breaker*, and Palfrey thought it "due to our personal relations" to inform Hale that he did not control the anti-Texas paper's editorials, nor had he ever written a word for it. Palfrey also assured his conservative friends that he had not sought notoriety by reason of his connection with slavery. Samuel A. Eliot, who had previously lectured Sumner on the social perils of violent reform activity, gave Palfrey similar advice. Palfrey was jeopardizing his "elevated and enviable" position on slavery through abolitionist contamination. The past was gone, but in the future he would do well to heed the proverb and "avoid bad company" if he wished to preserve the good opinion of his friends.[12]

Unknown to Eliot, conditions within the Texas Committee were such that Palfrey and his Whig associates were themselves fearful of being sucked into the abolitionist whirlpool. Palfrey, Adams, and Phillips all agreed that the abolitionists were "growing very wild." On December 19 news reached Boston that the Texas bill had passed in the House; three days later the Senate followed suit. Palfrey, ever-conscious of his Puritan forebears, noted with horror that the culmination of the Texas iniquity had come on Forefathers' Day: "It is the blackest 22d of December that . . . has risen on the race of the Pilgrims." [13]

There was nothing to do but to lay the Texas Committee to rest. The final meeting on December 30, 1845, was a surprisingly spirited session. Probably no one had seriously thought that Texas could be kept out, but the committee proved a valuable instrument of state politics. Men who in a few months were to be known as Conscience Whigs, and a few years later as Free Soilers, began to work together, appreciate one another, and cut their political teeth. Adams called more and more on Palfrey's "cool eye and judgment" in matters of publication and policy. The committee had fought a good if shadowy fight, but privately they were forced to agree with Andrews Norton, who commended the effort but concluded "in respect to the business of Texas, I fear we are compelled to say *actum est*."

The dissolution of the Texas Committee left the Whig

activists in a state of indecision. Palfrey feared that should they lapse into quietism, the abolitionists would seize the antislavery initiative. Yet he had no specific suggestions ready on how to prevent this. The Liberty party faction of abolitionism, on the other hand, pressed for the formation of an "Anti-Slavery League" designed to keep the men of the Texas Committee together. An appeal for further aid came directly to Palfrey:

. . . something should be done to rescue the moral and religious impulses of "Young" New England from the worldly-wise tutelage of the Dollars and Cents statesmanship now in vogue. . . . And from whence shall we expect such appeals to *heart*, as shall have power to counteract those to the pocket, if not from such thinkers and writers as yourself?

But Palfrey held himself aloof from the abolitionist embrace. Their ways and ideas were not his.[14]

*　　*　　*

Early in 1846 the Texas activists acquired the name they bore until the formation of the Free Soil party two years later. Henry Wilson presented resolutions in the state legislature cataloguing the alleged horrors of Slave Power domination. When a conservative Boston merchant remonstrated against resolutions which needlessly antagonized the South, young Ebenezer Rockwood Hoar of Concord snapped back that it was time the legislature began to represent the conscience as well as the cotton of the Commonwealth. From then on the antislavery Whigs of Massachusetts were known as Conscience Whigs.[15] (Another nickname, "Young Whigs," was hardly appropriate for Palfrey, who was fifty in May of that year.)

At the same time Adams began negotiations which brought the newly christened Conscience Whigs a daily means of public expression. In May the owners of the six-month-old Boston *Whig*, with a subscription list of only 200, decided to sell the paper. Palfrey bought a one-fifth interest, Adams two-fifths, and Stephen C. Phillips, the Salem merchant and ship-owner, the remaining two-fifths. Adams considered Palfrey the only person in whose judgment he could place complete reliance, and obtained from him the promise of frequent contributions. Adams' first editorial expounded his paper's *raison d'être*. Existing Boston papers were not true to Whig principles, he declared; the *Whig* would go beyond property rights to the question of right: "The times demand not merely a bold, but also a prudent, not merely an honest, but an energetic Newspaper." A fine beginning, yet even well-wishers doubted the *Whig*'s ability to stay in business.[16]

A week after the purchase of the *Whig*, Congress declared war against Mexico. War talk had been in the air for some time, and Boston Whigs feared that "many a young Jackson" in Washington was meditating expansion in the Southwest as the road to political fame. The vote on the declaration of war provided ammunition for political warfare in Massachusetts for years to come. Fourteen representatives voted against war, five of them (half the state's delegation) from the Bay State. In the Senate, Daniel Webster was absent from Washington, but the other Massachusetts senator, John Davis, was one of two men voting "No."[17]

"Verily, the American Eagle is a vile bird, which it would be almost a charity to the world to destroy," lamented a Conscience Whig, Lowell editor William S. Robinson. Many New Englanders echoed his reaction, refusing to give their support to the "war of aggression" against Mexico. Palfrey, writing in the Dedham paper of Edward L. Keyes, was delighted by the Commonwealth's response which gave "proof of a wide spread sense among the people that freedom and humanity are of more account than cotton prints." There could be no question of the survival of a nation rent by slavery: "The time is soon to come . . . when there will be *no slaves* in this country, *or else no freemen*." When a member of the nascent Native American party solicited Palfrey's aid, he was told that there was a far greater danger to America's free institutions than European immigration. In the Southwest, sixty thousand foreigners and their slaves had just entered the Union by Act of Congress. And additional Mexican provinces might be seized with their "foreign habits, and their nameless Indians and mongrel breeds." Palfrey would join no third party fighting tangential issues. The menace of the Slave Power demanded all the energies of free men.[18]

When Robert C. Winthrop voted for war supplies, he opened a Pandora's box of political evils for himself. Winthrop admitted that the preamble to the declaration of war ("war exists by the act of Mexico") was hard to swallow, but the national defense took precedence over everything else. Adams decided to commit the *Whig* to an all-out attack on Winthrop's vote. As Winthrop's friends rallied to his defense, William Hayden, co-editor of the conservative Boston *Atlas*, offered Winthrop his columns, scoring "a certain class of theorists about here, who are quite excited . . . and find no terms too harsh to use towards any one who speaks with the least calmness about . . . this Mexican War." The intense newspaper controversy which followed hastened the polarization of the Whig factions. Sumner's temporarily anonymous articles in the *Courier* led to a complete break with Winthrop, who recoiled in disgust from his accuser: "My hand is not at the service of any one, who has denounced it, with such ferocity, as being stained with blood." [19]

The Whig state convention, scheduled for the last week of September 1846, promised to be a lively affair. A month before, David Wilmot, a Democratic representative from Pennsylvania, had given the Conscience Whigs a secure peg on which to hang their antislavery sentiments by attaching a rider to a war appropriations bill, calling for the prohibition of slavery in any territory obtained from Mexico—the rider known as the Wilmot Proviso. "As if by magic," commented the *Whig*, "it brought to a head the great question which is about to divide the American people." The divergent emphases of the two groups emerged clearly at a preliminary meeting of Boston delegates. Abbott Lawrence told his fellow Whigs that there was no dearth of real issues, and he proceeded to list them with no mention of slavery or the war. Sumner replied, in a speech which Palfrey felt should be put in the hands of every convention delegate, that the paramount moral issue of slavery should not and could not be avoided. On the eve of the convention Stephen C. Phillips stood ready with strong resolutions reflecting the Conscience viewpoint.[20]

Palfrey led the Cambridge delegation at the convention. With Charles Hudson presiding, the conservatives ran things to their liking, renominating Governor Briggs by acclamation, and offering resolutions which went in the same direction, though not nearly so far as Phillips' proposals. The outcome of the convention forced John Quincy Adams to conclude with convenient oversimplification that "there are two divisions of the party,—one based on public principle, and the other upon manufacturing and commercial interests." [21]

Shortly before the convention Palfrey had mounted his first sustained effort in antislavery journalism. In keeping with his promise to aid Adams and the *Whig*, he wrote a series of twenty-four articles which appeared in the paper from July to September, under the title "The Slave Power." Palfrey, with pardonable exaggeration, later recalled the "hubbub they did make, as they appeared from week to week. . . . Nothing could exceed the rage of Milk Street and State Street. . . . A social anathema was proclaimed from the high seats of cotton merchandize." The articles, which soon reappeared as a pamphlet, were an extensive, though often overdrawn, exposition of the *Whig*'s Texas stand, as well as an indictment of Cotton Whig timidity in not accompanying antislavery professions with antislavery actions.[22]

The *Slave Power* pamphlet carried Palfrey's name, and he soon found himself embroiled in a controversy with Nathan

Appleton. Although Palfrey's publisher assured prospective purchasers that "these Articles have been highly commended, and by persons not generally termed Abolitionists," Appleton was not among the work's admirers. In one of his essays Palfrey had gone beyond his customary good taste in remarking of Appleton that it was "hard to make a statesman out of a calico merchant." Appleton requested that in any future edition of the pamphlet his explanatory letter of the previous November be included, since Palfrey gave the impression that he, Appleton, had brought on the Mexican War singlehanded. Palfrey's answer evaded his responsibility for introducing Appleton's name. Instead Palfrey pointed to attacks upon himself in the *Atlas*, and added disingenuously: "I do not allow myself to be pained by your overbearing language. . . . Doubtless in station and influence you have the advantage of me. But I, as much as yourself, am a free man of Massachusetts." Appleton replied correctly that he was not responsible for what appeared in the *Atlas*. He commended Palfrey's determination not to be overborne, but hoped that his adversary would remember to avoid injustice to others at the same time. A few weeks later Appleton published the exchange of letters.[23]

Palfrey's journalistic venture caused strained relations with other old friends. On October 19 Sumner called to relate painful facts about the reception of *Papers on the Slave Power*, and next day Palfrey found the door to Edmund Dwight's home closed to him. No one questioned Palfrey's right to speak on slavery, but his method and choice of vocabulary, particularly in reference to the Cotton Whigs, would not be tolerated. Harrison Gray Otis called it a "waspish & unmerited outbreak," answered by a "gentlemanly rebuke." Adams saw that Palfrey was visibly shaken by the "state of society," and was moved to sympathy for his sensitive friend.[24]

Palfrey found ostracism hard to bear. He was, in Andrews Norton's words, "preparing for himself great trouble and mortification." Of course he had made several new friends among the Conscience Whigs, but Palfrey's concern was the measure of his social insecurity. Whatever position he enjoyed in Boston society came not from distinguished ancestors or wealth, but from his own talents, or, rather, Boston society's opinion of them. Believing as he did that he had not used these talents to the fullest possible extent, Palfrey was uncertain of himself. Thus his unbending adherence to an exaggerated rectitude sprang not only from his moral sense, but from a desire to prove himself as well.[25] In the matter of being a Boston gentleman and worthy son of New England, Palfrey was determined to give lessons to *arriviste* State Street calico merchants and their political hired hands, however long and distinguished their lineages. But when truth to one's self brought the disapproval of those whose good opinion he craved, it left Palfrey battered, confused, and wavering.

To remedy the situation Palfrey called on Andrews Norton to discuss his position. Norton warned that the tone of the *Whig* articles was such that no good could come from them. Then came a withering letter from Samuel A. Eliot, which led Palfrey to seek solace in one of his old sermons on friendship. Did he recognize himself in Sparks's appraisal of what was needed for a successful career in politics? "You must either be silent . . . or be prepared for very rough usage. You will want strong nerves." Early in November a sudden but short-lived reconciliation with his estranged friends delighted Palfrey. He had a friendly talk with Francis C. Gray, and Mrs. Gray called again on Mrs. Palfrey. That same night ("Thanks to God!") a conciliatory letter came from Eliot, who saw a basis for friendship in the fundamental Whig conservatism of the two men, as long as they did not discuss the subject of antislavery politics. Palfrey wanted no interruption of his social life nor of his political activities; he naively thought one could continue without effecting the other. Late in November a second edition of the *Slave Power* essays appeared.[26]

Palfrey felt such intense pain over these incidents that one wonders why he became an active antislavery politician. Of course, the slavery issue had become far more prominent than before, but Palfrey had lived with the national sin of slavery for several decades with little discomfort before the emancipation crisis of the 1840's. And whatever the early hopes of would-be politicians with antislavery leanings in that decade, only the self-deluded believed that advancement on the antislavery political ladder would be easy. The careers of John Quincy Adams and Ohio's Joshua R. Giddings in the House of Representatives offered proof of that. Palfrey's main chance politically seemed to lie with the conservative Whigs who had eased him into Boston politics and had obtained for him the secretaryship.

Perhaps a partial explanation of his choice lies in Palfrey's feeling of personal failure. The constant changes of career, the unhappy final years at Harvard, and the *North American* disaster left him with a desperate need to bolster his self-esteem. To be on the periphery of Boston Whig politics had practical advantages, but little else for Palfrey, who still considered himself a man of letters and high principle. What better way to uphold his principles, in contrast to conservative Boston's alleged commercial and political capitulation to southern domination, than to champion the highest principle— human freedom? In this way Palfrey could assert his moral superiority over the merchants and politicians who ruled the society in which he lived, but for whom he harbored the contempt born of envy.

Impelled, probably unconsciously, by these feelings and armed with a genuine and unshakable abhorrence of slavery which had matured in the early 1840's, Palfrey went forward to do righteous battle.

* * *

Despite the antagonism he had created in conservative Whig circles, political expediency dictated Palfrey's advancement by the party. At the height of the Appleton controversy, Middlesex County Whigs nominated him to represent the Fourth Congressional district. Incumbent Whig Benjamin Thompson, never popular with the Liberty party, became doubly unpopular after his failure to vote against war with Mexico in May. With Conscience Whiggery strong in the county, especially in the smaller towns, no Cotton Whig could carry the district and with an almost evenly divided Thirtieth Congress predicted, the Whigs needed every seat. Better to support a possibly reconcilable Conscience man, thought the Whig managers, than to allow the Democrats to recapture the seat.[27]

Even before this nomination there was talk of running Palfrey as a Conscience Whig candidate for governor. But the insurgents' policy in Middlesex was to work through the regular party organization, and Palfrey vetoed the idea. When the Whig offer to run for Congress came, Palfrey turned it down, ostensibly for financial reasons. To risk losing his secretary's salary and submit to the dangers of popular election seemed a luxury beyond his means. As for accepting money from political supporters Palfrey rejected the idea haughtily: "I hope ten times Daniel Webster's greatness and fame would not tempt me to take Daniel Webster's annuity." In addition he was then revising more of his Old Testament lectures for publication. But his negative response stemmed primarily from the "visitation of public displeasure" he was then undergoing.

Palfrey's friends refused to accept the finality of his decision. Perhaps he had given hints that further entreaties would not be futile, and appeals came in many forms. Daniel P. King, Whig representative from Essex County, combined a request for a proper representative for the "University District" with assurances that Palfrey could actually save money on his Congressional salary. Rockwood Hoar raised the issue most likely to sway Palfrey: public duty, and the need for "a man of principle, a man of energy, a man of courage." At the district convention Palfrey received 74 of 90 votes on the first ballot. After a final plea by Adams two days later Palfrey agreed to run.[28]

Soon after the nomination a Liberty party committee called at Hazelwood to discuss the candidacy. They told Palfrey that they could not endorse him unless he gave specific antislavery pledges. Palfrey agreed that the manumission episode was not in itself sufficient cause for automatic Liberty votes; it had been "the simplest act of justice." As to pledges for future conduct, Palfrey stated his theory of government:

> The Representative is elected for the confidence entertained by his constituents in his principles and capacity; . . . while in office, his action is to be determined by the obligations of his conscience and his oath.

Liberty men uncertain of his views on slavery would find them clearly stated in the *Papers on the Slave Power*. The Liberty party found the reply unsatisfactory and nominated its own candidate, despite the belief of some that "a man who had made himself poor by emancipating slaves does not need to be asked many questions." [29]

In keeping with his conservative views of political propriety, Palfrey declined to make campaign speeches before the election, claiming that his secretary's job made such activity "indelicate." He also prevented Joseph T. Buckingham of the Boston *Courier* from using an account of the Louisiana affair in his behalf. The campaign proceeded, with the Conscience men convinced of Cotton duplicity by the spectacle of regular Whig support of Palfrey in Middlesex and solid opposition to the Conscience candidate, Samuel Gridley Howe, in Suffolk. Their newspaper propaganda conveniently ignored the fact that Howe was a splinter candidate running against Winthrop, the Whig nominee.[30]

The day after the election, Longfellow sighed gratefully that the contest was over, since "every body has been in a fever and ferment." But this first trial proved inconclusive, because Palfrey was 230 votes short of the necessary majority. The strong Liberty party showing prevented Palfrey's victory. Cornelius Felton lashed out at the Liberty men: "By defeating Mr. Palfrey, they have cast off the last rag of character, that partly hid their moral deformity. They are traitors to the cause which they dishonor by pretending to espouse." [31]

Palfrey responded characteristically to the setback. He offered to withdraw from the contest and allow someone more capable of bringing out the full Whig vote to take over. The offer, though it may have been regarded as a formality by party leaders, was sincerely made, as anyone familiar with Palfrey knew. Amos Lawrence, one member of the cotton-manufacturing Lawrence family who had not been antagonized, expressed concern over Palfrey's future:

> If those who *profess* to be his friends, will advise him to withdraw . . . he may still retain the office . . . for which he is so *admirably* qualified, but should he again be run for Congress, he will be *defeated, disgraced, & thrown aside*, as worthless *lumber*, & forgotten in three years—his family meantime losing cast [*sic*].

The Whig managers refused Palfrey's offer to step down, and advised him to await victory in the second trial. They assumed that enough Liberty men would swing to Palfrey and break the deadlock, although the abolitionists did not drop their separate ticket. On the eve of the second election the *Whig* urged the men of Middlesex not to leave the seat in Congress vacant, since questions of vital importance to all free men, questions pertaining to slavery and national expansion, were sure to be raised in the coming session.[32]

On December 28, two thousand fewer Middlesex men appeared at the polls than had in November. Despite a drop of 50 percent in the Liberty vote, Palfrey won the runoff election by only 50 votes. Disaffection among the more conservative Whigs produced this apparent contradiction. Adams commented indignantly that Palfrey had had almost too much to contend with—Cotton Whig treachery which spurred Democratic efforts, and Liberty party stubbornness; happily the masses had shown better judgment than the managers.

Thus Palfrey began 1847 as a member-elect of Congress, looking backward on a year which had made him well known in his community: "I have cooled & lost friends. On the other hand I have gained experience, &, I think, have gained confidence & moral strength." One of the cooled friends, Robert C. Winthrop, was not looking forward to welcoming his new colleague to Washington the following December. He doubted that Palfrey would do much in making a seat in Congress more desirable for others, and he sought consolation in Horace: "*Sed levis fit patientia, quicquid corrigere est nefas*"; whatever cannot be remedied is best borne with patience.[33]

*   *   *

Election in 1846 meant that Palfrey had nearly a year to wait before taking his seat in the Thirtieth Congress. He naturally wished to retain his position of Commonwealth secretary since this could be done for most of the year without conflict with Congressional duties. When he heard politically inspired doubts on the constitutionality of such a re-election, Palfrey sought legal advice. At the Whig caucus, Palfrey's friends worked hard and successfully for him. Secretary Palfrey won re-election, and he awoke next morning so happy that he could hardly believe it was true. Adams, who regarded the election as clearing up all "the personal questions which we had on hand," shared Palfrey's elation, since it left the Conscience Whigs an open field of operations. But the Cotton forces claimed that the principle of no plural officeholding had been violated on the pretext that Palfrey had been drafted into his Congressional seat.[34] Grudges were accumulating rapidly; each side viewed the other as destructive of "true Whig principles."

The first half of 1847 was not a time of intense activity for the Conscience Whigs. During February Palfrey occupied himself with speeches and articles soliciting contributions for Irish famine relief, but most of his political activity was of a sedentary nature—correspondence with potential political allies and speculation about the future, particularly on the chances of obtaining a Wilmot Proviso candidate for the presidency in 1848. In Congress the parties were floundering, with Proviso men from each side upsetting the best-laid plans of the party managers. As the Conscience Whigs followed the debates in Washington, their hopes of finding militant Proviso supporters rose and fell. Strong antislavery speeches from two Whigs, Massachusetts' George Ashmun in the House and Ohio's Thomas Corwin in the Senate, were received enthusiastically in Boston. Even some Democrats looked promising. The incipient Barnburner revolt of Proviso Democrats in New York delighted Adams, and Palfrey, too, hailed the growth of Free Soilism outside New England, particularly in Ohio.[35]

Much of the Conscience Whig attitude originated in apprehension that war in Mexico had created an unbeatable candidate, General Zachary Taylor. Early in 1847 Conscience men agreed that everything possible should be done to block the candidacy of the slaveholding general. Some of the Cotton forces shared the initial fears about Taylor. Webster realized that no effective opposition to the war hero was possible; better to let the mania run its course and hope it did so before the nominating convention in the spring of 1848. And other Cotton Whigs, especially those in Webster's camp, fumed against Taylor and the almighty sway of the Slave Power. Edward Everett, as Harvard's president temporarily retired from politics, saw clearly that "Scott is marching straight to Mexico;—Taylor straight to the Presidency." [36]

At the Whig state convention at Springfield in September 1847 Palfrey was the most prominent of the Conscience faction. During meetings held in August the Proviso Whigs decided to hinge their entire strategy on the coming presidential election. All agreed that any attempt by the Lawrence-Appleton forces to push Taylor's candidacy should be fought with every available resource. Palfrey sensed correctly that Webster, who "insisted on going to Springfield to look after his own interest," was a greater threat, since the Taylor men planned to wait for the national convention before moving. The Conscience men realized that any hope for victory lay in capitalizing on the Webster-Lawrence split, while for their part both regular Whig factions were angling for Conscience support. The increase in Conscience strength at Springfield (an increase in some cases arranged by Cotton managers) meant that there would be less harmony of viewpoint than before, but Conscience Whigs agreed on the Proviso as the *sine qua non* for support of any candidate.[37]

On September 29 approximately 600 delegates crowded into the convention hall. The first order of business put Representative George Ashmun, whom Palfrey thought a "skillful and unscrupulous" man, into the chair. Things proceeded slowly until Daniel Webster arrived with Winthrop "in his train." Stephen C. Phillips then introduced a resolution against making any presidential nomination, an obvious slap at Webster. Although the motion was tabled, the vote in Webster's favor was much less than a majority of the delegates. "The scene," crowed Sumner, "was humiliation" for the Webster men, which even the formal endorsement of Webster later could not erase. The first point of the Conscience program (and the first point of the Lawrence program as well), had been gained.

Meanwhile Palfrey as a member of the resolutions committee pushed his Proviso resolve. The resolution called for support of only those candidates who displayed an "uncompromising opposition to the extension of Slavery." Palfrey could do nothing in the committee, however. Webster was speaking when the committee members returned to the hall and friends told Palfrey that the longer the committee stayed out, the more antislavery Webster's words became. By the time he finished, Webster had all but claimed the Proviso as his own creation, if not in name, then in fact. As soon as the committee submitted its report, Palfrey moved from the floor to add his rejected resolution. This touched off the fiercest debate of the day. The Lawrence Cotton men, with General Taylor in mind for the presidency, awakened suddenly to the dangers of a strong Proviso stand, and Winthrop, "in Webster's train" no longer, "like a squib . . . made a violent speech in opposition." When Palfrey rose to defend his motion, a group of delegates began to shout and hiss, and it was some minutes before he could begin. Chairman Ashmun appointed special tellers to count the vote. The result brought defeat for Palfrey's resolution. The Lawrence-Webster rift had not gone far enough to bring a Conscience victory. The Conscience men left the convention convinced that the count had been fraudulent. Both Adams and Sumner were sure that they had attended their last political gathering as Whigs, and Palfrey reflected that "some more distinctness was given to the separating line between patriotism and servility, between Conscience and Cotton." [38]

* * *

Palfrey's role in the convention and his resolution served to increase sharply his popularity with antiwar and antislavery men in his county and elsewhere. Senator Thomas Corwin sent assurances from Ohio that before long all northern Whigs would adopt the grounds of Palfrey's resolution. Conscience men felt that they had carried their point, even in defeat at Springfield, thanks to Winthrop's "false step." Winthrop had to admit privately that Palfrey's Proviso resolution had a "plausible smack" to it and could not be ignored. Naturally, there was no increase of popularity for Palfrey among the Cotton Whigs, old or young. Harvard student Abbott Lawrence, Jr., came away from a social at Hazelwood complaining that it had been "The essence of stupidity and disgust—'Tea and Palfrey'—in connection—might give you a good idea of the amount of enjoyment." [39]

In preparing to leave for Washington, Palfrey decided to visit first the towns of his district. Since he had not campaigned he went unrecognized in most of them. Illness during most of November made it doubtful that he would be able to leave as scheduled, but he recovered with a week to spare. As he packed his trunks he may have remembered Daniel P. King's advice to take very little money or clothing with him, since Washington was "a den of thieves and the fewer temptations you afford them, the better."

By the end of the month, his desk tidy, and all farewell calls made, Palfrey was ready. He already had one friend waiting in Congress—Ohio's antislavery Congressman, Joshua R. Giddings. The two men had met twice before, and Giddings was delighted with Palfrey's Springfield performance: "I anticipate much pleasure at seeing him assume a portion of the responsibility that has so long rested upon a few of us." Sumner assured Giddings he would not be disappointed, since Palfrey was "true as steel." [40]

X

"He Knows Nothing about Politicks"

J OSHUA GIDDINGS stood near the shed which served as Washington's railroad station on the afternoon of December 4, 1847. Sumner had advised that despite Palfrey's firmness, he would welcome any show of sympathy or friendship. Feelings of gratitute were to be reciprocal, for Giddings, feeling the strain of his nearly isolated position, was happy to greet an ally. During the trip Palfrey had already encountered John P. Hale, newly elected senator from New Hampshire and the man who was to carry the antislavery burden in the upper chamber.[1]

In Washington Palfrey immediately heard whisperings about the House speakership and Winthrop's chances of occupying the chair. Conscience Whig opposition to Winthrop had been consistent since the war-supplies vote, and even before. Winthrop's re-election over Samuel Gridley Howe in 1846 made the Conscience men feel more acutely the necessity of blocking his advancement in the House.[2] Unlike Sumner, Palfrey was still on speaking terms with his colleague, but Winthrop's role at Springfield was not calculated to make Palfrey a supporter of the younger man's political aspirations.

The Whigs had been successful in the Congressional elections of 1846. While the Senate was still uncomfortably Democratic by a 32 to 22 margin, there were to be 117 Whigs and 110 Democrats in the House. This narrow Whig majority made party solidarity all the more important to the managers.

In the evening of the same day Palfrey arrived, House

Whigs held their nominating caucus. Both Palfrey and Giddings declined to attend, fearing that to do so might compromise them. They could not block the majority will, and their presence would leave them open to charges of having tacitly accepted the nominee. When Samuel F. Vinton of Ohio declined to be a candidate, the way was open for Winthrop.[3]

The issue was now joined. A Whig had been duly nominated by the party caucus; how would the Whig mavericks vote on Monday, the 6th? Giddings confessed to feelings of indecision, and in an effort to dispel doubts Palfrey took the initiative. After a talk with Giddings, he addressed a note to Winthrop inquiring about the organization of House committees. Would they be constituted so as to bring the Mexican war to speedy conclusion, bar slavery from any new territories, and insure trial by jury to alleged slaves? Giddings thought there was a chance that Winthrop would answer favorably, but the latter replied in few hours that he would give no pledges. He told Palfrey that his political views were in his speeches, and that nothing he could "get up for the occasion" would be better.[4]

On voting day, Boston Whigs worried over rumors of a cabal of a few untrustworthy Whig members which might deny Massachusetts her deserved honor. In the Capitol the galleries filled up early as anticipation of conflict over the speakership heightened the excitement which normally accompanies the opening of Congress. Palfrey entered the House conscious of the consequences of what he was about to do. On the first ballot Winthrop was only three votes short of the total needed. This strength showed that he was acceptable to the southern Whigs, who had been concerned about his position on slavery.[5] Palfrey had wanted to support Caleb B. Smith of Indiana, but he voted instead for his Massachusetts colleague, Charles Hudson, hoping to avoid stigmatizing Smith should Winthrop's candidacy fail. Giddings and Amos Tuck of New Hampshire[6] both voted for James Wilson of New Hampshire. The three men persisted in this course throughout the voting. Unfortunately for Winthrop's political position in Massachusetts his victory on the third ballot came about through aid from a southerner.[7] He picked up two votes on the second ballot, and the departure of South Carolinian Isaac E. Holmes decided the contest. Winthrop's good friend, editor William Schouler, could now detect "a vein of liberality and independence running through the South Carolina nullifying politicians." John Quincy Adams administered the oath of office, and Winthrop made a "sensible, dignified and pertinent" address. Palfrey, always taking things too seriously, found to his surprise that the whole affair had gone off good-naturedly.[8]

So much controversy arose over Palfrey's alleged desertion of state and party that the issue itself became lost in the din of charges and countercharges. Palfrey contended that while the liberties of all free men and their children were in danger from the political power of slavery, Winthrop was oblivious to the threat. Two years later the matter was still alive, and Palfrey explained again in an open letter:

> The Speaker is not merely the officer presiding. . . . By his high prerogative in the appointment of the committees . . . he exerts . . . an influence in all cases very material, and in a large proportion of cases no less than decisive. . . . I could not, without a sacrifice of my own integrity, help to entrust him with that power. He was no representative of the principles which had been solemnly affirmed by the Whigs who sent me to Congress.[9]

Adherence to the Wilmot Proviso was Palfrey's political litmus test. Palfrey knew Winthrop would not give the desired pledges.[10] His own experience with the Liberty party a year before was undoubtedly in his mind when he wrote the note to Winthrop. But he had to make the attempt before voting. The irritant which led to the clash was the fact that both men were nominally Whigs at a time when this term was beginning to lose its meaning. The Whig umbrella was not wide enough to cover such a diversity of views, and it was not long before events drastically remedied the situation.

Palfrey knew that storm clouds would soon roll in from Massachusetts, but before the onslaught he wrote Winthrop again, this time a letter of congratulation stating he hoped the speaker would fill the chair with honor. He also admitted to his family that he was not too displeased by the election, since a much worse speaker might have been chosen.[11]

Cotton Whigs and their supporters reacted immediately and vehemently. The Boston *Atlas*, chief Cotton organ, led the chorus in describing the widespread indignation in the city, and reported unctuously that when "first reported, there was no one willing to believe it could be true." The paper called on Palfrey to resign his seat. Specific criticism took many forms. One editor scored Palfrey's "unethical demand" for pledges; another declared the act was the result of private ill-will. A correspondent of the *Advertiser*, more concerned with Webster than with Winthrop, claimed that without a Whig speaker Webster's "great constitutional doctrine" of Congressional control of the executive could not be carried out.[12]

On the other hand, some papers supported the election of Winthrop, and agreed on the necessity for Whig control of the House, yet took a milder tack. Boston's most readable and fair-minded sheet, Joseph T. Buckingham's *Courier*, carried editorials far different from those of the *Atlas* and *Advertiser*. It did not question Palfrey's motives, but too much principle unleavened by some practicality seemed a liability. Sumner was still contributing occasional pieces to the *Courier*, and Buckingham printed Sumner's article praising Palfrey—merely affixing an asterisk to the title to indicate it was not his, Buckingham's, editorial. Buckingham's liberal policy annoyed Winthrop, but he decided not to make an issue of it: "These vindicators of Dr. Palfrey seem to forget that they are accusers of the whole of the rest of the delegation. If honor is to be rendered to J. G. P. for voting against me, then dishonor attaches to J. Q. A[dams] & the rest."[13] In Lowell,

the *Journal* called attention to personal considerations stemming, not from ill-will, but from honest differences, and
William S. Robinson, editor of the Lowell *Courier*, assured
Palfrey that he would have to do something much worse than
the Winthrop vote to earn the enmity of his paper.[14]

With the adverse clippings came strong letters of encouragement and admiration—admiration not confined to the close
circle of Conscience Whigs. Even Democratic chieftain Benjamin F. Hallett told Sumner that if Palfrey voted against
Winthrop he would have an "almighty great" respect for him.
Charles Francis Adams referred to "some barking in the Whig
papers" which would have made silence impossible despite
Palfrey's desire to keep press controversy at a minimum.[15]
Those who found Palfrey's conduct reprehensible or absurd
kept their mortification and disgust to themselves, or within
their own circles. Andrews Norton observed sourly that Palfrey's name had acquired a strong etymological significance,
but the man most concerned, Winthrop, claimed he bore no
grudge; on the contrary he averred that "nothing could have
been more fortunate for me and our party than the votes of
the three ultraists." Separation from the pollution of fanatical
antislavery men was best for the Whig party, thought Winthrop.[16]

Polemics aside, what if anything had been gained by Palfrey
and his friends Giddings and Tuck? If nothing else, publicity
or notoriety, depending on the views of the observer. Stephen
C. Phillips first called this to Palfrey's attention, alluding to
the conspicuousness which accompanied the censure. Adams
suggested that Palfrey act with his father, Giddings, and
Gamaliel Bailey, an Ohioan who was then editing Washington's abolitionist *National Era*, to coordinate antislavery activities in the capital. Recalling Palfrey's previous reluctance to
deal with abolitionists, Adams reminded him that his first day
in the House had "sealed the bond with the Antislavery men."
In South Carolina, the Charleston *Courier* noted that an

abolitionist clique had appeared in the House, with Palfrey, "a gentleman of undoubted talent and industry," at the head. Palfrey, then, was a marked man.[17]

Although he had no intention of abandoning his antislavery stand, Palfrey, unlike some of the Conscience men, still believed that something might be done within the Whig party. Phillips and Sumner had already urged him to burn all boats, and though Adams felt the break would come eventually he warned Palfrey not to make any hasty moves. Palfrey's natural caution meant he would follow this advice instinctively: "It does not follow because a man votes firmly, he can speak effectively." Palfrey still considered himself a Whig, and voted for most of the Whig nominees for the minor offices in the House. He was pleased by the courtesy shown him by other House Whigs, interpreting this as respect for his display of principle. Suggestions to bolt the party and boycott district and county conventions got no support from Palfrey: "Insist that we are the Whigs—so shows the record; the others are seceders." [18]

Good opinions meant more to Palfrey than good politics. He would have been highly gratified by Harvard librarian John L. Sibley's journal entry in the Winthrop vote: "It is a rare virtue in a politician to sacrifice his popularity by abandoning even the less of two evils and adhering to what is right in itself and to what conscience dictates." And James Russell Lowell used Palfrey's vote as the theme for one of the *Biglow Papers*. Palfrey, the "chap thet wuz chose fer a wig," was excoriated by one Increase D. O'Phace, Cotton Whig: "An', ez fer this Palfrey, we thought wen we'd gut him in, he'd go kindly in wutever harness we put him in." [19] Palfrey came into politics armed with little but an overriding sense of righteousness and the habits of a gentleman. The latter proved to be no armor at all; the politics of righteousness proved too difficult to sustain without the solid political base of the compromising, working politician.

Mary Ann Palfrey was proud when Palfrey won election to the House, although the unpleasantness of the Appleton controversy did not please her. But why should her husband differ with his Boston friends in a way that upset the family's social life and endangered her daughters' marriage prospects? If it came to a choice between social relations with conservative Boston and unyielding adherence to principle she was willing to see her husband yield a bit. The repercussions of the vote against Winthrop were too much for her. Palfrey, obviously shaken by his wife's reaction, asked Adams to call and explain the reasons for his vote. "My wife would cheer me to the stake," he declared in a vein of wishful thinking, "if she thought I ought to go, but she cannot see the occasion for it as I do." After Adams' visit, Palfrey noted a different tone in letters from his wife. But when Frank, who had entered Harvard the previous June, repeated his mother's doubts, Palfrey responded without annoyance that his son should think independently: "Respect your father's judgment. Look favorably on the reasons which influence him; but respect above all the integrity of your own mind." [20]

Palfrey had already told his family that opposition to Winthrop was a matter of principle, and that the speaker would conduct himself honorably. In the matter of committee assignment, Palfrey, as a new member, could not hope for an important post. Some of the Conscience men objected to Palfrey's "burial" on the Agriculture Committee, and the Democratic Boston *Post* laughed that this was the speaker's way of telling Palfrey to "go to grass." Winthrop said he would have liked to "heap coals of fire" on Palfrey's head by giving him more demanding assignments, but too many Massachusetts men had prime committee seats already. Palfrey was not insulted. When Winthrop sent George Ashmun to discuss committees, Palfrey told Ashmun that new men should not get the best posts for their own sake. Winthrop's acknowledged impartiality left no cause for complaint. [21]

Palfrey began the new year with a quick trip to Massachusetts. As secretary of state he had to attend the election of a successor. The trip also gave Palfrey a chance to get a firsthand reaction to his vote. When Secretary Palfrey opened the legislative session, a leading member, former *Atlas* editor William Hayden, ostentatiously turned his back on him. But the hostility was not unanimous; a few minutes after Hayden's snub, John C. Gray, another conservative Whig, marched to the platform and greeted Palfrey cordially.[22]

Palfrey had impaired his social position by his action, but he exaggerated the extent of his martyrdom. Francis Bowen, who was in a position to know, congratulated Palfrey on his ability to combine independence in Congress with friendly relations with many individuals who disagreed with him. Governor Briggs privately decried the newspaper attacks on Palfrey, saying "how much better to treat so good a man kindly and wait and see where he will come out." Throughout the spring Palfrey heard that Middlesex County was daily becoming prouder of its representative. After his return to Washington, he received a call from the chairman of the Whig district committee. Palfrey feared the meeting would not go well, but found the man friendly. This prompted Palfrey to advise his daughter: "To make other people think eventually that you do right, there is no way like doing what you think right yourself." [23]

Early in 1848 Palfrey confronted, then avoided, the issue of reconciling his antislavery activities and his brothers' slaveholding with his desire to maintain friendly family relations. William Palfrey was a difficult man to get along with under the best of circumstances. Gorham and Henry had already complained to each other of his lack of affection, and the tensions of the emancipation did nothing to remedy this deficiency. Palfrey inquired whether his Free Soilism was the cause of William's four-year silence. Since Gorham had raised the slavery issue, William replied frankly. Emancipation of property was Gorham's business and besides, observed William shrewdly, the emancipator had no choice; any New Englanders who wished to remain in that section could not possibly accept slave property. But Gorham's political activities were not so blameless:

> I do find fault with your placing yourself in the position of a *leader* of the *Abolition* Party. . . . You were making political capital of this transaction [emancipation] . . . and the capital . . . is made at the expense of your father's memory.
> . . . I do not see any emergency requiring you, for conscience sake, to take the zealous part in favor of this mischievous faction, whose mildest epithets towards all slaveholders without distinction are those of "murderers and thieves."

William did not defend slavery. It was an evil that the country would be fortunate to be rid of, but he saw no practical immediate remedy. Gorham found much in his brother's statements that he wished to correct. He resisted the urge and thanked William for his "manly and honorable tone" and whatever kindness lay behind his words. In March he received a more conciliatory note. The subject of slavery would not be mentioned again by the brothers for seventeen years.[24]

* * *

In Washington Palfrey soon became a member of an informal group of antislavery Congressmen that met frequently for political and social reasons. It included Giddings, Amos Tuck, Caleb B. Smith, Joseph M. Root of Ohio, and later Horace Mann, all of the House, and Senator John P. Hale. In addition editor Gamaliel Bailey joined them frequently, as did visiting Conscience Whigs. The men Palfrey saw most often were Giddings and Tuck. From the beginning of the session Giddings and Palfrey had been sizing each other up. Palfrey had no complaints about Giddings' courage or character, except that his overoptimism weakened his analytical powers—a failing noted by others. Giddings quickly perceived Palfrey's strong and weak points:

> He is a learned man. It is a feast to sit down and chat with him on any moral subject. In truth the Dr. & myself make a very good pair. *He knows nothing about politicks, but is exceedingly interesting on morals, religion, and science.* I am honored to call him my friend. Is it not curious that I should have been so long acting as it were by myself, and now the most learned man in Congress would be my most intimate friend and Companion?[25]

Late in December southern members had made allusions to the folly of certain northern antislavery Whigs. Thomas L. Clingman of North Carolina attacked the intrusion of abolitionism into national politics, and warned that the Union could not endure such strains. Palfrey listened carefully, and began drafting a speech which was ready near the end of January. "Never did I feel that I had a holier work in hand," he observed as he prepared to deliver his reply, "Political Aspects of the Slavery Question." In a complete rejection of Clingman's thesis, Palfrey told the House that the South, not the North, had injected slavery into national politics by the annexation of Texas. The power of slavery was subversive of American democracy, mocking as it did the right of petition, freedom of speech and the press, and due process. As for Clingman's sneering reference to the end of slavery in the British West Indies, Palfrey could hardly believe his ears:

> The failure of the West Indian emancipation! Do the gentleman and I speak the same language? . . . *Failure* when eight hundred thousand human chattels were quietly changed in a day to men and women endowed with the possession and care of their own bodies and souls, introduced to the relations of humanity, entitled to call their children their own, empowered to have husband and wife, brother and sister in some intelligible sense! This is a *failure!*

Clingman had spoken of the possible necessity for drastic measures in fighting antislavery campaigners; to Palfrey this smacked of disunion, something which Free Soiler Palfrey never advocated, and was unwise for the South: "If they insist that the Union and Slavery cannot live together, they may be taken at their word, but it is the Union that must stand." [26]

The speech, and its reception in the House, pleased Palfrey. He had easily conquered his early nervousness. There were no signs of hostility from his listeners, despite some antislavery remarks as strong as those which caused Giddings' censure in the House six years before. Giddings was thoroughly satisfied with the effort and John Quincy Adams reportedly remarked, "Thank God! The seal is broken," when Palfrey sat down. Sumner praised the "keen dialectic" of Palfrey's speech while exclaiming, "Honor to the breaker of the seal!" in the *Courier*. Even the *Atlas* ran the speech and praised its sentiments, not as something new, but as the oft-repeated views of all Massachusetts Whiggery. Sumner overheard a remark that within five years Palfrey would be the most popular man in Massachusetts.[27]

Palfrey could learn much about the perils of principle, of their effect on political popularity, from John Quincy Adams. Adams, feeble since a stroke in 1846, could not attend the meetings of the antislavery Congressmen. But there was no doubt about his stand. He told Giddings and Palfrey that he approved the votes against Winthrop, and voted for the speaker out of respect for the memory of Winthrop's father, who had once helped him during difficult times. Palfrey escorted "Old Man Eloquent" to the door of the House chamber several times. On February 21, 1848, Adams suffered another stroke. Palfrey telegraphed Charles Francis Adams, and he and several other members of the Bay State delegation attended the dying man almost constantly. When the vigil ended two days later Palfrey went with a few other members to inform the widow of Adams' death.[28]

In selecting a successor to fill the remainder of Adams' term Palfrey immediately thought of Charles Francis Adams. There seemed no other choice. Henry Wilson, who also wanted the place, was trustworthy, but intellectually Adams outranked any other Conscience Whig. Palfrey declared with sincerity that if his resignation meant a seat in Congress for Adams he would step down at once. Neither Adams nor Wilson succeeded, however. The Whig nomination went to Horace Mann, who accepted although he felt that taking John Quincy Adams' place was a "good deal like asking a mouse to fill the skin of an elephant." Both Cotton and Conscience camps immediately claimed Mann as their own. Palfrey had no objection to his new colleague. A Congressman from Tennessee told him that a New York paper referred to Mann as a "Palfrey man"; Palfrey retorted that he hoped it would soon be proper to call Palfrey a "Mann man." Soon after Mann's arrival Giddings remarked that there was antislavery work aplenty for those who wanted it.[29]

For a new member, Palfrey did more than his share of the antislavery work. After the speech in January, he spoke briefly but frequently in the House, arguing for a liberal policy on receiving petitions. (During an impromptu speech, Speaker Winthrop, with customary fairness, squelched several attempts to interrupt.) After the death of John Quincy Adams, Palfrey became the recipient of an increasing number of antislavery petitions. On February 17, he presented resolutions calling for an immediate end to the war with Mexico and the denial of funds to the executive beyond the precise amount needed for military withdrawal. Palfrey stirred himself that day because a large war loan was then on its way through Congress. The resolutions were tabled, and for the first time Palfrey experienced a display of rudeness from the "war side of the House," which snickered over his moralizing.[30]

This outburst was insignificant compared to what lay in store for Palfrey at the hands of a future president of the United States. Any Congress is a cross-section of American types, and the Thirtieth was no exception. Polished gentlemen and scholars sat with men who could make no claim to formal education and whose rough manners were their trademark. A Virginia observer of Congressional events, young William C. Rives, Jr., had predicted that Palfrey would be unceremoniously run over before the end of the session by some of the " 'half horse-half alligator' species who are the peculiar production of the Western & Southern states." [31]

In April Palfrey delivered a rambling speech on the evils of slavery, despite the fact that the subject under discussion was the revolution in France.[32] He described the favorable living conditions for Negroes in Massachusetts, and mentioned a young Negro, "a charming boy," who— Here southern members chortled and shouted back: "Charming! A Charming Negro!" Palfrey maintained his composure and went on: "The expression was unpremeditated, but the reception it meets only attracts my attention to its propriety. I do not know what there is that has a charm for rightly-thinking men if it be not moral and intellectual excellence." The youth died before he could enter Harvard College, where he would have been a classmate of his son Frank, and, Palfrey was sure, he would have been treated with respect and good will. At this point Andrew Johnson rose to ask the classic question of the Negrophobe: how would Palfrey like the "charming" boy to have married his daughter? Palfrey's answer was that he would introduce no person to the female members of his family who for whatever reason might prove a source of embarrassment to them. His reply was a partial evasion. Like most antislavery men of his time, Palfrey's hatred of slavery implied no desire to establish social relations with the people whose emancipation he sought. A few days later, during a revival of the issue, Johnson mocked the discomfited Palfrey: "Theory and practice must be very different from each other. . . . [Palfrey's] sense of honor, his nice, discriminating powers, and the high tone of his morality, would forbid and reject every idea of reducing such a theory to practice." Palfrey did not reply, and wanted no mention made in Massachusetts of the exchange, "for my poor daughters' sake." [33]

*   *   *

By that time the Conscience men had already been deprived of one of their chief arguing points, the Mexican war. The Senate's ratification of a treaty of peace on March 10 meant that the Wilmot Proviso was to emerge as the key issue of the next presidential election. What little unity existed between the Cotton and Conscience factions in Congress had been on the basis of opposition to the war; the Cotton Whigs were not eager to follow a militant Proviso policy. Palfrey gave a representative Conscience opinion, when he observed before the voting:

> I believe the Treaty will be ratified. It is an awful choice of evils. But I think the better view is—Peace at any rate. And then will begin a real anti-slavery-extension struggle,—to be renewed every time a new state Constitution is proposed.[34]

In mid-April the case of the schooner *Pearl* rocked Washington. On the 17th a ship captain named Daniel Drayton tried to steer seventy-eight Negroes down the Potomac to freedom. The *Pearl* was overtaken in Chesapeake Bay and brought back to Washington, where a prominent slavedealer purchased most of the Negroes for shipment, this time not to the North, but to the Deep South and a slavery much harsher than their previous servitude. Next day, Giddings called for a special House committee to determine why certain persons were in custody without having been charged with any crime. For two nights proslavery mobs formed in front of the jail and Bailey's *National Era* office. It appeared that Gamaliel Bailey might join Elijah Lovejoy in the ranks of abolitionist press martyrs. Giddings, displaying the courage even his enemies admired, visited the prisoners, ignoring threats from the same crowds which a few days before had been wildly celebrating the triumph of freedom in revolutionary France.[35]

At this point Palfrey entered the affair. On the day of the *Pearl*'s capture Giddings commented favorably on Palfrey's resoluteness: "He is precisely the man to fill the very place he occupies—We had no such man before he came. He is a reliable man at all times"; and his actions during the *Pearl* affair left nothing to be desired. Palfrey tried to frame the issue in terms of the personal safety of a member of Congress when he introduced resolutions calling attention to the threats against Giddings. The debate which he touched off was rambling but bitter. Southerners lashed out at New England's "vile hypocrites" who had fattened their purses in times past by slave-trading, and now presumed to act as keepers of the national conscience. Although Palfrey and Giddings responded spiritedly in their own defense, when the resolution came to a vote a few days later, the danger to Giddings had subsided. A large majority of the House agreed with the *Atlas* that Palfrey's move was "unnecessary and ill-judged." Yet the antislavery forces were satisfied. Bailey's *Era* crowed over the victory of the all-important principle of freedom of the press, and Palfrey believed that the week's events could not fail to enlighten the people of the North. He had no doubts about the corrupting influence of the southern way of life. When a fistfight between representatives from Georgia and Tennessee broke out on the House floor, he commented scornfully: "It was an ugly scene. But this comes of Southern blood, made rampant by the habitual despotism of Slavery." [36]

*   *   *

Whatever the political issue of the moment, 1848 was above all a presidential year. The quadrennial American sweepstakes began long before the official time for presenting candidates. The first exhilarating war victories had already created a contender: after Buena Vista and Resaca de la Palma, Zachary Taylor, "Ultra" Whig or not, was the man to beat. In Washington Palfrey heard rumors that Webster and Winthrop

were insinuating themselves into the Taylor movement. All
Conscience men agreed that General Taylor would not do.
Who, then, was both worthy of support and capable of being
nominated? John P. Hale possessed so little "availability"
that he was out of the question. The man regarded as available
and acceptable was Ohio's John McLean, an associate justice
of the United States Supreme Court.[37]

Palfrey sought to commit this politically minded judge to
a strong Proviso stand at several meetings. In January, Giddings took him to the justice's chambers for introductions.
McLean said he favored the restriction of slavery, but not the
Proviso. It was unnecessary, he contended, since the courts
(in a way he never detailed) would block slavery extension.
Palfrey replied that this was true in principle, but not in practice, and here the interview ended. A second meeting a month
later was equally unsatisfactory. Palfrey then asked McLean
to put his ideas on paper. Ever cautious, McLean extracted
Palfrey's promise not to publish his letter but merely show it
to friends. The judge would go no further then to reiterate his
stand on judicial restriction of slavery, which "cannot be
maintained for an hour, where the local law does not sanction
it. This is more than the Wilmot Proviso. It is much stronger,
for it is in the Constitution." Following the second meeting,
McLean heard from Ohio: "Do you know Palfrey? If not,
I hope you will make his acquaintance. He has influence. I
think . . . it is destined to grow." When Palfrey next met
McLean on the street the justice acted more cordial. He seemed
ready to consider an independent nomination should the
Whigs pass him over.[38]

McLean's fellow Ohioan, Salmon P. Chase, tried to drum
up enthusiasm for him in Massachusetts, but it was difficult
to reconcile the antislavery zealot of Chase's letters with the
cautious politician of the Palfrey interviews. Adams was not
convinced; McLean might be supported, not as the best man,
but as "the best we can get." Despite favorable reports, the

justice refused to commit himself further. Adams was right when he noticed that McLean did not have the heart of a leader.[39]

Another name frequently cropped up in Conscience Whig correspondence and councils, that of Daniel Webster. Outbreaks of the "Webster mania" hit some of the younger Conscience Whigs such as Rockwood Hoar, who quoted Webster as saying he would never support Taylor, "a *Swearing, fighting, Frontier Colonel.*" While most Conscience men expected nothing from Webster they considered his friends good material for recruits and listened hopefully to promises of defection by Webster men should Taylor receive the nomination. Palfrey thought these hopes unfounded, and as for Webster himself he was in perpetual thralldom to State Street: "They hold his game in their hands, or rather, in their purses." [40]

As the day for the Whig national convention approached, the Conscience Whigs knew that their policy hinged on the outcome of this meeting. Palfrey warned Sumner not to let immediate setbacks depress him as all eyes turned toward Philadelphia, site of the convention.[41]

XI

Down with Old Zack

THE Whig national convention of 1848 was not one of our great political gatherings. An irate but finally reconciled Horace Greeley dubbed it "The Slaughterhouse of Whig Principles." Indeed, for some time before the spring of 1848 many Whigs debated the advisability of holding no convention and merely placing Zachary Taylor's name on their ticket. The general's political inexperience and popularity combined to foster confusion; as late as mid-April Boston Free Soil Democrats were thinking of Taylor as a standard-bearer for their cause.[1]

In the weeks preceding the convention, the Massachusetts Conscience Whigs strove to influence the district conventions called to select national delegates. The same convention that had nominated Horace Mann for Congress named Henry Wilson a delegate to the national convention, and Wilson made no secret of his opposition to Taylor. In the Fifth District, which included the antislavery stronghold of Worcester, the Conscience men won a total victory. The convention selected Charles Allen as delegate, instructing him to vote for no man not publicly opposed to the extension of slavery into any territory then free.[2] Before leaving for the convention Allen sought Palfrey's advice on what course to follow, and asked for information on the status of Whig disaffection in other states. Palfrey urged militancy; if Allen put forth his strength, and others stood by him, the nomination of Taylor, which seemed to be "but too probable, will be but brute thunder."[3]

Palfrey's own Middlesex Fourth District presented a different picture, however. Rockwood Hoar sought vainly to represent the district, but the Charlestown meeting chose a compromise delegate. Hoar was equally unsuccessful in his attempt to gain support for Palfrey's rejected Springfield resolutions of 1847. These setbacks evoked the amused statement of a Democratic paper that apparently all "doughfaces" were not members of the Democratic party, and foreshadowed the trouble that Palfrey would face in his district. Adams called the convention an "abominable cheat" and hoped the method of choosing a Cotton delegate in the flimsy disguise of a compromise man would prove self-defeating.[4]

At Philadelphia the two Conscience Whig delegates expressed their disgust with the Whig party. On the fourth ballot Taylor won out over his rivals, Clay, Scott, and Webster. Massachusetts support for Webster was steady though unavailing, and when the contest ended Allen and Wilson refused to make the nomination unanimous. On the last day of the convention, Abbott Lawrence made his bid for the vice-presidency.[5] That was too much for Allen. He obtained the floor and amid hoots and catcalls shouted: "The Whig party is here and this day dissolved. . . . The free state of Massachusetts will despise the miserable boon of the Vice-Presidency. Let me here say that it will not do—that she will spurn the bribe." Wilson also declared to the convention that he was returning to Massachusetts to do all in his power to defeat the election of the Whig nominee. The Whigs thought it wiser not to put "Cotton" on both ends of their ticket (Taylor grew the staple on his Louisiana plantation, while Lawrence spun and wove it in his mills); the nomination went to Millard Fillmore of New York. Although the Massachusetts Cotton men held Allen and Wilson responsible, a day before their remarks Sumner had informed Palfrey of recurrent rumors of the probable scuttling of Lawrence's candidacy.[6]

"God bless your righteous soul for giving them such plain words at the Convention," Palfrey congratulated Charles

Allen, but the news of the presidential nomination was disappointing. His own reaction surprised Palfrey, for he realized that he should have expected nothing else. Unlike Giddings, he was not prone to be "overly sanguine"; why then his optimism before the convention? The answer seems to be a bad case of wishful thinking, a malady brought on by his reluctance to accept the fact that the Whig party was not to become a Free Soil party. Palfrey's avowed principles and his distaste for controversy were not easily reconcilable. The Whig presidential nomination made this fact clear. On the night of June 8, and well into the morning, Palfrey lay awake thinking of the nomination and the coming struggles.[7]

*   *   *

In Boston the Conscience men were ready for the news of the Taylor nomination, relieved that the period of indecision and doubt lay behind them. Rockwood Hoar had written a convention call which scored Taylor's political pretensions ("HE IS NOT A WHIG when tried by the standards of our party"), and called on all men opposed to the nominees of both major parties to meet in convention at Worcester on June 28.[8]

In the days following the Whig national convention Palfrey kept a closer watch on political affairs than usual. First reports from Cambridge informed him that many of his constituents would not vote for a slaveholder. Hoar's Worcester convention call delighted Palfrey, who wanted it sent to every minister in the state with the added exhortation: "Clergymen of Massachusetts! Ministers of truth & humanity! Give two days to your country. Give one day to collecting signatures to this call. On another give your presence at Worcester." Palfrey also concerned himself with events in other states. In March he had suggested a meeting of friends of the Proviso, but little was done. Taylor's nomination three months later made action imperative. Palfrey attended antislavery gatherings which decided to send emissaries to sound out opinions and estimate chances of a union of Proviso men of all parties. John P. Hale was to urge the Liberty party men of New England to coalesce with midwestern Free Soilers. And Amos Tuck went on a fact-finding trip to New York to learn how far the dis-affected Barnburner Democrats would go in revolt. So im-portant were events outside of Massachusetts to the Conscience men that they chose June 28 for their Worcester meeting so as to be able to gauge the results of antislavery meetings in Ohio and New York, both scheduled to meet a week earlier.[9]

Although there were "heartburnings" among the Cotton forces of Boston, particularly the Webster men, they had little trouble in adjusting to the Whig nominee. The *Atlas* did mention the fact that Webster, not Taylor, had been its pre-ferred candidate, but promised full support for the general. Winthrop declared that he would not hesitate in supporting him despite rumblings from his constituents. Cotton papers vented their spleen on the two convention renegades, Allen and Wilson, ridiculing Allen's remark about the dissolution of the Whig party and dismissing the coming meeting at Worcester. Let them go about their crazy business, counseled the Lowell *Journal,* but "staunch old-fashioned" Whigs would not be tricked into such nonsense. Instead they would crowd into Faneuil Hall on the night of June 16 for a well-attended Taylor ratification convention. Cotton editorialists stigmatized the organizers of the Worcester convention:

WHO ARE THEY? The grand sachems, who are to counsel the factious assemblage . . . are announced to be, Allen, Wilson, Giddings, Sumner, Phillips, Keyes, Hoar, and Adams—the very men who have been striving . . . to dissever the Whig party; and this by no open, square, manly fight, but by the pretense of holding to Whig doc-trines. . . . Happily, they have now assumed their proper attitude of real hostility . . . and it is the happiest result of Taylor's nomination.[10]

The Cotton blacklist did not include Palfrey only because he had remained in Washington until the close of the session.

A sincere believer in the nefarious strength of the Slave Power, and with territorial questions pending, he wished to stay in the capital. Besides, Giddings had agreed to visit the Yankees, and Palfrey knew he was no match for his friend in speechmaking. Although disappointed, his friends did not press him to appear as they never doubted his firmness. These were days of disappointment, as more and more men found it inexpedient to appear at Worcester. Whittier might worry over Horace Mann's hesitancy, but "Of Palfray [sic], I have no fear." Palfrey himself did not let individual defections trouble him: "Whether more or fewer of our old friends stand with us . . . God Almighty does, & I think things are safe in his hands." [11]

The Worcester convention marked the high point of the Massachusetts Conscience Whig movement. The word Whig is used advisedly, for although the call asked for nonpartisan support, the arrangements, handling, and speechmaking were primarily the work of disaffected Whigs.[12] June 28 was a day of ardent and righteous oratory. Whittier had advised the Conscience men not to "stultify yourselves by boasting of your Whiggery" since the Whig party was no more. Palfrey, in a letter to the convention, voiced his agreement:

> Many of us in Massachusetts have hoped & believed that in Whig principles there was an ark of safety. But the insolent Slave-Power has trampled them under foot in a National Convention professedly composed of Whig delegates. It is time for patriots to consider, & consult, & pray, & resolve, & act. It is time for Massachusetts freemen to take a stand.[13]

When the meeting adjourned that evening, the five thousand participants scattered, possessed of a new element to add to their feeling of righteousness. For the first time they felt that the path of Proviso politics would not be traveled alone. Many Liberty party men now believed in the sincerity and resolution of the Free Soil advocates, and the strong show of strength in the Bay State heartened antislavery men in other parts of New

England. Worcester was an effective political revival meeting; even realists like Adams began to believe in ultimate victory.[14]

* * *

However firm the Conscience leaders may have felt in their convictions, Mary Ann Palfrey remained troubled. Her husband, in addition to enduring the increasingly frequent snubs of Congressional Whigs, had to spend much time trying to calm her. He explained that to write fully about all the "aspects of the political sky" would take more sheets of paper than he could spare, and suggested to Mary Ann that she read the *Whig* daily. When George Ashmun published an attack on Palfrey which greatly distressed Mary Ann, Palfrey explained: "I have had the approbation of my deliberate judgement and sense of duty as much this summer as last winter, and I mean so to act as to continue to have it. I am satisfied that he who walketh uprightly, walketh freely." Mary Ann was also displeased by her husband's friendship with the blunt Westerner, Giddings, who had affronted conservative Boston in the first months of 1848 because of an acrimonious public controversy with Winthrop. Mary Ann considered Giddings little more than a western ruffian. Palfrey patiently defended his colleague:

I have lived here on the most intimate footing with him, and I have scarcely known the man whom I so entirely respect and esteem. With perfect firmness and some impetuosity, he has rare gentleness and delicacy of character, and all sustained by an enlightened and fervent piety. He looks rough, but the mildest elements are mixed up in him, and he fears God, and nothing else.

Mary Ann, mollified but ever practical, could not help observing that should the opposition to Taylor fail, the general-president would be "tempted to set his foot upon the necks" of the antislavery men.[15]

Palfrey's separation from home was not pleasant, but he

claimed that he had no time to think of his solitude. Many
hours a day went to his correspondence and to the chore of
franking government documents[16] to his constituents. The
work should have gone to a secretary, but Palfrey's budget
would not allow it. His reading was almost exclusively concerned with Congressional work. After a few days at a hotel,
Palfrey obtained two rooms in the house of a baker at 11th
and E streets. Despite reasonable rates, Palfrey stopped eating
dinner so that he would have more money to send home. On
several occasions, when guests stayed late, he missed his bachelor's solitude. But Palfrey did not suffer too much from isolation. At one reception he "circulated as much as anybody,
and talked as fast," and he gave several parties in his quarters
for his antislavery friends. When a cold confined him to bed
for a few days the number of callers who came to cheer him
up attested to his popularity.[17]

The two committees Palfrey sat on provided additional out-
lets for his energies. The House Agriculture Committee had
had a single meeting in the past thirteen years. The Whig
committee members found an offensive passage in President
Polk's annual message that dealt with the irreconcilable clash
between manufacturing and agriculture interests. The chairman turned the task of replying over to Palfrey. The resulting
report was the product of ten weeks of the usual Palfrey
industriousness. By the time he finished early in August he
had combed the available sources for data which supported
the "great doctrine of Protection." He franked all the available copies, hoping that his defense of a cardinal point of
northern Whig orthodoxy would soften the antagonism that
existed toward him. Though customarily there were large
printings of such reports, in this case only the statutory minimum number of copies left the press. Palfrey, thinking that
the Whigs wanted to keep the tariff question dormant until
after the election, was certain that the party did not intend to

allow him to be conspicuous, even while rendering valuable service to Whig principles.[18]

The Joint Library Committee met more regularly than the Agriculture Committee, and handled topics which had interested Palfrey all his life. He got a seat in this group following the death of John Quincy Adams in February. At its fortnightly meetings Palfrey sat with several men who later achieved fame as officials of the Confederacy. Senator James M. Mason, future Confederate ambassador to England, was particularly kind to Palfrey; Senator Jefferson Davis, "though not allowing himself to be offensive, was hard, with a soupçon of arrogance and superciliousness." Palfrey, the future historian, introduced a bill to appropriate $20,000 to purchase James Madison's personal papers. Luckily the House was "thin and good-humored" that day, and only Andrew Johnson put up any serious opposition. He scored the bill as a subterfuge to give Mrs. Madison a pension while the widows of many poor revolutionary soldiers received nothing. These soldiers had made a greater contribution than any philosopher. Johnson's anti-intellectualism brought forth an eloquent reply from Palfrey on the responsibility of all Americans to preserve their intellectual heritage. The bill was passed.[19]

*   *   *

While Palfrey fought to preserve the records of the past, current political issues demanded more and more attention. After the Worcester convention the main question in the minds of Free Soilers was the choice of a presidential candidate. Quick action was imperative since the New York Barnburners had nominated Martin Van Buren. Palfrey and most of the Conscience Whigs balked at the thought of supporting a hated Loco-Foco for the presidency. "From an early period . . . I had been . . . endeavouring to arrange what would have warded off [that] disaster." Thus Palfrey had made his un-

satisfactory contacts with Justice McLean in the hope of finding an acceptable Whig candidate.

Some Conscience Whigs, but not Palfrey, still regarded
Daniel Webster favorably. Webster, in the period following
the Taylor nomination, has been compared with Achilles'
sulking in his tent, since he retired to his home at Marshfield
to hide his disappointment and ponder his future course. Reports circulated that Webster's followers waited only for his
signal to declare their opposition to the Whig ticket; the signal
never came. Conscience overtures received some consideration,
but Webster concluded as a matter of strategy: "What could
it all come to?—I could not consent . . . with so little show of
strength as they now put forth." The Marshfield sulking continued although Webster had already decided upon acquiescence, and acquiescence it finally was.[20]

Horace Mann was another source of disappointment to the
Conscience Whigs. Palfrey and his antislavery friends in
Washington had welcomed Mann enthusiastically, but the
newcomer's conduct was too circumspect to please them. From
Boston Sumner sent a stream of insistent letters calling for
Mann to speak out at once on slavery. Mann knew the Taylor
nomination would "play great mischief" with Massachusetts
Whig politics, but he was not sure that the immediate results
made bolting worthwhile. He protested that as secretary of the
Massachusetts Board of Education: "I cannot say five words
in defense of the course I should take without . . . compelling
myself to bear . . . whereever I may go on educational errands,
a political badge." Sumner's reply went straight to the point:
if Mann could not act as a representative he ought to resign
his seat.[21]

The harried Mann went to see Palfrey, who after several
conversations put his ideas on paper. Palfrey recommended
a resignation, but from the Board of Education, not from
Congress. There was no obligation to engage in the presidential campaign, yet the demands of the two posts held by Mann

could not be reconciled. Mann should prepare a final educational report and then step down. Although Mann did not follow Palfrey's advice, and decided not to go to Buffalo, Palfrey still trusted him. He knew where Mann stood, but the latter's silence was difficult to accept; it would take the crisis of 1850 and the Fugitive Slave Law to make a Free Soiler of Horace Mann.[22]

Unlike the Barnburners, the Conscience Whigs had no man of presidential caliber. Furthermore the New Yorkers were formerly members of the well-knit Albany Regency. Although they declined to make any nomination at Worcester the realization grew that ultimately Van Buren would become their nominee because of the vacillation or weakness of his principal rivals. Palfrey viewed the prospect with alarm: "I can think of no expedient for checking the growth of slavery which would be so difficult as that of supporting Mr. Van Buren." But Adams stifled his reluctance, and prepared to accept the Red Fox. Sumner brushed aside objections; he was content to take Van Buren as the only means of "breaking the slave-power," and suggested that McLean be run for vice-president.[23]

Opposition to Van Buren mounted. In mid-July Adams asked him to issue a less equivocal statement on slavery than his letter to the Utica convention. Van Buren's reply, "the most enigmatic thing conceivable," offered nothing new. He stood squarely behind his Utica pronouncement, which could hardly be called a commitment to anything. Meanwhile Palfrey found it impossible to overcome his repugnance toward a man who he felt had done so much to corrupt American politics. He advised that firmness was the only safe policy in dealing with the Barnburners. Let the New Yorkers name a less objectionable man from their own ranks. Should they refuse, Palfrey would proceed with the Buffalo convention without them. Far better to preserve the hard core of true antislavery strength than to sacrifice matters of principle.[24]

The Conscience delegates and observers prepared for the journey to Buffalo in a state of anxiety and uncertainty. Palfrey's friend Richard Henry Dana best expressed the anxiety:

We do not ask that either the President or the Vice President should come from New England. We do not ask that the President should be a Whig. All we ask is that we be not required to vote for a man identified with everything we have opposed through life; whose name we have rebelled against.

The uncertainty led to a great deal of unwarranted optimism. Palfrey had long since abandoned McLean, but not others. The coy Ohioan kept his silence while, one after another, the antislavery Whigs paid court. Giddings was deferential; Stephen C. Phillips appealed to high principles; Sumner dangled the bait of the White House in 1852, if the judge settled for second place on the ticket.[25] McLean made no reply. Nothing could be done with such a "candidate." On the eve of the convention even such militant abolitionists as Whittier and Gamaliel Bailey were willing to accept Van Buren if he merely promised to support the abolition of slavery in the District of Columbia.[26]

The convention soon turned fears about Van Buren into realities. Palfrey believed that Salmon P. Chase of Ohio, a former Democrat and Liberty man, played the most important role in obtaining Van Buren's nomination, and that he did so to block the rise of his fellow Ohioan, McLean. This suspicious analysis overlooks both Van Buren's strength as the sole Barnburner candidate and McLean's personal and political weakness. To ease the Whig pain of supporting Van Buren, the convention nominated Charles Francis Adams for the vice-presidency. The unenthusiastic Adams accepted, but considered the venture valuable to him only "as it places me somewhat near the level of my father" and for the hopes it held out for the future. The Free Soil newspaper in Boston, which changed its name prophetically from the *Whig* to the *Republican,* showed its discomfiture by protesting too much that the Van Buren-Adams ticket was a "very strong one in every respect." [27]

Recently a historian referred to the Massachusetts men of this period as "Sumner's Conscience Whigs." This view, fostered by Sumner's subsequent fame, is incorrect. The early Conscience Whig movement was a group movement, and the work of Palfrey, Allen, Wilson, Phillips, Hoar, Dana, and others, while not so well known as the efforts of Sumner and Adams, was equally important. The Sumner of 1848 was not yet even *primus inter pares*. Dana's appointment as a Buffalo delegate instead of Sumner, who was not considered a "true Whig," made this clear. Years later Palfrey wrote Sumner's biographer: "It may be difficult now to understand but so it was, that Sumner, brilliant as his powers were already . . . was then a young man among the co-labourers." [28]

*   *   *

As the Congressional session stretched out through the summer, Palfrey felt tempted to visit Massachusetts and perhaps go on to Buffalo for the Free Soil convention. But the introduction of a territorial compromise bill by Whig Senator John M. Clayton of Delaware put an end to such thoughts. "The events of the last two or three days, the prospect of a miscalled *Compromise* . . . has given a new aspect to affairs, and the next fortnight will probably be a very critical period," warned Palfrey. The Clayton bill would organize Oregon as free territory, leaving the question of slavery in California and New Mexico to be settled ultimately by the Supreme Court, or, as its author phrased it, "by the silent operation of the Constitution itself." To an already heavily charged political atmosphere, the bill brought additional cause for agitation.

Since March, Palfrey had intended to speak on the territorial question. When the issue reached the House floor late in July, he was unprepared; yet he vowed to take the floor even if it meant a poor speech. He had relaxed a bit, if only for a moment: "I take all as coolly as a cucumber. Never was my equanimity more free from disturbance. . . . I am not responsible for the course [the world] takes." The Clayton Compromise squeezed through the Senate, but the House rejected it, tabling the measure without debate. "An hour sufficed to kill and bury it," Palfrey gloated.[29]

The failure of the compromise did not close the door on territorial legislation, however. Strong sentiment persisted in both houses in favor of organizing Oregon, and northerners in the House wanted to push ahead with the Proviso. Palfrey feared that a Senate compromise amendment would succeed through "executive corruption." This time he had a speech ready. But he could have saved his efforts; the only speaking he did in the last days of the session came during the time allowed for amendments to the Oregon bill, when members had to limit themselves to five minutes.[30] Palfrey twice tried to attach amendments. The first would have eliminated the words "free white" from the qualifications for voting and office-holding. He saw no reason to restrict suffrage to one color or make it dependent on complexion; Oregon did not require a better constituency than Massachusetts. Once again Andrew Johnson rose in opposition, and after the tabling of Palfrey's motion, a substitute motion struck out the word "free," since the bill as written created the impression that white men might be slaves. Palfrey was equally unsuccessful in moving that the fugitive slave law of 1793 ("the most abominable upon the statute book") be suspended in the Oregon territory, contending that in a frontier region, mistaken identity and hurried justice made the danger of the law's misapplication acute. The House disagreed.[31]

Passage of the Oregon bill in mid-August meant that Congress could go home. When it got through the House, with the Proviso included, Palfrey and his friends rejoiced. Despite early misgivings, the margin of victory proved a comfortable one: "The truth is, the Pro-Slavery men are beginning to take warning." Congress adjourned on August 14, and Palfrey started home the next day. At Springfield he met Dana, who had many stories to tell of Buffalo. When they exhausted their store of anecdotes, the men turned to the coming campaign in Massachusetts and the chances of defeating Old Zack.[32]

* * *

After a week of rest at home Palfrey returned to the political struggle. He accepted the chore of writing the address and resolutions to be presented at the Free Soil state convention early in September. Next day several acquaintances passed him in the street without a word or at most with a cold greeting. These snubs caused Palfrey great pain. Politics had left its mark on him. His face had aged noticeably, and there was an unaccustomed hardness in his look, as if he were striving to maintain his resoluteness at the expense of natural inclinations.[33]

Palfrey made two contributions to the first Massachusetts Free Soil convention. He prepared the address and resolutions which Sumner read for him, and also sent a copy of a letter received from John Quincy Adams in 1846 which declared: "Let us not be ashamed of the name of *Conscience* Whigs, but inscribe it on our banners.... Will they answer *Conscience* with a sneer?" This use of the term "Conscience Whigs" reflects the lack of unity among the segments of the Free Soil coalition. The pre-convention jockeying was full of factional considerations, with distrust greatest between the former Whigs and Democrats. Trouble arose over the gubernatorial nomination because of a dearth of candidates. Palfrey had already sounded out Governor Briggs to determine whether he was a possible bolter and Free Soil candidate, but the governor preferred to remain in the Whig party, saying he could not swallow Martin Van Buren.[34] The Conscience men were in control, yet none of them would step forward. After Samuel Hoar and Charles Allen declined to run, the convention turned to Stephen C. Phillips. John Mills, a Democrat from Western Massachusetts, balanced the ticket as the candidate for lieutenant-governor. The enthusiasm of Worcester and Buffalo had not entirely worn off; the Conscience men left the Boston meeting with visions of a statewide sweep for Free Soil in November. Adams anticipated the greatest political revolution since 1776.[35]

Palfrey was still the elected representative of the Fourth District Whigs, but soon after the Free Soil convention the Whigs read him out of the party. He refused to attend the Whig state convention, and although he declined in mild terms, his letter left no doubt about where he stood. A week before the district convention a Concord Whig, desiring to act "understandingly" at the meeting, asked him if he intended to vote for Van Buren and support the Free Soil ticket. In replying Palfrey avoided any mention of Van Buren, but as everyone knew his position on free soil, there was no need for explicit answers. To dispel any misinterpretations of his explanation, Palfrey appeared at a Free Soil rally in Cambridge soon after. The *Republican* that day called on Bostonians to march across the Charles in procession to hear "the great Free Soil champion of Middlesex." [36]

Despite his Free Soil activities, Palfrey felt that the Whigs might nominate him, thus insuring his re-election. The Conscience men considered the "Taylor party" the incarnation of political corruption and jobbery, and that if expediency dictated the selection of a Free Soiler they would do so with no regard to principles. Hoar pointed out that Palfrey's speeches were ill-advised in view of the impending district convention and counseled silence for a few days. When the Whigs met at Concord on October 3 they expected a stiff fight for the nomination. The regular party machinery worked smoothly, however, as Palfrey's Congressional predecessor, Benjamin Thompson, won easily. Before the balloting the chairman read Palfrey's letter pointing out that he was the author of the Free Soil Address and Resolutions; Palfrey received only 7 of 88 votes. William S. Robinson, new editor of the *Republican,* wrote bitterly that the Taylorites had finally aired their barely concealed grudge against a man who "trifled with property" by freeing slaves:

A man who could not be trusted to take care of his own property certainly would not look after their ships and factories with sufficient care. . . . A small knot of Taylor conspirators hate Mr. Palfrey. . . . The daily beauty of his life makes them ugly. He was elected despite their lukewarmness, and will be re-elected in spite of their open opposition.

Two days after the Whig convention, the Middlesex Free Soilers met at Concord to nominate Palfrey.[37]

Although Palfrey was himself a candidate, he reversed his stand of two years before, and campaigned vigorously for the Free Soil party. This time he saw no impropriety. He was no longer a state office holder and the many speeches he made concerned the presidential campaign, not his own candidacy. In the month before the presidential vote of November 7 Palfrey made nearly two dozen appearances in Middlesex and other counties, many of them with John P. Hale of New Hampshire. The two men made a good team since the caution of one complemented the enthusiasm of the other. Palfrey's political sermons were well received by the Middlesex Free Soilers; one reported after a meeting in Ashland: "The more John G. Palfrey is known, the better the people like him." But he had the greatest difficulty in justifying support for Van Buren. His own reluctance to vote for the ex-president could not be completely hidden by appeals to principles instead of men. Despite the force and frequency of Free Soil arguments, many Whigs refused to vote for their arch-enemy of so many years. S. C. Phillips exaggerated when he claimed that 25,000 potential Free Soil votes were thus lost, but the number was considerable.[38]

The election campaign was the most exciting Massachusetts

had seen since the Log Cabin campaign of 1840. The Whigs greatly feared the strength of Free Soilism and took no chances on losing the state through absent-mindedness. The many Whig rallies and torchlight processions heard addresses from the party stalwarts of the Bay State "promoting the great cause of conservatism," and from visitors, including a young Whig from Illinois named Abraham Lincoln.[39] Their efforts were effective; while the Free Soil party ran ahead of the Democrats, General Taylor carried Massachusetts.

A week later the state election revealed a similar pattern. Governor Briggs easily defeated S. C. Phillips, and most state offices and Congressional seats went to the Whigs as well. In Middlesex Palfrey had shown more strength than anticipated by his opponents. He led the field, 41 votes ahead of Thompson, but his 38 percent of the total vote fell far short of the required majority. Rockwood Hoar rushed to assure him that all would be well, or at least that "no man can be elected in the District while you live and will consent to run."[40]

The reassurances of friends did not keep Palfrey from becoming downcast. Senator John Davis apparently read his thoughts when, misinterpreting the first election returns, he reported with as much sympathy as glee:

Poor Palfrey is left out of sight—this is too good—How the poor man was deluded—He thought last summer . . . that there would not be a grease spot left of Whiggism and he would walk all over the course by acclamation, but now is the winter of discontent and no glorious summer in prospect.[41]

XII ~

Trial by Stalemate

There are, who triumph in a losing cause,
  Who can put on defeat, as 'twere a wreath
  Unwithering in the adverse popular breath,
Safe from the blasting demagogues' applause;
'Tis they who stand for Freedom and God's laws;
And so stands Palfrey now. . . .
            —JAMES RUSSELL LOWELL[1]

PALFREY had run far ahead of the Free Soil presidential ticket in Middlesex. This, and his small plurality, steeled his supporters for what they thought would be the victorious second effort. Rockwood Hoar appealed to Palfrey voters to take advantage of Democratic confusion and the expected drop in Whig enthusiasm by appearing at the polls *en masse*, from every Middlesex village and farm. Old Whig editorials praising Palfrey's rectitude and spirit of philanthropy appeared in the Free Soil press.[2]

Governor Briggs, who had often raised Conscience hopes that he might leave the Whig fold, did the Free Soilers a good turn by scheduling the elections for New Year's Day, 1849. Whigs were critical of Briggs' sense of timing; a spring election, with Taylor safely inaugurated and Whig Congressmen home repairing their own political fences, would have benefited the party. In addition to Palfrey's, two other seats in Congress were yet to be filled; elections in Essex and Worcester counties had been indecisive. In Worcester, Free Soilers were sure that Charles Allen would defeat the Whig candidate, Charles Hudson.[3]

The best Palfrey could hope for from the Whigs on election

day was indifference; but what of the Democrats, who had run third in the November elections? Already there were signs that Free Soilism and Democracy in the Bay State might move closer together for the purpose of ending the Whig reign. Sumner spoke of a "new alliance of principle" which would inevitably emerge. "Here in Massachusetts," he added, "the Old Democratic party is not merely defeated—but . . . irretrievably broken. . . . It must seek safety upon our Buffalo platform." Democratic chieftains sensed the possibilities of fusion, though they differed on its advisability.[4]

Would Palfrey be willing to make overtures for Democratic votes? A Cambridge Democrat put the question to him in mid-December, assuring him that he was not demanding Palfrey's adherence to the national Democracy. But, he argued, a Free Soil party that was no more than an antislavery version of ultra Whiggery had no future. Would Palfrey fight to emancipate the "slaves" of the "monied aristocracy" of the North as well as the slaves of the South? Palfrey's answer was straightforward but politically unwise. Although he agreed that an aristocracy of wealth existed and had controlled elections, he would make no pledges to fight against it except on the slavery issue; he would let his judgment guide his actions. As for democratic utilitarianism:

> You avow your aim to be "the greatest good of the greatest number." I accede cordially to . . . the spirit of your remark. But I would alter its terms. The greatest number is only the majority. I presume your aim includes the good of the minority also. We both aim at "the greatest good of the *whole*."

Palfrey's letter was no clarion call for fusion. When Adams read it he chided his friend patiently: "I know the embarrassment of your position, but surely the crisis in which we are all equally placed may justify half a dozen warm paragraphs which freemen owe to themselves . . . without subjecting you to the suspicion of courting votes." Adams knew that Palfrey could not win without the votes of "Conscience Democrats";

Palfrey knew it too, but he considered no political office worth the contamination of working with "Loco Foco dough-face leaders." When approached by Free Soilers who urged coalition, Palfrey threatened to withdraw. Nevertheless Whig newspapers alleged that such an arrangement existed.[5]

By this time Palfrey was simultaneously hoping for victory and anticipating the pleasures of honorable defeat. From Washington, where he had gone for the second session of the Thirtieth Congress, he kept a close watch on the Middlesex campaign, asking his son to send him clippings from the Whig press. As the year ended, Palfrey was happy that the "noise" he had made in 1848 had not interfered with keeping a good conscience. In a letter sent to arrive at Hazelwood on election day, he unburdened himself to Mary Ann, telling her not to expect victory. The future held little but a wearying series of inconclusive trials:

> I do not think the result to ourselves is of much importance, any way. Of course, a choice would be for the moment gratifying because it would be the more obvious expression of public confidence, and vindication of my character and of the principles I have sustained. But . . . the time is near at hand, when justice must be done me. And possibly that time might be hastened by the success of my opponents. For, should they succeed in removing me, they would permanently have to ask themselves what were the good souls' reasons for doing so; and this is a question which when the excitement of the election was over, and the time of reflection . . . comes, I fancy they would find mighty hard to answer to their own minds. . . .
>
> Should I go out, I should feel that I had done something useful and important by having been here, and that my course had been such as I would always look back upon without the slightest misgiving or regret.

Mary Ann appreciated her husband's high-mindedness, but vindication through electoral victory appealed to her more than the slower verdict of history. Nor had her practicality deserted her. "Let [the opposition] see that to be free soil is compatible with being a very agreeable, sensible person, and break down their prejudices. Much may be done in good natural talk." [6]

Meanwhile there had been much talk in Middlesex, though none of it calculated to soothe injured feelings. According to Free Soil speakers and editors, the fate of the Commonwealth hung on the outcome of the Congressional elections. On January 1, the South would learn why the antislavery professions of such men as Thompson and Hudson were not enough; it would "know why these men are defeated, and why John G. Palfrey is sustained." [7] Such was the promise; it came within 43 votes of fulfillment.

The second trial of January 1849 was the closest Palfrey was to come to re-election. As he approached the Capitol an Illinois Congressman stopped to congratulate him. News of a victory had just come from the *Globe* telegraph office. Palfrey had asked Adams to wire the result, but early telegraphic reports were so unreliable Palfrey decided to wait before telling his friends. His caution proved wise; final returns showed that although his vote far exceeded his opponents' he was still a few votes short of the elusive majority. Yet with 49.5 percent of the vote, Palfrey had clearly become the leader. [8]

Friends quickly stressed the positive side of his near-victory, and predicted an easy triumph in the next trial. As expected, Worcester had gone for Charles Allen and Free Soil. Many old Conscience men were sorry to see the fall of Charles Hudson, one of the fourteen who voted against war with Mexico, but not Palfrey. With Allen in the coming Congress his own presence was not so necessary. Massachusetts had done well, but it must not stop there: "The Southerners and dough-faces feel in their bones that 'the Campbells are coming.' The heavier & heavier tread beats awfully upon their ear-drums. . . . We shall not need to live much longer, to see better times." [9]

In the short second Congressional session, Palfrey and his colleagues accomplished little. Nevertheless, what he did satisfied him. In the selection of seats in the House Palfrey considered himself particularly fortunate. Representative Samuel

F. Vinton of Ohio, who had taken the desk last used by John Quincy Adams, wanted a change, and Palfrey eagerly accepted the venerated spot.[10]

Palfrey's principal efforts during this session concerned the question of slavery in the District of Columbia. On December 12 he moved for permission to introduce a bill abolishing slavery and the slave trade in the District. Because of a Senate debate between Calhoun and Benton, there were many absentees, and the motion went down 62 to 89. Yet Palfrey was not downhearted. He thought the move was important, and the *Republican* hailed him for standing in the "first ranks of freedom." He kept up his campaign by introducing a bill calling for the protection of trial by jury to all Negroes alleged to be runaways. To his delight, a motion to consider a District slave-trade abolition bill won out on its first reading on the 20th. Northerners friendly to the South were in a quandary. A vote favoring the slave trade was bad politics; therefore, many of them failed to answer the roll call. "It is the strongest blow ever dealt against Slavery in this House," claimed Palfrey. "The Southerners are more excited than they have been before this session. Well they might be uneasy." [11]

Southern anxieties were reflected in northern concern as well. Speaker Winthrop, apprehensive over the agitation of the slavery issue, had Giddings and Palfrey in mind when he scored those "men here bent on dissolving the Union." They stood at one pole of the magnet, while Calhoun stood at the other. In Massachusetts the Cotton press railed against the mischief of Palfrey and the other Congressional Free Soilers. The Lowell *Courier*'s praise of two years before had evaporated:

Mr. Palfrey has broken all his moral force . . . and isolated himself by his ultraism. . . . His movements, in company with those of Mr. Giddings, have shelved him in Congress, so far as any useful service can avail. . . . [The slavery question is too important to have any] such extreme, fanatical, dreamy man representing your interests.

The Free Soil victory was short-lived. What Palfrey termed

the "whole Taylor and Slavery machinery" went into operation to block the bill. Wavering members felt the pressure of
party whips. While legislation on slavery in the District would
have to wait until the omnibus compromise of 1850 the Whigs'
"wriggling efforts" denoted weakness.[12]

In addition to the capital's slave trade, Palfrey kept a sharp
eye out for other motions pertaining to slavery. There was the
affair of Lewis, a slave of one Pacheco, who had been hired
by the United States Army and taken to the Indian Territory.
When Lewis decided to remain there, Pacheco sued the government for the slave's value. Giddings led the opposition to
payment, and Palfrey seconded his efforts with individual
persuasion (he convinced an Ohio representative to change
his vote) and a speech of his own. He denied the southern
contention that slaves were legally property, since the Constitution always referred to them as persons. Nor did taxing
slaves make them property, since incoming aliens were taxed
by several states. He also warned the South that insistence on
this argument might bring Congressional regulation of slaves
as subjects of commerce. Although Mann thought the speech
was "not a very exciting affair," southern members were sufficiently roused to heckle Palfrey frequently.[13]

Satisfying his conscience meant that Palfrey continued to
propose unpopular reforms in Congress. He tried to change
the House rules giving committee chairmen almost dictatorial
powers over which bills reached the floor, and in the Library
Committee he suggested the Library of Congress purchase
Bailey's *National Era*. The first proposal died of instant
neglect; Jefferson Davis would have none of the second. Palfrey came close to leaving his mark on the history of the
cabinet. He was one of many persons who thought the newly
created Department of Interior should be called the Home
Department:

I told them they ought to be content with the English language ... ;
that they had got a schoolboy translation from the French, so literal

as to mean nothing. . . . I asked them . . . how Mr. Buchanan [the Secretary of State] . . . would like to be [be] called, the Secretary of the *Exterior*.

The House agreed at first, but the "schoolboys" later changed their minds. Palfrey reached the height of impracticality when he asked his colleagues to abolish the Congressional franking privilege as part of a comprehensive reform of the postal system, but he had better luck in the matter of the census of 1850. Just as the session closed, he reported a substitute census bill. The census of 1840 had been a failure, and Palfrey blamed the previous bill for much of the resulting incompetence and fraud. He convinced Congress that the authority for drawing up census-taking procedure properly rested with the executive. The result of his persuasiveness was that the census of 1850 was more inclusive and valuable than its predecessors; here Palfrey demonstrated the value of having a scholar in politics.[14]

After the rancor occasioned by incidents involving slavery in the District of Columbia had been partially diminished by time, Free Soilers lay back awaiting the next move of the "Slave Power." The challenge was sure to come on the territorial question—the question which since the Mexican War had become too important to ignore and too tangled to settle. David Wilmot came to Palfrey's rooms one evening early in February for an antislavery conference. He declared that there would be no betrayal from Democratic Free Soilers. Palfrey accepted Wilmot's promises warily: "If we had not lessons from the past teaching not to trust appearances, I should predict nothing will be done. But no one can tell." [15]

As in the case of the ill-fated Clayton Compromise of seven months before, the last days of the session saw frantic efforts to push a territorial bill through. These included Senator Isaac P. Walker's amendment to an appropriation bill which would have allowed slavery in the territories. Palfrey had already sketched a speech and joined the debate, speaking for an hour on February 26. Although his audience was "not sufficiently large to get up enough of the flow of extemporaneous harangue," the speech pleased those who shared Palfrey's point of view. Mann noted that remarks of certain southern politicians required the reply of a "scholar and a Christian," and Palfrey had answered beautifully. Sumner, with customary hyperbole, predicted that "even those distant Virginians and Carolinians, who wrap themselves so pleasantly in the garments of self-complacency" would be moved by the effort. As the sessions in both houses grew longer daily, Palfrey and his friends increased their vigilance. There was little spare time, even for essentials, he reported: "I said my prayers as fast as a Catholic does over his beads." The last day of the Thirtieth Congress extended through to seven o'clock of inauguration day. The Walker amendment went down: "Last night was like what is said in Exodus of the Passover, 'a night to be remembered throughout all our generations.' Almost beyond our most sanguine hopes, we defeated the slave-holding Senate." It was a perfect climax to what Palfrey suspected would be his final day in the House.[16]

Before leaving for home, Palfrey called on President-elect Taylor, the man whose rise to the presidency he and his friends had fought so strenuously. The general, the supposed tool of the Slave Power, engaged in a few minutes of inconsequential talk, and Palfrey came away impressed with Taylor's "intelligent and amiable" looks. In the Compromise crisis, Taylor would show that more than his looks merited the approbation of Free Soilers.[17]

During two sessions in the House, Palfrey had brought a remarkable amount of attention to himself, not only in Massachusetts but throughout the country. Even those who opposed him and lumped him in with the most fanatical abolitionists still respected the man's undeniable honesty. Much of his House activity was negative in character, because of the position of weakness from which the first Free Soilers were forced to operate. Giddings' estimate of Palfrey's political ignorance was a valid one, but Palfrey was a student, and he might be willing to learn. What he needed was victory in the Fourth District.

The day after the inauguration, while Palfrey was still traveling, five thousand Middlesex men appeared at the polls. "To elect you on the fifth of March will be a partial offset to the Inauguration of Old Zack," a supporter assured Palfrey. The Whigs, smarting over Hudson's defeat in Worcester, turned furiously on the Free Soilers of the Fourth District. With such "marvelous acrimony" neither Palfrey nor his managers were confident of victory, and the result showed no change, except that Palfrey's vote was down slightly, to 47.8 percent. "The election goes against me," wrote Palfrey wearily, "but what care I for that?" [18]

And so it went until the state elections of November 1849. Two more trials produced only minor decreases in Palfrey's percentage of the vote. Free Soilers tried everything to reverse the trend. Hoar questioned the legality of certain electoral procedures, and outside speakers, including New Hampshire's Senator Hale, came to help. But the basic factor in prolonging the stalemate became the inability to sustain voters' enthusiasm. Hoar's printed circulars predicting victory were by now tiresome. Sumner spoke of a "deceptive confidence" which had lulled many voters into forgetfulness, and Adams strained to draw something positive out of the situation:

> The Boston influence applied upon Charlestown and Cambridge defeated us—but there is good to be derived out of evil. The mode in which Mr. Palfrey is opposed ought to convince all reasonable men elsewhere of the hollowness of the Whig professions. Every failure to elect in the fourth District should be the means of gaining converts to our system, in every other District in the Free States.[19]

Palfrey had earlier suggested retirement, but this had been more an appeal for support than a threat. The agony of repeatedly indecisive elections would soon be unbearable. Hoar, who in order to accept a judgeship was on the point of resigning as chairman of the district committee, warned harshly: "Your withdrawal would be considered a proof of cowardice, and a yielding and sinking under the attacks made upon you." But by the end of the summer, Palfrey had had enough. He told Sumner, the state chairman, that the trial of September 10 would be his last. Sumner stalled for time, asking Palfrey to seek the opinion of his close friends, and consulted Adams, who replied that Palfrey's "nervous system is fast wearing under the unaccustomed pressure of political persecution." Nor did the "sharp and cruel attacks" in the newspapers do anything to improve Palfrey's nerves.[20]

For a variety of reasons Palfrey decided to continue to run. Chief among these was the improved showing he made in the total vote in September, when over 4,500 men refused to "bow to the knee to the image of Baal." Among the many exhortations from anxious Free Soilers, came a promise from Sumner that Palfrey had nothing to fear from any attempt at coalition which might seem to impeach Palfrey's antislavery position. The state convention had settled that matter; the party stood pledged to its original platform. In addition, the contest had become more than a county matter. Estes Howe, Hoar's successor as district chairman, pointed to the widespread national interest, and antislavery men from other states expressed their concern.[21]

The men who urged Palfrey on could not have known how troubled was his state of mind. His oversensitivity was again in command. Since the Whigs were "more truculent than ever, and feelings were very sore in all the circles" he thought it best to stop attending meetings of the Tuesday Evening Club. A painful snub came from the Unitarians. Palfrey received a ticket to the annual Unitarian Festival one day before the event although "every little pooch in office" had long since got one. This was particularly hard to bear since many of the new crop of Unitarian ministers had been

Palfrey's students at Harvard. He made a note of the insult, and added the fact that despite his twice having given sermons for Boston's Ancient and Honorable Artillery Company, their guest list for 1849 excluded him. And after thirty-one years, Nathan Hale canceled Palfrey's free subscription to the *Daily Advertiser*. Considering what the paper was printing about the Middlesex campaign, this was no loss.

Under the circumstances the best course for Palfrey would have been a program of concentrated work. But although he did work on his Old Testament lectures, masochistic brooding took up too many hours:

> Another wasted and sad day yesterday—nervous, brooding, helpless. . . . Where to turn, what to do, what system to follow, I know not. The constant calumny and hatred I am exposed to, particularly the estrangement of all my old friends, wears upon me now very much. And the greatest financial perplexity in which I am involved, almost distracts me.
>
> Good Lord, my mind is very much depressed, disordered, bewildered. It is, I presume, partial insanity, but I retain my self-control. Yet I feel no power within to woo back peace. May it please thee, blessed Parent, to compose and revive me!

Palfrey was a pathetic figure then. Although he could still call for continued struggle against slavery, "the great sin of the present day," and buoy up Sumner's spirits during the Roberts Case, the legal battle against racial segregation in Boston schools, he was close to a complete loss of faith in himself. He did little but sit, wait for election returns, and "beweep my outcast state." [22] Palfrey's problems were nearly compounded by the appearance of a more formidable potential rival for the seat in Congress, Edward Everett. The events of 1849 did nothing to change Palfrey's long-standing dislike of Everett. Early in the year, Everett acknowledged the failure of his Harvard administration by resigning; Sparks became the new president. In March Palfrey heard rumors that Everett, the "eloquent iceberg," would run against him, but Everett had concluded that he could not break Palfrey's plurality. Besides, Everett had his sights set on something higher than a seat in the House. Winthrop's plea that the Middlesex seat might determine the speakership in December left him unmoved.[23] Had Everett decided to enter the contest, Palfrey was ready to "follow the Western fashion" by challenging him to a series of public debates. The need never arose, and Palfrey recalled immodestly:

> The novelty of the proceeding, and his celebrity, would be sure to attract large audiences, and what with his daintiness and cowardice, and my own experience and knowledge in this department and reliance on the force of truth, I was quite confident of being able to defeat him. I think he may have heard of my purpose, and was not inclined to take the risk.

Everett later conceived a plan to aid Winthrop. On October 15, he called on Palfrey, and for several hours tried to convince his neighbor that if he announced he would vote for Winthrop as speaker, Everett would influence Whig voters in Palfrey's favor. The arrangement seemed "perfectly fair and honorable to Everett" since Palfrey was a good Whig in all but antislavery matters. Palfrey heard his guest out, then rejected the offer, "but he was not to be easily put off, and stayed and argued the question at tedious length, till I told him that we were made too much unlike for him to be able to understand me." Palfrey correctly reasoned that Everett's real intention was to break the power of the Massachusetts Free Soilers by luring Palfrey back into the Whig fold.[24]

The state elections of 1849 brought out an increased regular party vote, and Palfrey lost the lead for the first time, polling only 36 percent of the total. A new factor in the contest emerged, a Free Soil–Democratic coalition which appeared in several counties, including Middlesex. Palfrey's antislavery friends in Washington had already suggested that the possibilities of amalgamation should be weighed.[25] Palfrey was, as usual, cool to any such idea. Giddings urged that no honorable means be spared in Palfrey's behalf ("I shall be perfectly astonished if the Democrats continue their opposition to him"), but the Middlesex Democrats more than doubled the vote for their candidate. The result flattened Palfrey: "I am at my wits end," he confessed dazedly.[26]

Two weeks after his sixth trial, Francis Bowen appealed to Palfrey to step down, citing the necessity of keeping California free from slavery: "Sacrifice yourself. . . . Your public life really began with a noble personal sacrifice—the emancipation . . . let it end, at least for the present, by a similar act of self-renunciation." He also mentioned his belief that Palfrey's supposedly estranged friends remained friendly and were surprised by Palfrey's aloofness. In replying, Palfrey showed his confused state of mind. Despite his wishes of a few months before, he would not withdraw; a streak of stubbornness now appeared, a desire for melodramatic vindication or destruction. As for former friends, Palfrey rambled on irrelevantly about a certain door being closed on him, and ended, self-pityingly, with the lament that he had few close friends even among Free Soilers.[27]

The Thirty-First Congress opened in December 1849 with no representative from Massachusetts' Fourth District. The Free Soilers regarded the empty seat as Palfrey's, and reported events to him in the expectation that he would join them shortly. The struggle over the speakership was long and bitter. Once again Free Soilers opposed Winthrop's candidacy, and the result was the election, by a plurality vote, of a southern Democrat, Howell Cobb. Free Soilers were upset over several defections. Horace Mann and Amos Tuck went for Winthrop. Mann's action was not surprising, but Tuck's was. To elect a Whig with Free Soil votes, Tuck explained to Palfrey, would have meant influence over the Whig party, and would have insured Palfrey's election. Palfrey refused to be convinced; better to withhold Free Soil votes as a protest against the plurality fraud than to put Winthrop, the tool of the Boston doughfaces, back in the chair. Palfrey was glad that the speakership crisis had occurred. The structure of American political parties must be shattered. Reformation along the only logical lines—proslavery and antislavery—was inevitable. Controversy tended to "reconstruct parties upon their proper basis and bring names to represent things, instead of representing moonshine." [28]

Palfrey determined that he would not allow the electoral trials of 1850 to affect him. While Adams wrote another desperate appeal to Fourth District voters, and Sumner chanted "it is *money, money, money*, that keeps Palfrey from being elected," the candidate cultivated an air of indifference. The day after Trial Number Seven, Palfrey made no particular effort to obtain the returns: "I think I am a model of incuriosity." [29]

Attention focused on Washington, where the outlines of the Compromise of 1850 began to emerge. Free Soilers were unsure of what was to come, but never doubted that treachery was in the air. They hoped to use Washington events, such as Winthrop's dodge of a vote on the Proviso, to influence Middlesex electors. At a Free Soil convention in Faneuil Hall, speakers compared Winthrop with Palfrey, to the obvious disadvantage of the former. But the event of that year which shook Massachusetts politics more than any other was Webster's Seventh of March speech favoring compromise with the South. Palfrey had one word for it, "horrid," and many men from all parts of the political spectrum agreed. Even ardent Cotton Whig Joseph N. Brewer was stunned, and Schouler's *Atlas* came "down on the Godlike [Daniel] like a thousand bricks," although Whigs warned the editor that further criticism might elect Palfrey. [30]

The Whig split caused by Webster's speech had immediate results in the Fourth District. Palfrey was aware that some Free Soilers were now thinking of an arrangement with anti-Webster Whigs which would bypass Palfrey. He was ready to resign to forestall any such disgrace, but Adams persuaded him to delay his move, promising to investigate. At a meeting called ostensibly to discuss a new Free Soil daily the talk was all about Palfrey. Two Whig leaders were coming to bargain, and Adams noted sadly that Samuel G. Howe and Sumner were among the footdraggers. There was no deal with the Whigs, however; Free Soilers would not yet abandon Palfrey, and all knew that the candidate himself would reject any bargain. Meanwhile, Henry Wilson kept in touch with the Democrats, who were willing to aid Palfrey if the Free Soilers promised that Palfrey would serve only one more term in the House. Adams replied haughtily: "We had higher purposes in view." When the Democratic district convention made no nomination Free Soilers were sure this meant victory. But many Hunker Democrats reportedly voted for Thompson. Palfrey had once again come close (47.6 percent), but as Adams and the others knew, his last chance was gone.[31]

Jared Sparks, Everett's successor as Harvard president, rudely upset Palfrey's determination to keep cool about politics. The year before, Palfrey had greeted Sparks's elevation jubilantly. Although Sparks occasionally expressed concern over Palfrey's political trials, he did nothing in the way of helping to overcome them. In March 1850 Everett once again moved against Palfrey, this time using the pliable Sparks as his agent. Sparks called on Palfrey to say he was convinced that he was injuring the college by continuing to vote for a Free Soiler. Many conservatives felt that there was too much antislavery on the banks of the Charles for Harvard's good. Palfrey replied that Sparks must work for the benefit of the school, according to his own judgment. For several weeks afterward he brooded about the one-sided nature of his relationship with Sparks: "It is only the dispelling of a dream. . . . I see that the friendship has always been on my side. . . . I have had from him no attempt to aid, no syllable of encouragement."[32]

Despite the earlier failure to achieve an arrangement with

another party, Free Soilers talked of nothing but the possibility of coalition. Adams took the lead in opposing such action since the proposed union would most likely be with the Democrats. He, Palfrey, S. C. Phillips, and Dana became the core of anticoalitionist sentiment. Adams and Dana were able to check the rush to coalition momentarily at a meeting in September during which Henry Wilson attacked Palfrey and Adams, but the issue would not die. In mid-October Wilson made his first and last call at Hazelwood. He showed his ignorance of Palfrey's character by dangling the lure of the presidency of the state Senate before Palfrey if he left the Congressional race to run for the Senate on a Free Soil–Democratic coalition ticket. Palfrey refused, and from then on he had his political *bête noire*—Wilson, the unprincipled schemer. Nevertheless, the Middlesex convention narrowly approved a joint ticket for the legislature: the anticoalitionists spoke of "disgrace and defeat." Sumner, who had promised Palfrey that no compromise would be made, now defended amalgamation in terms of the balance of power. His arguments that antislavery men could most effectively wield power in Washington, not in the state government, were wasted on irerconcilables such as Palfrey to whom coalition, compromise, and corruption were synonymous. Nevertheless, there was logic in an arrangement satisfying both parties' primary interests. The Democrats who wanted state reform should concentrate on the state offices; since any real struggle with the Slave Power would be at the capital city, the Free Soilers should concentrate on Congressional seats.[33]

Palfrey would not budge. His only attempt to influence the November election was a pamphlet called *A Letter to a Friend*, an uncompromising defense of his political career. Palfrey achieved his purpose; letters of support from antislavery men poured in. Theodore Parker expressed his admiration for a man so obviously on the side of Mankind: "If you had secretly told the slaves you inherited & put the money in your pocket or drawn notes with it in State Street, I think your reputation would have been higher with the controlling men in Boston." Winthrop, who got a copy from Palfrey, reacted differently. He wrote John H. Clifford, a Whig friend:

> I have never seen such a medley of perversion, false imputation & unjust inference in my life. . . . It takes away all the little respect I had left for this Doctor of Divinity, & makes me almost ready to believe that instead of "his Country's, his God's, & Truth's,"—his only aims are for himself, the Devil, & falsehood. Harvard College Professors, certainly are, some of them, no Saints;—as you will have occasion to remember next Friday. Perhaps, however, I had better do with Palfrey what the Sheriff is going to do with Professor Webster— "give him rope" & let the whole thing drop.

Palfrey's pamphlet did not help in Trial Number Eleven. On the contrary, his intransigence on coalition caused his vote to drop to 34.6 percent, the worst showing he had yet made.[34]

Meanwhile Free Soilers pushed ahead plans for a new newspaper. After the failure of the *Republican* under Wilson, Palfrey's name cropped up often as a possibility for the editorship. Thomas Wentworth Higginson, then an abolitionist minister at Newburyport, urged Palfrey to consider the matter seriously; Higginson and J. G. Whittier had reviewed Palfrey's qualifications and found them more than adequate. Whittier sent a message: "Tell Mr. Palfrey . . . that it is worth two seats in Congress & a dozen pulpits!" Palfrey was receptive but tried to appear coy, saying he was not cut out for "a daily trial of temper." Late in November the project began to materialize, this time under the auspices of a board of trustees headed by Samuel Gridley Howe. Palfrey would be editor-in-chief of the daily, which after much deliberation the Free Soil leaders christened the *Commonwealth*.[35]

XIII ～

Defeat

FOR a man with political ambitions, Palfrey had learned little about the practical necessities of politics. Soon after obtaining the much-needed post of *Commonwealth* editor he again demonstrated his ineptitude as a politician.

The vehicle for this demonstration was a printed but supposedly confidential letter to the Free Soil members of the newly convened legislature. The state elections of November 1850 gave the Whigs a plurality of votes but not enough to elect major state officers. Only fusion of two parties could break the impasse. Sumner and Wilson worked for coalition with the Democracy, while Palfrey and other conservative Free Soilers reacted with horrified incredulity. Their Moral Crusade was to be defiled by unreliable, last-minute converts to the antislavery cause, the Loco-focos—the party of social upstarts and political apostates.

The first points of business before the General Court of 1851 were to be elections of state officers and United States senators. Everyone already knew the general terms of the Free Soil–Democratic arrangement when Palfrey sat down to draft his letter two days before Christmas. The Democrats were to have the principal state offices and the short-term senatorship, while a Free Soiler would go to the Senate for a full six-year term. Palfrey, in seeking to stop the bargain, called on the members to act as individuals: "I know of no existing compact or understanding, to restrain the free action of either [Free Soilers or Democrats]." Stephen C. Phillips, Free Soil candidate for governor in November, should not be deserted in favor of George S. Boutwell, Democratic de-

fender of the Fugitive Slave Act. Palfrey called such an abandonment of principle too high a price to pay for a Senate seat.
Besides, the bargain depended too much on Democratic good
faith. With Boutwell safely in office the "allies" would deny
their commitment. Fearing misinterpretation, Palfrey wrote
that under no circumstances would he be a candidate for
senator, and appealed for faith in the strength of an unham-
pered Free Soil party.[1]

Before dispatching the letter, Palfrey sought the opinions
of his friends, although he was determined to go ahead with
his plan whatever their reactions. Dana and Adams approved
of the substance of the piece, but Adams sharply criticized
the wisdom of such an act. He argued that Palfrey would
accomplish nothing but political suicide. Palfrey listened carefully, as he always did to Adams' advice, but declared that he
was willing to take the chance; the personal hazard was unimportant compared to the principle involved. He mailed
the circulars.[2]

Palfrey began the new year happy over the "prospect of
useful employment, and of a better provision" for his family,
but his career as an editor did not survive forty-eight hours.
His first day at the office went well. It seemed to him that the
circular had created little rancor. But the surge of resentment
among the coalitionists soon came to the surface. His first
editorial, a characteristic piece about the usurpations of the
Slave Power, predicted inevitable triumph of God and Right:
"Liberty is never in extreme peril, so long as its friends are
true." Yet he denied all taste for personal controversy, and
asked his readers' indulgence for early mistakes, since he had
had only four days' notice. The new editor looked harassed
immediately; Adams, whose office Palfrey used to write his
pieces, was not optimistic about his friend: "He is in a false
position which will inevitably do him harm." [3]

Palfrey did not have to wait long for the inevitable harm.
On the same day of the first editorial, William Jackson, one

of the trustees, came to tell Palfrey that party solidarity required his resignation. Thus began his "disgrace with [Henry] Wilson and his set, who had arranged the famous Coalition with the Democrats, a most discreditable business." Palfrey rushed to see Howe and Bird, but they would do nothing except assure him that his retirement would last only as long as the legislature debated the distribution of offices. With coalition matters safely behind them, Free Soilers would recall Palfrey. There was nothing Palfrey or his friends could do to sway the paper's trustees.[4]

Meanwhile Boston editors played a lively guessing game over the identity of the *Commonwealth* editors. Palfrey's name had never appeared on the masthead, and the day after his dismissal *Commonwealth* subscribers read a plea to judge the paper by its merits and not the names of its editors. For those perceptive enough to see it, there was an immediate change in the *Commonwealth*'s editorials. The leading piece of January 3 began with a personal attack on Rufus Choate, and by the end of the month an editorial chastised the editors of the Whig Salem *Gazette* in terms which Palfrey would never have employed. The *Atlas* rightly claimed that Palfrey had left in disgust after two days, but it was wrong in describing the separation as voluntary.[5]

*   *   *

Another election in Middlesex took place a few weeks after Palfrey's dismissal. The now coalitionist *Commonwealth* supported him, but without enthusiasm. It told Free Soilers that Palfrey had committed a "sad mistake" in opposing coalition, but that this was an error of judgment on the part of a man of proven principles. Palfrey's attack on the coalition did not spare him the virulence of the Whig press. "Advertizer poison still working yesterday," noted the candidate sadly two days before the election. This attack caused a break in the nearly healed personal relations between Palfrey and the family of

Nathan Hale, editor of the *Advertiser* and former Brattle Street parishioner. Palfrey went to Adams for sympathy, and the latter noted: "The truth is that Palfrey's whole career has been martydom of the spirit." Nor was the end in sight; the next election could not help but bring further disappointment. On the 20th only one third of the voters went for Palfrey.[6]

While Palfrey floundered toward defeat, the course of coalition politics worked in favor of Charles Sumner. Palfrey was one of many names mentioned as a candidate for the Senate, but in the serious bargaining at the State House Charles Sumner clearly led his Free Soil competitors. The Free Soilers ignored Palfrey's circular[7] and complied with their part of the bargain in supporting Boutwell for governor, but as Palfrey had predicted, getting Democratic votes for a Free Soil senator proved difficult. A group of "Hunker" Democrats under Caleb Cushing fought Sumner's candidacy, delaying the outcome for months. Whig hopes that the legislature would adjourn without an election disappeared late in April when Sumner received the exact number of votes required. Howe had observed bitterly that Palfrey would not work for Sumner's election. Nevertheless, Palfrey suppressed his anticoalition principles long enough to write a pro-Sumner article for the *Commonwealth*.[8]

As Sumner's friends congratulated him, excitement over the enforcement of the Fugitive Slave Act reached a high point. Massachusetts had been one of the first states to pass personal liberty laws; nor was it now backward in attempting to nullify the power of the new fugitive law. Early in 1851 Boston conservatives looked around them and saw a country moving toward peace and Unionism. Samuel A. Eliot had no doubt that "there will be peace," and that politicians would follow Daniel Webster or lapse into deserved obscurity. The circumstances attending the rescue of the runaway slave "Shadrach" in February and the successful rendition of Thomas Sims two months later shattered such peaceful expectations.[9]

During these exciting events Palfrey came closer to establishing friendships with Boston's abolitionists than ever before. Wendell Phillips introduced him to Garrison and to an equally famous abolitionist, English Member of Parliament George Thompson. Palfrey joined a committee of correspondence which attacked the fugitive law, contributing to the vigilance committee fund despite the always shaky state of his finances. On April 4 his old friend John P. Bigelow, then the mayor of Boston, called out troops to forestall Sims's rescue. Palfrey shared the anguish of other antislavery men over their impotence in this case, although he was not among the group who followed the military procession which returned Sims to bondage. As Boston bubbled with meetings and denunciations of the Slave Power and its northern toadies, Palfrey attended and listened, nodding his agreement, sometimes speaking out himself. It seemed proper to him that Daniel Webster should be refused the use of Faneuil Hall, the Cradle of Liberty. If slaveholders deserved no quarter, little pity should be wasted on northern traitors.[10]

The thirteenth runoff election in Middlesex occurred during the Sims case. The affair helped Palfrey make a more respectable showing, but both leading candidates were still as far from a majority vote as ever. After each of the early trials both parties had assumed that the next contest would be the last; by the spring of 1851 such assumptions had been discarded. Only a plurality law could break the stalemate. Palfrey's district was the most spectacular of many examples of deadlocked elections, at that time and long before, and the vicissitudes of Massachusetts politics produced demands for a plurality law, first from one party, then another.[11] At length the legislature agreed, in passing such a law, that Trial Number Fourteen in Middlesex would be the last.

Following the publication of the anticoalition circular, Palfrey again offered to resign. The Free Soilers ignored his suggestion, and most of them put their best efforts into this final campaign. Ralph Waldo Emerson was among the newly enlisted and most ardent Palfrey supporters. Sumner, repaying Palfrey's previous inactivity, confined himself to private encouragement. He told Palfrey he would "go into Sackcloth and ashes" should there be defeat, but he would not campaign. Another "slacker" was Henry Wilson, in whose every act, or failure to act, Palfrey now detected conspiratorial intent. Wilson, as state committee chairman, was in the best position to help, but, claimed Palfrey, he "was inefficient, if not treacherous." Wilson communicated with the candidate only once, to encourage him to speak. At the same time he warned that Democratic votes were hard to come by because of the circular letter and Palfrey's known scorn for the Democracy.[12]

Many of these normally Democratic votes were in the hands of the recently arrived Irish. The heavy Irish immigration of the late 1840's had made that group an important factor in Massachusetts politics. Many of them lived in Cambridge and Charlestown, and even Palfrey realized the desirability of obtaining their votes. But he would sanction no imaginative methods of electioneering among this group. Palfrey contented himself with claiming that some of the Cambridge Irish were among "our best and stubbornest and most active friends," and reminding his friends that during the worst of the potato famine he had been active in raising funds for Irish relief. The veto of a harbor-flats construction bill by coalition Governor Boutwell proved anathema to the Irish and costly to Palfrey. The Whigs seized upon this as political ammunition, telling the Charlestown Irish, many of whom worked as laborers in Boston, of an alleged intimacy existing between Palfrey and Boutwell.[13]

The knowledge of the finality of Trial Number Fourteen brought as many voters to the polls as normally appeared during a November election. With the Democratic candidate practically out of sight, the contest was between Palfrey and Thompson. On election day a Free Soiler from Bolton reported Palfrey's vote there as higher than ever in that village, and that the "abominable F[ugitive] Sl[ave] law will not go down with our honest yeomanry," but in most of the larger towns and cities Palfrey ran far behind. Thompson won with a plurality of 87 votes, of over 13,000 cast.[14]

That evening dejected Free Soilers came to Hazelwood in procession to commiserate, and next day Palfrey wrote to Thompson: "I do not doubt that we feel a similar gratification in seeing the end of this long contest, and being relieved from the various *unpleasantnesses* incident to such a state of things." After two and a half years of struggle, Palfrey felt that all the "unpleasantnesses" had not been a waste: "I feel sure that our stubbornness in this prolonged contest, will prove permanently serviceable to the great cause." The news staggered Adams, who was then in New York. He wrote a comrade's letter of encouragement, pointing to the injustice of the outcome and to the good services that Palfrey could yet perform for the Free Soil cause. But Adams' private reaction went beyond disappointment. That men pretending to intelligence and patriotism deliberately selected a "cypher where they might have had a man," provided food for thought. Anticipating his son Henry's observations on the decline of democratic government, and with himself in mind as well, Adams mused: "It is incident to all republican governments not entirely to appreciate their best men." [15] Sumner saw hope in the fact that the returns of Lancaster's 79 Whig votes had been improperly sealed and might be thrown out. These and a few more votes might change the outcome. Palfrey's reply again left the professional politicians shaking their heads ruefully; he threatened to resign should his election be obtained that way. What could be done with such a man—this politician who turned his back on office? [16]

*   *   *

One expedient was the careful use of Palfrey's writing talent and popularity with anticoalition Free Soilers. He could not be trusted as chief editor of the *Commonwealth*, but as a contributing editor Palfrey's displays of principle might be controlled. The coalitionists knew that Palfrey needed money and would not refuse any offer that appeared honorable. He agreed to write four columns weekly for $1,000 a year. Adams, who a few months before had bought some of Palfrey's land out of sympathy, feared Palfrey was being used as a lure for capital from himself and S. C. Phillips. Howe, no longer a friend of coalition, did all he could to get full control for Palfrey, but the trustees refused.[17]

The paper continued to drift under the management of Bird and Elizur Wright through the spring of 1851. At this point a new publisher, Joseph Lyman, appeared. Sumner assured Palfrey that within five years Lyman would make the paper worth $100,000 and that there was no reason why Palfrey should not share in the profits. In April Lyman detailed his plans for Palfrey's employment: an annual salary of $1,200 for five columns of material weekly, with generous provisions for salary increases to match the expected boom in circulation. Palfrey's friends encouraged him to accept. T. W. Higginson, one of the first to suggest newspaper work to Palfrey, urged him on: "you *are* needed very much here. . . . A Free Soil paper in Boston with 10,000 readers—and no editor! It is almost incredibly unfortunate." Palfrey would give the paper the consistency of position and energy it lacked. The coalitionists fought the transfer tenaciously, but in mid-June Lyman got the *Commonwealth*, and Palfrey his job, a "loose relation" as contribution editor. His first editorials were cheering: "The ship is fairly launched and will now, I hope, sail true to the wind." [18]

Palfrey's second effort as a newspaperman lasted longer than the first, but ended as unhappily. He got along well with Lyman, who regarded his assistant highly, and had no trouble in keeping abreast of his contracted five columns. Among these were antislavery articles entitled *Five Years Progress of the Slave Power*, a continuation of the series which had appeared five years before in the *Whig*. The events of those years furnished Palfrey with all the incidents he needed for constructing his picture of southern ascendancy through violence and subornation. As for the future, he believed the Slave Power would try to extend itself through the Caribbean and to the Isthmus of Panama, and that "this might suffice for the present century." Though he worried about responsibility for all that appeared in a paper with his name on the masthead, he began to feel at home at the office. But this long-sought security quickly vanished. His verbal agreement with Lyman did not bind the other investors. Early in September Howe called to tell Palfrey that Lyman would not last and that with his protector gone, he could not expect to remain long.[19]

To add to Palfrey's woes, Frank, a Harvard graduate that summer, decided to play the young man-about-town. Frank's final year at school had been an additional trial to his parents. He coupled unsatisfactory work at Harvard with untruthfulness at home. Once he entertained some friends at Hazelwood, and Palfrey noted uneasily that the group drank six bottles of wine. The *bon vivant*, who had suffered "rustication" some years before when his poor grades brought exile to Cape Cod as a schoolteacher, was to be rehabilitated in a similar manner, although this time closer to home. Adams agreed that Frank should tutor his son, Charles Francis, Jr., thus aiding Frank personally and his father financially. The experiment, according to the younger Adams, was not a success: "his and my thoughts were far more intent on parties, social life and dissipation than on our studies." On the same day that Palfrey learned of his shaky tenure on the *Commonwealth*, Frank came to announce the price of dissipation, debts of several hundred dollars. Palfrey was not surprised, but his sorrow and mortification were so great that in his autobiography he mentioned the incident only cryptically. He felt he had been too lenient with Frank; a series of stern talks followed, talks which Palfrey disliked as much as Frank although they had good results.[20]

* * *

The Free Soil–Democratic coalition had operated pragmatically in the legislature. The two parties were not fused: each would nominate a full slate of candidates for the elections of November 1851. But everyone knew that the Free Soil candidacy for governor was a sham. The agreement to send Sumner to Washington for six years also meant the re-election of Governor Boutwell after the expected stalemate in November. Who then was to be the Free Soilers' sacrificial lamb? Stephen C. Phillips, their gubernatorial candidate since 1848, refused to be considered, since the election of Boutwell early that year had left him bitter and in no mood for further sacrifice. The problem for the Free Soilers was to find an incorruptible yet hopefully naive man who would inject some principle into an election which, barring a miraculous Free Soil upsurge, was already decided. The man was John G. Palfrey.

Palfrey responded immediately to offers of the nomination. That politicians were toying with him is evident from the fact they extracted no concessions. Anyone schooled in political operations would have reacted apprehensively; Palfrey took it as a compliment.

Everything was apparently arranged. Henry Wilson called on Palfrey to tell him that he was to preside over the convention at Worcester which would nominate him for the governorship. But at the last moment, Wilson decided the nomination might be of some use to himself. Perhaps he thought that sharp bargaining with coalition Democrats might bring an abandonment of Boutwell. The first step in the attempt to eliminate Palfrey was to put someone else in the chair. This was done with little difficulty, and Horace Mann, at the moment a procoalition Free Soiler, took the assignment. Wilson failed to halt Palfrey's nomination, however; either he had given himself too little time to reverse the nomination instructions, or the delegates felt momentarily disillusioned with coalition and chose to nominate Palfrey as a form of protest. The first and only ballot went overwhelmingly in Palfrey's favor. Despite Wilson's warnings about Palfrey's unavailability, most delegates voted for the "good Doctor." [21] Palfrey's motives in agreeing to run produced speculation and some consternation among his friends. T. W. Higginson was one of many Palfrey's admirers who could not justify Palfrey's tacit support of coalition practices if not principles:

Mr. Palfrey has now found some way of refuting his arguments, (far more applicable this year than last,) and accepts the nomination. . . . This I cannot understand. The Dr. and I are like the Christian and Mohammedan lovers who mutually convinced each other and were then as far apart as ever.[22]

Palfrey based his actions upon exactly those impulses his political enemies knew they could rely on. In his own mind no capitulation to the coalition had occurred. Palfrey was incorruptible in the normal meaning of the term, but his political naiveté and ambition fostered the dream that he could elevate both himself and the tone of Massachusetts politics simultaneously.

The nomination did little to improve Palfrey's low standing with the party leadership. To be sure, the Free Soilers went through the motions of supporting their man, but ten days after the convention Palfrey learned that his separation from the *Commonwealth* was to come within a few weeks. The reason given was that Palfrey's candidacy could create too many embarrassments from the conflict of his viewpoint and that of the paper's trustees. Palfrey was helpless:

I did not see this, and my real poverty made me unwilling to relinquish the little income. But I was soon given to understand, with some abruptness, that I had scarcely an option, and I withdrew.

His letter of resignation represented as much facesaving as possible under the circumstances. Palfrey thought he would at least be allowed to finish out the month of October, but on the 8th he received a half-month's pay from Howe. Palfrey, knowing that Howe had fought the removal, felt sorry for his friend.[23]

The temperance crusade, an issue of fluctuating importance in Massachusetts politics for several decades, became an important factor in the election of 1851. Palfrey had dabbled in this reform since the days of the Brattle Street ministry, but in a moderate way. Always fond of his glass of Madeira, he had little sympathy for those who demanded total abstinence. The temperance movement, now rallying round the standard of the "Maine Liquor Law" (more properly, the Maine prohibition law), showed political possibilities that Free Soil managers quickly gauged and which made the Whigs apprehensive. Some Free Soil newspapers inaccurately referred to Palfrey as an abstainer. To widen his appeal as much as possible, Palfrey agreed to sacrifice himself by giving up all alcoholic drinks, though he would sign no formal pledge.[24]

Any informed politician could have told Palfrey that he stood no chance of election, but the candidate preferred to deceive himself with hopes for a miracle. In addition to Boutwell, who was to be re-elected by the coalition in the legislature, Palfrey's old Congressional antagonist, Robert C. Winthrop, opposed him. This was Palfrey's chance to justify his vote against Winthrop in 1847 by surpassing the ex-speaker's total. Despite the newly instituted secret ballot, the "free yeomanry" of the Bay State did not rise up and throw off the shackles of State Street and Hunkerdom by voting for Palfrey. Instead he ran a poor third behind his hated rivals, with only 21 percent of the vote. Winthrop did surprisingly well; although short of a majority, his 47 percent was the best individual showing. Palfrey had nothing to cheer about; only in Worcester, the faithful antislavery stronghold, did he come close to carrying a county. The prolonged periods of depression that followed the election were the measure of Palfrey's miscalculation and disappointment.[25]

The sacrificed candidate might have had a consolation prize had he been willing to accept a job from the coalition. The Free Soilers had the office of secretary of state at their disposal, but Palfrey haughtily spurned his old post, fearing that this was a scheme for shelving him, though such stratagems were hardly necessary by this time. This offer was honestly made and repeated when the legislature met in January 1852. Palfrey again refused, authorizing Dana to turn down all bargains. The coalition majority in the legislature was slender, and this situation led to recurrent rumors that Palfrey might gain the governorship with the aid of Whigs. Wilson, no stranger to political deals, feared that Palfrey would join with the Whigs and carry enough Free Soilers with him to break the coalition. The prospect certainly appealed to Palfrey's friends. "I do not pretend to deny," admitted Adams, "that it would give me unmixed satisfaction to see Mr. Palfrey our Governor in lieu of [Boutwell] the doublefaced trimmer who rejoices in our support." Some Whigs tried to make contact with anti-coalitionist Free Soilers, but no one developed these overtures. Palfrey would never have sanctioned a bargain; this partially explains his friends' inactivity. All they had left to them was the dubious pleasure of privately expressing complaints.[26]

*   *   *

Instead of maintaining the optimism of 1848 the Free Soilers of 1852 were badly divided on matters of strategy. Abbott Lawrence snorted derisively: "Where is their free soil party now?—just where all such parties should be—*dying out*—where is Mr. Charles Allen, Mr. Palfrey, Mr. Sumner and others, who made such a figure four years ago[?]" Some of the younger Free Soilers could pretend that nothing had happened to the party, but it appeared to Joshua Giddings that the antislavery feeling which he and John Quincy Adams had nurtured in the early 1840's was being diverted if not perverted. Palfrey was equally pessimistic, and friends noted that he did not look well. He was, sighed Howe, "growing rapidly into an old man, thin, wan, and sad. He is a noble, a beautiful spirit." Adams, alarmed by his friend's seclusion, sought Palfrey out as often as possible, and then was doubly alarmed to find him harboring political ambitions. These, Adams knew, could bring only further grief.[27]

Palfrey's position on the fringe of party affairs fed his hopes. He presided over a commitee to prepare resolutions for a Free Soil convention at Worcester in July, and a month later he did the same for a gathering at Faneuil Hall. Only with the perspective of many years did he realize that his participation meant little with regard to political power, which had clearly shifted into other hands. The "best of the party" were his friends, and to let Palfrey preside over an occasional meeting was an easy way to placate anticoalition feeling. Such realism lay in the future, however; in 1852 Palfrey did notice things which caused "disgust and dismay," but he clung to the conviction that an "honest and brave spirit possesses the masses of our party." As the time for the Free Soil nominating convention approached, he expected that "in the regular course of things" he would be renominated. This was nothing more than the honest reward for his sacrifice of the previous year. After two years, Governor Boutwell was to step down, and, according to Palfrey's information, the Free Soil candidate would succeed him. These assumptions were correct; all the more reason for the party managers to keep Palfrey out. The *Commonwealth* began to mention other candidates and listed them alphabetically.[28]

Shortly before the convention, Robert Carter, a coalitionist and one of the *Commonwealth* trustees who had dismissed Palfrey from the paper, called at Hazelwood. Carter noted that many Free Soilers looked to Horace Mann as the best candidate and asked Palfrey to withdraw for the good of the party. Palfrey replied that he would voluntarily step down only if S. C. Phillips were reinstated as Free Soil candidate. Carter then went to see Adams, who upbraided him for abandoning Palfrey because there was now a chance for success. When Adams heard that Carter still dangled the lure of a minor state office before Palfrey's eyes, he exploded: "This to Palfrey of all men! What is their treatment of men of lower grade?" In his perplexity Palfrey appealed to Rockwood Hoar for advice, and Hoar's reply that no Free Soiler had a chance if Palfrey insisted on running was a crushing blow. Phillips refused to be considered, leaving Palfrey in even more of a quandary.[29]

Palfrey's indecision was short-lived because of the strength of the new candidate, Horace Mann. Mann apparently knew of no commitment to renominate Palfrey, for he immediately agreed to suggestions that he run. The announced reason for the change was Mann's better standing with the antiliquor men, and many of Palfrey's friends prepared to switch for fear that Wilson would get the nomination. By this time Palfrey was ready to step aside. Although a teetotaler in fact, he was not so in writing, fearing that to sign a pledge at such a late date would be construed as political scraping. When Phillips came to urge Mann's selection, Palfrey made his decision. Adams and Dana were to take his letter of withdrawal to the convention and use it at their discretion, although Palfrey had no objection to a convention fight if Adams thought it worthwhile.[30]

Adams and Dana soon realized that Palfrey's letter would have to be used at Lowell. The delegates Adams queried on the train showed no enthusiasm for Palfrey. Because Mann was the only outspoken supporter of the Maine Liquor Law among the anti-Wilson faction, the issue reduced itself to a choice between Mann or Wilson. Mann's supporters pressed

Adams to release Palfrey's declination at once, since Wilson men were already distributing ballots. Dana read the letter to the delegates, assuring them of what they already knew, that Palfrey always meant what he said. The convention went on to nominate Mann while Palfrey's friends took comfort in the fact that Wilson's domination over the party was not so complete as they feared.

Mann rushed to inform Palfrey that he had not sought the nomination, and that he thought Palfrey far more entitled to it than himself. For his part, Palfrey replied graciously. He was satisfied with his friends' course, if not with the general course of events. Palfrey had been sidetracked, but men whose opinion he valued admired his conduct. "It increases my respect and regard for him," wrote Howe, "and makes me feel almost ashamed of association with men who overlook his high claims, and take advantage of his modesty and generosity." Perhaps Palfrey had been done a good turn, for unfortunately for Mann, 1852 proved a year of Whig resurgence. The Whigs under John H. Clifford, won the election and recaptured the state government.[31]

The final demolition of Palfrey's political career came a month later. Surely the party would not deny him the Congressional nomination after all the trials of 1848 to 1851? Dana was one of those who anticipated no opposition to the nomination and did not bother to attend the convention. But Henry Wilson was there, and a poorly attended convention nominated John A. Bolles, former Democrat and avowed coalitionist, by a few votes. Palfrey told Dana his apologies for missing the meeting were unnecessary; Dana should banish all regrets, as he himself had done. This display of cold-blooded practicality on the part of the Middlesex Free Soil politicians led Adams to reflect on Palfrey, the politician: "Men like him do not see the outside world as it is, so much as how they think it should be. . . . Yet I value his upright views of things, as beyond all price." What a pity Palfrey could not borrow some of Henry Wilson's flexibility.[32]

*   *   *

During the struggle to adopt a new state constitution in 1853, Palfrey made his last significant appearance on the Massachusetts political scene. Despite many amendments and a previous attempt to begin anew (by way of the constitutional convention of 1820) the Massachusetts constitution of 1780 was still in force. This conservative document had blocked the way of reform in many fields; in 1853 coalition politicians thought the moment propitious for replacing it with a constitution which might help restore them to power. The chief obstacle to coalition domination was the general ticket system which obtained in the cities and practically insured Whig control of the lower house of the legislature. The question of representation was also of vital importance. It was imperative that the small towns maintain or even increase their overrepresentation if the coalition were to continue to capitalize on the antislavery and anti-Whig-merchant sentiments of the rural areas. In addition to these matters the coalitionists proposed to alter the life tenure of the state's judges. Although the Whigs had done well in the elections of 1852 and organized the legislature, the voters decided to call a constitutional convention for the following year.[33]

With the elections of convention delegates approaching, Palfrey, who had been inactive for months, felt compelled to do something. His mind was working overtime again on the subject of Henry Wilson, the plotter. Palfrey urged Adams to join him in opposing the coalitionists openly and to dispute the process of selecting delegates from the small towns, since a delegate need not be a resident of the town he represented. But Adams hedged, indicating that he had no stomach for what would surely be a losing fight.[34]

The March elections brought victory to the Free Soilers

and Democrats. A few days before the voting, the Whigs had stupidly rammed through a bill which effectively abolished the secret ballot; this, and a variety of other issues including the failure to pass a ten-hour labor law, resulted in the party's defeat. Palfrey was not among those chosen to be Free Soil delegates; he claimed that the outcome revealed Wilson's "paltry plan of constituting a subservient party." How true was Palfrey's charge? Although some absentee Free Soil delegates won election, their victories had not come easily. "There has been great difficulty," reported Howe, ". . . in persuading small towns to take strangers." Wilson certainly did not strain himself to include Palfrey, but neither did he deliberately sabotage Palfrey's candidacy, as Adams inferred from the failure to obtain a place. Wilson proposed Palfrey to several towns, but they all declined.[35]

In Palfrey's mind no pressing need for constitutional reform existed. Certainly it should not come for reasons of partisan political advantage, and he later viewed the convention proceedings scornfully:

> In it [Wilson's] heterogeneous followers had everything their own way. The opposition were discouraged, timorous, confounded, divided, and feeble. Choate was there and talked, but to little purpose. My noble friends, Sumner, Dana, and Allen seemed to have lost their heads. Banks presided. Boutwell was the master spirit, and guided a compact majority. The result was such as might not have been unreasonably apprehended from men, most of whom had either no stake, or no clear discernment of their stake in the permanent well-being of the Commonwealth.

The opposition was not so docile as Palfrey pictured them (Dana tried actively to block excessive reform), but the large anticonstitution majority insured the triumph of the chief coalition aims. According to Palfrey, such a prolongation of coalition power, involving as it did a compact with Democratic Hunkerdom, meant the death of Massachusetts antislavery.[36]

Late in August Palfrey obtained a copy of the proposed constitution, found it wanting, and immediately drafted an outline of a critical article. For several weeks he studied the constitution of 1780, mentally blocking out his arguments. When Adams heard of Palfrey's plan he warned his friend of the probable consequences. Palfrey replied that a sense of duty would be his only consideration. Wilson's nomination for governor a few days later banished any doubts, since it seemed to solemnize the triumph of a "new set who seem to have more sail than ballast.... A party of dirty, negotiating, trading politics." On the day of publication, October 21, Palfrey wrote resignedly: "Now I shall hear the music."

The pamphlet was an excellent exposition of conservative fears about the dangers of rapid constitutional change. Palfrey, as many former Whig friends frequently noted, remained a good conservative Whig in everything but the matter of political antislavery. He began by extolling the existing constitution, which "to a rare extent" had given the state good government for so many decades; any imperfections could be remedied through the amending system. The provisions for representation in the House were unwise; overrepresenting the small towns smacked too much of rotton boroughs. The only solution was districting, but Palfrey showed his conservatism by refusing to surrender completely to the logic of this view. Cities should not get full representation according to population; a sliding scale, with each additional city representative requiring more voters, would help keep the power of the city rabble in check. But Palfrey's main objections centered upon the judiciary section, especially the abolition of life tenure for judges. The proposed ten-year term meant the end of the independence of the judiciary and the spectacle of judges "dancing attendance in the Governor's anti-chamber" as their terms expired. And Palfrey had come to consider the judiciary all-important, with the Chief Justice of the United States Supreme Court the most important individual in the country.

Palfrey did not agree completely with Whig arguments, however. Revising his opinion of ten years before, he now supported the secret ballot because of the election day abuses of the Cotton Magnates' mill managers. But, he told his fellow Free Soilers, partisan considerations had no place in such a fundamental question as the constitution; Massachusetts must not be disgraced for the sake of punishing Whigs. History furnished abundant lessons for those capable of learning: "Florence, before her frolics of this kind were brought to an end by the Grand Ducal despotism, had at one time . . . five Constitutions in ten years. It was not the way to a quiet life." [37]

The first five hundred copies of the *Remarks* left the press with no identification on the title page other than "By a Free Soiler From the Start." The Whigs, apparently crushed by the coalition domination of the convention, reposed in an apathetic state. Soon after the appearance of the pamphlet they began to show some life, although Palfrey's objections were not the sole cause of the Whig revival of spirit. Yet he provided the spark. The Whig press commented favorably; Whig leaders discussed the pamphlet, guessed correctly that Palfrey was the author, and decided to print many more copies. They urged Sparks to contact Palfrey and obtain authorization for new signed editions:

Thousands of persons would procure the pamphlet and will read it with pleasure and profit, if they can see the name attached to it, for whom they entertain so great regard and respect as they do for Dr. Palfrey, whereas if it come out without a name . . . its influence will be comparatively limited. If Dr. Palfrey will append his name to the pamphlet . . . I think this very thing will be decisive of the fate of the new constitution.

Palfrey had no objection. He withdrew his copyright and all claims to remuneration, with only one condition, that no unauthorized changes be made. Soon more than 17,000 copies were in print.[38]

On election day Palfrey confessed that he had no hope of the constitution's defeat, but to his delight the new document failed at the polls. The jubilant Whigs sent a brass band to serenade their party leaders, but the musicians did not stop at Hazelwood. Political neglect made Palfrey more than ever convinced that he had swung the balance against the constitution: "Whoever, in time to come, shall have occasion to think himself better off in consequence of his case having been passed by independent judges, owes me . . . a kind remembrance." Many of his friends agreed that his action was the all-important factor. A Democratic politician placed Palfrey's *Remarks* third in a list of reasons for defeat which included the opposition of administration Democrats, antiprohibition men, and Catholics (because of the denial of state funds for parochial schools). Sumner's list of reasons for the "catastrophe of our state and the country" put Palfrey's name at the top.[39]

Sumner fumed over Palfrey's "unexpected and eccentric" action. In a Faneuil Hall speech he assured Free Soilers that the constitutional issue would not be forgotten, nor did he hide his anger with those responsible for the result. At a frosty dinner at Adams', Palfrey, Sumner, Dana, and the host avoided all mention of current politics. Sumner left for Washington without seeing Palfrey, and he ignored Palfrey's friendly overtures. Adams told Palfrey that he had done everything a man might honorably do to placate Sumner's hostility. The rest was up to Sumner and time.[40]

*   *   *

"Palfrey is politically defunct, an obsolute nonentity," intoned a coalitionist fiercely, "my motto is 'Death to the traitors'." William S. Robinson, former editor of the *Republican*, lashed out angrily in the New York *Post* against Palfrey and Adams for their anticonstitution stand. Their arguments were "calculated to bring a satirical smile upon the faces of

those who knew that their real object was to revenge themselves upon Henry Wilson." If Palfrey thought that the
"anathema" of Cotton in 1846 had been harsh, the proscrip-
tion of his own people after 1853 was anything but gentle:

> They calumniated me abusively, perseveringly, and without stint.
> But since the 14th day of November, 1853, I have been clear in the
> conviction that it was not for no purpose that I was sent into the
> world.

Palfrey's political career had not given him the financial
security nor the fame he dreamed of. His later denials of
ambition and his claims that he had been pushed into politics
against his will are not valid. On the positive side, Palfrey's
role as one of the early Free Soil vanguard was an important
and creditable one.[41] His failure stemmed from his attitudes
toward compromise, at any level, and his refusal to adjust
himself to the changed conditions of Massachusetts life.

By the 1850's it was not enough to be a Whig gentleman,
not even an antislavery Whig gentleman, to succeed in Bay
State politics. The mode of operations, if not the formal rules,
had changed. Industrialization and immigration had shattered
the homogeneity of the commercial-agrarian, Anglo-Saxon
Commonwealth. The world of Palfrey's young manhood,
which seemed to offer so much along easily predictable lines,
no longer existed. The happy days of certainty and compara-
tive repose were certainly dead by the 1850's, and even in the
previous decade (the decade of Palfrey's initial political
activity), the discerning ones noted the presence of all the
factors of disintegration.

It is not surprising, then, that in his frustration Palfrey
found a scapegoat, a man to exemplify all that was new (and
thus reprehensible) in Massachusetts politics. The villain was
Henry Wilson. While Everett and Winthrop represented to
Palfrey good New England stock, soured and seduced by
the blandishments of the Slave Power, Wilson was a man of
no background, without even a name (he was born Jeremiah

Colbath in a New Hampshire hut).[42] Palfrey and the other gentlemen Free Soilers thought Wilson a capital fellow as long as he minded his minor business while tending to organizational errands. But the political upheavals of mid-century gave Wilson a chance to exercise real power and finally to run the state's Free Soil party. Each setback convinced Palfrey that Henry Wilson existed only to block his ambitions. While Wilson capitalized on the changed conditions superbly, Palfrey stood aside dazed by the rapidity of events. It was Palfrey's fault that he was too poor a politician to perceive the nature of the transformation and accommodate himself to it.

Accommodation was not in him. Even though his failures were as much his own fault as any one else's, Palfrey would not have had it differently. Sumner's claim that he was "in morals, not politics," applies more appropriately to Palfrey. Refusal to compromise nonessentials doomed him politically, so that his public career was one of constant pain. The anodyne which kept the pain bearable was the New England Puritans' knowledge that God's Way is a thorny one. If Palfrey had not taken himself so seriously, he would have called the political chapter of his autobiography "Wrecked by Rectitude."

XIV ~

Political Twilight and the Puritan Past

BECAUSE Palfrey felt that political behavior should be governed by high ethical principles he naturally adorned his political utterances with references to the moral precepts of Old New England. He attributed his political failure not to personal shortcomings, but to his neighbors' abandonment of the pathways laid out by Puritan forebears. The best way to halt this moral decline was to remind the people—those who had roots in the Puritan past—of the still useful lessons of New England's origins.

This interest in the past was deeply rooted. Palfrey's lectures and writings on the Old Testament, while more respected than enjoyed, evidenced his literary ambitions. During the 1840's, he first toyed with the idea of writing a history of colonial New England.[1] While serving as Commonwealth secretary he had in his charge colony records and had cooperated with Sparks in obtaining transcripts of colonial documents from foreign archives. This intimate association with the primary materials of history awakened a long-felt interest. His forced withdrawal from politics heightened the interest.

But more than scholarship was involved here. Palfrey had not yet acquired a reliable income. The immense popularity of the Boston historians, Sparks, Bancroft, Prescott, and Parkman, showed that history could be profitable. And the prestige which came with the authorship of a major work of history was an additional reward which Palfrey craved.

An increasing sense of isolation impelled him to seek new

fields of action. Twice, in the year before his final political fall, Palfrey almost broke away from the frustrations of his unhappy role of political martyr. A Harvard overseer, seeking a successor for Sparks as professor of history, approached Palfrey with the advice that an end to political activity might get him the post. Palfrey demurred, and the selection of another man convinced him that "the Milk Street and State Street interest" had again blocked his aspirations. A similar preliminary consideration, this time for the post of Harvard treasurer, produced an identical result. Conservatives felt that the college must remain a national institution. This could not be done if Palfrey were hired because of his "peculiar position" as a leader of a political party anathematized by the South. Palfrey never learned the precise grounds of rejection, but the reasons were not hard to surmise. "The dispensers of money-favors and of social attentions did not corrupt, and did not threaten"; they simply let the ambitious know that advancement would come only to those who agreed to "burn incense to the obscene Pro-Slavery idol of the day." [2]

*   *   *

If Palfrey had any doubts as to where he stood with his former political associates, the Kansas-Nebraska crisis quickly erased them. Free Soilers and Whigs called conventions to protest Senator Stephen A. Douglas' attempt to repeal the Missouri Compromise. A scant three months had passed since the defeat of the proposed state constitution, and Whigs remembered gratefully Palfrey's role in that struggle. Two weeks before the Free Soil meeting a bound volume of anti-constitution tracts, including Palfrey's *Remarks*, appeared. This publication angered Wilson and the coalitionists. Howe, standing halfway between the party men and the "principled faction," admitted to Palfrey that many Free Soilers wanted to keep Palfrey and Adams silent at the convention. At a meeting of the state committee Wilson sought the exclusion of the two mavericks, claiming that his "boys" would not permit Palfrey and Adams to speak.[3]

Palfrey's reaction of melancholy acquiescence deepened when he saw that his name was not on the list of Free Soil delegates from Cambridge. He thought of attending as a spectator, with the hope of being asked to speak by the audience, thus testing the "question whether a meeting of Free Soilers would disown me. But if I carried the point . . . it would have to be through a row, and this would be so unedifying a spectacle for the public." A floor fight at a political convention an unedifying spectacle! Palfrey's political kingdom was not of this world.[4]

Disillusionment with politics did not mean abandonment of antislavery activity. Palfrey drew nearer to the abolitionists, those who did not speak of coalitions or practicality, but adhered to their ideals whatever the results. While rejecting Theodore Parker's theological heresies he felt that there could be no caviling about the man's contributions in the fight against the Slave Power. And Palfrey promised the editor of a new antislavery monthly that he would send articles whenever time permitted. From Harriet Beecher Stowe, whose *Uncle Tom's Cabin* had become the chief literary vehicle of abolition, came a request that he deliver a series of antislavery lectures. Palfrey had already spoken several times in New York in December 1853, and he was happy to repeat his condemnation of slavery at home.[5]

No event of 1854, not even the Kansas-Nebraska Act, did more to inflame antislavery sentiment in Boston than the rendition of the fugitive slave, Anthony Burns. Before the trial of the hapless Negro, Palfrey sought out probate judge Edward G. Loring, who also served as federal commissioner to administer the Fugitive Slave Law. Palfrey had been instrumental in obtaining a Harvard law professorship for Loring several months before. It would be better for the judge to resign his commission, Palfrey argued, than to take part in such a degraded proceeding. When Loring said nothing, Palfrey hinted that a deserved ostracism awaited him if he ruled against the fugitive. Each day of waiting increased the tension. Palfrey joined the crowds around the jail, and glimpsed Burns, his head in his hands, peering resignedly through the bars of his cell at the people below. Dana's arguments for the defense, and the hopes of Boston, went down before the letter of the hateful law. When Palfrey returned home on the afternoon of June 2, Mary Ann could read the commissioner's decision in his face.[6]

After Burns's return to Virginia, antislavery elements in Boston had little difficulty in sustaining the feeling of indignation. As the number of converts to antislavery increased, even the "Hunker" Pierce-administration Democrats were temporarily silenced. Numerous conversions to a "better state of mind" impressed Palfrey; Dana relayed reports of former proslavery men cursing their own shortsightedness. Howe, who had seen no hope for antislavery when the year began, exulted over the "great revolution" that had come to Boston. He could be forgiven his enthusiasm; how else to describe the sight of Samuel A. Eliot, late defender of the fugitive bill, advocating disunion should the Kansas-Nebraska Act stand?[7]

The election of antislavery men caused them to view former antagonists with a more tolerant eye. The thaw extended to Washington and Senator Sumner, who knew of Palfrey's desire to restore their old friendship. If Cotton men were worthy of forgiveness, surely old Free Soilers merited the same dispensation. In March Sumner sent Palfrey a volume of his printed speeches, and Palfrey praised the senator's conduct in Washington. Sumner was conciliatory but the old hurt, while forgiven, was not forgotten: "Freedom in Massachusetts has received from you a more deadly blow than from any other living citizen of our Commonwealth." When Congress adjourned in August, Sumner visited Hazelwood, behaving "just the same as if he had not been queer." The reconciliation pleased Palfrey enormously, since it gave him hope for the future.[8]

The idea of ultimate political vindication did not blind Palfrey to the impossibility of achieving anything positive at once. Though Sumner was mollified and John A. Andrew assured him that unity and forgiveness were now bywords among sincere antislavery men, Palfrey's caution made him decline to attend the meetings which organized the Republican party in the Bay State. He claimed that his presence would only hamper the effort since so many politicians distrusted him. However, he gave advice freely: the Republicans would be fools to throw away the "hand which has just been dealt to us by the joint action of the Knavish Democrats and the silly Whigs," by setting up "soldiers of fortune" for candidates; antislavery purity required the nomination of Stephen C. Phillips for governor.[9]

But all plans for the redemption of Massachusetts ran afoul of a new political party. The Native Americans, or Know-Nothings, capitalized on old grievances by channeling them into one specious but easily grasped issue, fear and hatred of the Irish immigrant as a visible scapegoat for the social and political ills which accompanied the Commonwealth's industrialization. As early as 1844 Massachusetts Whigs had lamented the supposed connection between foreign votes and the defeat of Henry Clay. The following year Boston elected a Nativist mayor, and Free Soilers feared this new group would prevent the proper reorganization of state politics along antislavery lines.[10] The rise of the slavery issue as a divisive political factor coincided with the enormous increase in Irish immigration. While the antislavery crusade maintained its initial intensity, the political uses of anti-immigrant feeling lay dormant, but by 1854 the effective stalemate of coalition had created unbearable political pressures. Nativism burst upon Massachusetts that year, inundating the existing parties. The Know-Nothings won all the major state offices, and all but three seats in the legislature. The political log jam had been broken with a vengeance.

Palfrey would have been as unprepared for this electoral revolution as the politicians of Massachusetts had it not been for Henry Wilson's role in the triumph of Henry J. Gardner, the new Nativist governor. When he heard, in September, that Wilson would support Gardner in exchange for election to the Senate by a Know-Nothing legislature, Palfrey sadly predicted the success of this scheme. He had too much respect for Wilson's political talents to discount the power of any movement he joined.[11]

After the first shock of Wilson's defection and the Know-Nothing landslide had worn off, dazed Republicans looked for compensations. Although Palfrey would join no secret society, he thanked Providence that the two old corrupt parties of Massachusetts had been smashed and relegated to "eternal sunset." As for the new party, he believed it contained "large numbers of honest men," who joined it from a desire to escape their old party associations, something they found easier to do with the "advantage of partial secrecy." Despite the extent of the Nativist victory, Palfrey felt the issue of Irish immigration must inevitably bow to the moral predominance of the struggle against slavery.[12]

*   *   *

The life of a semi-public man, which Palfrey had been leading since his return from Washington in the spring of 1849, provided a good deal of time for work and reflection. With his political ambitions in abeyance, he turned to his old scholarly interests, but not before his first, unfortunate venture into history. In 1852 he entered a controversy between Sparks and Britain's Lord Mahon, whose *History of England* contained an attack on Sparks's editorial practice of altering Washington's letters and making improvements in the general's grammar. Though Sparks defended himself in print he also suggested that his friend aid him with a defense of the *Writings of Washington*. Palfrey, anxious to renew a friendship which had cooled for political reasons, agreed. Soon Palfrey regretted his involvement in "that awful piece of work." In July the *North American* carried Palfrey's barely anonymous apologia —a lame effort, tendentious instead of authoritative, shrill instead of reasoned. Despite the contrary evidence, Palfrey contended that Sparks's editorship had not altered the basic Washington. Everett justifiably observed that whatever points Palfrey made against Mahon were lost through the "bad spirit . . . and bitterness" of his commentary.[13]

A series of lectures on New England two years later provided a less controversial preparation for the forthcoming historical work. Antislavery lectures answered a fine moral purpose but provided little money, unlike the well-paying Lowell lectures during the winter of 1854 which paid $1,000 for a dozen Boston appearances. The research required for the lectures proved pleasant. Palfrey found library work and field trips far easier than the "dreadfully hard" criticisms of the Old and New Testament. He approached the Boston lectern with his usual unfounded fears. In a hall packed with socially prominent listeners, he told the Bostonians what they wanted to hear. According to his daughter Anna the subject, "New England Character," afforded an opportunity to "utter some truths for other people to apply." This verbal preview of the *History of New England* also helped balance the family budget for the year.[14]

*   *   *

Palfrey had declined to participate actively in the formation of the Republican party, but Wilson's defection to Know-Nothingism allowed him to renew part of his faith in the state's antislavery party. In January 1855 he attended a Republican meeting which Howe called a "rallying of the relics of the old Liberty and Free Soil party under the old banner."

Nativism, or the "new coalitionism," fared badly at the gathering. The Free Soil "relics" came out for clear opposition to the Know-Nothings.

A renewed interest in politics did not mean a full-scale re-entry into the political game, however. Palfrey, by this time, was too happy in his new role of historian and too conscious of past defeats. Yet all he learned about the New England past reinforced his conviction that without a return to established principles, political activity represented little more than organized amorality. No arguments about practicality could shake his belief in Free Soil. Merely to oppose the repeal of the Missouri Compromise was pointless. To Palfrey, the term "Slave Power" meant the political aggressions of slavery beyond its localized domains. He would allow the existence of the institution where it was already established, since such iniquity could not permanently sustain itself in a world of moral progress.[15]

Palfrey did, however, refuse to support radical means for the attainment of antislavery ends. In March 1855 the state legislature attempted to remove Judge Loring because of his role in returning Anthony Burns to slavery. Though Burns's freedom had been bought by the Negro community of Boston, the feeling against Loring would not be stilled. Despite his previous role as Burns's defender, conservative Richard Henry Dana hastened to defend the judiciary in the person of the unhappy Loring. Palfrey approved of Dana's course, as much from concern over the removal precedent as from sympathy for Loring. When the legislature rceommended removal, Governor Gardner did not comply, a decision which surprised Palfrey as much as it pleased him.[16]

With much of the radicalism of Massachusetts antislavery committed to Nativism, old Free Soil conservatives thought they saw an opportunity to realign parties along conservative-radical lines. In 1855 Palfrey, styling himself "An Old Conservative," wrote a pamphlet appealing to individual Whigs to abandon an organization which mouthed Free Soil phrases while serving the Slave Power. To speak of the Whig party now as "a national party . . . is the very extravagance of balderdash." A Whig vote could not be a vote for principle since the terms were mutually exclusive. Palfrey would neither attack nor defend the Know-Nothings: "Let that party vindicate or shrive itself." Every Massachusetts conservative must support Republicanism as the only defense against the depredations of the Slave Power, or the Union would ultimately dissolve. The Massachusetts electorate was not conservative enough to heed his advice. They wanted more of the "Paddy hunt," and Nativism won again. The pamphlet proved a dud because, as Palfrey put it, "the Know-Nothing movement had marshalled its prodigious force, and Wilson, Banks, and company, had joined it." [17]

The second Nativist victory confused Palfrey. The election of 1854 might be regarded as the aberrant behavior of a confused electorate, but Gardner's re-election could not be dismissed. The unmistakable inferences to be drawn from the result gave Palfrey much to ponder. Henry Wilson and Nathaniel P. Banks, the "Natick Cobbler" and the "Waltham Bobbin Boy," were the two men who symbolized Palfrey's conception of the working politician—men of quick handshakes and pliable principles. These same men, one originally a Whig, the other originally a Democrat, led the group which had captured the state government and prevented those whom Adams called "people of our sort" from playing a meaningful political role. When looking back on these events, Palfrey directed his scorn at these individuals instead of Governor Gardner, probably because both Wilson and Banks went on to national prominence as Republican politicians after the fall of political Nativism.[18]

But at the end of 1855 Nativism seemed permanently triumphant, so much so that even Palfrey momentarily relaxed his previously rigid sense of political rectitude. When Banks became speaker of the United States House of Representatives, Palfrey wrote to congratulate the "country and the cause of Freedom" on his election; and on another occasion he had nothing but praise for a speech on slavery by Henry Wilson, erstwhile schemer and traitor.[19]

*   *   *

"The politician's grim part was played through. I retired to dress for another." By 1856, Palfrey had been reading the sources of New England history for nearly two years and had sketched some early chapters. But with this early work came the realization that a thoroughgoing treatment required research in English archives. Once he decided on a trip Palfrey lost no time in making his arrangements, booking passage on a steamer leaving Boston late in March 1856.

Palfrey hoped that the material in the British archives would provide much of the substance of his narrative, but the youthful state of historical investigation in primary sources posed problems. Among these was uncertainty over what he could expect to find and what to look for. To help guide his inquiries, Palfrey asked the opinion of New England's historians and antiquarians. Which incidents of colonial history suffered most from lack of documentation? Had collections of private papers survived? Historically minded friends responded with many suggestions, but supplied few definite leads about the location of materials.[20]

Jared Sparks, an experienced archival researcher, was one of the many who thought Palfrey should travel as an official representative of the state. It annoyed him to see that several other states had gone further than Massachusetts in publishing colonial documents from foreign archives. Palfrey met a Know-Nothing member of the legislature, offering to supervise transcriptions if the state government paid the copyists' fees. The lower house appropriated $500, but in the Senate "some of the Knowing ones thought that they smelled a rat," and ignored the project.[21]

From Liverpool Palfrey hurried to London, where the researcher's desire to confront the manuscript sources immediately ran afoul of bureaucracy. For several weeks he waited for permission to enter the Public Record Office. Finally, with help from American Minister George M. Dallas, he "got through the Circumlocution office," and the archives of the Privy Council were opened.[22]

That official London began to take notice of him was partly the result of Palfrey's socializing and his many letters of introduction. Sumner had recommended him to the Duchesses of Sutherland and Argyll, who responded at once with invitations. Joseph Parkes, former M.P., dined with Palfrey often and got him a complimentary membership at the Reform Club. Mary Ann lectured her husband like a schoolboy on how to behave in the presence of a duchess: "I hope you will not be so afraid of accepting her politeness as to give her an impression that her attentions are not appreciated. . . . Dukes, and Duchesses belong to the human family." Palfrey admitted that all the efforts of noble ladies to put him at his ease had not entirely succeeded.[23]

Palfrey's work days consisted of five hours at the Public Record Office, beginning at ten A.M., with evenings reserved for reading at one of the clubs open to him. The well-indexed volumes of the Privy Council proceedings were easy to handle, but when he shifted to the massive and unsorted records of the Board of Trade, all hopes for an early conclusion to his research disappeared. Anticipating the feelings of hundreds of successors at the Public Record Office, he wished the hours might be lengthened to allow him more time for research. The "amplitude of the materials," intimidated him; nor did it help to reflect on the additional untapped mountains of research material which lay beyond the P.R.O.

Gradually the data began to fall into consistent patterns. While Palfrey did not seem to appreciate the dangers of deductive reasoning, his "knowledge of what is mainly to be looked for" enabled him to use research time economically.

His reverence for the past intensified as he picked his way through contemporary documents. A few weeks made it clear that nothing worthwhile could have been accomplished without such research. There was no other way to do justice to the richness and complexity of New England history.[24]

*   *   *

The life of colonial New England did not monopolize Palfrey's attention. News of the growing political power of the antislavery movement filled letters and newspapers crossing the Atlantic. Future generations of historians would accept the task of debating the causes of struggle more fundamental than the morality of the slave system; to the observers of 1856 the primacy of the slavery issue seemed clear. Palfrey, of course, had long viewed American political events through an antislavery lens. The Kansas battle and the caning of Charles Sumner by a South Carolina Congressman on the floor of the United States Senate corroborated the nefariousness of the Slave Power conspiracy. Letters from Palfrey's son, coupling the assault on Sumner with reports of the sacking of Lawrence, Kansas, by pro-Southerners, seemed to leave no hope for the Union. "I am very fond of peace," intoned Frank, "but if it must be slavery or war, why, war cannot come too soon." Palfrey relayed information about the convalescent senator to antislavery members of the aristocracy and supplied them with copies of the Sumner speech which had provoked the attack.[25]

But opposition to slavery did not foster any particularly friendly feelings towards Negroes in Palfrey. Acutely conscious of race, he could not rid himself of the feeling that dark skin and inferiority were bound together. The awarding of medical degrees at King's College astonished Palfrey in one respect. There were three Negro graduates, and he could not ignore the fact that despite being particularly black, and in features "an uncommonly pronounced Negro," one of the three won honors, nor that the men mixed easily with the other students.[26]

With more and more work behind him, Palfrey found himself a willing victim to pleasant distractions. Invitations to rambling English breakfasts came frequently, and he accepted as many as came. When the royal household regiments returned from the Crimea "there was no doing otherwise, than to go with all the world" to Hyde Park for the parade and review. In July Richard Henry Dana arrived for a short London visit, and he shared Palfrey's Regent Street lodgings.

A quick tour of the Continent capped Palfrey's European stay. To connect it with his work, he began by inspecting Leyden, the Dutch site of Pilgrim residence, and Delft, their port of embarkation. Then to Heidelberg, Cologne, and up the Rhine to Switzerland. In Paris there were inquiries to be made for Francis Parkman concerning Canadian history, and time for reassessment of impressions of Old World civilizations. In 1826 Palfrey had found England cold and France friendly. But the attentions of British aristocracy and the conservatism of thirty more years changed that. Westminster Abbey mastered the reserve of the New Englander: "It is too grand and too touching. Again and again I found the tears in my eyes." Paris, on the other hand, presented a spectacle of splendid luxury, but no spiritual fulfillment. It was a trap for young men, all the more dangerous for its surface attractiveness.[27]

By late October Palfrey was back in Cambridge. The trip had been of great value. He had gained confidence in his potential as a historian through the research, and the break from his withdrawn existence at Hazelwood had revitalized him in a way which delighted the family. Francis Parkman expressed the feelings of confidence and expectation with which Boston greeted Palfrey the historian: "Politically, socially, and religiously considered, your subject is the precise opposite of mine. . . . I hope that the history of New England

and the history of New France may see the light in some sort simultaneously." Palfrey left England earlier than planned so that he might campaign for Frémont and Republicanism in the final two weeks before the election. He had to be satisfied with presiding over a "non-partisan" Kansas meeting, and marching in the procession which greeted Sumner early in November. The crowd responded with "Three cheers for Mr. Palfrey," but the hoped-for speaking engagement never came. All Palfrey could do to swing the Bay State into the Frémont column was to cast his individual vote and to rejoice with this family over the many old "Hunker-conservatives" who had seen the light and voted for Free Soil and Frémont.[28]

The disappointment of the election and the elevation of pro-southern Democrat James Buchanan to the presidency were not easy to bear. With the Slave Power strong in White House councils, and political Free Soilism unresponsive to his offerings, Palfrey once more began to flirt with abolitionism. He responded effusively to Mrs. Stowe's second antislavery novel, *Dred: A Tale of the Dismal Swamp*, telling her that "the services you are rendering to humanity are of unspeakable worth." And Palfrey's old friend and former parishioner, Lydia Maria Child, appealed to him to encourage a Kentucky girl of nineteen who tried to free the slaves she owned. The fact that she was a minor prevented the emancipation; all she accomplished was her own ostracism. Mrs. Child urged Palfrey to tell the girl of his own venture into emancipation. Palfrey responded at once with praise for Miss Griffith's resolve and for her outspoken antislavery writings. Virtue was an integral part of genius, he observed, and the virtue of emancipation was no exception: "Before anti-slavery took hold of you, did you dream you could write as you have now done? . . . The abolition vein is the source of all that is best in American poetry." Even disunion, the extreme antislavery measure which provided the best argument to those dismissing abolitionism as pernicious fanaticism, did not then horrify Palfrey.

When Thomas Wentworth Higginson invited him to attend an abolitionists' disunion convention at Worcester, Palfrey declined to come, but expressed his admiration for Higginson's earnestness in the cause of freedom.[29]

* * *

The years between his return from Europe and the outbreak of civil war were outwardly uneventful ones for Palfrey, now committed to full-time work on the *History*. The London research revealed the inadequacy of the sections of narrative already sketched, and rather than attempt to repair the draft chapters, he decided to begin again. The end of political opportunities made success as a historian all the more important. Although he could have had a volume through the press by the end of 1857, Palfrey decided to proceed carefully. The caution meant a year's delay.

"I rejoice that the History of New England is about to be redeemed from the dominions of dullness, and of narrowness of view," exalted young Charles Eliot Norton. After examining several chapters of proofsheets Norton became one of Palfrey's most enthusiastic readers, and consequently of relatively little value to the flattered author as a critic. Not all the responses were learned backslapping, however. Francis Bowen, in a society which equated minced words with propriety, got to the point immediately: "Your tone in reference to the Puritan fathers seems to be uniformly apologetic and laudatory. After all, they were mortal men; they made blunders, they shared the errors of their times." Boston lawyer William H. Gardiner phrased it differently; though not particularly well-disposed toward the Puritan worthies, he had to admit they were "excellent people to have come *from*." [30]

On one important question Palfrey remained adamant. Roger Williams, the disruptive fugitive from the Puritan Zion in the Wilderness, would get no coddling in his pages. Despite the passage of two centuries, Palfrey viewed Williams with a Puritan's eye—as a threat to their settlement and its principles. Several readers reacted to the seemingly one-sided presentation. One inquired plaintively if Williams' banishment in the middle of winter did not merit some sympathy. When Palfrey's first volume appeared, a Providence editor contended that Williams "discovered religious freedom just as much as Harvey did the circulation of the blood." The argument was wasted; a year before Palfrey had committed himself to "putting Roger Williams in his right place." [31]

From the start, the *History of New England* produced financial disappointment. The author had himself partially to blame, for his overgenerous policy of sending several hundred free copies to friends cut into his potential market. Naturally, Palfrey dreamed of large royalties and literary fame, but acceptance and mere approval on the part of those who mattered was return enough for him should the fame and profits fail to materialize. "Palfrey is well," Longfellow informed Sumner, "his history is very successful, and he is at work on the second volume." But the poet had not seen the Palfrey family accounts for the previous year.

The voice of practicality, Mary Ann, was not ecstatic over the situation: "I don't like the idea of his making such a slave of himself for nothing." As if to emphasize her point, a man who received a complimentary copy sent four barrels of potatoes in payment; unfortunately, he was an exception. Francis Bowen, with his usual good sense, explained that Palfrey could not expect the ordinary popularity for writing "by far the best *American* history that has yet been published. . . . Half as much research and ability given to a broad and attractive theme, that admitted of picturesque or romantic details, such as the history of Spain, Italy, or Holland, would have created a more saleable book." Such were the facts, and Palfrey declined to become downcast. In closing out 1859, he reflected that because of the generally favorable reception of his work the year had been the happiest of his life. This was no surprise for a man who considered the purpose of civilized institutions the protection of "life, liberty, reputation, and property." [32]

*   *   *

The satisfaction which Palfrey felt over his literary reputation, while shared by his family, did not bring happiness at home. Sarah and Mary had made adjustments of a sort, the former by writing poems and romantic novels, the latter by a seemingly inexhaustible expenditure of "animal spirits." Shortly after Anna's last potential suitor had been dismissed from Hazelwood, John told Frank that she was a sick woman and must be protected from herself. All the residents of Hazelwood were in some way affected:

> It is a wicked life they live at home. . . . It is sufficient to break down a strong man like Father, although three quarters of his life has been bound up in his books; and what must be its effect on women? You have never really lived at home since the trouble began. . . . I was warped by it for life two years before going to College, and I can appreciate its influence better than you. I hope, I am sure, that Father will not let the house relapse into its old monotony after he gets home.

One source of family pride was the fact that John, who from Harvard entered West Point, was graduated at the head of his class of 1857. The rivalry—hatred, rather—which had grown up between the antislavery cadets and the more numerous southern and pro-southern boys made the victory of the Black Republican student all the sweeter.[33]

John had observed that one way to break the "old monotony" at home was to increase the family income. But neither of the sons could do this quickly, and Palfrey knew his writing would not bring wealth. Expedients such as the sale of a portion of his land or the galling necessity of accepting gifts were part of Palfrey's life. From Amos Lawrence had come $1,000 to aid in the Harvard education of Frank and John. "In walks entirely apart from those of politics," lamented Palfrey to a benefactor, "unfriendly politicians have . . . closed against me opportunities which occurred for earning something." [34] Palfrey purchased his literary reputation at the price of threadbare gentility. But what else could he do?

*   *   *

Throughout the late fifties Palfrey kept an ear cocked for political news, although he told Sumner in 1858: "Of political movements, I know nothing." But it was not easy, after years of participation, to see the political current sweep past. To Sumner's suggestion that Palfrey's retiring character had aggravated his isolation, he replied that desires alone were no substitute for effective political power. He would simply do his best in his chosen field; after all, "the Puritan salt has been hitherto the preservation of this people against loathsome corruption." Though it had lost some of its savor, the salt of Puritanism was too valuable to be thrown away.[35]

The state elections of 1859 provided Palfrey with opportunities for a modest amount of political activity and for the growth of the self-esteem through electioneering. He spoke at a few rallies in the Third District in support of the candidacy of Charles Francis Adams for Congress. His friend's victory was cause for satisfaction. Massachusetts politics and the old Free Soil principles of the 1840's seemed to be one now—but the basic irritant had not been eliminated. He warned Adams that "you and I do not much esteem what is called policy—which is generally nothing else but a departure from principle for some delusion or transient advantage." [36]

During the presidential campaign of 1860, Palfrey watched carefully and waited. He attended many Republican meetings and parades, making no effort to speak at them. Palfrey's old Congressional colleagues, Giddings and Root of Ohio, proposed a tour of several midwestern states. The notion, but not the physical hardships, of such "disinterment" intrigued the scholar. After a few days' musing he decided that instilling ancient virtues through the pages of his books was all the contribution he could make.[37]

"Honest Abe seems to be as good as chosen," wrote Anna happily in November. Palfrey never doubted that Lincoln would win, what with three other candidates in the field. He dismissed the Constitutional Unionists as the resuscitators of Websterian compromise long discredited by the events of the preceding decade. The election had sounded the death knell of slavery, wrote Sumner from Washington; Palfrey agreed and greeted the prospect with equanimity, since slavery was the only intolerable evil in the United States. "I am as cool as a cucumber," he replied to the senator, as the nation prepared to cleanse itself in its own blood.[38]

XV ✐

War Against the Slave Power

THE Republican victory in 1860 signaled the start of the customary race for offices. There was no shortage of scoundrels to be turned out for the benefit of patriotic, deserving Republicans. Palfrey saw an opportunity for himself in Lincoln's victory, although he knew he could not merely sit back and be recognized by those newly come to power. Late in January he made a five-day visit to the agitated capital city in search of an appointment. Out of the patronage melée of the secession winter Palfrey emerged with one of the state's most lucrative and desirable offices. How a man without political power could have been so fortunate affords a revealing insight into politics of patronage.

Senator Sumner and Representative Adams, Palfrey's colleagues of Conscience Whig days, were the chief Massachusetts patronage dispensers in Washington. Adams would of course do what he could; Sumner, now ostensibly a friend, had forgiven Palfrey his conduct of 1853, but Palfrey doubted his willingness to help. He was doubly uneasy because Sumner and Adams were then disputing over what policy should be pursued toward the rebellious South. Palfrey, quick to attach importance to the "tone" of social relations, took heart when Sumner greeted him effusively on the Senate floor, and escorted him to the anteroom where he called in half a dozen senators to meet the visitor.[1] But he soon wearied of being part of the anonymity of the Congressional galleries, since former members no longer enjoyed House floor privileges. Shortly before departing, Palfrey sought out Benjamin O. Tayloe, his old Harvard chum. Tayloe, a Virginian, responded

cordially. Palfrey was glad to learn that southern fire-eating
had not vanquished his friend's gentility and sense of hospitality.[2]

Palfrey returned to Massachusetts uncertain of the usefulness of his trip. He had little to rely on but the friendship of
his potential benefactors; there was nothing to do but wait.
He did, however, do his best to further Dana's advancement
by presiding over a Republican meeting in Cambridge, at
which Dana was the principal speaker, and by recommending
him to Sumner as a candidate for federal district attorney.
Hearing that a younger man was pushing hard for the job,
Palfrey, now sixty-five, expressed the concern of the old guard
at being shunted aside; the young man in question could
afford to wait.[3]

That the great secession crisis would blow over without
bloodshed Palfrey never doubted. The calm with which Dana
and Palfrey discussed the situation in the library at Hazelwood astonished Mary Ann, understandably concerned about
her soldier son. When Adams made a speech hoping that war
could be avoided by reasonable men, Palfrey responded with
high praise and a prediction that Adams' oratorical effort
would turn the tide. Late in February, Palfrey stood convinced
that only time, and not too much of that, was needed to heal
the rift. The Peace Convention would fail to present acceptable legislative proposals or constitutional amendments. If true
men in the North held firm, there was nothing a little time
could not cure. Palfrey's opinion reflected the antislavery mind
at work. He could not credit the South with resoluteness, or
even a strong belief in the desirability of the slave system.[4]

With inauguration day fast approaching, Palfrey grew im-
patient, then panicky about an appointment. He forced himself
to importune in terms which his stiff rectitude would have
rejected a few years before, explaining that he had not profited
from the *History*, that his major source of steady income was
Mary Ann's inheritance, and that he would be sixty-nine at

the end of the Lincoln administration. Nor should the past be forgotten: "I bore my share in the burden and heat of the day, when it was a 'day of small things' as to achievement and even prospect, but not small as to labor, annoyance and loss." Adams had it in his power to insure Palfrey "a bright revival of ease and comfort" in his last days. A similar letter to Sumner so embarrassed Palfrey that he asked that it be returned, since "the begging attitude it takes is odious." [5]

Initially, Palfrey hoped for a diplomatic appointment, and to some this seemed an excellent idea. "He is said to be impracticable as a politician," admitted James Freeman Clarke, "but this would not be an objection to a Mission." While in Washington Palfrey mentioned to Sumner his desire for a "minor foreign mission," even specifying Belgium as the proper assignment. But Sumner demurred, and revealed that with another Boston historian, John Lothrop Motley, slated for a diplomatic post, it would not do. When inauguration day brought no word, Palfrey did not share Anna's enthusiasm over the accession of "honest old Abe." He found his own affairs too engrossing.[6]

Sumner was the key man. Lincoln, thinking the senator from Massachusetts might be miffed at the appointment of Adams as minister to Great Britain, decided to give Sumner a virtually free hand in state appointment. "I cannot forget your life," Sumner assured Palfrey, "and I long to serve you!" But the problem was to find a proper post. The place-seeker rushed to disclaim high pretensions; any place "honorable and remunerative" would do.

Complaining of this "weary work," Palfrey doggedly followed newspaper reports which alternately raised and dimmed his hopes. The question of an appointment absorbed all his attention: "May I not be pensioned? The stake for my dear family is great." [7] Happily for the Palfreys, Charles Sumner was at the moment obtaining a place which would entail, not an ocean voyage, but a short move across the Charles.

The Boston postmastership, with its control of 127 clerk-ships, was a position well worth the avarice of hungry politicians. This plum was not to be disposed of lightly. Senator Sumner queried his lieutenant Frank Bird: "Who *under all circumstances* should be Postmaster of Boston? Politicians, editors are competitors. . . . Write me frankly." Palfrey had put in his first bid for the office only two weeks after Lincoln's election, but when he saw Sumner in January they barely mentioned the place. On the same day he wrote to Bird, Sumner received Charles Francis Adams, Jr., and noted playfully that in the Boston post office he had "drawn an elephant," difficult to dispose of. Young Adams quickly suggested Palfrey to Sumner as the ideal man. Later the elder Adams supported Palfrey's claim at a dinner with Sumner.[8]

Bird's response was equally encouraging for Palfrey. All earnest Republicans would be satisfied, in an act showing that the party could have the courage to do the decent thing. As for caviling from the little politicians and editors, they would soon quiet down during the dispensation of patronage. Most men had forgotten and forgiven the hurts of 1853. Bird was not the calculating politician in giving this advice. He knew that, politically, such an appointment would need much explanation behind the scenes, but "such a recognition of Mr. Palfrey's service to our cause would be a proud thing for any man to do. . . . When I remember '46, '47 at Springfield—'49 to '51, my heart is stirred." [9]

Old loyalties aside, Palfrey had half a dozen rivals for the job.[10] The strongest challengers, Charles A. Phelps, Otis Clapp, and L. K. Pangborn, were all loyal and active party workers. This job meant political bread and butter, a pro-Pangborn man bluntly reminded Sumner. Pangborn was a poor man who had worked hard for the party; Palfrey lived well and had contributed nothing to the Republican victory. Old Times be damned! William Claflin, a future governor of the Commonwealth, thought Palfrey should get another, less important, job. The appointment of New Hampshire's

Amos Tuck to the office of Naval Officer made the local politicians touchy. "This is a local office," Claflin warned, "if we are to have a party in Boston we must appoint somebody who *represents the party*." He urged further consultation with the Massachusetts Congressional delegation.[11]

While these and similar accounts of political realities came to Sumner's desk, many regarded Palfrey's appointment as something pleasantly reminiscent of the "good old days" when solid qualifications for office determined selections. Lamented Howe: "Our politicians are *below* the average of morality in the community and they are getting worse. This custom of rewarding party hacks with office is a fertile source of evil." Another friend urged Palfrey's appointment as a proof to Massachusetts that respectable men were not proscribed politically, and Bird, wishing to clear the air stale with the breath of job-hunting hacks, pleaded for an appointment that would "assure the community that the reign of the subterraneans and the pigmies is over. Give us some one who is not in the market!" Palfrey, true to his character, thought a postal appointee should know something about post-office affairs. He suggested that Sumner, then in the middle of the secession crisis, consult the *Congressional Globe* and read Palfrey's 1848 speech on the postal system! His patrician friends joined the chorus, citing Palfrey's supposed "masterly business and administrative talent." [12]

Governor John A. Andrew led the opposition to Palfrey's appointment. He made it clear that he thought Palfrey politically unstable, a man whose "crochets" might prove embarrassing. "Good and Noble Dr. Palfrey, with his freaks and whims and his qualms, would tip over the party in six months," the governor warned. "Send him to Spain, or Turkey:—where they have no politics." Andrew had two other men in mind, but when he learned that reports of his anti-Palfrey activities had reached Washington, he became fearful of antagonizing Sumner, who would make up his own mind in any case, and explained he would be happy with any "manifestly good man." [13]

Palfrey's agony ended late in March. Sumner informed Postmaster General Montgomery Blair of his choice, "after the most careful consideration"—John Gorham Palfrey. The fact that the appointee lived in Cambridge, not Boston, presented a short-lived difficulty, but Palfrey made immediate plans to move to Boston. On the 26th, after a two-hour talk with Sumner, Blair took the recommendation to the cabinet session. Next day he returned to Sumner's room bearing the recommendation endorsed "Appoint, A. L." The news reached Cambridge by telegraph, informing Palfrey he would have to post bonds of $40,000. Sparks and Peleg W. Chandler came forward as the first of many volunteers ready to supply the money. [14]

In naming Palfrey, Sumner expected reverberations from Boston. But he knew he could silence the dissidents with little effort. Criticism from editors who had been pushing their own candidates quickly evaporated. Sumner had urged that Dana, soon to receive the federal district attorney's post, prepare the pro-Palfrey case for publication: "Dwell on his business talent; his success as Secy. of the Commonwealth; his industry; his order; his knowledge; his conscientiousness; his ability in details; and all those things which will make him the best Postmaster Boston has ever known. . . . A few positive articles in season will fix public opinion." Edward L. Pierce, eager to serve Sumner, visited several Boston editors, and all was smooth. [15]

The appointment of such an unlikely candidate as Palfrey presented a puzzle. Boston Republicans, close to Sumner's interest, had urged upon him the necessity of keeping a close watch over the post-office patronage if he wished to control the party in Boston. Palfrey, with no power of his own would be a perfect political satrap, incapable of giving any trouble beyond the embarrassment of an occasional display of excess rectitude. The venerable figurehead would do nicely, and would be more easily handled than a younger, energetic politician. To Dana, Sumner could speak of Palfrey's past services to The Cause, but with Andrew, he wasted no words: "Would not his name give satisfaction all around and eclipse others?" [16]

The appointment meant moral and monetary salvation. Palfrey counted for something again. A few hours after the telegram arrived from Washington the first office seekers were at Hazelwood. Palfrey's bearing and disposition changed at once. No worries now about fatigue, or attacks of melancholia. It was like the old Congressional times, with each mail heavy with correspondence. "He seems already many years younger," reported Frank, "his appetite comes back, his whole manner changes—and he chirps like a cricket." Three days before the attack on Fort Sumter, Palfrey received his commission. [17]

*   *   *

Once in office, Palfrey sought to prove that his friends had not been mistaken about his administrative abilities. The office had a bureaucratic life of its own and the new postmaster moved cautiously, not wishing to disrupt established procedures without careful study. Mail agents, a constant source of worry, proved lax in their duties, but Palfrey limited himself at first to reprimands. The public did not get off so easily. When the new postmaster had the clear authority of a postal regulation behind him, enforcement proceeded precisely according to the law. If hardship resulted, as when Palfrey prohibited bulk mailings without prepaid postage stamps, he would do no more than request a ruling from the department. Sometimes department regulations made Palfrey unpopular. In mid-1862, when the shortage of coins caused widespread use of postage stamps for change, Washington decided to restrict sale of stamps. Palfrey found that a five-dollar daily limit per person ineffective because businessmen sent several messengers to the office. This made necessary a further reduction of the limit to fifty cents. "Complaints have been less than I anticipated," he told his chiefs, "though sufficiently annoying." [18]

From the beginning, the problem of patronage was a primary concern. He learned that his clerks feared that he might make a clean sweep. With appeals for jobs frequent and insistent, Palfrey found this aspect of business wearing, but he did not yield to partisan demands for wholesale firings. Some misjudged their man by hinting about salary kickbacks; one desperate person offered his first quarter's pay for a place. Sumner's recommendations demanded attention and prompt action. Palfrey did not have to be told how to show his sense of gratitude. When Sumner endorsed an application: "This is a very strong case and I recommend it most cordially," Palfrey responded at once.[19]

Pressure on the new postmaster was lightened by enlistment of clerks after Lincoln's call for volunteers. The first time a departing clerk asked if he would later have a place, Palfrey impulsively assured him that if he were still postmaster the clerk would have nothing to fear. But upon reflection Palfrey realized that such requests, sure to mount when the clerk told his fellows, could bring about an unmanageable situation. The collector of customs advised Palfrey to make no further pledges, since the circumstances at the time of mustering out would have to determine his conduct. From then on Palfrey curbed his patriotic inclinations.[20]

With the country locked in battle with the Slave Power, Palfrey was acutely conscious of the need to keep the Confederates from using the United States mails. Palfrey relished this aspect of his job, since it meant a break in office routine and gave him a sense of participation in the struggle. Two months after war began, several businessmen requested that foreign mail addressed to their southern agents be transferred to them. Palfrey refused and sent the offending correspond-

ence to the Dead Letter Office in Washington. No quarter to
the Slave Power! He also warned express companies that
agents who received letters to be carried to or from the "so
called Confederate States" would be arrested. Most of these
alarms concerned innocuous personal letters or imaginary spy
scares. Palfrey's only real contact with rebel mail came when
bags arrived from Fort Warren, the army prison in Boston
harbor. But wartime fervor could be useful in patronage
matters. Cleaning out Democratic clerks (on orders from the
Republican leaders) took on new dignity, with a postmaster
convinced that the men dismissed were "positively and actively
disloyal and attached to the rebel interest." [21]

Unhappily, the pleasures of "counter-espionage" yielded
precedence to Washington's demands for economy. Early in
1862, the department sent its chief clerk to inspect Boston
operations. In a report which Palfrey knew would cause
trouble, the inspector concluded that retrenchment could save
$6,500 a year. After several days of attempting to agree upon
the expendable jobs, Palfrey had had enough of this "very
tiresome . . . business of Post-Office reform." He took an early
train for Washington to protect his clerks' and his own interests.

In the capital Palfrey conferred with John A. Kasson of
Iowa, the first assistant postmaster general. The two men
reviewed the proposed economies item by item and agreed
that too much had been demanded of the Boston office. They
scaled down the economies to a manageable $3,000. Palfrey
delightedly offered to show that his office could be "reformed"
to that amount, and at the same time revealed his almost complete lack of patronage control. With one exception, there was
"no one employed in this office in whom I have the slightest
personal interest. I was acquainted with one of them before
I came into the office." Further Palfrey could save money by
dispensing with his chief clerk. He claimed this would increase
efficiency since he would deal directly with his section heads.[22]

Although the department had ordered the elimination of some jobs and a reduction of payroll, Palfrey keenly felt the needs of his clerks and carriers. The postmaster had discretionary power to reduce clerks' salaries. This was a power Palfrey used gingerly, often resorting to a reduction instead of dismissing an offender. Later, with more confidence in himself and less confidence in his employees' hard-luck stories, he extended the reduction scheme to carriers. The usual cut was five dollars a month (the average wage was $50–$60 monthly), and by 1864 when economy was no longer taken so seriously, Palfrey gave the five dollars to an especially deserving clerk.

Requests for better pay for his workers filled Palfrey's departmental correspondence. After the first economy drive had passed, increased business and wartime inflation meant that not only were more men needed, but that payroll had to be raised. As always, prices ran ahead of wages. In report after report, Palfrey stressed these facts to his superiors, since many clerks earned less than $500, and very few made much more than $800:

Boston is an extremely expensive place to live in. For a very modest house of twenty-two feet front, and not in one of the choicest streets, I pay a rent of $1000, and the humbler tenements which clerks occupy cost more than this compared with the accomodation. I pay for beef from eighteen to twenty-two cents a pound, and for mutton sixteen or eighteen. How often can a clerk earning $500 or $600 a year, after providing shelter and clothing for his family, afford to give them a meat dinner? And what can he be expected to reserve for sickness or other casualty?

He proposed as a matter of business efficiency that no man earn less than $700. Competent men would not stay at the post office for less. Each month that passed made his employees' needs more acute. Late in 1863, Palfrey estimated that it cost one third more to live than it had three years before. Low wages were an invitation to theft since the clerks knew that many letters contained currency. Because Palfrey did not ask for an increase in his own salary of $4,000, he could press the issue. Often he tried the domestic approach on the Washington bureaucrats: "I do not look after my household supplies, but seeing a turkey of moderate size on my table a little while ago, I had the curiosity to inquire about it and learned that the cost was $3.30." When the department finally authorized a raise of 20 percent for the clerks, Palfrey expressed thanks, but reminded Washington that the same "weighty reasons" for raises applied to the carriers.[23]

*　　*　　*

Palfrey's post-office benefactor, Charles Sumner, became his most vexing problem. The senator displayed his usual ability to stir up arguments, and also his compulsive inability to overlook small matters. The first signs of trouble came in October 1862, when a clerk warned Sumner that many of his co-workers opposed his re-election. Sumner sent the letter to Boston with no comment, and Palfrey assured the senator that the informant was "a sort of moon-stricken person, so taken up with spiritualism" that he hardly found time for his work, and that he had invented the charges out of personal spite.[24]

The incident which brought out the worst in Sumner concerned a postal clerk and the senator's franking privilege. Sumner learned that several letters bearing his signature had gone out from Boston, postage due, and convinced himself that this was no mistake, but political spite—a conviction doubtless strengthened by the "moon-struck" letter he had received earlier. Palfrey tried to question the reliability of Sumner's evidence, but the latter retorted gruffly that the man "ought to have been dismissed from the Post-Office before night. Every hour that he remains there affects the standing and honesty of the office. . . . I do not see two sides to the case."

Palfrey played for time, refusing to follow Sumner's orders without further investigation. But he could not help reminding the senator that the tone of his letter was "scarcely suitable to be used to a public officer supposed to be sensible of his obligations." The results of Palfrey's investigation were inconclusive, and on that account he refused to discharge the alleged offender. Anticipating Sumner's wrath, Palfrey swore he would not quarrel whatever the provocation. Sumner would admit of no doubts in the case ("I have known nothing anywhere so flagrant"), yet he claimed he would forget it; there were too many other important things unattended.[25]

But Sumner refused to abandon the demand for the clerk's scalp. Later, when Palfrey rebuffed a job hunter, the man claimed that not only would he denounce Palfrey before the Republican Committee of Boston, but that Sumner had told him to come and say so.[26] Palfrey could laugh this off as the audacity of a desperate man, but he learned next day that Sumner himself had been summoning postal clerks to inquire about the franking incident. For a man unsure of his status, there was only one conclusion: there was an intrigue afoot to oust him, and Sumner was wavering. Despite assurances of confidence from the department, Palfrey nervously queried his close friends. Peleg W. Chandler was hardly reassuring: "So far as Sumner is concerned nothing will surprise me. Unless a man is willing to be chained to his triumphal car, he cannot be sound, in the estimation of him and such as him." [27] Palfrey saw little of Sumner after that, and several months later he was shaken by a curt note. Sumner, whose brother had drowned shortly before, commented on Francis Palfrey's serious and slow-healing war wounds: "I am sorry to hear that Frank is troubled still. But when I think of my poor brother's case Frank's seems very trifling." [28]

The franking incident was but one of several disagreeable encounters with Sumner. In the fall of 1864 Sumner repulsed an invitation, saying that since Palfrey had been avoiding him for two years, his self-respect would not permit a visit. In fact, Palfrey had seen the senator on several occasions and

called on him on many more. But Sumner would not be
reasoned with. A meeting at the Boston Anthenaeum ended
abruptly when Sumner turned away muttering angrily about
false friends. Palfrey unburdened himself to Dana, and noted
sadly: "It is the madness of the moon. His nervous system is
sadly disordered." [29]

*   *   *

Whatever the annoyance of his relationship with the senator,
Palfrey willingly accepted them as the price for retaining his
lucrative office. Though the work at the office was not "dignified or pleasant in its details," the Palfreys lived in a style
unknown to them for twenty years. Wartime wealth was
everywhere evident in Boston. Shops had no trouble selling
luxuries; fine carriages and livery were common; many made
a sport of ostentatious spending. Even charities received increased donations. "I think you would be surprized at the
aspect of things in Boston," Palfrey told Adams, now minister
to Great Britain. And Adams would have witnessed nothing
more surprising than his friend's financial status. When he took
office, Palfrey had rented a house on Boston's Chestnut Street.
As if to indemnify Mary Ann for her patience, an increase in
family income, hardly imaginable a few years before, accompanied the return to Boston. When he closed out his first year
as postmaster, he could hardly believe his luck. At each succeeding Thanksgiving, he felt more and more indebted to the
Lord. "My regular pursuits are agreeable, and I earn, much
more easily than is allowed to most people, more money than
we have an occasion to spend. And this is as unspeakable, as
it is a novel, comfort." With a salary of $4,000 itself enough
for comfortable living, Palfrey struck a gold mine on his
commissions from the sale of revenue stamps. Wartime taxa-
tion through the required use of such stamps brought additional profits to the sales agents, and Postmaster Palfrey occupied a strategic position. He needed little capital, since

banks loaned readily with postage stamps as security. In 1864
earnings on stamp commissions exceeded twice his regular
salary, giving him a total income of over $12,000. Even the
inflation did not keep Palfrey from living the good, material
life. Instead of appeals to friends for money, Palfrey could
now pay old debts. The *nouveau riche* of the war prosperity
was an object of scorn, but the fact remained that "never was
money so easily earned," and Palfrey benefited as much as
anyone.[30] Throughout the war Palfrey could rejoice both in
the rebirth of his financial freedom and in the death of the
Slave Power.

*   *   *

The war for the Union was to Palfrey a moral struggle
between virtue and vice, between Puritan New England and
the Plantation South. To the extent that Ohio, Michigan, and
other western states rallied to the Union standard, they
demonstrated how deep had been the penetration of New
England principles. Palfrey clung to this view with patriotic
tenacity. Early in the war, for example, a newspaper referred
to Confederate general Mansfield Lovell as Massachusetts-
born. Palfrey countered that while the man did come from a
Bay State family on his father's side (and "the more is the pity
and the shame"), his mother, of Hudson, New York, had had
the bad sense to raise him in the District of Columbia. This
rebel, Palfrey thought, was "one of the many sad examples of
the effect of education and residence in the national capital to
overcome the generous tendencies of wholesome Massachusetts blood." [31]
     With two sons of military age, one of them a graduate of
West Point, the Palfrey family's involvement in the war
would doubtless go beyond the seizure of rebel mail at the
Boston Post Office. Lieutenant John Palfrey, stationed at
Portland, Maine, soon received orders to proceed to Fortress
Monroe on the Potomac.

As new regiments formed daily John almost made the jump from lieutenant to colonel at once. Governor Andrew suggested that if he resigned his regular commission, he would get a command in the Massachusetts volunteers. Palfrey advised his son to accept nothing less than a regiment, for "with a half-baked Colonel, you could not be sure of doing yourself justice," [32] and he took up the negotiations. A resignation was out of the question, but if the Corps of Engineers granted John a leave of absence, Andrew had any number of regiments in need of competent officers. Palfrey saw the governor several times, and sent many letters to Washington. Secretary of War Simon Cameron put an end to the plan, however. Sumner, who had pushed for the leave, confided that Commanding General Winfield Scott had the highest regard for John, but the resignation of southern officers had created a particular shortage of engineers.[33]

While family fears centered upon the professional soldier, Frank saw action first. As a result of his militia service, Frank became lieutenant colonel of the Twentieth Massachusetts, the "Harvard Regiment." Many of the officers were Harvard graduates, although the commanding officer, William R. Lee, was a West Pointer from Boston. With the regiment encamped south of Boston, news of Bull Run came to shock the North from its dreams of a bloodless punitive expedition which would erase the stain of rebellion. Gloom and humiliation overcame Palfrey. Perhaps the infusion of "wholesome Massachusetts blood," when such regiments as the Twentieth reached the lines, would remedy the situation. The men, equipped with gaudy, gray overcoats and new British Enfield rifles, felt they were ready for anything. When asked if his regiment had everything it needed, Lee retorted: "My regiment, sir, came from Massachusetts." [34]

Illusions about Massachusetts invincibility went up in the smoke of Ball's Bluff. Frank Palfrey's introduction to war proved a fearful lesson for the neophyte regiment. The inflated hopes of the Twentieth and their fathers drowned with many of the men in the bloodied water of the Potomac, as the Union troops fled across the river. Colonel Lee was one of several officers captured by the rebels, leaving Frank the regiment's commanding officer. Much as Palfrey desired his son's advancement, this carnage seemed too high a price to pay. All Palfrey could muster in the way of fatherly advice to a son after his first battle was the mildewed exhortation of the home front about Trust in God and Dry Powder.[35]

War enthusiasm was easily sustained in Boston, but the men in the Maryland and Virginia mud knew better. The city might go wild in welcome for Captain Wilkes, the captor of Confederate emissaries Mason and Slidell, but from the "crusaders" at the South came disquieting letters. A month after Ball's Bluff:

> The rain makes me very cross. How precious little people know about soldiering. The mass of mankind do not think about any thing. Of those who think at all, probably the vast majority think that the only sacrifice soldiers make is exposing themselves to the chance of death or wounds in battle, captivity, or sickness in Camp. How far this is from the truth. I don't suppose one tenth part of our army has been in action in all these months, and the percentage of sickness in Camp is not great. It's under five with us, and generally a good way under— People think little of the thousand and one discomforts and privations of every day life. My position is a good one, and there is much to enjoy, but I should like to go back tomorrow, and put my bones down to lawyer's work—wearing decent clothes, living under a roof, seeing some people, reading some books, and making some approach to leading the life of a gentleman.

By February 1862 the understandable dejection of the civilian at war deepened and acquired an added bite:

> You would be surprised to know the bitterness of feeling growing up, as much in the minds and hearts of good Republicans as of others in the Army, against reckless, virulent politicians, and the profligate press. The soldier . . . is not well-pleased at reading the abuse heaped on the officers whom he trusts and honors . . . by nameless men, comfortably cocktailing in all the bar-rooms of Washington.

On the eve of Antietam the feeling of betrayal was complete:

I am getting to be an old soldier now, and I see little reason to think that the end of the campaign is near. When parents get tired of having their children die by thousands in camps and in the field, when all who have any money get tired of paying it for nothing, then the war will be so conducted as to bring victory near, and, with victory, peace, prosperity, and happiness. Thus far, our blood and money have gone in electioneering schemes, and Messrs. Wilson, Sumner, Wade, Andrew, Stanton, &c., have managed matters so as to make the Peninsula a graveyard, every other house a house of mourning, and—to suit themselves. If I could have known a year ago, how things were to be managed, I never would have taken up arms.[36]

Frank's disillusionment with politicians originated in his controversy with Governor Andrew over promotion and charges that his regiment was "slavecatching," or returning runaway Negroes to their Maryland masters. Boston watched the Twentieth closely. Regimental promotions were a favorite topic of conversation, and none more so than the colonelcy, vacant since Lee's capture. When, at the end of 1861, Palfrey journeyed to Camp Benton, Maryland, to present a flag to the regiment from its many friends, he first heard of the slave-catching charges against his son, the same charges which had earlier been made against Lee.[37]

Garrison's *Liberator* and the Boston *Journal* made references to the use of the Twentieth as "blood-hounds." Both Sumner and Andrew picked up the scent. Frank's denial satisfied Sumner, but Andrew used the matter as a pretext for postponing a decision on the command of the regiment. Frank deserved promotion, and the regiment had become restless from this denial of confidence in its acting commander. Frank was especially insulted that Andrew credited the charges without confronting him first, and he asked his father to talk to those in power in Boston and force a quick decision. Palfrey saw Andrew immediately, labeling as nonsense a report that Lieutenant Colonel Palfrey had personally arrested two of the fugitives. Perhaps some of Frank's own officers were acting through jealousy, speculated Palfrey; or Andrew's military secretary might have delusions of front-line glory; or the governor himself might be to blame: "I do not pretend to understand him directly. . . . When I was considerable, [and] he was not, he was my enthusiastic supporter." The fortunes of politics had changed that; Andrew had not only opposed Palfrey's appointment, but paid little attention to him once in office. Despite the governor's previous offer of a regiment for John, the self-conscious Palfrey was willing to see a general scheme to strike at him by punishing his son.[38] Andrew was exasperating. Colonel Lee (now paroled, but not exchanged) asked that Frank succeed him, but the governor would not budge from his wait-and-see policy.

As to the origin of the slavecatching rumors Frank thought the informer (a member of his regiment), was "an atheistical, marriage-despising disciple of Wendell Phillips," but did not name him. Palfrey kept his peace, not interrupting his now-frequent visits to the Emancipation League, until Phillips in a speech in April repeated the charge about a slavecatching Boston lieutenant colonel. Palfrey wrote the short note which customarily begins acrimonious exchanges, but Phillips would not fight because of "the life long respect I have felt for you." The Brahmin abolitionist refused to let misunderstanding grow; he insisted on seeing Palfrey and satisfying him completely that his speech had been an honest mistake.[39]

*   *   *

The disappointments of militia politics had not dampened Palfrey's ardor for the great cause. He showed this in several ways. To Senator Lyman Trumbull of Illinois went congratulations for a speech supporting a bill confiscating rebel property with a bit of autobiography concerning his own anti-slavery political activity a decade before. Palfrey believed the importance of northern grain far outweighed the economic power of southern cotton, and European talk of intervention would come to nothing:

> Statesmen understand that it is well to think twice before quarelling with a nation which has in the field more than a half million of expert and well provided soldiers, and at sea half a thousand well built and well manned ships of war, especially when that nation commands virgin resources, and when it is inspired by one of those *enthusiasms* (fanaticisms, if you like), which a few times in the succession of the ages, have made a harder pushed nation able to remodel the world.

Palfrey was no pacifist. Citing the example of Charles Martel's defeat of Islam at Tours, he believed that many times in human history the fate of civilization—"all the best and good which Divine Providence designed for man"—hinged on the outcome of a war.[40]

As the armies of North and South fought during the bloodiest day of the war at Antietam, Palfrey waited for news of the Twentieth. The dread, always half-expected, news came on September 19, two days after the battle. Frank had been "slightly" wounded.[41] The day after the news arrived, Palfrey left for the South to find his son.

Washington was all confusion. Palfrey went blindly from office to office, but no one could give him any information about the removal of the Twentieth's wounded. Two days of anxiety followed, each day increasing the chance that Frank was one of the two thousand Union dead. Finally, word came that Frank was alive, convalescing in the Philadelphia home of merchant Morris Hallowell, whose two sons had also been wounded in the fight. Hallowell had better luck than Palfrey in finding his boys, and with field hospitals overcrowded, he decided to take Frank along. The generous act had saved Frank's life; "he got Frank out of a camp hospital, and over the road, in the face of obstacles which only Quaker stubborness would surmount."[42]

Frank's wound (grape-shot had shattered his shoulder) was

too severe to allow a move from Philadelphia. He lost much blood, and the doctors debated the advisability of amputation. Hallowell insisted that on no account should the man be moved while any risk of complications existed. Hallowell declined Palfrey's offer to pay the expenses of Frank's seven-week stay in Philadelphia.[43]

One positive result of the Antietam action was Lincoln's Preliminary Emancipation Proclamation, released five days later. Palfrey greeted it approvingly, though he saw many problems ahead before emancipation would have any meaning. Military defeat of the rebels was but one of the problems. Yet he rejected the pessimism of some of his friends on the extent of "social derangements" sure to come. His son John, however, was not pleased by the change in the status of many Negroes. John, now stationed at Ship Island, Mississippi, and on his first visit to New Orleans, rode in trains filled with Negro officers. The West Pointer complained that although he was a good abolitionist, the sight of so many "black and yellow men who very likely could not sign their names" and who outranked him was hard to bear.[44]

When New Orleans fell to the Union forces the Boston Palfreys imagined that their erring Louisiana relations would welcome the occupation in the spirit of repentant sinners. Mary Ann blithely instructed John to visit: "If you see Brother Henry or any of the family do give our love to them." In December John went to the city, not as a conqueror, but as an invalid. He stayed at the home of a Union officer while fighting a fever. Learning that his uncle Henry had returned to the city on parole after his capture and lived a few doors away, he wrote to him, "it being Christmas time, and Secesh feeling having a little subsided here." Henry made no reply, but a week later a Mr. Blanc, Henry's son-in-law, came to call, apologizing for his father-in-law's silence. Blanc explained that Henry would not visit a man who had come down to fight him. Blanc was so friendly that John invited him to call again, if he were so inclined, and sent regards to Cousin Maria. Here the visitor paused, and indicated that his wife's response would match her father's. "I had a good mind," John recalled, "to get up and kick him, and tell him I would not go near his secession shanty for $50,000." [45]

Palfrey did not react harshly, as did his wife and daughters. Looking for silver linings, he claimed to be glad that relations had not been restored prematurely. But should he see Henry, Palfrey told John, he wished his brother to know he had written twice since the war began. "He has an excellent heart, and I know it gives him pain not to seek you." [46] Palfrey had never been a good hater.

Confederate deserters finally brought news of William Palfrey. His plantation was a total loss. The armies battled several times on his land; his barns and fences had long since been burned for firewood; all the slaves were gone. John could be philosophical: "I pity the old gentleman, but I think it is rather cool the universal expectation these people have that they will be secured in their property by our little army." Palfrey did not take the news so casually. He asked John to send along news of his brothers. The memories of his good relations with Henry would not die; the animosities of the hour, he was sure, would.[47]

*   *   *

The Boston postmastership was not a full-time job, so Palfrey tended to affairs which ranged from writing history to protecting his sons' interests. During his talks with Frank about returning to the army, Palfrey had the wild idea of asking Governor Andrew for a regiment for himself. But his mind had not slipped so far as to entertain that thought for more than a moment. Palfrey felt some guilt over having only one son at the front, and in 1864 he paid $125 to hire a substitute, Lewis Williams, Private, 53rd United States Colored Infantry.[48]

Throughout the war Palfrey maintained his correspondence with his British friends of 1856. Joseph Parkes, former M.P. and an influential behind-the-scenes figure in British politics, valued Palfrey's views on American affairs, and he replied with frequent and massive letters on Anglo-American relations. Palfrey thought so much of them that he sent copies to Secretary of State Seward. As reports of British sympathy for the Confederacy increased, Palfrey attempted to combat the spread of southern ideas by sending reprints of his Slave Power pamphlets to prominent Englishmen. John Stuart Mill's acknowledgement particularly pleased Palfrey:

Had but such a book as yours been in the hands of our people at the commencement of the present contest, I think that it would have saved many from disgracing themselves and their country by sympathising with the atrocious slaveholding conspiracy. . . .

I feel the warmest sympathy with the tone and spirit of your book, and the highest admiration for the band of men of whom you are one, who founded and led the Anti Slavery party in the United States in still worse times than these. And I have found myself often exclaiming, as I read your book, that the noble Commonwealth of Massachusetts will yet redeem America and the world.[49]

Palfrey's official position and, even more, the salary and commissions it gave him allowed for full participation in the social life of Boston. Leading politicians came to dine, as did Harvard student Robert Todd Lincoln, the "Prince of Rails." Nobody took Palfrey seriously on political matters, but he was a useful chairman at testimonial banquets when Republican unity, strained by the piebald nature of the coalition of 1860, threatened to dissolve. One such delicate affair was a dinner for General Benjamin F. Butler on his return from New Orleans, since many Bostonians shared the opinion of the general held by the New Orleans rebels. While Palfrey was in a sense above politics—outside of it, rather—his office remained political; the Republican state treasurer did not forget to assess him for a $500 "voluntary contribution" to the campaign fund of 1864.[50]

The happiest aspect of the wartime feeling of amity was the burial of most of the old hatreds stirred during the Free Soil days. Although Eliot and Everett died in those years without reconciling, Palfrey was no longer the enemy of the Hale family, or of Winthrop. "So pray let us let the past go," proclaimed Edward Everett Hale. Palfrey wanted nothing more. The past had taken care of itself in this Boston of the 1860's, a Boston composed exclusively of abolitionists and men who claimed they had been "free soilers from the start." [51]

In the year that saw the southern Slave Power finally crushed, John Gorham Palfrey became the president of the American Unitarian Association, a selection which contrasted happily with his church's earlier neglect. The conclusion of four years of civil war found the Palfrey family prospering. Boston sons were breveted brigadier generals; Frank was about to marry a Boston heiress, and several textile corporations were already seeking John's services. Mary Ann, happy in Boston, had three daughters for company, and the ladies seemed reconciled to spinsterhood, "fixtures in our house." [52] Palfrey had survived patronage squalls and Sumner's paranoic behavior. Money problems seemed as far in the past as the data for the *History of New England*. The only cause for regret was Frank's wound, but the sacrifice could be balanced with "the vast blessing of the abolition of the horrible pest and curse of slavery,—a blessing worth the great woes which its acquisition has cost us."

With the Confederacy expiring in April 1865, Boston strained to hear the news of final victory. Word of Lee's surrender came on April 11; that night Palfrey stayed late at the Union Club. But the celebrants were soon chastened. The morning of the 15th brought reports of the "horrible Washington tragedy" of the night before. Two days later Palfrey sat on the stage of Faneuil Hall as Boston mourned the death of Lincoln, the "wise, courageous, humane, and patriotic statesman," as Palfrey described America's secular saint.[53]

XVI

The Celebrated New Englander

THE months immediately following the war were busy ones for Palfrey. Many matters occupied his time, particularly those concerning his family, North and South. Family fortunes in Massachusetts and Louisiana rose and fell with the state of each section's war effort. While Palfrey had been relieved of money worries, his brothers were struggling to re-establish a semblance of their prewar world. In contrast, the prospects of the northern Palfreys seemed limitless.

The first order of business was civilian employment for John. The available job, that of superintendent of Lowell's Merrimack Mills, carried with it a salary in the neighborhood of $5,000. Not only would John display his talents in a way which commanded an initial high price, but who could tell of the future? "The money-coining treasury-ship of one of the corporations" John learned from his impressed father, "looms dimly in the distance." [1] If Palfrey recalled his earlier denunciations of the Massachusetts cotton interests, he did not bother John with retrospection. The war had made Cotton and Conscience one. With John then in Texas, Palfrey negotiated with the mill owners. The army was reluctant to give up its regular officers, particularly engineers. [2] Military red tape forced a hurried trip to Washington. Palfrey went to Secretary of War Edwin M. Stanton, who received him graciously despite his, Stanton's, reputation for irascibility. Though Stanton made no commitment then, the engineers found a replacement for John in September. John proved more than capable at his work; his responsibilities and income both increased at a geometric rate. And Frank, after some faint attempts to practice law, married a girl who inherited a fortune.

"Never did a closing year find me . . . so prosperous," observed Palfrey gratefully, "One son agreeably married; the other home from the perils of war and eligibly established near us; my daughters good, affectionate and happy. . . . And so farewell to my good friend *1865*." [3]

*   *   *

Despite the wartime breakdown of relations between the northern and southern branches of the family, Palfrey refused to allow the bitterness to fester. As soon as the war ended he sounded William out. His attempt at kindness took a specific form, an offer of $2,000. If William could not respond in friendship, he need not answer: "I shall understand your silence. And it will be only with sorrow."

William's reply was a masterpiece. It provided him with an opportunity to vent his grievances, placing the blame for his calamities where he thought it rested, while at the same time he kept the door ajar for reconciliation. Gorham's hesitancy offered the point of departure:

I beg, my dear brother, you will dismiss from your mind, these doubts and misgivings.—my breast was never the abode, for any length of time, of hateful feelings towards any one; and now age and recent severe misfortunes have so chastened and subdued my spirit that unnatural resentments can find no place there.—However antagonistic our positions are in regard to the public topics of the day, however different have been the results of these positions to you and to me, I feel myself reminded that

"The same fond mother bent at night,
O'er each calm sleeping brow."

Although Gorham's politics had reflected discredit on his brothers and on the memory of John Palfrey, he was forgiven. William then detailed his sufferings during "a war that I did my utmost in a humble way to prevent." His lot became invasion, confiscation of property and disease.

And now let me ask, who has been benefitted by all this: the South has been destroyed, but has the North gained any thing?—Have the unfortunate Creatures, whose condition it has been the pretext to improve, have they gained by it? Let their present destitute, squalid condition answer that question.

William contrasted the confusion among former masters and slaves, with his prewar paternalism and concern. Though his "poverty and privation" were undeniable, he would not take the money Gorham offered. The Divine Provider, he reminded the former clergyman, could always be relied upon.

And now farewell my brother—when you sit down to a full and dainty meal or lay your head on your soft downy pillow, (long may these comforts be yours) do not let your thoughts revert to the condition of those who are reduced by these cruel events to the slender crust and the hard couch of poverty. Shut your eyes and close your recollections to the slow, snake-like progress with which these fiendish [abolitionist] theories have crept to their final accomplishment, and then you will sleep the sounder, and eat with a better appetite.[4]

Mary Ann did not see William's indictment. Her husband sent only extracts of the letter to their Nahant summer retreat, for fear of another explosion among the womenfolk. Palfrey was still determined to regain William's friendship ("I cordially recognize your integrity, conscientiousness, honor, and humanity"), and to break the ice with Henry, still unheard from although he had passed through Massachusetts early in 1865.[5]

Gorham got his chance to help when William sought the restoration of his civil rights. The mild Johnson Reconstruction program of speedy restoration and restitution of political rights offered some hope to William, who was to sit in the state Senate at the coming session of the legislature. To do so required a presidential pardon. The necessity of purging himself of treason against the United States was hard to accept, but ex-Confederates possessing over $20,000 of taxable property had to obtain a pardon before holding public office. "If I were to be asked what was my guilt or the nature of it I should be at a loss to answer," complained William. He had opposed secession, but Yankee invasion had to be met with resistance.[6] Word that the pardon had been granted came just as Gorham was about to leave for the capital to rescue the application from bureaucratic limbo. William was appreciative, but said he felt like the husband constantly acccused of infidelity by his wife, who agreed to confess to end the persecution.[7]

"And now will you permit me to introduce a rather delicate subject?" asked William in May 1866, referring to Henry. With old age upon them, William thought "it would be but natural at least, that we should (metaphorically speaking) go out of the world hand in hand, harmoniously, as we came into it." Henry was willing to see Gorham "as of old," but would not make the first overture. He would be at Niagara Falls that summer, and wanted Gorham as the victor to take the initiative; "there is certainly water enough in the Falls to wash out all animosity." [8]

Gorham responded immediately with a friendly letter to his estranged brother. Henry invited him to visit the Falls, adding, "The unhappy and unnatural Civil War is now terminated and the ladies of my family (like myself) have assumed the duties of loyal citizens." They finally met in September when Henry canceled plans for a European trip and passed through Massachusetts on his way to a homeward-bound steamer. Gorham went to meet him at Springfield, and the two men came to terms with each other and the past. "Both our tongues worked vigorously," reported Gorham happily. "We were very glad to see each other." [9]

A few days later news came of Henry's death. The *Evening Star*, four days out of New York, foundered in heavy seas off the Florida coast. Over 250 persons died, inclduing Henry, his wife, and two children. The tragedy, so soon after the reconciliation at Springfield, helped bring some of the members of the family closer together. Henry's surviving children found solace in the brothers' meeting. Henry's son George mused: "It seems as though he had some foreknowledge of events, in that he arranged all his affairs here before leaving and was suffered to meet you again." [10] Gorham's only regret was that he had gone to Springfield alone. His wife and daughters still considered Henry an unreconstructed rebel and would not travel to greet him.

William continued to write. Although the advent of Military Reconstruction gave him more than enough to grumble about, he suppressed most recriminations. He had predicted calamity in 1867, but then allowed himself a cautious optimism the next year. That summer, although troubled by a heart condition, William made a northern trip, visiting Gorham for three weeks. Mary Ann was not impressed by her brother-in-law, but she silently tolerated his pro-southern remarks. The case of Henry's son George, who happened to be in Boston at the time, was different. Henry's death had not erased the memory of the New Orleans snub. Although John reminded his sisters that "the house is Father's and not ours," Mary Ann and Anna would not relent. Palfrey had to meet his nephew in Boston and leave a note explaining why he could not invite him to Hazelwood.[11]

Back in Louisiana by September, William reported an improving situation; crops were abundant, and there were no cases of yellow fever near him. He had hopes that the "relentless oppression" of Reconstruction would not last. Two months later he died.[12]

* * *

In 1865, when the war was moving into its bloody concluding stage, Palfrey had been as much concerned about his ability to keep the postmastership as with the fortunes of

Union generals. His liking for the job had not increased; the petty details was anything but exhilarating. But at least the quarterly household accounts no longer provided occasions for melancholia.[13]

Would the volatile Sumner support the reappointment? Palfrey listened fearfully to rumors of removals with a credence bordering on masochism. Every windblown straw, favorable or unfavorable, provided the basis for doubt. Palfrey asked his friends for help. Peleg W. Chandler reassured him all was well, adding that Palfrey ought to take Sumner's temperamental pyrotechnics in stride. Bird visited Washington and cautioned that Sumner, sensitive about having less political power at the moment than he thought he deserved, was unhappy over Palfrey's inquiries to third parties. The Boston post office was a matter strictly between Sumner and the appointee.[14]

That was in February 1865. Two months later Lincoln was dead and Andrew Johnson became president. Palfrey's only contact with him had been in 1848, when Johnson had taunted him in Congress with the question about a Negro marrying into the Palfrey family. The incident, forgotten by all but Palfrey, was the last thing in the president's mind. The Boston post-office patronage was not to be disturbed, not yet. William Dennison, the new postmaster general, approached Sumner to learn if he wished any change, noting that Palfrey had the confidence of Boston merchants and most of the politicians including Henry Wilson.[15] Sumner replied tersely at the end of June: "I desire the commission to be renewed." [16]

Palfrey had more cause to worry about President Johnson than the volatile senator. The rift between Johnson and the Congressional Radicals made Palfrey's tenure precarious, and fear of removal prompted him to establish his revenue stamp counter in a room next to the post office. Rumors of impending removal found their way into Boston newspapers. They included reports that a discharged army officer would be appointed. Palfrey, who had made it his policy to hire only veterans as new clerks, countered with details of his sons' wartime service. In December 1865, Maine Senator William P. Fessenden asked the president point-blank if Palfrey was to go. Johnson said he had no reason to change, that he knew Palfrey well, having served in Congress with him.[17]

Despite assurances, Palfrey knew that each month might be his last. Sumner remained outwardly calm about the alleged danger: "The Boston Post Office is considered, according to the common phrase a 'piece of patronage' belonging to the Senator who resides in Boston." An anonymous writer, claiming to be a survivor of the Confederate prison, Andersonville, boasted that 50,000 veterans were ready to keep Palfrey in office by force if necessary. But frequency of removal rumors reduced Palfrey to an attitude of resigned expectancy by the fall of 1866.[18] Profits from stamp sales and his salary had already created an economic cushion which allowed him to wait calmly.

The president settled the matter in the spring of 1867. On April 13, to the surprise of Sumner and his friends, Johnson nominated William L. Burt. Burt was a young lawyer and politician close to the late Governor Andrew, and wartime brigadier general.[19] Bird urged Sumner not to object to the change since the Boston Radicals thought that Burt, far from giving trouble, would be valuable in the showdown with Johnson. The Republican press claimed Burt as a Radical. William H. Gardiner observed wryly to Palfrey: "You are not quite radical enough for the Republican Senate—nor conservative enough for the Republican President." [20]

Palfrey was not sure why he had been replaced. Although he said he would not whine over the decision, he insisted on dragging in the Congressional incident in 1848, as well as the hostility toward Sumner. The senator tried to explain it as a move intended exclusively against him. Palfrey admitted he would have liked a year or two more, but contented himself with the idea of continuing the revenue stamp business. Burt objected vehemently in the newspapers, but he was legally helpless to cut Palfrey off from this valuable source of income. Burt then abandoned belligerence and suggested reaching a reasonable compromise. Palfrey ignored him.[21]

Economic independence allowed Palfrey to ease his disappointment through travel. This time he took his daughter Mary on a tour of England and the Continent—an excursion which cost well over $2,000. The trip's highlight was participation in the International Anti-Slavery Conference, which met in Paris in August 1867. Palfrey spoke to the group in French creditably enough to please him, but annoying to William Lloyd Garrison, who had been forced to sit, uncomprehending, through endless addresses in French only to hear his American neighbor join the Gallic chorus.[22] Once again Palfrey found London most attractive. "Like every other true Bostonian," as Henry Adams put it, "he yearned for the ease of the Athenaeum Club in Pall Mall or the Combination Room at Trinity." And the Public Record Office was there, with the masses of documents yet to be studied. Although Palfrey worked hard there were not enough days at his disposal. He could not neglect Mary too much, so he hired a clerk to digest selected documents after he had gone. Once again the "independence" provided by the post office had proved useful. Palfrey returned home by late November, but not unscathed. "He was hurled down by a cab in London, and has an Influenza—" recorded Longfellow, "both bad for a gentleman of seventy." [23]

*   *   *

The loss of the postmastership in 1867 forced Palfrey to take stock of his life. For nearly fifty years he felt he had been taxing his powers "to their utmost force." The time for relaxation had come. He could now read and write at his own pace, and put aside notions of becoming a "mover" in the world. Besides, "a very different world than that which I began in," existed now; a world "much less respectable." Better to sit back and count blessings than to seek the "gratuitous trouble of distressing myself about what I cannot change." These feelings had prompted Palfrey, a year before, to interrupt his *History* for the luxury of autobiography. "A Tragi-Comedy in Several Acts," he called it deprecatingly, and told Adams it was not to be published.[24] His strong desire for vindication in the eyes of moral and resepectable men belies that claim.

Introspection also meant further withdrawal. Winthrop invited him to rejoin the Massachusetts Historical Society, but Palfrey cut off ties with all but charitable societies which required only the payment of dues. While the presidency of the American Unitarian Association did not come under this heading, the pleas of the association's secretary kept Palfrey from stepping down during the middle of his term. In May 1867 the executive board accepted his resignation. Another factor influencing the decision was the appointment of former Transcendentalist sympathizers such as John Weiss to the board in 1866. Palfrey had planned an immediate resignation, but he remained on the board hoping to give it conservative ballast, since the liberal theology of his youth had been all but mastered by a more liberal Unitarianism.[25]

The "errors" of the new Unitarians saddened Palfrey, not only because of the harmful effects of such "irreligion," but because their spread reflected unfavorably upon the generation which had created Boston Unitarianism. There was little future for the older ideas, certainly not in Palfrey's lifetime: "I see only the loose ruins of what I laboured . . . with flattering and exulting hopes to build up." A walk through Boston brought the sight of demolished buildings which had once been Unitarian churches, or what was worse, the sight of such church buildings which had been acquired by Catholics. Even the Brattle Street Church could not survive. At a service in 1869 Palfrey was one of only fifteen persons present. In 1873 the society moved to Back Bay, and struggled on for thirty years more before selling its property to a Baptist church.[26]

Nor was modern infidelity confined to religion. As the fervor of the antislavery crusade ebbed, Palfrey became increasingly disillusioned with the Republican party, but while Andrew Johnson occupied the White House Palfrey suppressed his doubts. Sumner asked him to Washington as his guest to witness a few days' "amusement," as Johnson stood trial in the Senate. Palfrey showed no sympathy for Johnson or concern that an impeachment and conviction might set the precedent for future political purges. Instead he wrote of social triumphs in Sumner's train. The height of Palfrey's giddiness came when he tried to join the vultures hovering around Johnson's carcass. He suggested that after the president's removal Sumner have him appointed postmaster general for the remaining months of the term. The president's acquittal saved Sumner the trouble of replying.[27]

In 1868 Palfrey supported Grant enthusiastically, and the following year he published six hopeful articles in the *Advertiser* called "Let Us Save Peace." The series began with a defense of Radical Reconstruction. Southerners could not, for their own sakes, be allowed to slip from insurrection to self-government. They first had to prove that the secession delirium had worn off. And Palfrey reminded the North that in freeing "the blacks" it was white America which freed itself of complicity in the crime of slavery. Now that three distracted years of conflict between the branches of government were over, peace would come at once if restive southerners woud only join the march of northern progress, with Grant in the lead: "Under his wise and upright administration, it may be reasonably hoped that the business of political jobbers and plotters will languish, and that a renovated and increased public integrity, strength, wealth and wisdom will LET US HAVE PEACE!" [28]

Palfrey made no effort to hide his authorship, and praise from other hopeful Republicans came in steadily. From Washington Henry Adams sent compliments and reservations:

I have read them with much pleasure, although I estimate the influence of our corrupt tendencies at a rather higher rate than you do. How a mere change of administration is to help us, I cannot see, and am rather inclined to think that it will only improve our affairs so far as to make the system endurable, and so blind our people to the necessity of true reform. The idea that democracy in itself, by the mere fact of giving power to the masses, will elevate and purify human nature, seems to me to have now turned out one of those flattering fictions which have in all ages deluded philanthropists.

Yet Palfrey looked forward to Grant's inaugural, an expectation sweetened by the news that Rockwood Hoar was to be attorney general.[29] There were personal expectations as well. The change of administrations might jar loose some office holders in the diplomatic service. Palfrey wished to be considered a candidate for a minor mission, as he informed countless friends and acquaintances.[30]

Political events soon convinced Palfrey that the political Messiah had not arrived. Within five months he wrote Grant off and swung over to the position of the insurgent Liberal Republican movement. Hoar's forced retirement from the cabinet was symptomatic of the malaise prevailing in Washington. By 1870 Palfrey felt that there was little to choose between the "vicious principles" of the Democrats and the "vicious practices" of the Republicans. Grant stood helpless and bewildered, "meaning well in a rude, indistinct way." That year Palfrey declined to vote, hoping that a reduced vote would chasten the party leaders.[31] As the next presidential election approached, Palfrey's opposition to Grant intensified when Henry Wilson became the Republican vice-presidential candidate. He tried to interest state Republicans of Liberal persuasion to seek Grant's withdrawal and the nomination of Charles Francis Adams. The other major candidate, Democratic nominee Horace Greeley, was an eccentric whose trumpet gave off uncertain sounds, and Grant was out of the question since prudent men could not "help place Henry Wilson where there will be one life btween him and the Government of the country." On election day Palfrey did not vote for presidential electors; the "vein of impracticality" was still there.[32]

*   *   *

The final decade of Palfrey's life witnessed a steady mental and physical decline. Consciousness of both these processes made him uneasy, and the "fear of imbecility" drove him to undertake further work in the *History* even though, at times, he found the project a tyrant. To stop altogether, after years of diligent application, argued Palfrey (forgetting his long periods of unproductive brooding), was to invite "decay of the mind" more rapidly than necessary. A serious illness in 1869 had already alerted Palfrey to what might come at any time.[33]

Before retiring into his Cambridge study, Palfrey decided to made what proved to be his final European trip. Not that he thought death was so close as to demand an immediate departure; but once again he wished to investigate primary sources, and his copyist was not qualified to search the documents. The trip became a family gala. Mary Ann vetoed a full Grand Tour, but agreed to go for the summer of 1871, an enormous concession in view of her previous Boston-Cambridge insularity. After all the trip seemed "not much more than going to Nahant or Beverly, after one sets about it." Of course, all the Misses Palfrey accompanied and ministered to their mother, whose health was always "delicate" throughout her ninety-eight-year life span. And to add to Palfrey's pleasure, John left the Lowell mills for a month of continental touring.

Palfrey enjoyed himself enormously. The seventy-five-year-old patriarch showed his clan the sights. And when the females asked for a rest, he ducked into the Record Office for the best diversion of all. The only upsetting sight on the Continent was the thousands of swaggering Prussian troops occupying the French city of Dijon, since the tour coincided with the aftermath of the Franco-Prussian War.[34]

When he returned home, Palfrey had to face a family crisis, Mary's final suitor was deemed unsuitable. Palfrey had several uncomfortable chats with the man, while Mary Ann comforted her daughter with strong, frank words: "On the weighty subject of matrimony . . . I don't think you know how much you have to be thankful for; nor how much you have escaped." [35]

*   *   *

In the final third of his life Palfrey invested all his creativity and most of his energy in historical scholarship. He felt the need to repay New England all it had done for him. His five-volume historical eulogy was a reflection of himself; it had to be written.

Foremost among the *History of New England*'s characteristics, which included diligence, seriousness, and gentility, was its unabashed willingness to judge and censure wrongdoing. Scholarship divorced from morality was a monstrosity. This pedantic amorality, although prevalent among some supposedly reputable historians was nevertheless shocking: "Is humanity never to be spared the woes propagated from age to age by accomplished writers who extol or extenuate villainy practised in the most exalted positions?" Palfrey asked angrily. He considered Carlyle's *Frederick the Great* the worst offender among many, a "most detestably immoral" book, clearly inspired by the "evil one." [36] Such amorality was out of the question in an author like Palfrey, who considered "virtue" the most important word in the dictionary.[37]

"Palfrey always defends whatever the Puritans did," complained an otherwise friendly New Yorker, "and his bias is so great that he seems incapable sometimes of weighing evidence." [38] The bias certainly existed, but it does not follow that Palfrey's *History* contained nothing but Puritan apologetics. He could and often did weigh evidence and discuss the credibility of historical sources with authority.[39] Palfrey believed that whatever was scientific (or logically sound) in history had to do with verification of data. The historian should not "frame justifications for acts which he records," a maxim he often honored in the breach. "But he should endeavour to produce the true explanations of whatever is perplexing." [40]

In many respects the *History of New England* was a history of Massachusetts. Most of the text concerned the Bay Colony, and the character sketches dealt primarily with her sons or those who came from England to rule in Boston. Plymouth, New Hampshire, and the Maine section of Massachusetts were not important enough for detailed treatment. Rhode Island and Connecticut affairs received more space, although the handling was not smooth. They entered the narrative at predictable points, where the reader, after a heavy dose of Massachusetts politics, might wonder about the rest of the area. The overemphasis on Massachusetts brought criticism, but the greater power of the Bay Colony made such handling at least defensible.

Before establishing Boston's dominance Palfrey had two subjects to dispose of: the Indian and the Pilgrim. A savage first chapter grappled with the noble-savage myth. He gave the Indian no quarter, and the benefit of not one doubt. The aborigines were, morally, so much filth and were defiling the North American continent. Fortunately, their only virtue, small numbers, made it simple for the civilized white man to push them aside. "I suppose we must give him up," admitted Longfellow, the creator of Hiawatha, sadly after reading Palfrey, "and the 'noble savage' must become a myth of the imagination!" As for the Plymouth settlers, Palfrey admired their religious fervor, but correctly resisted any impulse to inflate the importance of this small, poor, and socially backward band. They did act forcefully in putting down Merrymount's Thomas Morton, the "witty and knowing, but shiftless, reckless, graceless, shameless rake." Yet Plymouth's contribution was that of example, especially in demonstrating that a properly motivated colony could survive at a time when Virginia's Jamestown settlement "flickered toward extinction." [41]

The event which assured the permanency of English colonization was the Puritan migration of 1828–1830. From Salem and Boston they branched out, establishing the Zion in the Wilderness which was to provide most of what was estimable in the American character. The antislavery moralism of his generation represented to Palfrey only the continuation of Puritan religiosity. The Puritan was a Scripturalist and a moralist, and in his natural opposition to royal pretensions to godhead he was the liberal of his day. [42]

That Puritan liberalism did not include a tolerant spirit troubled Palfrey. But he resolved the problem in terms of a retrospective realism which could have helped him in his own attempts to cope with an imperfect world. Incidents of repressive exclusiveness such as the expulsion of Anne Hutchinson and Roger Williams, and especially the execution of Quakers in Boston, required all the considerable leeway Palfrey willingly granted his ancestors.

Both Hutchinson and Williams were cut from the same cloth. Their theology might vary, but not their spirit of fanatical contentiousness which made them threats to Massachusetts Bay. Palfrey maintained that the exclusion was not solely for religious reasons. Obviously Williams' denial of tenurial rights and the threat to the charter could not be tolerated, and Mrs. Hutchinson's antics were as much a threat to political stability as matters of pure theology. It was a question of security. With much land available, and most of it wilderness, what matter that Roger Williams moved from Salem to Narragansett Bay? This new England firebrand might be a "single-hearted lover of God and men," but he and other troublemakers could not be allowed to tear down the colony's fragile edifice.

The case of the Quakers was a painful exercise in historiographical discomfiture. These willful—all too willful—disturbers of the peace refused to be banished. The confused, allpowerful yet impotent government could do nothing but answer their search for martyrdom with the ultimate severity. Aside from delineating the absolute fanaticism of the victims, Palfrey did not, of course, defend the "sad scene" done in jail with few witnesses. Massachusetts should have admitted defeat at the hands of Quaker pertinacity. They were no real threat, for "their oddities and dreams were proved to be not at all to the taste of the sober mass" of the New England people. Instead of executing them, it would have been better to open "their hospitable drawing-rooms to naked women, and have suffered their ministers to ascend their pulpits by steps paved with fragments of glass bottles." If Winthrop had been alive, perhaps his wisdom woud have seen through the law to the greater wisdom of restraint.[43]

In contrast to the disruptionists, Palfrey found his hero in John Winthrop, the leading architect of the Massachusetts Puritan state. Although he might at times appear overbearing, this Boston Moses did more than any single individual to make the terms of the Cambridge Agreement the guide lines for Puritan success in the New World. "The influence of his genius and character have been felt through seven generations of a rapidly multiplying people." His wise administration was the fruit, and Massachusetts Revolutionary patriotism was the blossom of the Puritan tree.

Consientiousness is not always the writer's best asset. Palfrey's explanations of involved events did not always come gracefully. His prose is, of course, dated for our tastes. The plethora of commas, the constant use of phrases where a word will do, the involved forms ("they did not wholly disrelish"), the Nice-Nellyisms (the Boston massacre was a "sanguinary collision"), all combine to make much of the writing appear opaque. His tangled accounts of colonial boundary disputes were just as dull as any boundary dispute in history. Palfrey knew it, and apologized to the reader, but the *History* was not intended for amusement. One Baltimore reader who admired Palfrey's "subtle power of elaboration," must not have been thinking of the boundary disputes, which even the author was happy to terminate.[44]

The colonies of Connecticut and Rhode Island, so unlike each other in social fabric and religious institutions, allowed a perfect juxtaposition of opposites. The Rhode Island settlement never knew stability in government or traditionalism in religion. They had to learn that social order was inconsistent with runaway individualism: "If the New England settlements had all been 'Providence Plantations' New England would have proved a failure." The colony sinned badly in experimenting with paper money and probably infected Massachusetts with that delusion. But the "Steady Habits" of Connecticut were commendable in every detail. Palfrey imagined a "Connecticut Idyll." Its homogeneity, social sobriety, and relatively equitable property distribution, assured placid and responsible self-government. "Frugality and industry, friends to rectitude and content, secured a comfortable living, . . . and rendered a life of blameless morals easy and attractive." It was the happiest colony.[45]

The heart of the *History* lay in the three volumes covering the span 1628–1689, and published between 1858 and 1864. They culminated in Governor Andros' overthrow in the aftermath of the Glorious Revolution. This was New England's revolution as well. The section secured liberty for itself; not all it wanted, but enough to assure development relatively free from overseas oppression. The struggles of the following century were meant to secure these liberties.

The two volumes which followed were in a sense anticlimax. The Adams clan might praise Palfrey's ability to make sense out of the "extreme barrenness" of New England's history in the first half of the eighteenth century,[46] but the author knew better. The events of that century were too complex for him to master in the two volumes he had not originally intended to write. As his energies flagged, he resorted to longer and longer documentary quotations and inserted a plea for the reader's indulgence in the preface to the last, posthumously published, volume.

Palfrey reserved his greatest scorn for those New Englanders who betrayed the interests of their "country." In particular he singled out Joseph Dudley and Thomas Hutchinson. Not only was Dudley Andros' henchman, but by insinuating himself at court he later returned to govern Massachusetts. He was the symbol of the successful politician, one who "united rich intellectual attributes with a grovelling soul." In a wiser world, such perversion of talents would receive merited scorn. Nor could Hutchinson claim the forgiveness of his injured homeland. He ended his days in the worst way, unsustained by "any consciousness of upright endeavour in behalf of a righteous cause." [47] Although he mentioned no contemporaries by name, it was clear that he had such as Daniel Webster in mind.

These traitors provided Palfrey with materials for his only attempt at periodization. He theorized that there were cycles in New England history of eighty-six-year duration which ended in betrayal. After the beginning of Stuart rule in 1603 first came Dudley's defection of 1689; than Hutchinson's in 1765; and in 1861 the betrayal of the nation by the Slave Power.[48] Though his nativism was guarded and not political, the Irish domination of twentieth-century Massachusetts politics would probably have qualified in Palfrey's mind as a betrayal of ancient New England virtues. In 1947, eighty-six years after the last betrayal Palfrey described, the mayor of Boston, James Michael Curley, began serving a sentence in a federal penitentiary for mail fraud.

"I think of my History of New England with satisfaction," mused Palfrey. "It will never be much read. But I think it will help to keep future students and writers fairly informed, and on the right track." [49] As usual, Palfrey assessed his own work with judicious modesty. Contemporaries who read little if any of it praised the *History* excessively, and for several decades it held its own. Turn-of-the-century students considered this the work of an amateur in history, produced at a time when history was moving haltingly toward professionalization, a valuable regional study. Subsequent disuse came as a result of the rise of liberal historiography and distaste for the Puritan oligarchy, and in the process natural supersession by more modern studies such as Osgood's and Andrews'. Placed in historical context, Palfrey's *History* represents a commendable contribution to a fledgling discipline, a model of intensive and honest research in the available primary sources, at a time when much that passed for history was the product of the author's imagination.

Palfrey looked backward for precepts, for guides to moral action. "His work," wrote Henry Adams with his customary cogency, "was rather an Apologia in the Greek sense; a justification of the ways of God to Man, or, what was much the same thing, of Puritans to other men." [50] In a post-Puritan age it could not be popular.

* * *

Long a nonparticipant in political life, Palfrey was no longer even an interested observer. The defeat of Liberal Republicanism, and Henry Wilson's election as vice-president, made Republican politics anathema to him. What was worse, Wilson had turned historian. His *Rise and Fall of the Slave Power* was well received and ran through several editions. Even Wilson's staunchly antislavery tone and praise of Palfrey did not change the latter's mind about the vice-president. A complimentary copy of Wilson's second volume came to Hazelwood with a terse note which Palfrey endorsed sarcastically, "A specimen of high courtesy." [51]

Deaths among Palfrey's restricted circle of friends drew him closer to those who remained. Sparks had died in 1866, and with the death of Charles Folsom in 1872, the social and literary club which Palfrey joined over fifty years before was reduced to four members. His closest friend was still Adams, who reminisced about their relationship: "There has never been the slightest shadow of a shade between us. . . . I see nothing but genial and softened sunshine." In March 1873 the Palfreys celebrated fifty years of marriage, a gay affair which brought out many "people so old, that, like ourselves, they have done going anywhere." By this time Palfrey had established a relaxed tempo of writing, and spent a good deal of time reading novels. It was, he admitted happily, "rather a Sybarite existence." [52]

Palfrey, by now "Good Old Doctor Palfrey," a respected figure identifiable on his infrequent outings by his full white beard, was no longer the object of any man's jealousy or hatred. Health became the only problem. A Thanksgiving Day stroke partially paralyzed his right side. He was strangely pleased with the thought that the Almighty might claim him in this plainless way, and spare him the agony of "cancer or stone." For the next two years, while still feeling the effects of the attack, he continued a curtailed but basically unaltered routine.[53]

From his eightieth year, Palfrey lived with death in his mind. "I approach the end surrounded by all conceivable circumstances of comfort. . . . I cannot be too thankful that . . . I am unassailed by positive ailments of any form."

By September 1877 there were neither activity to warrant nor mental strength to allow continuation of his journal. A final entry concerned the unfinished fifth volume of the *History*.[54] As a general debility slowly overcame him, he had to be carried up and down stairs and use a wheelchair. In 1880 he visited Harvard for the last time, and his speech was so incoherent that Sarah translated for librarian John L. Sibley. When his eyes failed, he often sat on his bed, now placed in the library, and scarcely moved for hours.[55]

In April 1881 relief came. On the 24th, he suffered a particularly bad day of hiccoughing and choking, which left him enervated. Two days later, early in the morning, he died in his sleep. As far as John could tell, his breathing had simply stopped.

He had no pain, of mind or body, to speak of, throughout . . . he was always cheerful, and the excitement of company ever made him gay, though his articulation was much embarrassed, and his memory was slow. Since his greater seclusion, his mind has been unsettled, and there has been some difficulty in managing him. . . . But of late he has been so feeble, that he has been perfectly content to lie still. I do not learn that there was any distinct re-access of his complaint, as his end approached. He simply faded away, and went out. His family were all about him, and he recognized . . . for a little while, his youngest son. . . . In his failing years he was very happy in the recent good prospects of his children.[56]

This description of a gentle end was written by Palfrey in 1872, after he had witnessed Charles Folsom's death. Every detail fits Palfrey's own death-scene in the library at Hazelwood nine years later.

* * *

"DEATH OF A CELEBRATED NEW ENGLAND-ER," mourned the *Evening Transcript* next day, informing its readers that a man who had served Boston and Massachusetts all his life "always with his conscience, his honor, and his marked convictions" was no more. The Democratic press ignored the event, and Palfrey would not have objected since the Democracy and corruption had always been synonymous to him. But Republican editors lauded his historical work, and in their sympathetic enthusiasm linked him with Carlyle and Ranke as well as the great names of American historiography. The *Transcript* went further in retelling some of the incidents of Conscience Whig days to help draw its picture of Palfrey, the man of principle.[57] This was a moral vindication that Palfrey craved so desperately, and had always known would come.

To be true to one's conscience—little else mattered. Charles Francis Adams, Jr., who had known Palfrey during the last third of his life, and learned about the earlier years through the admiration and affection his father felt for Palfrey, thought that it was not possible for a man to live "more consistently up to conscientious ideals. . . . He was almost morbidly victim to the terrible New England Conscience." A victim yes, but a willing victim, even though his ideals of rectitude had undoubtedly produced much unhappiness. For as Palfrey put it, using terms of phrenological determinism, his "bump of conscientiousness," [58] too prominent to allow the luxury of moral laxity, had preserved what was truly important, his self-respect.

Manuscript Collections Cited

Palfrey's Books and Pamphlets

Notes

Index

Manuscript Collections Cited

ADAMS, CHARLES FRANCIS, Mass. Hist. Society, Boston
ANDREW, JOHN ALBION, Mass. Hist. Society
APPLETON, NATHAN, Mass. Hist. Society

BANCROFT, GEORGE, Mass. Hist. Society
BANCROFT-BLISS FAMILIES, Library of Congress, Washington
BANKS, NATHANIEL PRENTISS, Essex Institute, Salem, Mass.
BIGELOW, JOHN PRESCOTT, Houghton Library, Harvard Univ.,
    Cambridge
BIRD, FRANCIS WILLIAM, Houghton Library
BRYANT, WILLIAM CULLEN, New York Public Library
BURTON HARRISON COLLECTION, Library of Congress

CARTER, ROBERT, Houghton Library
CHAMBERLAIN COLLECTION, Boston Public Library
CHASE, SALMON PORTLAND, Library of Congress
CUSHING, CALEB, Library of Congress

DANA, RICHARD HENRY, JR., Mass. Hist. Society
DAVIS, JOHN, American Antiquarian Society, Worcester
DEANE, CHARLES, Mass. Hist. Society

FOLSOM, CHARLES, Boston Public Library
———, Houghton Library

GASTON, WILLIAM, Univ. of North Carolina, Chapel Hill
GARDINER, WILLIAM H., Mass. Hist. Society
GIDDINGS, JOSHUA REED, Ohio Hist. Society, Columbus
GIDDINGS-JULIAN FAMILIES, Library of Congress
GORDON, GEORGE WASHINGTON, New York Public Library

HALE, ARTEMAS, Library of Congress
HALE, JOHN PARKER, New Hampshire Hist. Society, Concord
HALE FAMILY, Library of Congress
HARVARD DIVINITY SCHOOL ARCHIVES, Cambridge
HARVARD UNIVERSITY ARCHIVES, Widener Library
HAVEN, SAMUEL FOSTER, Amer. Antiquarian Society
HIGGINSON, THOMAS WENTWORTH, Houghton Library
HOADLEY COLLECTION, Conn. Hist. Society, Hartford
HOAR, GEORGE FRISBIE, Mass. Hist. Society
HOWE, SAMUEL GRIDLEY, Houghton Library
HUDSON, CHARLES, Amer. Antiquarian Society

LAWRENCE, AMOS, Mass. Hist. Society
LAWRENCE, ABBOTT, Houghton Library
LEAVITT, JOSHUA, Library of Congress
LEE-PALFREY FAMILIES, Library of Congress
LONGFELLOW, HENRY WADSWORTH, Houghton Library
LORING, CHARLES GREELEY, Houghton Library

MANN, HORACE, Mass. Hist. Society
MAYER, BRANTZ, Maryland Hist. Society, Baltimore
MCLEAN, JOHN, Library of Congress

NORCROSS COLLECTION, Mass. Hist. Society
NORTON, ANDREWS, Houghton Library
NORTON, CHARLES ELIOT, Houghton Library

PALFREY, JOHN GORHAM, Houghton Library
———, Louisiana State Univ. Library, Baton Rouge
———, D. H. Stiel, Franklin, La.
PARKMAN, FRANCIS, Mass. Hist. Society
PARSONS, THEOPHILUS, Houghton Library
PAYNE, JOHN HOWARD, Columbia Univ. Library, New York
PHILLIPS, WILLARD, Mass. Hist. Society
PIERCE, EDWARD LILLIE, Houghton Library
PIERCE, HENRY LILLIE, Mass. Hist. Society

RIVES, WILLIAM CABELL, Library of Congress

SCHOULER, WILLIAM, Mass. Hist. Society
SIBLEY, JOHN LANGDON, Harvard Univ. Archives, Widener Library
SPARKS, JARED, Houghton Library
STORY, JOSEPH, Library of Congress
SUMNER, CHARLES, Houghton Library

TRUMBULL, JAMES HAMMOND, Conn. Hist. Society
TRUMBULL, LYMAN, Library of Congress

VAN BUREN, MARTIN, Library of Congress

WASHBURN COLLECTION, Mass. Hist. Society
WEBSTER, DANIEL, Library of Congress
WESTON FAMILY, Boston Public Library
WHITTIER, JOHN GREENLEAF, Houghton Library
WINTHROP, ROBERT CHARLES, Mass. Hist. Society
WINTHROP-WESTON FAMILIES, Yale Univ. Library, New Haven

MANUSCRIPT ELECTION RETURNS, Congress and Governor, State House, Boston

Palfrey's Books and Pamphlets

1820

Letter From a Congregationalist to a Friend, on the Subject of Joining the New Episcopalian Church (Boston: Wells & Libby).

Review of the Rev. Jared Sparks' Letters on the Protestant Episcopal Church, in Reply to Dr. Wyatt's Sermon (Baltimore: N. G. Maxwell).

1823

A Sermon Preached to the Society in Brattle Square, June 8, 1823, the Lord's Day after the Interment of the Late Hon. John Phillips (Boston: Munroe & Francis).

1824

The Young Child's Prayer Book (Boston: O. Everett).

1825

The Prospects and Claims of Pure Christianity; a Sermon Preached at the Dedication of the 12th Congregational Church in Boston, October 13, 1824 (Boston: W. W. Clapp).

A Sermon Preached in the Church in Brattle Square, in Two Parts, July 18, 1824 (Boston: O. C. Greenleaf).

1827

The Child's Prayer Book (Boston: [no publisher]).

Discourses on Intemperance Preached in the Church in Brattle Square, Boston, April 5, 1827, the Day of Annual Fast, and April 8, the Lord's Day Following (Boston: N. Hale).

1828

(ed.) *The New Testament in the Common Version, Conformed to Griesbach's Standard Greek Text* (Boston: Daily Advertiser Press).

1829

A Sermon Occasioned by the Death of John Gorham, M. D., and Preached in Boston, April 9, 1829 (Boston: S. G. Goodrich & Co.).

1830

A Sermon Preached in the Church in Brattle Square, Boston, August

1, 1830, the Lord's Day after the Decease of the Hon. Isaac Parker (Boston: N. Hale).

A Sermon on the Use of Poisoned Drinks (Boston: Bowles & Co.).

1831

An Address Delivered Before the Society for Promoting Theological Education, June 5, 1831 (Boston: Gray & Bowen).

A Harmony of the Gospels on the Plan Proposed by Lant Carpenter (Boston: Gray & Bowen).

An Oration Pronounced Before the Citizens of Boston, on the Anniversary of the Declaration of American Independence, July 4th, 1831 (Boston: J. H. Eastburn).

Sketch of a Plan for a Sunday School (Boston: [no publisher]).

1832

A Discourse Delivered in the Church in Brattle Square, Boston, August 9, 1832, the Day Appointed for Fasting and Prayer in Massachusetts on Account of the Approach of Cholera (Boston: Gray & Bowen).

1833

A Sermon Preached December 1, 1833, the Lord's Day After the Decease of Miss Elizabeth Bond (Boston: [no publisher]).

1834

The Claims of Harvard College Upon its Sons; a Sermon Preached in the Chapel of that Institution, on Lord's Day Afternoon, July 13, 1834 (Cambridge: J. Munroe).

A Sermon Preached at the Installation of the Rev. Samuel Kirkland Lothrop, as pastor of the Church in Brattle Square, Boston, June 18, 1834 (Boston: [no publisher]).

Sermons on Duties Belonging to Some of the Conditions and Relations of Private Life (Boston: C. Bowen).

The Worthy Student of Harvard College. A Sermon Preached in the Chapel of that Institution, on Lord's Day Afternoon, March 23, 1834 (Cambridge: J. Munroe).

1835

Elements of Chaldee, Syriac, Samaritan, and Rabbinical Grammar (Boston: Crocker & Brewster).

A Letter to the Corporation and Overseers of Harvard College on the Proposed Change in the Constitution of that Seminary. By an Alumnus (Boston: [no publisher]).

A Plea for the Militia System. In a Discourse Delivered Before the

Ancient and Honorable Artillery Company, on its CXCVIIth Anniversary, June 1, 1835 (Boston: Dutton & Wentworth).
A Sermon on Self-Denial (n. p.: [no publisher]).

1836

Divinity School of the University of Cambridge (Cambridge: [no publisher]).
Efficacy of Prayer (Boston: [no publisher]).

1838

Academical Lectures on the Jewish Scriptures and Antiquities, 4 vols. (Boston: J. Munroe & Co., 1838–1852).

1839

The Theory and Uses of Natural Religion; Being the Dudleian Lecture Read Before the University of Cambridge, May 8, 1839 (Boston: F. Andrews).

1840

A Discourse on the Life and Character of the Reverend John Thornton Kirkland . . . Late President of Harvard College; Pronounced on Thursday, June 5, 1840, in the New South Church in Boston, Before the Pupils of President Kirkland, and the Government and Students of the University (Cambridge: J. Owen).
A Discourse Pronounced at Barnstable on the Third of September, 1839, at the Celebration of the Second Centennial Anniversary of the Settlement of Cape Cod (Boston: F. Andrews).
Remarks Concerning the Late Dr. Bowditch . . . with the Replies of Dr. Bowditch's Children (Boston: C. C. Little & Co.).

1843

Lowell Lectures on the Evidences of Christianity. 2 vols. (Boston: J. Munroe & Co.).

1845

Life of William Palfrey, Paymaster-General in the Army of the Revolution (Boston: Little & Brown).

1846

Abstracts from the Returns of Agricultural Societies in Massachusetts for the Year 1846, with Selections from Addresses . . . (Boston: [no publisher]).
An Address to the Society of Middlesex Husbandmen and Manufacturers, Delivered at Concord, Oct. 7, 1846 (Cambridge: Metcalf & Co.).
Correspondence between Nathan Appleton and John G. Palfrey, In-

*tended as a Supplement to Mr. Palfrey's Pamphlet on the Slave
Power* (Boston: Eastburn).

*A Discourse on the Life and Character of the Revd. Henry Ware . . .
Pronounced in the First Church in Cambridge, Sept. 28, 1845*
(Boston: Crosby & Nichols).

Papers on the Slave Power, First Published in the "Boston Whig"
(Boston: Merrill, Cobb & Co.).

*Statistics on the Condition and Products of Certain Branches of
Industry in Massachusetts, for the Year Ending April 1, 1845.
Prepared from the Returns of the Assessors, by John G. Palfrey,
Secretary of the Commonwealth* (Boston: Dutton & Wentworth).

1848

*Report from the Committee on Agriculture, U. S. House of Repre-
sentatives, 30th Congress, 1st Sess.* (Washington).

*Speech of Mr. Palfrey of Massachusetts, on the Political Aspects of
the Slave Question. Delivered in the House of Representatives,
January 26, 1848* (Washington: J. & G. S. Gideon).

1849

Speech on Postage Reform, Delivered in the House, February 21, 1849
(Washington).

*Speech on the Bill Creating a Territorial Government for Upper
California, Delivered in the House, February 26, 1849* (Washington).

1850

A Letter to a Friend (Cambridge: Metcalf & Co.).

1851

*To the Free Soil Members of the General Court of Massachusetts for
the Year 1851* (Boston).

1852

*A Chapter of American History. Five Years' Progress of the Slave
Power; a Series of Papers First Published in the Boston "Common-
wealth" in July, August, & September, 1851* (Boston: B. B. Mussey
& Co.).

*Review of Lord Mahon's History of the American Revolution. From
the North American Review for July, 1852* (Boston: Little, Brown
& Co.).

1853

Notice of Professor Farrar (Boston).

*Remarks on the Proposed State Constitution. By a Free-Soiler from
the Start* (Boston: Crosby, Nichols & Co.).

1854

The Relation Between Judaism and Christianity, Illustrated in Notes on Passages in the New Testament containing Quotations from, or References to the Old (Boston: Crosby, Nichols & Co.).

1855

The Inter-State Slave Trade (New York: American Anti-Slavery Society).

Letter to a Whig Neighbor, on the Approaching State Election, by an Old Conservative (Boston: Crosby, Nichols & Co.).

1856

A Decade of the Slave Power, Facts for the People (Washington).

1857

A Review of Mr. Banks' Political History; by a Free-Soiler from the Start; Designed for the Information of the People of Massachusetts (Boston).

1858

History of New England. Vol. I (Boston: Little, Brown & Co.).

1860

History of New England. Vol. II (Boston: Little, Brown & Co.).

1864

History of New England. Vol. III (Boston: Little, Brown & Co.).

1866

A History of New England, From the Discovery by Europeans to the Revolution of the Seventeenth Century, Being an Abridgement of his "History of New England During the Stuart Dynasty." 2 vols. (New York: Hurd & Houghton).

Report of the Commissioners Upon the Subject of Placing Statues in the Old Hall of the House of Representatives (Boston).

1872

A Compendious History of the First Century of New England. 3 vols. (Boston: H. C. Shepard).

A Compendious History of New England from the Revolution of the Seventeenth Century to the Death of King George the First (Boston: H. C. Shepard).

1873

A Compendious History of New England from the Accession of King

George the Second to the First General Congress of the Anglo-American Colonies (Boston: H. C. Shepard).

1874

Thoughts on Providence and Prayer, in a Letter to a Serious Doubter (Boston).

1875

History of New England. Vol. IV (Boston: Little, Brown & Co.).

1890

History of New England. Vol. V, Francis W. Palfrey (ed.) (Boston: Little, Brown & Co.).

Notes

The following abbreviations are used in the notes:

ARP   Anna Russell Palfrey
EP   Edward Palfrey
FWP   Francis Winthrop Palfrey
GP   George Palfrey
HWP   Henry William Palfrey
JP   John Palfrey
JCP   John Carver Palfrey
JGP   John Gorham Palfrey
MAP   Mary Ann Palfrey
MGP   Mary Gorham Palfrey
SHP   Sarah Hammond Palfrey
WTP   William Taylor Palfrey

CFA   Charles Francis Adams

HUA   Harvard University Archives
SPTE   Society for the Propagation of Theological Education

MS-A   Manuscript Autobiography
MS-D   Manuscript Diary
MS-J   Manuscript Journal

I: The Child

1. JGP, MS-A, Notes, p. 10. When no location is given for a manuscript source it is from the Palfrey Papers, Houghton Library, Harvard University, Cambridge.

2. Susan Lee to William Lee, May 16, 1796, Lee-Palfrey MSS, Library of Congress, Washington.

3. JGP, MS-A, p. 2.

4. Jared Sparks to JGP, Dec. 3, 1840.

5. Joseph B. Felt, *The Annals of Salem* (Salem, 1827), p. 7; James Duncan Phillips, *Salem in the Seventeenth Century* (Boston, 1933), p. 27.

6. JGP to JP, May 10, 1834.

7. Herbert S. Allen, *John Hancock* . . . (New York, 1948), pp. 94, 122.

8. George M. Elsey (ed.), "John Wilkes and William Palfrey," Colonial Society of Mass., *Transactions*, XXXIV (February 1941), 411–428.

9. JGP to JCP, Mar. 24, 1848.

10. Harrison Gray Otis to JGP, Aug. 20, 1845; Joseph Nourse to JGP, Aug. 27, 1835.

11. JGP, *Life of William Palfrey* . . . (Boston, 1845); this slight biography is vol. VII of the Second Series of Jared Sparks' *Library of American Biography*. Not all the Palfreys were Revolutionary patriots. The colonel's brother, a captain in the British Colonial Marines, was captured early in the war by the rebels, paroled, and allowed to return to his home in Boston where he remained throughout the duration of the conflict; JGP to JP, June 25, 1833; JP to JGP, Feb. 25, 1834.

12. JP to Gardiner Greene, Sep. 7, 1794, Lee-Palfrey MSS.

13. JCP, undated memorandum; JGP, MS-A, pp. 5-11; U. B. Phillips, *Life and Labor in the Old South* (Boston, 1929), pp. 292-296.

14. JGP, MS-A, p. 12.

15. On one of these voyages he was captured by a French privateer and taken to Martinique for three weeks. Rough treatment caused him to observe that French hospitality was something he would not wish on his most inveterate enemy; JP to Susan Lee, Apr. 17, 1798, Lee-Palfrey MSS.

16. Mary G. Palfrey to Susan Lee, Jan. 14, 1798, Lee-Palfrey MSS; Nathaniel Kidder to JP, July 22, 1798.

17. Bradford & Palfrey, Partnership Agreement, Jan. 1, 1801.

18. Bradford to JP, [August 1801].

19. JGP, MS-A, pp. 13-16.

20. *Ibid.*, pp. 16-17.

21. JP to Susan Lee, Dec. 19, 1802, Lee-Palfrey MSS.

22. JGP, MS-A, pp. 18-23. Palfrey suggested that his father's bachelor life as a Demerara slave-holder may have added to his selfish and arbitrary ways.

23. JGP, MS-J, Jan. 31, 1871.

24. JP to William Lee, Nov. 17, 1803, Lee-Palfrey MSS.

25. JGP, MS-A, p. 30.

26. JP to JGP, Apr. 30, 1803.

27. Grace Overmyer, *America's First Hamlet* (New York, 1957), pp. 33-35.

28. W. Payne to Taylor, Nov. 18, 1804.

29. W. Payne to Taylor, May 8, 1805; Gay to Taylor, Aug. 20, 1805.

30. JGP, MS-A, p. 41.

31. JP to JGP, Mar. 25, 1805; JP to William Lee, Apr. 20, 1805, Lee-Palfrey MSS.

32. JP to JGP, Nov. 20, 1806.

33. JGP, MS-A, pp. 33, 40; J. H. Payne to JGP, Jan. 12, 1806; Boston *Evening Gazette*, May 29, 1852.

34. Yet a few years later he wrote to John Howard, inquiring about

the alleged bully, Thatcher, and asking to be remembered "most affectionately" to him. When William Payne died in 1812, Palfrey wrote: "I never felt so sensibly the obligation I was under to him & the affection I entertained for him, as since I have known they were to be the last he would ever impose and inspire, nor ever reflected so fully upon the happiness I enjoyed while an inmate of your family, nor the gratitude I owe to every member of it." Such contradictory statements mean either that Palfrey was a master of the hypocritical letter of condolence, or, more probably, that his attitude toward the Paynes was an ambivalent one. On many later occasions he noted that his had been an unhappy childhood, and this conviction, carried into maturity, tended to warp his perspective. JGP to J. H. Payne, Mar. 15, 25, 1812, Payne MSS, Columbia University Library, New York.

35. JP to JGP, Mar. 31, Aug. 14, 1806.

36. JP to JGP, Dec. 12, 1806; William Palfrey to Susan Lee, July 4, 1806, Lee-Palfrey MSS.

37. JGP, MS-A, p. 43; JP to JGP, July 15, 1807.

38. Charlotte Gorham to JGP, Aug. 7, 1807.

39. JGP to Charles J. Hoadley, July 7, 1866, Hoadley Collection, Conn. Hist. Society, Hartford.

40. JGP, MS-A, pp. 43–45.

41. JGP to JP (draft), October 1808; Charlotte Gorham to JGP, Jan. 30, 1809; Overmyer, *First Hamlet*, p. 76.

42. "I shall always esteem & regard Mrs. Phillips for her kind and friendly interference." Charlotte Gorham to JGP, Apr. 21, 1809.

43. Emily Phillips to JP, Mar. 4, 1809.

44. Pickard to JP, Mar. 14, 1809; JGP to Emily Phillips, Apr. 10, 1809, Hoadley Collection.

45. W. Payne to JP, Mar. 30, 1809.

46. Pickard to JP, Apr. 28, 1809; Emily Phillips to JP, June 16, 1809; JP to JGP, Aug. 18, 1809; Charlotte Gorham to JGP, Aug. 22, 1809.

47. Emily Phillips to JGP, Apr. 26, 1809; JGP to Thatcher Payne, June 10, 1809, Payne MSS.

II: The Student

1. Herbert B. Adams, *The Life and Writings of Jared Sparks*, 2 vols. (Boston, 1893), I, 27.

2. JGP, MS-A, p. 51.

3. *Ibid.*, p. 53.

4. Sparks to JGP, July 3, 1834.

5. JGP, MS-A, p. 56.

6. Lawrence M. Crosbie, *The Phillips Exeter Academy* ([Exeter, N. H.], 1923), pp. 30–70; Myron R. Williams, *The Story of Phillips Exeter* (Exeter, N. H., 1957), pp. 32–38.

7. JGP, MS-A, p. 59.

8. JGP to H. Sheafe, Oct. 17, 1809; Adams, *Sparks*, I, 32–33; JGP, receipted bill, April 1810.

9. JGP to Pickard, Dec. 15, 1809.

10. Pickard to JGP, Sep. 10, 1809; JGP to Sheafe, Oct. 17, 1809.

11. Emily Phillips to JGP, Oct. 12, 1809.

12. Emily Phillips to JP, Dec. 18, 1809; Pickard to JGP, Apr. 9, 1810.

13. JP to JGP, Apr. 18, 1810.

14. H. Johnson to JP, Aug. 27, 1810.

15. Pickard to JP, Aug. 27, 1810.

16. HWP to JGP, Nov. 9, 1810, Jan. 17, 1811.

17. JGP to Emily Phillips, May 27, 1811, Hoadley Collection.

18. Pickard to JP, Nov. 5, 1810; JGP to JP, Nov. 9, 1810; JP to Pickard (copy), [December 1810].

19. Emily Phillips to JGP, Mar. 1, 1811; Emily Phillips to JP, Mar. 14, 1811.

20. Adams, *Sparks*, I, 44; JGP, MS-A, p. 62.

21. EP to JGP, Jan. 23, 1811; HWP to JGP, Mar. 10, 1811.

22. Pickard to JGP, July 19, 1811.

23. Folsom to Sparks, July 21, 1811, Sparks MSS, Houghton Library, Harvard Univ.; JGP, MS-A, p. 64; "Insurance Policy," July 1811.

24. Emily Phillips to JP, Sep. 13, 1811.

25. Samuel Eliot Morison, *Three Centuries of Harvard, 1636–1936* (Cambridge, 1937), p. 196.

26. JGP, MS-A, Notes, pp. 22–23.

27. JGP, MS-A, p. 68; Emily Phillips to JGP, Dec. 9, 1811.

28. JGP to Emily Phillips, May 27, Oct. 15, 1811, Mar. 5, 1812, Hoadley Collection; Morison, *Harvard*, p. 201.

29. JGP to Emily Phillips, Nov. 11, 1813, Hoadley Collection.

30. He also received a part (a Latin dialogue with Davis) in that year's college exhibition; Records of the Class of 1815, HUA.

31. JGP, MS-A, pp. 70–71; JGP to Emily Phillips, Oct. 15, 1811, Hoadley Collection.

32. Folsom to Sparks, July 4, Nov. 18, 1812, Sparks MSS.

33. JGP to Sparks, Oct. 18, Dec. 13, 1812, Sparks MSS.

34. Eliza Buckminster Lee, *Memoirs of Rev. Joseph Buckminster, D.D., and of his Son, Rev. Joseph Stevens Buckminster* (Boston, 1851).

35. Emily Phillips to JGP, Dec. 9, 1811, July 19, 1812.

36. JGP to JP, Dec. 20, 1812. John Palfrey finally replied in March 1813 that he was too weighed down by his misfortunes to write, and had waited vainly for some good news to communicate. He authorized Pickard to sell some lands he owned in Massachusetts to pay part of his debts; JP to JGP, Mar. 20, 1813.

37. Charlotte Gorham to JGP, Apr. 16, 1812; HWP to JP, Apr. 11, 1812.

38. JGP to JP, Sep. 15, 1812; HWP to JP, Dec. 7, 1812, Jan. 19, 1813.

39. Records of the Class of 1815, HUA; JGP to Sparks, Aug. 27, 1814, Sparks MSS.

40. HWP to JP, Jan. 19, 1813.

41. Emily Phillips to JP, Feb. 17, 1814; John T. Kirkland to I. Davis, Feb. 12, 1813, College Papers, VIII, 44, HUA.

42. JGP, Draft of Petition, May 2, 1814.

43. JGP, MS-A, p. 70.

44. Morison, *Harvard*, p. 203.

45. "We proceeded to canvass characters from the junior Class. Mr. Theodorick T. Randolph was first ballotted, &, for a variety of reasons excluded by ten, out of twelve votes. . . . [Sparks, William Warner, and Convers Francis were admitted.] Several others were tried without success." Harvard ØBK Society, Minutes of the Recording Secretary, July 15, 1814, HUA; JGP to J. H. Payne, Oct. 18, 1812, Payne MSS.

46. JGP to Sparks, July 11, Aug. 27, 1814, Sparks MSS.

47. Bruce to Sparks, Oct. 27, 1814, Sparks MSS.

48. Harvard ØBK, Secretary's Minutes, Mar. 10, 24, 1815, HUA; JGP, MS-A, pp. 75–80.

49. Morison, *Harvard*, pp. 213–214; JGP to Emily Phillips, June 17, 1814, Hoadley Collection.

50. JGP to HWP, Feb. 26, 1813; JGP to JP, June 17, 1814.

51. JGP to HWP, Feb. 26, 1813; JGP to Sparks, Jan. 18, 1815, Sparks MSS.

52. JP to EP, Jan. 19, 1815; EP to JGP, Jan. 27, 1815.

53. HWP to JGP, Jan. 27, 1815; JGP, MS-A, p. 83.

54. JGP to Sparks, Jan. 18, 1815, Sparks MSS.

55. JGP to Emily Phillips, Apr. 1, 1815, Hoadley Collection; JGP, MS-A, p. 82.

56. JGP to Emily Phillips, May 23, Sep. 25, 1813, Hoadley Collection.

57. JGP, MS-A, Notes, pp. 32–33, 40–41.

58. Boston *Columbian Centinel*, Sep. 2, 1815; Faculty Records, IX, 32, HUA.

59. Rice to JP, Aug. 10, 1815.

III: LIBERAL THEOLOGY

1. Octavius B. Frothingham, *Boston Unitarianism* . . . (New York, 1890), p. 23.

2. JGP to Pickard (draft), Sep. 4, 1815. Channing's solution to this problem had not gone unnoticed: "Mr. Channing, the Rev., is going to be married in spring to Miss Gibbs of Newport, and a hundred thousand dollars"; JGP to Emily Phillips, Dec. 26, 1813, Hoadley Collection.

3. Edward Everett left the Brattle Street Church in March 1815; Paul Revere Frothingham, *Edward Everett* (Boston, 1925), p. 34.

4. Sparks to JGP, Sep. 18, 1815.

5. JGP, MS-A, p. 84; JGP to Emily Phillips, Nov. 12, 1815, Hoadley Collection.

6. Rice to JGP, Sep. 15, 1815.

7. JGP to JP, Oct. 30, 1815; JGP to Emily Phillips, Nov. 12, 1815, Hoadley Collection; JGP to Sparks, Nov. 19, 1815, Sparks MSS; Sparks to JGP, Dec. 23, 1815.

8. Sparks to JGP, Dec. 7, 1815.

9. JGP to Emily Phillips, Dec. 26, 1815, Hoadley Collection; JGP, MS-A, p. 84, JGP to Sparks, Dec. 28, 1815, Sparks MSS.

10. JGP, MS-J, Feb. 2–11, Mar. 1–3, 1816.

11. JGP to Sparks, Mar. 6, 1816, Sparks MSS.

12. Eliza Sumner to JGP, Jan. 19, 1816.

13. JGP, MS-J, June 5–July 16, 1816; J. A. Lowell to JGP, July 5, 1816.

14. JGP, MS-J, Sep. 2, 1816.

15. William Ellery Channing, *Works* (Boston, 1896), p. 408.

16. George Willis Cooke, *Unitarianism in America* (Boston, 1902), p. 102; Earl Morse Wilbur, *A History of Unitarianism in Transylvania, England, and America* (Cambridge, 1952), p. 417.

17. Perry Miller, "The Marrow of Puritan Divinity," in *Errand Into the Wilderness* (Cambridge, 1956), ch. iii.

18. This discussion of eighteenth-century Arminianism is based largely on Conrad Wright's exemplary monograph, *The Beginnings of Unitarianism in America* (Boston, 1955).

19. Wilbur, *Unitarianism*, p. 400.

20. *Ibid.*, pp. 401–408; the best treatment of the Hollis controversy is in Wright, *Beginnings of Unitarianism*, ch. xii.

21. SPTE, Trustees Records, pp. 3–5, HUA.

22. JGP, MS-J, Oct. 15, 1816; John Ware, *Memoir of the Life of Henry Ware, Jr.* (Boston, 1868), pp. 91–92; SPTE, Trustees Records, p. 13, HUA.

23. JGP, MS-J, Nov. 7, 1816; College Papers, VIII, 30, HUA.

24. JGP, MS-A, pp. 88–89.

25. JGP to B. O. Tayloe, Oct. 17, 1816, JGP, Quinquennial Folder, HUA; JGP, MS-A, p. 89.

26. See *The William and Mary Quarterly*, 3rd ser., XV (January 1958), 93–94.

27. EP to JGP, May 15, 1817. Edward died four months later of yellow fever; JGP to W. E. Channing (draft), October 1817.

28. A. Norton to S. Norton, Dec. 30, 1817, A. Norton MSS, Houghton Library, Harvard Univ.; Sparks to JGP, Dec. 26, 1817; JGP, MS-A, p. 92; College Faculty Records, IX, 125, HUA.

29. JGP to Sparks, Nov. 19, 1815, Sparks MSS; Sparks to Miss Storrow, Feb. 21, 1817, Sparks MSS.

30. JGP to Tayloe, June 8, 1817, JGP, Quinquennial Folder, HUA; JGP, MS-A, Notes, p. 41.
31. JGP to Emily Phillips, Apr. 17, 1817, Hoadley Collection; JGP, MS-A, Notes, pp. 42–43.
32. JGP to Emily Phillips, Dec. 12, 1817, Hoadley Collection; Emily Phillips to JGP, Mar. 11, 1818.
33. JGP to JP, Nov. 24, 1817.
34. JGP, MS-A, p. 93; JGP to Emily Phillips, Feb. 16, 1818, Hoadley Collection.
35. S. Higginson to Sparks, Nov. 7, 1816, Sparks MSS; Tayloe to JGP, Nov. 14, 1816; Rice to JP, Dec. 10, 1816.
36. Rice to JGP, Feb. 9, 1818; Dr. Warren to JGP, Jan. 12, 1818.
37. Briggs to Sparks, Feb. 22, 181[8], Sparks MSS.
38. Thacher to JGP, Mar. 17, 1818; *The Manifesto Church, Records of the Church in Brattle Square, Boston* (Boston, 1902), pp. 62–63.

IV: BRATTLE STREET

1. Van Wyck Brooks, *The Flowering of New England, 1815–1865* (New York, 1937), p. 38.
2. JGP, MS-A, pp. 95–99.
3. *Ibid.*, p. 95.
4. I have used this term throughout, as the most common name for the church. The official records are those of "The Church in Brattle Square," while Lothrop's history of the church refers to "The Brattle Street Church."
5. Samuel Kirkland Lothrop, *A History of the Church in Brattle Street, Boston* (Boston, 1851); Adams to Thomas Jefferson, Oct. 28, 1814, Everett MSS, Mass. Hist. Society, Boston.
6. "The salary they offer, or rather encouragement, for we in N[ew] England . . . like to avoid even in names the appearance of anything mercenary in these matters . . ."; JGP to JP, Apr. 30, 1818; Record of the Meeting, Apr. 26, 1818; *Brattle Records*, pp. 62–63.
7. JGP to Emily Phillips, May 4, 1818, Hoadley Collection; Bradford to JGP, May 4, 1818; JGP to Brattle Street Church, May 5, 1818, *Brattle Records*, pp. 63–66.
8. Bradford to Chelsea Church, May 18, 1818, Chamberlain MSS, Boston Public Library; Channing to JGP, [May] 1818.
9. JGP to Emily Phillips, May 4, 1818, Hoadley Collection; Emily Phillips to JGP, June 1, 1818; Emily Phillips to JP, June 22, 1818.
10. JGP, MS-J, June 21, 1818; *Brattle Records*, p. 66.
11. MS Creed, June 17, 1818.
12. Lothrop, *Brattle Church*, pp. 110–112; Lee, *Buckminster*, p. 211; Sullivan to JGP, May 19, 1818; Thacher to Sullivan, July 7, 1818.
13. Andrews Norton noted: "A Boston clergyman suffers almost as much in seasoning as one who goes to an unhealthy climate"; Norton

to George Bancroft, March 1819, A. Norton MSS; JGP, MS-A, pp. 102–103.

14. Bradford to Sparks, July 4, 1819, Sparks MSS; JGP, MS-J, Nov. 29, 1819.

15. S. Higginson to Sparks, Jan. 2, 1820, Sparks MSS; R. Bartlett to Sparks, Feb. 10, 1821, Sparks MSS; JGP, MS-A, p. 108.

16. One series of calls was particularly embarrassing. A woman parishioner seemed to be dying of dropsy and Palfrey called frequently. But after a few months the young lady's illness was suddenly cured when she gave birth. Though she afterward married William A. Warner, one of Palfrey's Harvard classmates, this "shameless intrigue" ruined them; JGP, MS-A, pp. 109–111; Notes, pp. 60–61.

17. H. G. Otis to JGP, Jan. 20, 1820; Ware, *Ware*, I, 149–150; JGP, MS-A, pp. 109–111.

18. JGP to JP, Dec. 22, 1818; S. A. Eliot to Sparks, July 26, 1819, Sparks MSS; GP to JP, Aug. 14, 1819; JGP to Sparks, Sep. 8, 1819, Sparks MSS.

19. S. Hammond to JGP, Apr. 18, 1819; S. A. Eliot to Andrews Norton, May 6, 1819, A. Norton MSS; Adams, *Sparks*, I, 138–141; JGP, MS-A, p. 107.

20. JGP to Sparks, May 18, 1819, Sparks MSS; Sparks to JGP, May 22, June 7, 1819.

21. JGP, MS-J, May 23, 1818; Charles Lyttle, "An Outline of the History of the Berry Street Ministerial Conference," *Meadville Theological School Quarterly Bulletin*, XXIV (July 1930), 3–27.

22. Frank L. Mott, "The *Christian Disciple* and the *Christian Examiner*," *New England Quarterly*, I (April 1928), 197–198; JGP, "For the Daily Advertiser," Jan. 12, 1819; Ware to Joseph Allen, March 1819, quoted in Ware, *Ware*, I, 129; JGP, "Communication," 1819; Norton to JGP, March 1819.

23. JGP to Norton, Dec. 27, 1819, Jan. 11, 1820, A. Norton MSS; Norton to JGP, Jan. 1, 1820; Norton to Sparks, Jan. 6, 1820, Sparks MSS.

24. Sparks to JGP, Nov. 9, 1819, Jan. 11, Feb. 3, 1820, Apr. 30, May 28, 1821; JGP to Norton, Feb. 24, 1821, A. Norton MSS; S. A. Eliot to Sparks, July 9, 1821, Sparks MSS.

25. JGP to Sparks, Apr. 11, 1822, Sparks MSS; Sparks to JGP, Jan. 22, 1821, June 13, 1822.

26. JGP to JP, Dec. 22, 1818; JGP, MS-J, Nov. 10, 1822; Lothrop, *Brattle Street*, p. 188.

27. Norton to JGP, Sep. 11, 1818, A. Norton MSS; JGP, MS-J, June 1, 1819.

28. Norton to Bancroft, Dec. 27, 1820, A. Norton MSS; JGP, MS-J, Oct. 8, 1820; Webster to JGP, Oct. 20, 1820.

29. JGP to WTP, Apr. 17, 1821.

30. [JGP], "Carrier's Address," Jan. 1, 1822.

31. JGP, MS-J, Jan. 3, 1819; W. H. Gardiner to JGP, June 8, 1817, Gardiner MSS; JGP, MS-J, Aug. 9, 1818; W. H. Gardiner, MS-D, Nov. 19, 1819, Gardiner MSS.

32. Eliot to Sparks, Aug. 31, 1819, Sparks MSS; JGP, MS-J, Sep. 7, 1819; Thacher to JGP, Sep. 14, 1819; JGP to WTP, Dec. 9, 1819; JGP, MS-A, p. 113.

33. Rice to JGP, Dec. 4, 1820; *Brattle Records*, pp. 67–68; G. Bond to JGP, June 1, 1821; J. Davis to JGP, May 3, 1821.

34. JGP to B. Tayloe, Oct. 12, 1817, JGP, Quinquennial Folder, HUA; JP to JGP, June 17, 1818.

35. JGP, MS-A, pp. 113–115, Notes, pp. 53–55; Frothingham, *Everett*, p. 76; JGP to Miss Davenport (two undated letters ca. 1821), Misc. MSS, Louisiana State Univ. Library, Baton Rouge.

36. JGP, MS-J, Dec. 12, 1819, 1820 *passim*.

37. JGP, MS-A, p. 116; JGP to Hammond, Feb. 8, 1822; JGP, MS-J, Feb. 26, 1822.

38. A. G. Storrow to Sparks, Feb. 3, 1822, Sparks MSS; Mary Ann Hammond to JGP, [1822].

39. Some of the notes are in Hannah Palfrey Ayer (ed.), *A Legacy of New England, Letters of the Palfrey Family* (n.p., 1950), I, 61–70; JGP, MS-J, Mar. 17, 1823; JGP to Sparks, Apr. 10, 1823, Sparks MSS.

40. JGP, MS-J, Dec. 15, 1823, Mar. 28, June 12, 1825; F. Parkman to JGP, Jan. 19, 1824; MAP to JGP, July 1, 1825.

41. JGP, *A Sermon Preached . . . in Two Parts, July 18, 1824* (Boston, 1825); JGP, MS-J, July 20, Nov. 21, 1824.

42. "Out Dana went, and out went with him any hope that the *North American* would ever understand the new generation"; Brooks, *Flowering of New England*, p. 115; JGP, MS-A, pp. 105–107; Sparks to JGP, Sep. 26, 1819.

43. JGP, MS-A, Notes, p. 54; JGP to Everett (draft), [January 1820]; Everett to JGP, [November 1821].

44. Everett to JGP, [February 1823]; JGP to Sparks, Nov. 12, 1822, July 29, 1823, Sparks MSS; JGP, MS-J, Sep. 1, 1823.

45. Ware to J. Allen [Autumn] 1822, quoted in Ware, *Ware*, I, 167; Sparks to JGP, Nov. 24, 1822; JGP to Sparks, Nov. 12, 1822, Apr. 10, 1823, Sparks MSS; JGP, MS-J, Sep. 1, 1823; JGP to Folsom, Jan. 13, 1853, Folsom MSS, Boston Public Library.

46. Mott, "*Christian Disciple*," p. 198; *Christian Examiner*, I (January 1824), 2–4; JGP, MS-A, p. 105; JGP to Oliver Everett (draft), June 20, 1825. While Palfrey was in Europe the magazine languished; A. Norton to Dr. Parker, Aug. 15, 1825, Washburn MSS, Mass. Hist. Society.

47. JGP to JP, May 17, 1825; Bond to JGP, May 5, 1825; Robert E. Spiller, *The American in England . . .* (New York, 1928), p. 224.

48. Bond to JGP, June 24, 1825; JGP, MS-A, p. 122; JGP, MS-J, Dec. 27, 1869.

49. Arthur W. Brown, *Always Young for Liberty, a Biography of William Ellery Channing* (Syracuse, 1956), pp. 143–152; JGP to H. Ware, July 29, 1825; JGP, MS-A, p. 119; JGP to MAP, Aug. 20, Sep. 20, 1825.

50. JGP to MAP, Oct. 19, 1825; JGP to Henry Ware, Oct. 21, 1825.

51. JGP to MAP, Oct. 22, 1825; JGP to A. Norton, Dec. 7, 1825.

52. JGP to MAP, Aug. 27, 1825; JGP to Sparks, Sep. 9, 1825, Sparks MSS; MAP to JGP, Sep. 16, 1825.

53. JGP to Sparks, Feb. 24, 1826, Sparks MSS; JGP to MAP, Mar. 18, 25, Apr. 4, 8, May 14, 1826.

54. JGP to MAP, June 3, 1826; JGP to W. H. Gardiner, June 19, 1826, Gardiner MSS.

55. JGP to MAP, Nov. 22, 1825; JGP to J. Gorham, [1826]; Hammond to JGP, July 30, 1828; Amos Lawrence to JGP, Dec. 12, 1828.

56. JGP, MS-A, p. 122; N. Hale to JGP, Mar. 23, 1827; JGP, MS-J, May 6, 1827; *Christian Register*, IX (Aug. 28, 1830).

57. JGP, MS-A, pp. 124–127; Edward Everett Hale, *A New England Boyhood* (Boston, 1927), pp. 107–108; JGP to D. Webster, Apr. 17, 1828, Webster MSS, Library of Congress.

58. WTP to JGP, Nov. 16, 1827; JGP to WTP, Mar. 11, 1828.

59. JGP, MS-A, Notes, p. 65; JGP to N. Appleton, Jan. 29, 1829, Appleton MSS, Mass. Hist. Society; Sparks to JGP, Mar. 30, 1827; JGP to Sparks, Mar. 20, 1827, Sparks MSS.

60. Sparks to JGP, Apr. 17, 1827, Feb. 29, 1828; C. Bowen to Sparks, Feb. 23, 1828, Sparks MSS; JGP to Sparks, Apr. 10, 1828, Sparks MSS; Eliot to Sparks, Dec. 24, 1828, Sparks MSS; Everett to JGP, Feb. 7, 1829.

61. JGP, MS-A, pp. 128–129; J. Tuckerman to JGP, Feb. 1825, Divinity School, MS Dean's Papers, HUA; S. Higginson, Jr. to JGP, Mar. 8, 1825; JGP, MS-J, Sep. 3, 1826.

62. J. Walker to JGP, Aug. 31, 1827; JGP, MS-J, Mar. 30, 1828; J. Walker to F. C. Gray, July 3, 1828, MS College Papers, 3rd ser., III, 49, HUA; SPTE, MS Misc. Papers, I, 87, HUA; JGP to Sullivan (draft), July 18, 1828.

63. JGP to Sparks, Aug. 20, Dec. 30, 1828, Sparks MSS; Ware to Second Church, Mar. 27, 1829, quoted in Ware, *Ware*, II, 25.

64. JGP to Norton, [March 1830], A. Norton MSS.

65. Ware to JGP, July 30, 1830.

66. F. Parkman to J. Quincy, Sep. 1, 1830, SPTE, MS Misc. Papers, II, 8, HUA; JGP to Ware, Jr. (draft), Oct. 24, 1830; SPTE, MS Misc. Papers, II, 10–11, HUA; JGP to Quincy, Nov. 12, 21, 1830, MS College Papers, 2nd ser., IV, 140–155, HUA; F. C. Gray to JGP, Dec. 16, 1830.

67. Bond to JGP, Nov. 12, 1830; JGP to Bond (draft), Dec. 11, 1830.
68. JGP, MS-A, p. 131; JGP to CFA, Dec. 16, 1847, Adams MSS, Mass. Hist. Society.
69. JGP to HWP, Dec. 27, 1830; JGP, MS-J, June 18, 1869.

V: DEAN PALFREY

1. JGP, Inauguration Oath, [1831]; JGP, Report, SPTE, MS Misc. Papers, II, 7, HUA.
2. J. Pierce to JGP, June 5, 1828; Conrad Wright, "The Early Years, 1811–1840," ch. i of George H. Williams (ed.), *The Harvard Divinity School* (Boston, 1954), pp. 29–35; SPTE, MS Misc. Papers, II, 12, HUA.
3. *Ibid.*, II, 10; JGP, MS-A, p. 142.
4. *Ibid.*, pp. 143–144.
5. MS College Papers, 2d ser., IV, 201–202, HUA; Ware to JGP, Oct. 9, 1830, Divinity School, MS Dean's Papers, HUA; Divinity School, MS Faculty Records, May 30, 1831, May 3, 1833, Andover-Harvard Library, Cambridge.
6. JGP to Ware, Jr., July 30, 1831, Divinity School, MS Dean's Papers, HUA; Williams, *Harvard Divinity School*, pp. 37–42, 57.
7. JGP to Quincy, Oct. 26, 1831, MS College Papers, 2d ser., V, 28, HUA; Charles Follen, *Works* (Boston, 1841), I, 287–289.
8. JGP, MS-A, pp. 147–149; Ware to Quincy, July 6, 1832, MS College Papers, 2d ser., V, 129–130, HUA.
9. JGP to Quincy, June 3, 1831, *ibid.*, IV, 266; Quincy to JGP, June 26, 1832; JGP, MS-A, p. 147; Ware to Carpenter, Aug. 20, 1833, July 28, 1834, quoted in Ware, *Ware*, II, 109, 111.
10. JGP to Everett (draft), Dec. 21, 1830; JGP to Quincy, Feb. 12, 1831, MS College Papers, 2d ser., IV, 193, HUA. Hazelwood still stands, surrounded by the Harvard cyclotron, and is used by the School of Education.
11. JGP to WTP, June 21, 1831; JGP, MS-A, Notes, p. 66; JGP, MS-J, Jan. 15, 1832; JGP to HWP, Jan. 17, 1832.
12. JGP, MS-A, p. 161, Notes, pp. 69–70; Lawrence to JGP, Mar. 12, 1832; JGP, MS-J, Mar. 19, 1832.
13. Webster, *et al.*, to JGP, Oct. 27, 1833; J. T. Austin to JGP, Oct. 30, 1833; MS Record of Theological School, pp. 56–58, Andover-Harvard Library; Students to JGP, Oct. 29, 1833.
14. JGP to Austin, Nov. 2, 1833, Norcross MSS, Mass. Hist. Society; JGP, MS-A, pp. 162–165; JGP to J. Walker, July 23, 1835, MS College Papers, 2d ser., VIII, 126–136, HUA; Howard to J. Story, July 23, 1838, Story MSS, Library of Congress.
15. See the next chapter.
16. J. F. Clarke to E. L. Pierce, Aug. 22, 1875, Sumner MSS, Houghton Library; JGP, MS-J, Oct. 20, 1822, Mar. 4, 11, 1833, May 26, 1834; JGP to JP, Jan. 26, 1817; JGP to JP, Oct. 25, 1819, Palfrey

Family MSS, in the possession of Mr. D. H. Stiel, Franklin, Louisiana.

17. Charles T. Brooks to J. S. Dwight, May 26, 1834, Autograph File, Houghton Library; JGP, MS-J, June 1, July 6, 1834; Ware, *Ware*, II, 147–154; *Boston Daily Advertiser*, July 4, 11, 1834.

18. JP to JGP, June 2, 1830; HWP to JGP, June 16, Sep. 20, Oct. 27, 1834.

19. JGP, MS-J, Nov. 29, 1835; JGP to MAP, Jan. 2, 19, Feb. 18, 1836; JGP to G. Ticknor, Sep. 28, 1836, Chamberlain MSS.

20. Clarke to JGP, Aug. 1, 1836.

21. W. O. White to JGP, Nov. 1, 1865; Andrew P. Peabody, *Harvard Reminiscences* (Boston, 1888), pp. 110–111.

22. *Ibid.*, p. 109; JGP, MS-A, pp. 155–159; Charles T. Brooks to J. S. Dwight, Jan. 20, 1834, Misc. MSS, Houghton Library.

23. Emerson to W. Emerson, Oct. 23, 1836, Ralph L. Rusk (ed.), *The Letters of Ralph Walto Emerson* (New York, 1939), II, 42; JGP to G. Ticknor, Sep. 28, 1836, Chamberlain MSS; J. Ware to JGP, Jan. 14, 1838.

24. Emerson was protesting in part against the acknowledged pulpit ineptitude of Barzallai Frost; see Conrad Wright, "Emerson, Barzallai Frost, and the Harvard Divinity School Address," *The Harvard Theological Review*, XLIX (January 1956), 17–43.

25. Ralph Waldo Emerson, *Works* (Boston, 1904), I, 117–148.

26. MS Record of the Theological School, p. 98, Andover-Harvard Library; JGP, MS-J, July 16, 1838; H. W. Longfellow to Clara Crowninshield, July 28, 1838, photostat in Longfellow MSS, Craigie House, Cambridge; Jean Holloway, *Edward Everett Hale* (Austin, 1956), pp. 39–40; JGP, MS-J, July 18, 1838.

27. This point is well developed by C. H. Faust, "The Background of the Unitarian Opposition to Transcendentalism," *Modern Philology*, XXXV (February 1938), pp. 297–324.

28. *Boston Daily Advertiser*, July 26, 1838; A. Norton to C. Robbins, Oct. 22, 1838, A. Norton MSS.

29. JGP to G. E. Ellis (draft), Oct. 16, 1843.

30. In 1838 Palfrey published the first of four volumes of *Academical Lectures on the Jewish Scriptures and Antiquities*.

31. W. D. Wilson, *et al.*, to JGP, July, 1838.

32. JGP to J. Walker, Jan. 11, 1839, MS College Papers, 2d ser., IX, 159–163, HUA; *ibid.*, p. 183; JGP, MS-J, Mar. 30, 1839; Quincy to JGP, Apr. 2, 1839.

33. JGP to Quincy, Apr. 5, 1839, MS Corporation Records, HUA; Quincy to JGP, Apr. 30, 1839; JGP to Quincy, Aug. 23, 1839, MS College Papers, 2d ser., IX, 308, HUA.

34. "A story got into the papers that when I left the school, I said that it was made up of mystics, skeptics, and dyspeptics. I do not think that I was the author of any such saying, nor was it witty enough for me to be inclined to claim it"; JGP, MS-A, Notes, p. 72.

35. JGP to Sumner, Feb. 6, 1837; JGP, MS-J, June 18, 1869; William R. Hutchison, *The Transcendentalist Ministers* (New Haven, 1959), p. 1.

36. H. W. Longfellow, MS-J, Apr. 8, 1839, Longfellow MSS, Houghton Library.

VI: THE NORTH AMERICAN

1. JGP, MS-J, Mar. 23, 1835; Frank Luther Mott, *A History of American Magazines, 1850–1865* (Cambridge, 1938), p. 234; JGP, MS-A, p. 166.

2. E. Everett to his wife, Jan. 13, 1835, Everett MSS; E. Everett to JGP, Mar. 21, 1835; A. H. Everett to E. Everett, Mar. 28, 1835, Hale Family MSS.

3. E. Everett to JGP, July 25, 1835.

4. JGP to Lawrence (draft), Sep. 1, 1835.

5. JGP, MS-J, Sep. 20, 1835; JGP to JP, Oct. 9, 1835.

6. JGP, MS-A, Notes, p. 70; JGP, MS-J, Oct. 5, 1835; JGP, MS-A, p. 168.

7. E. Everett to JGP, Dec. 8, 1835; JGP to Cushing, Sep. 20, 1836, Cushing MSS.

8. JGP to Longfellow, Oct. 18, 1835, Longfellow MSS; Prescott to JGP, Dec. 8, 1835; Prescott to W. H. Gardiner, [1837], Gardiner MSS; JGP to H. A. Bullard, Sep. 18, 1837, Burton Harrison Collection.

9. *Graham's Magazine*, XIX (November 1841), 224–225, 234; George E. Woodberry, *The Life of Edgar Allan Poe*, 2 vols. (Boston, 1909), I, 312–313.

10. JGP to CFA, Sep. 20, 1838; CFA to JGP, Feb. 5, 1839; both in the Adams MSS.

11. JGP to Bancroft, Oct. 3, 1835, Bancroft MSS; Bancroft to JGP, Oct. 6, 1835; JGP, MS-J, Jan. 10, 1838.

12. JGP to Bancroft, Mar. 11, 1838, Bancroft MSS; Prescott to JGP, Mar. 21, 1838; Sparks to Bancroft, Apr. 1, 1838, Bancroft MSS; *North American Review*, XLVI (April 1838), 483; *ibid.*, XLVII (July 1838), 262.

13. H. W. Longfellow, MS-J, Apr. 2, 27, 1838, Longfellow MSS; *Boston Daily Advertiser*, Apr. 27, 1838; JGP to Clarke (draft), June 18, 1838; Russel B. Nye, *George Bancroft* (New York, 1945), pp. 118–119.

14. J. Pickering to JGP, Aug. 1836; Brooks, *Flowering of New England*, p. 114; J. Story to J. S. Jones, July 30, 1834, William Gaston MSS.

15. Mott, *American Magazines, 1850–1865*, p. 237.

16. JGP to CFA, Feb. 7, 1839, Adams MSS.

17. JGP to Folsom, Feb. 22, 1839, Folsom MSS, Boston Public Library; Norton to JGP, Apr. 13, 1840, A. Norton MSS; JGP to

Cushing, June 23, 1838, Apr. 3, 1839, Cushing MSS; JGP to [CFA?] (draft), Nov. 29, [1841].

18. Lydia M. Child to JGP, [1837]; E. Quincy to JGP, June 9, 1838; CFA to JGP, May 15, 1842, Adams MSS.

19. JGP to Folsom, Feb. 25, July 1, 1840, Folsom MSS, Boston Public Library; Folsom to JGP, Dec. 21, 1840, Letterbook, Folsom MSS, Houghton Library; JGP to Cushing, June 27, 1838, Cushing MSS; JGP to Longfellow, Jan. 11, 1841, Longfellow MSS.

20. JGP, MS-J, Jan. 14, Mar. 10, 1837, July 13, 1838; JGP, MS-A, pp. 181–182; JGP to Otis, Broaders & Co., Nov. 27, 1837.

21. HWP to JGP, Mar. 4, May 7, Aug. 3, 1837; JGP, MS-J, Sep. 29, 1837.

22. JGP to JP, June 12, Aug. 24, 1839; JP to JGP, July 9, 1839. The Louisiana Palfreys had their financial troubes too. Henry, who had withstood the Panic of 1837, was the worst sufferer. In 1842 he went bankrupt, having lost $200,000 in four years. Gorham scraped together a few hundred dollars in the way of temporary relief. Henry, one of the most resilient businessmen of the New South, was not a man to be kept down. Before long he resumed a business career which was a series of spectacular booms and busts; HWP to JP, Apr. 15, 1837, June 2, 1842, Jan. 23, 1843.

23. H. W. Longfellow, MS-J, Nov. 12, 1838, Longfellow MSS; JGP to JP, Nov. 15, 1838.

24. J. Lowell to JGP, Mar. 18, 1839; Folsom to JGP, Jan. 20, 1840; CFA, MS-D, Sep. 16, 1840, Apr. 23, 30, 1841, Adams MSS.

25. E. Quincy to JGP, Jan. 23, 1840. Circulation was down to 1,802 by 1840. (In 1830 it had been 3,200.) JGP, Statement, Nov. 10, 1840; Mott, *American Magazines, 1850–1865*, p. 231; S. A. Eliot to JGP, Nov. 14, 1840; JGP, MS-A, p. 184, Notes, pp. 73–75; E. Everett to JGP, Feb. 21, 1842.

26. JGP to Sparks, Jan. 1, 1841, Sparks MSS; CFA to JGP, Feb. 28, 1841, Adams MSS; JGP, MS-J, Oct. 15, 1842; JGP to Stackpole (draft), Nov. 1, 1842; *Boston Daily Advertiser*, Jan. 5, 10, 1842; Sumner to Longfellow, Aug. 29, 1842, Longfellow MSS.

27. JGP to B. O. Tayloe, Dec. 30, 1842, Misc. MSS, New-York Hist. Society; JGP, MS-J, Dec. 17, 31, 1842, June 18, 1869.

VII: The State House

1. JGP, MS-A, p. 187.
2. JGP, MS-J, Aug. 20, 1840.
3. *Ibid.*, Sep. 11, 1840; JGP to MAP, May 26, 1840; SHP to JP, Nov. 2, 1840; Arthur B. Darling, *Political Changes in Massachusetts, 1824–1848* . . . (New Haven, 1925), p. 262.
4. JGP, MS-J, Dec. 7, 1841, Jan. 5, 1842.
5. *Boston Daily Advertiser*, Jan. 6, 1842; CFA, MS-D, Jan. 5, 1842, Adams MSS.

6. *Mass. Leg. Documents, House 1842, No. 40* (Boston, 1842).
7. JGP, MS-J, Jan. 15, 27, 1842.
8. *Boston Daily Advertiser,* Jan. 20, 1842; *Mass. Leg. Documents, House 1842, No. 13* (Boston, 1842).
9. CFA, MS-D, Jan. 27, 1842, Adams MSS; *Boston Daily Advertiser,* Jan. 28, 29, 1842.
10. *Ibid.,* Feb. 8, 11, 12, 1842.
11. *Mass. Leg. Documents, House 1842, No. 20* (Boston, 1842); *Boston Daily Advertiser,* Feb. 17, 1842.
12. CFA, MS-D, Jan. 19, 1842, Adams MSS; *Boston Daily Advertiser,* Jan. 21, Feb. 16, 1842.
13. *Ibid.,* Mar. 3, 1842; CFA, MS-D, Mar. 2, 1842, Adams MSS.
14. JGP, MS-A, pp. 184–185; Mann to T. Robbins, Mar. 8, 1842, Hoadley Collection.
15. Barnard to JGP, Mar. 8, 1842; Mann to C. E. Stone, Mar. 15, 1842, Mann MSS, Mass. Hist. Society; Louise Hall Tharp, *Until Victory, Horace Mann and Mary Peabody* (Boston, 1953), p. 176.
16. JGP to Mann, Apr. 16, [1842], Mann MSS; JGP to G. E. Ellis (draft), Oct. 16, 1843.
17. *Boston Daily Advertiser,* Mar. 4, 1842; JGP to JP, May 20, 1842.
18. JGP, MS-J, Apr. 2–15, 1842; Saltonstall to JGP, Aug. 12, 1842.
19. Darling, *Political Changes in Mass.,* pp. 169–170, 259.
20. JGP, MS-J, July 13–Aug. 13, 1842.
21. *Ibid.,* Aug. 22–29, 1842.
22. CFA, MS-D, Sep. 5, 1842, Adams MSS; Martin B. Duberman, *Charles Francis Adams* . . . (Boston, 1961), p. 76; JGP, MS-J, Sep. 6, 1842.
23. *Ibid.,* Sep. 7–8, 1842; *Boston Daily Advertiser,* Sep. 9, 14, 1842.
24. Lawrence to R. C. Winthrop, July 12, 1841, Winthrop MSS, Mass. Hist. Society; CFA, MS-D, Aug. 12, 1841, Adams MSS.
25. Boston *Daily Atlas,* Sep. 1, 1842; JGP, MS-J, Aug. 31, 1842.
26. *Ibid.,* Sep. 9, 12, 1842; Boston *Daily Atlas,* Sep. 15, 1842. Palfrey joked so seldom, at least in writing, that it is a pity the "hits" were not recorded by the *Atlas* correspondent.
27. JGP to Willard Phillips, Sep. 17, 1842, Phillips MSS, Mass. Hist. Society; JGP, MS-J, Sep. 30, 1842.
28. *Ibid.,* Nov. 11–12, 1842; Darling, *Political Changes in Mass.,* p. 289n.
29. *Ibid.,* pp. 290–293; *Boston Daily Advertiser,* Dec. 31, 1842, Jan. 3, 1843.
30. JGP, MS-J, Jan. 12, 1843. This is uncharacteristic of Palfrey's political behavior, as his later adherence to a politically suicidal sense of rectitude amply demonstrated. He would have agreed with Whig Congressman Charles Hudson, who called Morton a "*talented,* but *miserable,* whispering demagogue"; Hudson to G. N. Briggs, June 8, 1843, Washburn Collection, Mass. Hist. Society.

31. CFA, MS-D, Feb. 18, 1843, Adams MSS.
32. *Boston Daily Advertiser*, Mar. 3, 1843; JGP to J. Story, June 28, 1843, Story MSS.
33. *Boston Daily Advertiser*, Jan. 17, 1843; Marquis James, *Life of Andrew Jackson* (Indianapolis, 1938), p. 264; CFA, MS-D, Jan. 21, 1843, Adams MSS.
34. *Ibid.*, Feb. 17, 1843, Adams MSS; *Boston Daily Advertiser*, Feb. 20, 1843; *Mass. Leg. Documents, Senate 1843, No. 11* (Boston, 1843).
35. JGP, MS-J, Mar. 2, 1843; CFA, MS-D, Mar. 13, 1843, Adams MSS; *Boston Daily Advertiser*, Mar. 27, 1843.
36. JGP, MS-A, p. 189.
37. For example, JGP, MS-J, Jan. 29, Dec. 7, 1842.
38. *Ibid.*, Aug. 7, Sep. 8, 11–14, 1843.
39. *Ibid.*, June 28, 1843; JGP, MS-A, Notes, p. 76.
40. *Ibid.*, p. 189; JGP, MS-J, Aug. 28–29, Oct. 6, 1843.
41. JGP, MS-A, p. 189.
42. Kinnicutt to JGP, Nov. 23, 1843. This constitutional aversion to everything pertaining to the Democracy goes far in explaining Palfrey's refusal eight years later to sanction the Free Soil–Democratic coalition.
43. JGP, MS-J, Jan. 5, 7, 1844; CFA, MS-D, Jan. 4, 9, 1844, Adams MSS; *Boston Daily Advertiser*, Jan. 10, 1844; Bolles to JGP, Jan. 9, 1844.
44. JGP, MS-A, p. 190.
45. *Mass. Leg. Documents, Senate 1844, Nos. 85 and 94* (Boston, 1844).
46. JGP to J. P. Bigelow, Mar. 14, 1844, Bigelow MSS; CFA, MS-D, Jan. 8, 1844, Adams MSS; JGP to G. N. Briggs (draft), Sep. 9, 1844.
47. JGP, *Third Annual Report to the Legislature Relating to the Registry and Returns of Births, Marriages and Deaths . . . 1844* (Boston, 1845); *Mass. Public Documents, No. 15, 1848* (Boston, 1849); JGP to W. H. Hoadley, July 24, 1846, Hoadley Collection.
48. *Mass. Leg. Documents, Senate 1843, No. 44* (Boston, 1843); *Mass. Leg. Documents, House 1848, No. 2* (Boston, 1848); JGP to President of Mass. Hist. Society (draft), Jan. 1, 1846.
49. JGP to CFA, Feb. 3, 1845, Adams MSS; JGP to B. P. Poore, Nov. 16, 1847, Misc. MSS, New York Public Library.
50. JGP, MS-J, May 22, 1845; JGP, MS-A, p. 190.

VIII: A Practicing Abolitionist

1. HWP to JGP, Dec. 4, 1838; JGP to HWP (draft), Jan. 11, 1839.
2. JGP, MS-A, p. 193.
3. JGP, MS-J, Oct. 30, 1842; E. G. Loring to JGP, Dec. 27, 1842; Henrietta Buckmaster, *Let My People Go* (Boston, 1959 ed.), pp. 124–125.
4. JGP, MS-A, p. 187.

5. SHP to ARP, Apr. 30, 1843; JGP to MAP, May 8, 1843.

6. WTP to JGP, Oct. 19, 1843.

7. WTP to JGP, Nov. 4, 1843; HWP to JGP, Nov. 11, 1843.

8. JGP, MS-J, Nov. 21, 24–25, Dec. 2–3, 1843; JGP to T. W. Higginson, Feb. 22, 1868, Higginson MSS, Houghton Library; JGP, Codicil, Dec. 13, 1843.

9. I have been unable to establish any previous connection between Palfrey and Giffen. Miss Marcelle F. Schertz, of the Archives Department, Louisiana State Univ., informs me that Giffen was Louisiana state treasurer immediately after the Civil War.

10. JGP to Giffen (draft), Dec. 9, 1843; Giffen to JGP, Dec. 29, 1843. Palfrey also told Giffen of the $1,000 he had borrowed from his father in 1839, and asked to have his inheritance account debited. Since John Palfrey had returned the promissory note, no record of the loan existed.

11. HWP to JGP, Jan. 12, 1844; Giffen to JGP, Jan. 19, 1844.

12. JGP to Giffen (drafts), Jan. 22, Feb. 6, 1844.

13. Giffen to JGP, Feb. 8, Mar. 2, 1844.

14. The inventory of slave property in "Allotment Number One" was as follows:

Anna, 32; and her four children, Mana, 9;		
Charles, 6; Caroline, 4; William, 2.	5 persons	$1,500
Sarah, 11.	1	400
Betsy, 30; and her child Ralph, 5.	2	850
Frankey, 11.	1	400
Maria, 22; and her child Emily, 2.	2	650
Margery, 20; and her infant child.	2	550
Little Sam, 27.	1	300
Amos, 61.	1	350
Clara, 55; and her child Amos, 9.	2	550
Old Sam, 65.	1	150
Jose, 40.	1	500
Rose, 12.	1	400
		$6,600

Notarized Affidavit (copy), Mar. 8, 1844.

15. JGP to Senate and House of Louisiana (draft), Feb. 27, 1844; JGP to Morse (draft), Feb. 27, 1844.

16. New Orleans *Courier*, Mar. 12, 1844 (clipping in Palfrey Papers); Giffen to JGP, Mar. 12, 1844.

17. JGP to Giffen (draft), Mar. 14, 1844.

18. Giffen to JGP, Jan. 19, 1844; JGP, MS-J, Mar. 23–24, Apr. 16, 1844.

19. *Ibid.*, Apr. 18, 1844; Lydia M. Child to JGP, Apr. 18, 1844.

20. JGP to Clay (draft), Apr. 26, 1844.

21. JGP to ARP, May 11, 1844; Quincy to Caroline Weston, Sep.

17, 1844, Weston MSS, Boston Public Library; JGP, MS-A, pp. 191–192.

22. *Ibid.*, p. 192.

23. JGP to Giffen (drafts), June 13, Nov. 26, 1844.

24. Giffen to JGP, Mar. 22, 1845; JGP to Giffen (draft), May 31, 1845.

25. Giffen to JGP, Aug. 5, 1845; JGP to Giffen (copy), Aug. 30, 1845. In his final accounting with Palfrey, Giffen explained that expenses, including "influencing" the Police Jury, had been heavy; Giffen to JGP, Mar. 20, 1846.

26. Ayer, *Legacy of New England*, I, 145.

27. A. Ballou to JGP, Mar. 12, 1846; JGP to T. W. Higginson, Feb. 22, 1868, Higginson MSS; JGP, MS-A, Notes, p. 77.

28. E. Farrar to Maria Weston Chapman, Sep. 5, 1844, Weston MSS; Quincy to Caroline Weston, Sep. 17, 1844, Weston MSS.

29. Loring to JGP, Mar. 24, 1845; Felton to JGP, Sep. 11, 1845; Boston *Free State Rally and Texas Chain-Breaker*, Nov. 20, 1845.

30. Account of Estate of John Palfrey, Palfrey MSS, Louisiana State Univ. Library.

31. Clara to Master Gorham [JGP], Feb. 6, 1847.

32. Phillips, *Life and Labor in the Old South*, p. 300.

33. Samuel J. May to JGP, Sep. 29, 1863.

IX: Conscience and Judgment

1. Whittier to S. E. Sewall, Aug. 8, 1837, Norcross Collection; Everett to R. C. Winthrop, Sep. 30, 1837, Winthrop MSS.

2. C. Hudson to I. M. Barstow, Mar. 19, 1844, Hudson MSS; Webster to Winthrop, Apr. 28, 1844, Winthrop MSS.

3. JGP, MS-A, pp. 194–195; Sumner to S. G. Howe, May 21, 1844, Sumner MSS.

4. JGP, MS-J, July 1, Sep. 9, 12, Nov. 7-12, 1844; JGP, undated MS draft of speech, [1844]; C. Hudson to C. Allen, Nov. 14, 1844, Hoar MSS.

5. Phillips to C. Allen, Dec. 29, 1844, Hoar MSS; Webster to Winthrop, Dec. 13, 29, 1844, Jan. 10, 1845, Winthrop MSS.

6. C. G. Thomas to JGP, Jan. 26, 1845; CFA, MS-D, Jan. 29-30, 1845, Adams MSS; M. Brimmer to L. H. Sigourney, Feb. 1, 1845, Hoadley Collection; Webster to Winthrop, Jan. 11, 1845, Winthrop MSS; Saltonstall to Winthrop, Jan. 30, 1845, Winthrop MSS; Donald, *Sumner*, p. 156.

7. CFA, MS-D, Mar. 4-25, 1845, Adams MSS; JGP, MS-J, Mar. 10, 1845; Phillips, Allen, and CFA to Winthrop, June 25, 1845, Winthrop MSS; Winthrop to Clifford, July 11, 1845, Winthrop MSS.

8. JGP, MS-J, Feb. 7, Apr. 6, 1845; JGP, MS-A, pp. 196–197; Pierce, *Sumner*, II, 342-343, 355, 357; JGP to Sumner, Sep. 8, 1845.

9. C. Cushing to G. W. Gordon, Oct. 5, 1845, Gordon MSS; CFA,

MS-D, Sep. 24, 1845, Adams MSS; JGP, MS-J, Sep. 22, 1845; W. Phillips to S. E. Sewall, Oct. 14, 1845, Norcross Collection.

10. CFA, MS-D, Oct. 30, Nov. 15–17, 1845, Adams MSS; JGP, MS-A, p. 196; CFA to Lawrence, Nov. 13, 1845, Letterbook, Adams MSS; Appleton to CFA, JGP, and Sumner, Nov. 10, 1845, Sumner MSS.

11. *Free State Rally and Texas Chain-Breaker*, Nov. 15, 1845; CFA, MS-D, Nov. 14, 1845, Adams MSS; H. L. Pierce to Editor of Taunton *Democrat*, Nov. 22, 1845, H. L. Pierce MSS.

12. JGP to CFA, Nov. 21, 1845, Adams MSS; JGP to Hale (draft), Dec. 8, 1845; JGP to Eliot (draft), Dec. 10, 1845; Eliot to Sumner, Aug. 19, 1845, Sumner MSS; Eliot to JGP, Dec. 13, 1845.

13. JGP to CFA, Dec. 22, 1845, Adams MSS; JGP, MS-J, Dec. 19, 28, 1845.

14. CFA, MS-D, Dec. 19, 1845, Jan. 19, 1846, Adams MSS; Sumner to F. Lieber, Nov. 19, 1845, Sumner MSS; Norton to JGP, [Dec., 1845]; S. Higginson to JGP, Jan. 20, 1846.

15. Boston *Daily Atlas*, Feb. 4, 27, Apr. 14, 1846; Boston *Daily Whig*, Sep. 29, 1846; George F. Hoar, *Autobiography of Seventy Years*, 2 vols. (New York, 1903), I, 134.

16. JGP, MS-J, May 5, 20–23, 1846; CFA, MS-D, May 2, 19–28, June 1, 1846, Adams MSS; Boston *Daily Whig*, June 1, 1846; W. S. Robinson to W. Schouler, June 12, 1846, Schouler MSS.

17. J. Davis to JGP, Jan. 16, 1846; *Cong. Globe*, 29th Cong., 1st Sess., p. 795. The five representatives were John Quincy Adams, George Ashmun, Joseph Grinnell, Charles Hudson, and Daniel P. King. Professor Bemis incorrectly calls them "the famous Conscience Whigs." Adams died before the election of 1848, and the other four supported the Cotton candidate, General Taylor; Samuel F. Bemis, *John Quincy Adams and the Union* (New York, 1956), p. 498.

18. Robinson to W. Schouler, May 25, 1846, Schouler MSS; H. W. Longfellow, MS-J, May 27, 1846, Longfellow MSS; *Norfolk County American*, June 20, 1846 (clipping in Palfrey Papers); JGP to J. Mann (draft), July 30, 1846.

19. Winthrop to Clifford, May 15, 1846, Winthrop MSS; CFA, MS-D, July 15, 1846, Adams MSS; Boston *Daily Whig*, July 16, 1846; Hayden to Winthrop, July 23, 1846, Winthrop MSS; Winthrop to Sumner, Aug. 17, 1846, Sumner MSS.

20. Boston *Daily Whig*, Aug. 15, 19, Sep. 10, 1846; JGP to Sumner, Sep. 11, 1846; Phillips to Sumner, Sep. 15, 1846, Sumner MSS; CFA, MS-D, Sep. 22, 1846, Adams MSS.

21. Boston *Daily Whig*, Sep. 21–26, 1846; J. Q. Adams, MS-D, Sep. 23, 1846, Adams MSS.

22. JGP, MS-A, pp. 198–199; JGP, *Papers on the Slave Power, First Published in the "Boston Whig"* (Boston, 1846); JGP to JCP, Jan. 27, 1868.

23. Boston *Daily Whig*, Oct. 10, 1846; Appleton to JGP, Oct. 15, 24, 1846; JGP to Appleton (draft), Oct. 17, 1846; *Correspondence Between Nathan Appleton and John G. Palfrey* . . . (Boston, 1846).

24. JGP, MS-J, Oct. 19–20, 1846; J. L. Sibley, MS-J, Oct. 20, 1846, HUA; Otis to Appleton, Nov. 1846, Appleton MSS; CFA, MS-D, Oct. 21, 1846, Adams MSS.

25. Norton to Appleton, Nov. 4, 1846, Appleton MSS. Van Wyck Brooks's remark about Sparks, the gentleman-editor, fits Palfrey perfectly: "the high-minded Sparks, who, had made his own way in a world that worshipped manners, could hardly have been expected to underrate them"; Brooks, *Flowering of New England*, p. 125.

26. JGP, MS-J, Oct. 21, 23, Nov. 1–2, 1846; Norton to JGP, Oct. 29, 1846; Sparks to JGP, Oct. 31, 1846; Eliot to JGP, Nov. 2, 1846.

27. Thompson to W. Schouler, Nov. 18, 1848, Schouler MSS; JGP, MS-A, p. 199.

28. JGP, MS-J, Feb. 14, Sep. 15, Oct. 3–5, 1846; JGP to E. R. Hoar (draft), Sep. 21, 1846; JGP, MS-A, p. 200; King to JGP, Oct. 2, 1846; CFA, MS-D, Sep. 26, Oct. 2, 8, 1846, Adams MSS; Hoar to JGP, Oct. 1, 1846; Boston *Daily Whig*, Oct. 6, 10, 1846; JGP to J. T. Buckingham (draft), Oct. 12, 1846.

29. JGP to Liberty Party Committee (draft), Oct. 12, 1846; E. Everett to A. H. Everett, Oct. 30, 1846, Letterbook, Everett MSS; E. Wright to J. G. Birney, Feb. 8, 1847, Dwight L. Dumond (ed.), *Letters of James Gillespie Birney* . . . , 2 vols. (New York, 1938), II, 1039.

30. JGP to Whigs of Westborough (draft), Nov. 2, 1846; JGP, MS-J, Nov. 8, 1846; C. Stetson to Sumner, Nov. 7, 1846, Sumner MSS.

31. H. W. Longfellow, MS-J, Nov. 9–10, 1846, Longfellow MSS; MS Election Returns, Congress 1828–1852, pp. 225–226, Mass. Archives; Felton to Sumner, [Nov.] 11, 1846, Sumner MSS.

32. JGP to H. P. Fairbanks (draft), Nov. 21, 1846; Lawrence to S. Lawrence, Nov. 21, 1846, Schouler MSS; H. Wilson to W. Schouler, Nov. 26, 1846, Schouler MSS; Boston *Daily Whig*, Dec. 12, 26, 1846.

33. MS Election Returns, Congress 1828–1852, pp. 236–237, Mass. Archives; CFA to J. R. Giddings, Dec. 30, 1846, Letterbook, Adams MSS; JGP, MS-J, Dec. 31, 1846; Winthrop to Clifford, Dec. 21, 1846, Winthrop MSS.

34. Clerk of Mass. Senate to JGP, Jan. 13, 1847; CFA, MS-D, Jan. 13, 1847, Adams MSS; Curtis to Winthrop, Jan. 17, 1847, Winthrop MSS.

35. JGP, MS-J, Feb. 18–Mar. 8, 1847; Artemas Hale, MS-J, Jan. 27, 1847, A. Hale Papers; CFA to Ashmun, Jan. 10, 1847, Letterbook, Adams MSS; Sumner to Chase, Mar. 12, 1847, Chase MSS; JGP to J. W. Taylor, June 8, 1847, Misc. MSS, New-York Historical Society.

36. Sumner to Giddings, Feb. 1, 1847, Sumner MSS; Webster to J. A. Hamilton, June 16, 1847, Misc. MSS, New York Public Library;

C. Hudson to Schouler, June 28, 1847, Schouler MSS; Everett to Winthrop, May 31, 1847, Winthrop MSS.
37. CFA, MS-D, Aug. 11, 21, Sep. 28–29, 1847, Adams MSS; JGP, MS-J, Sep. 21, 25, 1847; an excellent account of the convention is in Donald, *Sumner*, pp. 156–159.
38. JGP, MS-A, pp. 203–205; Sumner to Giddings, Oct. 1, 1847, Giddings MSS; Sumner to Chase, Oct. 1, 1847, Chase MSS; Duberman, *Adams*, pp. 126–127; Fuess, *Webster*, II, 180.
39. Sumner to Bird, Oct. 6, 1847, Bird MSS; Corwin to Sumner, Oct. 25, 1847, Sumner MSS; JGP, MS-J, Nov. 2, 1847; Winthrop to Clifford, Oct. 3, 1847, Winthrop MSS; Lawrence, Jr. to W. C. Rives, Jr., Nov. 10, 1847, Rives MSS.
40. JGP, MS-J, Oct. 5–18, 1847; King to JGP, Sep. 21, 1847; Giddings to Sumner, Oct. 8, 1847, Sumner MSS; Sumner to Giddings, Nov. 1, 1847, Giddings MSS.

X: "He Knows Nothing about Politicks"

1. Sumner to Giddings, Dec. 1, 1847, Giddings MSS; JGP to MAP, Dec. 4, 1847.
2. Harold Schwarz, *Samuel Gridley Howe* (Cambridge, 1956), p. 163; Giddings to Sumner, June 2, 1847, Sumner MSS.
3. R. C. Winthrop, MS-D (fragment), Dec. 4, 1847, Winthrop MSS; A. Hale, MS-J, Dec. 4, 1847, A. Hale MSS.
4. Giddings to Sumner, Dec. 4, 1847, Sumner MSS; JGP to Winthrop, Dec. 5, 1847, Winthrop MSS; Giddings to Mrs. Giddings, Dec. 5, 1847, Giddings MSS; Winthrop to JGP, Dec. 5, 1847. Professor Nevins, citing the memoir of Winthrop by his son, and a South Carolina newspaper, gives a distorted account of the affair. Palfrey was the only man to write to Winthrop, and his note cannot be regarded as a demand for personal control of specific House committees. Winthrop did not refuse "indignantly," his note was a "friendly answer, declining to reply . . . with the common reasons for so doing"; JGP to CFA, Dec. 6, 1847, Adams MSS; Allan Nevins, *Ordeal of the Union*, 2 vols. (New York, 1947), I, 16; Winthrop to C. Deane, Aug. 27, 1872, Winthrop MSS.
5. *Boston Daily Advertiser*, Dec. 6, 1847; Charles A. Cole, *The Whig Party in the South* (Washington, 1913), pp. 123–124.
6. Tuck, a former Democrat, gained his seat as an independent in the same New Hampshire upheaval that sent John P. Hale to the Senate; Charles R. Corning, *Amos Tuck* (Exeter, 1902), pp. 32–33.
7. *Boston Daily Whig*, Dec. 11, 1847; Robert C. Winthrop, Jr., *A Memoir of Robert C. Winthrop* (Boston, 1897), p. 71.
8. *Boston Daily Atlas*, Dec. 6, 1847; *Cong. Globe*, 30th Cong., 1st Sess., p. 2; A. Hale, MS-J, Dec. 6, 1847, A. Hale MSS; JGP to CFA, Dec. 6, 1847, Adams MSS.

9. JGP to A. R. Thompson (draft), Dec. 20, 1847; JGP, *A Letter to a Friend* (Cambridge, 1850), p. 12.

10. *Ibid.*, p. 19.

11. JGP to Winthrop, Dec. 6, 1847, Winthrop MSS; JGP to SHP, Dec. 6, 1847.

12. Boston *Daily Atlas*, Dec. 10, 1847; *Boston Daily Advertiser*, Dec. 10, 11, 1847; Lawrence *Courier*, Dec. 25, 1847.

13. Boston *Courier*, Dec. 11, 20, 1847; Winthrop to Clifford, Dec. 26, 1847, Winthrop MSS.

14. Lowell *Journal*, Dec. 17, 1847; Robinson to JGP, Dec. 17, 1847.

15. Sumner to JGP, Dec. 8, 1847; CFA to JGP, Dec. 8, 1847, Letter-book, Adams MSS.

16. Mrs. M. Torrey to Mrs. G. Bancroft, Dec. 11, 1847, Bancroft-Bliss MSS; H. W. Bellows to Norton, Dec. 24, 1847, A. Norton MSS; Winthrop to Clifford, Dec. 14, 1847, Winthrop MSS.

17. Phillips to JGP, Dec. 9, 1847; CFA to JGP, Dec. 11, 1847, Adams MSS; Charleston *Courier*, quoted in Salem *Gazette*, Jan. 7, 1848.

18. CFA to JGP, Dec. 11, 1847, JGP to CFA, Dec. 9, 15, 1847, Adams MSS; *Cong. Globe*, 30th Cong., 1st Sess., pp. 4, 14–15, 24. Palfrey's vote for chaplain, which "scandalized" his friends of the Massachusetts delegation, was directed against John Quincy Adams' nominee Rev. R. R. Gurley because that clergyman had been secretary of the American Colonization Society; JGP, MS-J, Dec. 8, 1847; Donald W. Riddle, *Congressman Abraham Lincoln* (Urbana, 1957), pp. 29–30.

19. J. L. Sibley, MS-J, Dec. 16, 1847; Arthur Voss, "Backgrounds of Lowell's Satire in 'The Biglow Papers,'" *New England Quarterly*, XXIII (March 1950), 47–64.

20. Abbott Lawrence, Jr. to William C. Rives, Jr., Jan. 9, 1848, Rives MSS; JGP to CFA, Dec. 13, 22, 1847, Adams MSS; JGP to FWP, Dec. 11, 1847.

21. JGP to CFA, Dec. 15, 1847, Adams MSS; JGP to Sumner, Dec. 14, 1847; Winthrop to Clifford, Dec. 14, 1847, Winthrop MSS; *Cong. Globe*, 30th Cong., 1st Sess., p. 60.

22. S. H. Jenks to F. W. Bird, Dec. 30, 1847, Bird MSS; JGP to J. P. Bigelow, Jan. 12, 1848, Bigelow MSS; JGP, MS-A, Notes, p. 80.

23. Bowen to JGP, Jan. 18, 1848; A. R. Thompson to JGP, Jan. 24, 1848; JGP to SHP, Feb. 14, 1848.

24. WTP to JGP, Jan. 5, Feb. 20, 1848; JGP to WTP (draft), Jan. 22, 1848; JGP, MS-J, Mar. 6, 1848.

25. JGP to MGP, Feb. 19, 1848; JGP to Sumner, Jan. 19, 1848; JGP to CFA, Dec. 18, 1847, Adams MSS; Giddings to Mrs. Giddings, Jan. 30, 1848, Giddings MSS (italics added).

26. JGP to SHP, Jan. 24, 1848; *Cong. Globe*, 30th Cong., 1st Sess., Appendix, pp. 133–137.

27. Giddings to Sumner, Jan. 26, 28, 1848, Sumner MSS; Sumner to

Chase, Feb. 7, 1848, Chase MSS; Boston *Courier*, Feb. 1, 1848; Boston *Daily Atlas*, Feb. 7, 1848; Sumner to JGP, Feb. 14, 1848.

28. Giddings to Mrs. Giddings, Jan. 9, 1848, Giddings MSS; JGP to CFA, Jan. 13, 1848, Adams MSS; JGP, MS-A, pp. 209–210.

29. JGP to Sumner, Feb. 28, Mar. 2, 1848; Mann to E. W. Clapp, Mar. 11, 1848, Mann MSS; Sumner to Giddings, Mar. 28, 1848, Sumner MSS; JGP to SHP, Mar. 27, 1848; Giddings to Sumner, Apr. 17, 1848, Sumner MSS.

30. *Cong Globe*, 30th Cong., 1st Sess., pp. 329–330, 368, 370; JGP to CFA, Feb. 10, 1848, Adams MSS. The petitions are in the MSS of the 30th Congress, Box 12, Bundle 64, and Box 17, Bundle 101, National Archives.

31. Rives to Abbott Lawrence, Jr., Dec. 25, 1847, Rives MSS.

32. Palfrey was too active in the House. On several occasions, having just entered the chamber, he plunged into debate without full knowledge of what had gone before, a course which sometimes led to embarrassment; for example, see *Cong. Globe*, 30th Cong., 1st Sess., p. 610.

33. *Ibid.*, pp. 609–610, 637; JGP to Sumner, Apr. 19, 1848.

34. *Cong. Globe*, 30th Cong., 1st Sess., p. 456; Giddings to Sumner, Mar. 13, 1848, Sumner MSS; JGP to Sumner, Mar. 5, 1848.

35. Boston *Daily Whig*, Apr. 20, 21, 1848; *Cong. Globe*, 30th Cong., 1st Sess., p. 641.

36. Giddings to Sumner, Apr. 17, 1848, Sumner MSS; Boston *Daily Atlas*, Apr. 26, 1848; Washington *National Era*, Apr. 27, 1848; JGP to Sumner, Apr. 29, 1848; JGP to JCP, Mar. 10, 1848.

37. CFA to Giddings, Dec. 30, 1847, Letterbook, Adams MSS; JGP to CFA, Jan. 24, 1848, Adams MSS; C. D. Cleveland to Sumner, Feb. 7, 1848, Sumner MSS.

38. JGP to CFA, Jan. 13, Feb. 3, 8, Mar. 10, 1848, Adams MSS; JGP to McLean, Feb. 4, 1848, McLean MSS; McLean to JGP, Feb. 7, 1848; M. C. Vaughan to McLean, Feb. 11, 1848, McLean MSS.

39. Chase to Sumner, Feb. 19, 1848, Sumner MSS; CFA to JGP, Feb. 12, 20, 1848, Adams MSS; C. B. Smith to McLean, Mar. 29, 1848, McLean MSS; Francis P. Weisenburger, *Life of John McLean* (Columbus, 1937), pp. 136–138.

40. Hoar to E. L. Pierce, May 23, 1892, Sumner MSS; Sumner to JGP, Apr. 23, May 24, 1848; JGP to CFA, May 31, 1848, Adams MSS.

41. JGP to Sumner, May 22, 1848.

XI: Down with Old Zack

1. Glyndon G. Van Deusen, *Horace Greeley* (Philadelphia, 1953), p. 122; C. D. Denison to J. Van Buren, Apr. 14, 1848, Van Buren MSS.

2. Myron Lawrence to Allen Bangs, Apr. 1, 1848, Hoar MSS; J. N.

Brewer to W. Schouler, May 21, 1848, Schouler MSS; Boston *Daily Whig*, Apr. 29, 1848.

3. Allen to JGP, May 22, 1848; JGP to CFA, May 29, 1848, Adams MSS.

4. E. Howe to JGP, Mar. 30, 1848; Moorefield Storey and Edward W. Emerson, *Ebenezer Rockwood Hoar* (Boston, 1911), p. 52; Worcester *Palladium*, Apr. 5, 1848; CFA to JGP, Apr. 5, 1848, Adams MSS.

5. With Lawrence the leading contender for the post, Conscience Whigs directed much criticism at him. Lawrence returned the sentiments, remarking early in the year: "The *Conscience Whigs*, alias the Abolition Party appear to have lost some of their strength—the odour of their insidious attacks has vanished—and I cannot but hope we may now drive them from the Whig Party—We gain nothing by allowing any portion of those people to attend our primary and other political meetings"; Lawrence to Winthrop, Feb. 4, 1848, Winthrop MSS.

6. Alonzo Hill, *Memoir of Charles Allen* (Cambridge, 1876), pp. 56–57; Boston *Daily Whig*, June 12, 1848; Worcester *Palladium*, June 14, 1848; Nathan Appleton, *Memoir of Abbott Lawrence* (Boston, 1856), p. 10; Sumner to JGP, June 8, 1848.

7. JGP to C. Allen, June 11, 1848, Hoar MSS; JGP to MAP, June 9, 1848; JGP to ARP, June 12, 1848.

8. Shortly before the Whig convention, the Democrats nominated Lewis Cass of Michigan for the presidency. Cass was unacceptable to Proviso men; CFA, MS-D, June 8, 1848, Adams MSS; Boston *Daily Whig*, June 10, 1848; G. F. Hoar, *Autobiography*, I, 148.

9. JGP to CFA, June 11–13, 1848, Adams MSS; Giddings to Sumner, Mar. 18, 1848, Sumner MSS; JGP, MS-J, June 15, 1848; Sumner to Chase, June 12, 1848, Chase MSS.

10. I. P. Davis to Louisa Bancroft, June 13, 1848, Bancroft-Bliss MSS; Boston *Daily Atlas*, June 12, 13, 17, 1848; Winthrop to Mrs. Gardner, June 13, 1848, Winthrop MSS; Salem *Gazette*, June 23, 1848; CFA to JGP, June 20, 1848, Adams MSS; Lowell *Journal*, June 16, 27, 1848.

11. JGP to CFA, June 23, 1848, Adams MSS; Giddings to Sumner, June 21, 1848, Sumner MSS; Whittier to Sumner, June 20, 1848, Sumner MSS; JGP to Sumner, June 24, 1848.

12. Adams found a good many Democrats in sympathy with the convention's aims, but Amasa Walker was the only well-known Democrat who spoke at Worcester. The regular Democratic papers exulted over the difficulties the Worcester committeemen had in finding Democratic leaders for their organization; CFA to JGP, June 20, 1848, Adams MSS; Boston *Post*, June 29, 1848.

13. Whittier to Sumner, June 20, 1848, Sumner MSS; JGP to Allen, Wilson, and Sumner (draft), June 24, 1848.

14. W. Jackson to Mann, June 28, 1848, Mann MSS; A. Willey to J. P. Hale, July 6, 1848, J. P. Hale MSS; CFA, MS-D, June 28, 1848, Adams MSS.

15. JGP to CFA, June 16, 1848, Adams MSS; JGP to MAP, June 19, 23, July 2, 1848; MAP to JGP, July 3, 1848.

16. Palfrey should have been called "The Conscientious Whig." He mailed a letter under his franking privilege for a friend, and then paid postage on the next letter home, to ease his troubled conscience; JGP to FWP, Apr. 13, 1848.

17. JGP, MS-A, pp. 206–207; JGP to CFA, Mar. 28, 1848, Adams MSS; JGP to MGP, Apr. 9, 1848.

18. JGP, MS-A, pp. 207–208; JGP to W. Phillips, Aug. 7, 1848, Willard Phillips MSS; JGP to JCP, Jan. 27, 1868; Boston *Daily Republican*, Aug. 26, 1848.

19. JGP, MS-A, pp. 208, 211; JGP to Sparks, Mar. 25, 1848, Sparks MSS; *Cong. Globe*, 30th Cong., 1st Sess., p. 786. Two months later Palfrey defended the purchase of the Jefferson and Hamilton Papers. When a member objected that there would be no end to such requests, and that soon they would have to buy John Quincy Adams' 100 volumes of papers, Palfrey denied with "some warmth" and as an intimate friend of the Adams family that Congress would ever be asked to buy that collection; *ibid.*, p. 919.

20. JGP, MS-A, p. 211; JGP to CFA, June 7, 1848, Adams MSS; Sumner to JGP, June 8, 1848; Keyes to Mann, June 12, 1848, Mann MSS; Webster to D. F. Webster, June 10, 16, 19, 1848, C. H. Van Tyne (ed.), *The Letters of Daniel Webster* (New York, 1902), pp. 367–369.

21. Mann to Mrs. Mann, June 14, 1848; Mann to Sumner, June 28, 1848; Sumner to Mann, June 21, 25, July 2, 1848; all in Mann MSS.

22. JGP to Mann, July 8, 1848, Mann MSS; JGP to Sumner, July 20, 1848. Mann's latest biographer has written that in 1848 he "wisely minded his own business and kept his own counsel" (Tharp, *Until Victory*, p. 237). This is hardly an adequate handling of a difficult problem, and the question immediately arises, what was his business? As a representative Mann had political obligations. His conception of his post as a kind of federal educational commissioner was not valid, since a seat in Congress and political neutrality are mutually exclusive.

23. Dana to Allen, July 28, 1848, Hoar MSS; CFA, MS-D, June 27, 1848, Adams MSS; JGP to CFA, July 4, 1848, Adams MSS; Sumner to Whittier, July 12, 1848, Sumner MSS.

24. CFA to Van Buren, July 16, 1848, Van Buren MSS; CFA, MS-D, July 28, 1848, Adams MSS; Van Buren to CFA, July 24, 1848, Adams MSS; JGP to CFA, July 20, 23, 1848, Adams MSS.

25. Dana to J. Willson, July 26, 1848, Dana MSS; Phillips to JGP,

July 17, 1848; Giddings to McLean, July 13, 1848, McLean MSS; Phillips to McLean, July 17, 1848, McLean MSS; Sumner to McLean, July 31, 1848, McLean MSS.

26. Whittier to M. A. Cartland, July 27, 1848, Whittier MSS; Bailey to Van Buren, Aug. 2, 1848, Van Buren MSS.

27. JGP, MS-A, Notes, pp. 81–82; CFA, MS-D, Aug. 10, 1848, Adams MSS; Boston *Daily Republican*, Aug. 12, 1848.

28. Arthur M. Schlesinger, Jr., *The Age of Jackson* (Boston, 1946), p. 464; Dana to Mrs. Dana, July 21, 1848, Dana MSS; JGP to E. L. Pierce, Mar. 8, 1875, Sumner MSS.

29. JGP to ARP, July 13, 19, 1848; *Cong. Globe*, 30th Cong., 1st Sess., p. 950; JGP, MS-J, Mar. 28, 1848; JGP to MAP, July 27, 28, 1848.

30. This was not wholly unwelcome to Palfrey. His brother William was in the capital that week, and the two men got along surprisingly well considering the animosities engendered by the emancipation in 1844. "I had made up my mind that I could not in faithfulness and Honor . . . spare a single word fit to be spoken, though my brother should stand across the Hall, looking me in the face." Fortunately, he did not have to meet this test; JGP to MAP, Aug. 11, 1848.

31. JGP to CFA, July 28, 1848, Adams MSS; JGP to SHP, Aug. 1, 1848; *Cong. Globe*, 30th Cong., 1st Sess., p. 1019.

32. Mann to Mrs. Mann, Aug. 11, 1848, Mann MSS; JGP, MS-J, Aug. 14–15, 1848.

33. W. M. Bassett to JGP, Aug. 21, 1848; JGP, MS-J, Aug. 22, 1848; H. W. Longfellow, MS-J, Sept. 3, 1848, Longfellow MSS.

34. JGP to Sumner, Sept. 7, 1848; J. Q. Adams to JGP, Nov. 4, 1846, Adams MSS; for a sneering definition of Conscience see Salem *Register*, Aug. 10, 1848; Briggs to JGP, Aug. 24, 1848.

35. Phillips to Sumner, Sept. 5, 1848, Sumner MSS; Boston *Republican*, Sept. 7, 1848; E. L. Keyes to H. Mann, Sept. 11, 1848, Mann MSS; CFA, MS-D, Sept. 5, 7, 30, 1848, Adams MSS.

36. JGP to N. W. Coffin (draft), Aug. 22, 1848; JGP to J. S. Keyes (draft), Sept. 27, 1848; Boston *Republican*, Sept. 28, 1848.

37. Hoar to JGP, Sept. 29, 1848; Boston *Republican*, Oct. 4–6, 1848; J. G. Carter to JGP, Oct. 5, 1848.

38. C. Mason to Hale, Oct. 4, 1848, J. P. Hale MSS; Boston *Republican*, Oct. 9, 17, 1848; D. Perkins to F. W. Bird, Aug. 21, 1848, Bird MSS; Phillips to S. P. Chase, Oct. 19, 1848, Chase MSS; Palfrey's Whiggery came through in a speech which attacked the Independent Treasury, and Henry D. Gilpin of Pennsylvania, a former Democrat, complained to Sumner of Palfrey's inability to favor reform in any field but antislavery; Gilpin to Sumner, Nov. 2, 1848, Sumner MSS.

39. I. P. Davis to Mrs. G. Bancroft, Oct. 31, 1848, Bancroft-Bliss MSS; Abbott Lawrence to N. Appleton, Aug. 11, 1848, Abbott Lawrence MSS.

40. MS Election Returns, Congress 1828–1852, pp. 243–244, Mass.

State Archives; T. W. Higginson to L. Higginson, Nov. 14, 1848, Higginson MSS; Hoar to JGP, Nov. 13, 1848; Boston *Republican*, Nov. 18, 1848.

41. CFA, MS-D, Nov. 17, 1848, Adams MSS; Davis to J. P. Bigelow, Nov. 14, 1848, Bigelow MSS.

XII: Trial by Stalemate

1. The poem first appeared in the *National Anti-Slavery Standard;* the Boston *Republican* reprinted it on Nov. 21, 1848.

2. Hoar to Free Soil Voters (printed circular), Nov. 22, 1848; Boston *Republican*, Nov. 23, 1848.

3. CFA to JGP, Dec. 9, 1848, Adams MSS; Winthrop to Clifford, Dec. 11, 1848, Winthrop MSS.

4. Sumner to S. P. Chase, Nov. 16, 1848, Chase MSS; B. F. Hallett to C. Cushing, Nov. 21, 1848, Cushing MSS; E. Hale to C. Cushing, Nov. 30, 1848, Cushing MSS.

5. JGP to J. Russell (draft), Dec. 19, 1848; CFA to JGP, Dec. 25, 1848, Adams MSS; JGP, MS-A, p. 215.

6. JGP to MAP, Dec. 27, 1848; JGP, MS-J, Dec. 31, 1848; MAP to JGP, Jan. 5, 1849.

7. Boston *Republican*, Dec. 28, 1848.

8. JGP to ARP, Jan. 2, 1849; MS Election Returns, Congress 1828–1852, pp. 254–255, Mass. State Archives.

9. Sumner to JGP, Jan. 4, 1849; Hoar to JGP, Jan. 5, 1849; JGP to Sumner, Jan. 8, 1849.

10. JGP to CFA, Dec. 5, 1848, Adams MSS; Winthrop to Clifford, Dec. 11, 1848, Winthrop MSS.

11. *Cong. Globe*, 30th Cong., 2nd Sess., pp. 31, 56, 38; Boston *Republican*, Dec. 14, 1848; Giddings to Sumner, Dec. 22, 1848, Sumner MSS; JGP to MAP, Dec. 20, 1848.

12. Winthrop to Everett, Dec. 23, 1848, Everett MSS; Lowell *Courier*, quoted in Boston *Republican*, Dec. 29, 1848; JGP to JCP, Dec. 29, 1848; Everett to Winthrop, Dec. 30, 1848, Winthrop MSS.

13. JGP to MGP, Jan. 6, 1849; Mann to Mrs. Mann, Jan. 12, 1849, Mann MSS; *Cong. Globe*, 30th Cong., 2nd Sess., pp. 240–241.

14. *Ibid.*, pp. 85, 577, 638–639; Boston *Republican*, Feb. 3, 1849; JGP to FWP, Feb. 15, 1849; Riddle, *Congressman Lincoln*, p. 155.

15. JGP to CFA, Jan. 29, 1849, Adams MSS; JGP to Sumner, Feb. 16, 1849.

16. JGP to SHP, Feb. 26, 1849; Mann to Sumner, Feb. 27, 1849, Mann MSS; Sumner to JGP, Mar. 28, 1849; JGP to MGP, Mar. 4, 1849.

17. JGP to MAP, Feb. 28, 1849.

18. E. Howe to JGP, Feb. 13, Mar. 1, 1849; CFA, MS-D, Feb. 24, 1849, Adams MSS; JGP, MS-J, Mar. 8, 1849; MS Election Returns, Congress 1828–1852, pp. 258–259, Mass. State Archives.

19. *Ibid.*, pp. 259–262; Hoar to G. N. Briggs, May 7, 1849, Wash-

burn MSS; JGP to Hale, Apr. 24, 1849, J. P. Hale MSS; Sumner to Giddings, June 29, 1849, Giddings-Julian MSS; CFA to G. Bailey, June 15, 1849, Letterbook, Adams MSS. In both cities Palfrey's vote fell off sharply, while Thompson's held firm; MS Election Returns.

20. Hoar to JGP, June 29, 1849; Sumner to JGP, Aug. 31, 1849; CFA, MS-D, Sep. 1, 1849, Adams MSS; JGP, MS-J, Sep. 8, 1849.

21. JGP to MAP, Sep. 11, 1849; Sumner to JGP, Sep. 13, 1849; Howe to JGP, Sep. 13, 1849; J. Jay to Sumner, Sep. 22, 1849, Sumner MSS.

22. JGP, MS-A, p. 215; JGP, Memorandum, May 28, 1849; JGP, MS-J, Apr. 11, June 13–19, 1849; JGP to S. May, Jr. (draft), July 27, 1849; JGP to Sumner, Dec. 12, 1849.

23. J. N. Barbour to JGP, Mar. 7, 1849; Everett to Webster, Apr. 18, 1849, Everett MSS; Everett to Winthrop, Sep. 20, 1849, Winthrop MSS; Winthrop to Everett, Sep. 22, 1849, Everett MSS.

24. JGP, MS-A, pp. 216–217; JGP, MS-J, Oct. 15, 1849; Everett to G. Morey, Oct. 11, 15, 1849, Letterbook, Everett MSS; JGP to Everett (draft, not sent), 1849.

25. Tuck to JGP, June 6, 1849; Giddings to Sumner, June 21, 1849, Sumner MSS.

26. CFA, MS-D, Oct. 4–12, 1849, Adams MSS; Sumner to Giddings, Oct. 19, 1849, Giddings MSS; Giddings to Sumner, Oct. 29, 1849, Sumner MSS; JGP, MS-J, Nov. 13, 1849; MS Election Returns, Congress 1828–1852, pp. 262–263, Mass. State Archives; Boston *Republican,* Nov. 15, 1849.

27. Bowen to JGP, Nov. 26, 1849; JGP to Bowen (copy), Nov. 28, 1849.

28. Giddings to JGP, Dec. 4, 1849; CFA to JGP, Dec. 10, 1849, Adams MSS; C. Allen to JGP, Dec. 23, 1849; Tuck to JGP, Jan. 13, 1850; JGP to Tuck (draft), Jan. 18, 1850; JGP to J. P. Hale, Dec. 13, 1849, J. P. Hale MSS.

29. CFA, MS-D, Jan. 14, 1850, Adams MSS; Sumner to Longfellow, Jan. 24, 1850, Longfellow MSS; JGP, MS-J, Jan. 23, 1850.

30. Giddings to Sumner, Feb. 15, 1850, Sumner MSS; Brewer to W. Schouler, Mar. 8, 1850, Schouler MSS; A. W. Fletcher to W. Schouler, Mar. 13, 1850, Schouler MSS. "Mr. Palfrey met Wendell [Phillips] in the street this morning, and told him he thought he had in his '*Review [of Webster's Speech on Slavery]*', completely served Mr. Winthrop up!"; S. May, Jr. to Caroline Weston, Apr. 12, 1850, Weston MSS.

31. JGP, MS-J, Apr. 28, 1850; CFA to JGP, Apr. 29, 1850, Adams MSS; CFA, MS-D, May 1–29, 1850, Adams MSS; C. Allen to JGP, May 22, 1850; B. Thompson to W. Schouler, May 29, 1850, Schouler MSS.

32. JGP to Sparks, Jan. 27, Feb. 8, 1849, Sparks MSS; JGP, MS-J, Mar. 4, 17–19, 1850; C. Cushing to Sparks, Sep. 8, 1850, Sparks MSS.

33. CFA, MS-D, Aug. 10, Sep. 5, 10, Oct. 8, 1850, Adams MSS; JGP, MS-J, Oct. 15, 1850; JGP, MS-A, p. 220; Sumner to JGP, Oct. 15, 1850; Donald, *Sumner*, pp. 199–200.

34. Parker to JGP, Sep. 9, 1850; Winthrop to Clifford, Aug. 25, 1850, Winthrop MSS; MS Election Returns, Congress 1828–1852, pp. 278–279, Mass. State Archives. Winthrop alluded to Professor John W. Webster, soon to hang for the murder of a Harvard colleague; Morison, *Three Centuries of Harvard*, pp. 282–286.

35. Higginson to JGP, Aug. 21, 1850; JGP to Higginson (draft), Sep. 2, 1850; Higginson to W. Higginson, Sep. 2, 1850, Higginson MSS; Schwarz, *Howe*, p. 177.

XIII: Defeat

1. JGP, MS-J, Dec. 23, 1850; [JGP], *To the Free Soil Members of the General Court of Massachusetts for the Year 1851* (Boston, 1851).

2. CFA, MS-D, Dec. 26, 1850, Adams MSS; CFA to JGP, Dec. 26, 1850, Adams MSS.

3. Howe to Mann, Dec. 27, 1850, Howe MSS. Professor Schwartz errs in attributing this first editorial to Howe (Schwartz, *Howe*, p. 178); Palfrey wrote the first two. JGP, MS-J, Dec. 31, 1850; CFA, MS-D, Jan. 1, 1851, Adams MSS; Boston *Commonwealth*, Jan. 1, 1851.

4. JGP to Dana, Mar. 15, 1854, Dana MSS; JGP, MS-J, Jan. 1–2, 1851; CFA, MS-D, Jan. 2, 1851, Adams MSS.

5. Boston *Commonwealth*, Jan. 3, 29, 1851; Boston *Daily Atlas*, Jan. 6, 1851.

6. Boston *Commonwealth*, Jan. 13, 16, 1851; Boston *Daily Advertiser*, Jan. 17, 1851; JGP, MS-J, Jan, 17–18, 1851; JGP to E. E. Hale (draft), June 29, 1854; MS Election Returns, Congress 1828–1852, pp. 299–200, Mass. State Archives.

7. "Palfrey, who with all his moral excellence had an element of impracticability in him, addressed the members in an open letter. . . . Annoying as this interference was, it had little effect on the members"; Pierce, *Sumner*, III, 236.

8. Abbott Lawrence to N. Appleton, Feb. 14, 1851, Abbott Lawrence MSS; Howe to Mann, Feb. 6, [Apr. ?], 1851, Howe MSS; Sumner to JPG, [March 1851]; JGP, MS-J, Mar. 29, 1851.

9. Eliot to Sparks, Jan. 21, 1851, Sparks MSS; Harold Schwartz, "Fugitive Slave Days in Boston," *New England Quarterly*, XXVII (March 1954), 197–202.

10. Bigelow to C. L. Holbrook, Apr. 4, 1851, Bigelow MSS; JGP, MS-J, Jan. 30, Apr. 4–8, 1851; Webster to Everett, Apr. 23, 1851, Everett MSS. The fugitive slave issue was too serious to Palfrey for him to joke about as Winthrop did: "You left your *cane* here. . . . You need not resort to the Fugitive Law to reclaim it, though I doubt not you could have a Commissioner's Warrant for taking it back to service or labor"; Winthrop to J. Davis, June 2, 1851, Davis MSS.

11. W. Parmenter to G. Bancroft, Jan. 4, 1839, Bancroft MSS; Boston *Republican*, Feb. 8, 1849; J. Morse to C. Cushing, June 27, 1850, Cushing MSS.

12. J. Leavitt to R. H. Leavitt, Apr. 4, 1851, Leavitt MSS; Ralph L. Rusk, *The Life of Ralph Waldo Emerson* (New York, 1949), p. 367; Sumner to JGP, [May 1851]; Wilson to JGP, May 19, 1851.

13. JGP to Sumner, May 23, 1851; JGP, MS-A, pp. 223–224.

14. J. Sawyer to Sumner, May 26, 1851; MS Election Returns, Congress 1828–1852, pp. 322–323, Mass. State Archives.

15. JGP to Thompson (draft), May 27, 1851; JGP to S. P. Chase, June 16, 1851, Chase MSS; CFA to JGP, May 28, 1851, Adams MSS; CFA, MS-D, May 27, 1851, Adams MSS.

16. Sumner to JGP, May 27, 1851; JGP to Sumner, May 28, 1851.

17. JGP to CFA, Nov. 9, 1850, Adams MSS; CFA, MS-D, Feb. 11–13, 1851, Adams MSS; Howe to JGP, Feb. 14, 19, 23, 1851.

18. Sumner to JGP, Mar. 31, 1851; Lyman to JGP, Apr. 1, 1851; Howe to Sumner, [May 1851], Howe MSS; JGP, MS-J, May 24, 28, 1851; Higginson to JGP, May 27, 1851; CFA, MS-D, June 11–18, 1851, Adams MSS.

19. JGP, *A Chapter of American History, Five Years Progress of the Slave Power* . . . (Boston, 1852); JGP to CFA, June 16, 1851, Adams MSS; JGP, MS-J, June 18, Sep. 2, 1851; CFA, MS-D, July 5, 21, Sep. 2, 1851, Adams MSS; JGP to F. D. Huntington (copy), Aug. 24, 1851; J. Lyman to R. Carter, Oct. 1, 1851, Carter MSS.

20. JGP, MS-J, Jan. 20, June 22, July 7, Sep. 2, 1851; Charles Francis Adams, [Jr.], *An Autobiography* (Boston, 1916), p. 23; H. Sargent to Anna W. Weston, July 29, 1851, Weston MSS.

21. JGP to Dana, Mar. 15, 1854, Dana MSS; JGP, MS-J, Sep. 10–15, 1851; CFA, MS-D, Sep. 12–22, 1851, Adams MSS; JGP, MS-A, Notes, pp. 87–89.

22. Higginson to Mrs. Higginson, Oct. 30, 1851, Higginson MSS.

23. JGP, MS-A, p. 225; JGP to Editor of *Commonwealth* (draft), Sep. 30, 1851; JGP, MS-J, Sep. 29–30, Oct. 7–8, 1851.

24. JGP, MS-J, Oct. 1, 1851; Winthrop to J. Davis, Sep. 30, 1851, Davis MSS. Palfrey's drought lasted four years. He returned to wine while in England in 1856; JGP, MS-A, Notes, p. 88.

25. JGP, MS-J, Nov. 10, 29, 1851; Winthrop to J. Davis, Sep. 2, 1851, Davis MSS; Winthrop to Clifford, Aug. 10, Nov. 15, 1851, Winthrop MSS; MS Election Returns, Governor 1851, Mass. State Archives.

26. Howe to Sumner, Dec. 12, 1851, Jan. 10, 1852, Howe MSS; JGP, MS-J, Jan. 14, 1852; Wilson to Sumner, Dec. 15, 1851, Sumner MSS; CFA to Sumner, Jan. 1, 1852, Sumner MSS; CFA, MS-D, Dec. 27, 1851–Jan. 14, 1852, Adams MSS.

27. Lawrence to N. Appleton, July 9, 1852, Abbott Lawrence MSS; Giddings to G. W. Julian, June 30, 1852, Giddings-Julian MSS; Howe

to Sumner, Mar. 15, 1852, Howe MSS; CFA, MS-D, Jan. 27, June 5–6, 1852, Adams MSS.

28. E. Hopkins to G. F. Hoar, June 18, 1852, Hoar MSS; J. W. Stone to Sumner, July 3, 1852, Sumner MSS; JGP, MS-A, pp. 227–228; JGP to Sumner, July 5, 1852. Palfrey's painting of Wilson's machinations employs no half-tones. His memory grants Wilson no mercy, though Sumner, another coalitionist, is forgiven all his errors. Palfrey would probably have drawn something conspiratorial from the knowledge that Wilson favored him as a vice-presidential candidate in 1852; Wilson to Sumner, July 22, 1852, Sumner MSS.

29. JGP to Dana, Mar. 15, 1854, Dana MSS; CFA, MS-D, Sep. 3–7, 1852, Adams MSS; Hoar to JGP, Sep. 7, 1852.

30. Mann to Howe, Aug. 16, 1852, Howe MSS; JGP to Convention, Sep. 14, 1852, Adams MSS; JGP to CFA, Sep. 14, 1852, Adams MSS.

31. CFA, MS-D, Sep. 15, 1852, Adams MSS; T. W. Higginson to JGP, Sep. 16, 1852; JGP, MS-A, p. 229; JGP to Mann, Sep. 18, 1852, Mann MSS; Howe to Sumner, [1852], Howe MSS.

32. Dana to JGP, Oct. 20, 1852; JGP to Dana, Oct. 21, 1852, Dana MSS; CFA, MS-D, Nov. 10, 28, 1852, Adams MSS; Horace Gray to G. F. Hoar, Oct. 21, 1852, Hoar MSS.

33. D. W. Alvord to Sumner, Aug. 21, 1849, Sumner MSS; J. Leavitt to R. H. Leavitt, Dec. 18, 1850, Leavitt MSS; Samuel Shapiro, "The Conservative Dilemma: The Massachusetts Constitutional Convention of 1853," *New England Quarterly*, XXXIII (June 1960), 207–224.

34. JGP to Sumner, Jan. 28, 1853; CFA, MS-D, Feb. 10, 23, 1853, Adams MSS.

35. Michel Brunet, "The Secret Ballot Issue in Massachusetts Politics from 1851 to 1853," *New England Quarterly*, XXV (September 1952), 358; JGP, MS-A, p. 234; Howe to Sumner, Feb. 8, 1853, Howe MSS; CFA, MS-D, Mar. 9, 1853, Adams MSS; Wilson to Sumner, Mar. 5, 10, 1853, Sumner MSS; Wilson to Free Soil Town Committees, Feb. 26, 1853, Carter MSS.

36. JGP, MS-A, p. 235; JGP to J. Jay (draft), Jan. 4, 1854.

37. JGP to Dana, Mar. 15, 1854, Dana MSS; JGP, MS-J, Aug. 28, Sep. 15, Oct. 21, 1853; CFA, MS-D, Sep. 2, 12, 1853, Adams MSS; JGP to S. P. Chase, Dec. 7, 1864, Chase MSS; [JGP], *Remarks on the Proposed State Constitution . . .* (Boston, 1853).

38. C. W. March to C. Cushing, Oct. 14, 1853, Cushing MSS; Boston *Daily Advertiser*, Oct. 25, 1853; G. Morey to Sparks, Oct. 27, 1853, Sparks MSS; JGP to Sparks, Oct. 26, 1853, Sparks MSS; JGP to J. Wilson & Co., Oct. 27, 1853, Folsom MSS.

39. JGP to JCP, Nov. 14, 1853; JGP, MS-A, p. 237; J. Willard to JGP, Nov. 22, 1853; F. A. Hildreth to C. Cushing, Nov. 17, 1853, Cushing MSS; Sumner to E. L. Pierce, Dec. 18, 1853, Sumner MSS.

40. G. Walsh to C. Cushing, Nov. 15, 1853, Cushing MSS; W. W. Winthrop to E. Winthrop, Nov. 27, 1853, Winthrop-Weston MSS;

JGP to Sumner, Nov. 29, 1853; CFA, MS-D, Dec. 5, 1853, Adams MSS; Donald, *Sumner*, pp. 248–249.

41. T. P. Chandler to Sumner, Dec. 16, 1853, Sumner MSS; William S. Robinson, *"Warrington"* Pen-Portraits (Boston, 1877), p. 204; JGP, MS-A, p. 238; JGP to JCP, Jan. 27, 1868.

42. I am indebted to Mr. Ernest McKay of Manhasset, L. I., New York, for allowing me to see his manuscript life of Wilson, a work still in progress.

XIV: POLITICAL TWILIGHT AND THE PURITAN PAST

1. JGP, MS-J, July 31, 1845.

2. E. Peabody to JGP, Sept. 29, 1852; CFA, MS-D, Jan. 27, 1853, Adams MSS; C. G. Loring to Sparks, Aug. 10, 1853, Sparks MSS; JGP, MS-A, pp. 230–232.

3. JGP, MS-J, Feb. 2, 1854; Howe to JGP, Feb. 10, 1854; CFA, MS-D, Feb. 11, 13, 1854, Adams MSS.

4. JGP, MS-J, Feb. 8, 1854; JGP to Dana, Feb. 13, 1854, Dana MSS; Howe to Sumner, Feb. 16, 1854, Howe MSS.

5. JGP to Parker (draft), Jan. 27, 1854; JGP to F. H. Underwood, Nov. 22, 1853, Palfrey MSS, Louisiana State Univ.; Mrs. Stowe to JGP, Dec. 27, 1853.

6. JGP, MS-J, May 26–28, 1854; CFA, MS-D, May 29, 1854, Adams MSS; JGP, MS-A, Notes, p. 168; Samuel Shapiro, "The Rendition of Anthony Burns," *The Journal of Negro History*, XLIV (January 1959), 34–51.

7. JGP to JCP, June 9, 1854; Howe to Sumner, Jan. 18, 1854, Howe to Mann, June 18, 1854, both in Howe MSS.

8. JGP to Sumner, Jan. 3, June 1, 1854; Sumner to JGP, June 6, 1854; JGP to Longfellow, July 8, 1854, Longfellow MSS.

9. Andrew to JGP, June 8, 1854; JGP to S. Hoar (draft), July 3, 1854; JGP to J. W. Thompson (draft), Aug. 18, 1854.

10. A. Abbott to W. Schouler, Nov. 16, 1844, Schouler MSS; CFA, MS-D, Jan. 6, Feb. 22, 1845, Adams MSS.

11. R. C. Winthrop to J. H. Clifford, Sept. 16, 1854, Winthrop MSS; D. W. Alvord to F. W. Bird, Sept. 10, 1854, Bird MSS; CFA, MS-D, Sept. 15, 25, 1854, Adams MSS.

12. S. G. Howe to H. Mann, Nov. 14, 1854, Howe MSS; JGP to J. R. Giddings, Dec. 2, 1854, Giddings MSS. The Palfreys were not overly sympathetic to the newly arrived Irish. The Irish maids at Hazelwood gave much trouble, though one suspects that native farm-girls would not have improved the situation. Mary Ann attended Catholic Mass once when her curiosity overcame her fear: "I should not like to be in a Hibernian atmosphere long, this cholera season." Palfrey joined the anti-slavery Know-Nothings in identifying a great portion of the Irish Democratic voters with the Doughface politicians who bowed to the Slave Power, and in his memoirs he referred to

Boston's servants as "that Irish rabbledom"; MAP to ARP, Aug. 19, 1849; JGP, MS-A, p. 258. See also JGP, *Hist. of New England*, IV, 100.

13. JGP, MS-J, March–June 1852; George H. Callcott, "The Sacred Quotation Mark," *The Historian*, XXI (August 1959), 409–420; [JGP], "Lord Mahon's History of England," *North American Review*, LXXV (July 1852), 185–208; Everett to W. B. Reed, Sep. 18, 1852, Letterbook, Everett MSS.

14. JGP, MS-A, p. 239; MAP to JCP, May 1, Apr. 30, June 18, Dec. 16, 1854.

15. CFA, MS-D, Jan. 19, 1855, Adams MSS; Howe to Sumner, Jan. 19, 1855, Howe MSS; JGP to S. Bowles (draft), Aug. 12, 1855.

16. JGP to Dana, Mar. 23, 1855, Dana MSS. When the issue reappeared in 1858 Governor Banks had no scruples about the removal; Adams, *Dana*, I, 347.

17. [JGP], *Letter to a Whig Neighbor, on the Approaching State Election by an Old Conservative* (Boston, 1855); E. L. Pierce to S. P. Chase, Nov. 9, 1855, Chase MSS; JGP to JCP, Jan. 27, 1868.

18. JGP to CFA, Oct. 29, 1855; CFA to JGP, Oct. 31, 1855, both in Adams MSS.

19. JGP, MS-A, p. 240; JGP to Banks, Feb. 5, 1856, Banks MSS; JGP to Sumner, Mar. 1, 1856.

20. JGP, MS-A, p. 242; JGP to Charles Deane, Mar. 3, 1856, Deane MSS; JGP to S. F. Haven, Mar. 3, 1856, Haven MSS.

21. Sparks to JGP, Feb. 26, 1856; JGP to Haven, Oct. 22, 1860, Haven MSS.

22. JGP to MAP, Apr. 18, May 8, 1856.

23. Parkes to JGP, Apr. 19, 1856; C. R. Weld to Longfellow, May 2, 1856, Longfellow MSS; MAP to JGP, Apr. 11, 1856; JGP to MAP, Apr. 22–23, 1856.

24. JGP to MAP, May 15, 18, 29, 1856; *The Times* (London), Jan. 9, 1861 (clipping in Palfrey Papers).

25. FWP to JGP, May 27, 1856; JGP to Sumner, June 11, 1856; Carlisle to JGP, June 7, 1856; JGP to Duchess of Argyll (draft), June 20, 1856.

26. JGP to MAP, May 15, June 11, 1856; JGP, MS-J, May 11, 29, 1856.

27. JGP to MAP, July 3, 9–10, 20, Aug. 4, 13, 1856; R. H. Dana, MS-J, July 15, 1856, Dana MSS; JGP to Parkman, Aug. 22, 1856, Parkman MSS.

28. Parkman to JGP, Sep. 14, 1856; JGP, MS-J, Oct. 29, Nov. 4–5, 1856; JGP to Giddings, Aug. 4, 1860, Giddings MSS.

29. JGP to Harriet B. Stowe (draft), Dec. 19, 1856; Lydia M. Child to JGP, Jan. 28, 1857; JGP to Mattie Griffith (draft), Feb. 2, 1857; JGP to Higginson, Jan. 12, 1857, Palfrey MSS, Louisiana State Univ. Library.

30. Norton to JGP, Oct. 15, 1857; JGP to Deane, Dec. 17, 1857, Deane MSS; Bowen to JGP, Jan. 30, 1858; Gardiner to JGP, Dec. 22, 1858.

31. H. W. Torrey to JGP, Dec. 27, 1857; H. B. Anthony to JGP, Jan. 11, 1859; JGP, MS-J, Nov. 21, 1857.

32. Longfellow to Sumner, Apr. 25, 1859, Longfellow MSS; MAP to JCP, Nov. 29, 1859; E. A. Newton to JGP, Oct. 30, 1860; Bowen to JGP, Sep. 6, 1860; JGP, MS-J, Dec. 31, 1859; JGP, *Hist. of New England*, I, 37.

33. JCP to FWP, Oct. 22, 1856; ARP to JCP, Jan. 8, 1857; JCP to JGP, Mar. 15, 27, 1857.

34. S. H. Russell to JGP, Oct. 12, 1859; JGP, Sons' College Accounts; JGP to Miss A. P. Jones (draft), July 4, 1858.

35. JGP to Sumner, Aug. 16, 1858, Jan. 18, May 2, 1859.

36. JGP to CFA, Dec. 8, 1859, Feb. 23, 1860, Adams MSS.

37. Giddings to JGP, July 13, 1860; JGP to Giddings, Aug. 4, 1860, Giddings MSS.

38. ARP to JCP, Nov. 8, 1860; Sumner to JGP, Dec. 10, 1860; JGP to Sumner, Dec. 15, 1860.

XV: War against the Slave Power

1. Donald, *Sumner*, pp. 373-382; JGP to MAP, Jan. 19, 1861.

2. JGP to MAP, Jan. 19, 21, 23, 1861.

3. H. R. Harding to JGP, Feb. 11, 1861; JGP, MS-J, Feb. 12, 1861; JGP to Sumner, Feb. 20, 1861.

4. MAP to JCP, Jan. 13, 1861; JGP to CFA, Feb. 4, 1861, Adams MSS; JGP to Sumner, Feb. 20, 1861.

5. JGP to CFA, Feb. 15, 20, 1861, Adams MSS; CFA to Sumner, Mar. 8, 1861.

6. Clarke to Sumner, Dec. 8, 1860; JGP, MS-J, Mar. 5, 1861; drafts of letters to Lincoln, and Secretaries Seward and Chase, all dated Mar. 6, 1861.

7. Sumner to JGP, Mar. 9, 1861; JGP to Sumner, Mar. 12, 1861, Sumner MSS; Donald, *Sumner*, p. 384; JGP, MS-J, Mar. 9-16, 1861.

8. JGP to Sumner, Nov. 26, 1860; Sumner to Bird, Mar. 10, 1861, Bird MSS; CFA, Jr., *Autobiography*, pp. 100-102.

9. Bird to Sumner, Mar. 13, 1861, Sumner MSS.

10. The Sumner MSS include a bulky letter file devoted entirely to the politics of the Boston post office appointment.

11. Howe to Sumner, Mar. 13, 1861; W. C. Brown to Sumner, Mar. 14, 1861; Claflin to Sumner, Mar. 14, 1861; all in Sumner MSS.

12. Howe to Sumner, Mar. 13, 1861; G. L. Stevens to Sumner, Mar. 16, 1861; Bird to Sumner, Mar. 18, 1861; JGP to Sumner, Mar. 13, 1861; all in Sumner MSS.

13. Dana to Sumner, Mar. 13, 1861; Andrew to Sumner, Mar. 11, 18, 21, 1861; all in Sumner MSS.

14. Sumner to Blair, Mar. 23, 1861 (copy); Sumner to JGP, Mar. 29, 1861(telegram); JGP to W. H. Gardiner, Nov. 12, 1864, Gardiner MSS.

15. Sumner to Dana, Mar. 29, 1861, Dana MSS; Pierce to Sumner, Apr. 2, 1861, Sumner MSS.

16. J. E. Lodge to Sumner, Mar. 15, 1861, Sumner MSS; Sumner to Andrew, [March 1861], Andrew MSS; Donald, *Sumner*, p. 385.

17. JGP, MS-J, Mar. 29, Apr. 9, 17, 1861; FWP to Sumner, Apr. 2, 1861, Sumner MSS.

18. JGP to 3rd Asst. PMG, July 22, 1862, P. O. Letterbooks, I, 110-111.

19. JGP, MS-J, June 3, 15, 1861; JGP, MS-A, Notes, pp. 108-109; JGP to Sumner, Mar. 30, 1861; W. Thayer to Sumner, Apr. 17, 1861 (endorsed to JGP).

20. JGP to J. Goodrich, Apr. 20, 1861; J. Goodrich to JGP, [Apr. 21, 1861].

21. JGP to PMG, June 7, 1861, P. O. Letterbooks, I, 13, 32; JGP to Bird, Aug. 29, 1861, Bird MSS; Keyes to JGP, Sep. 2, 1861; JGP, MS-A, p. 252.

22. JGP to 1st Asst. PMG, Apr. 8, 1862, Feb. 6, 1863, P. O. Letterbooks, I, 77-81, 169; JGP, MS-J, Mar. 14-17, 1862. Palfrey spoke with President Lincoln briefly at the White House during this trip.

23. JGP to 1st Asst. PMG, July 22, 1862, Nov. 23, 1863, June 2, 1864, P. O. Letterbooks, I, 108, 293-294, II, 99, 156.

24. George A. Bacon to Sumner, Oct. 15, 1862; JGP to Sumner, Oct. 18, 1862.

25. JGP to Sumner, Nov. 4, 5, 1862; Sumner to JGP, Nov. 5, 7, 1862; John Lewis to JGP, Nov. 6, 1862; JGP to CFA, Nov. 9, 1862, Adams MSS.

26. Palfrey later developed a formula for insistent office seekers. The *Boston Daily Advertiser* of July 7, 1864, carried his statement that being overage, he would gladly hire any applicant as his substitute in the Army of the Potomac.

27. JGP, Memorandum, Nov. 20, 21, 1862; Chandler to JGP, Dec. 19, 1862.

28. J. H. Butler to Andrew, June 30, 1862, Andrew MSS; Sumner to JGP, Aug. 2, 1863.

29. JGP, MS-J, Sep. 9, 1864; JGP to Dana, Sep. 12, 1864, Dana MSS.

30. JGP, MS-A, pp. 253-255; JGP to CFA, Dec. 25, 1863, Adams MSS; JGP to Sparks, May 29, 1863, Sparks MSS; JGP to JCP, Nov. 19, 1863, Sep. 11, 1864.

31. JGP, Draft of article signed "P" for Salem *Gazette*.

32. H. Lee, Jr. to JGP, June 14, 1861; JGP to JCP, June 15, 1861.

33. Cameron to JGP, June 21, 1861; Sumner to JGP, June 26, 1861.

34. George A. Bruce, *The Twentieth Regiment of Massachusetts Volunteer Infantry, 1861-1865* (Boston, 1906). Frank Palfrey "was

Boston to the bone"; Catherine D. Bowen, *Yankee from Olympus, Justice Holmes and His Family* (Boston, 1944), p. 149. Bruce Catton, *Mr. Lincoln's Army* (Garden City, N.Y., 1951), pp. 75–76.

35. FWP to JGP (telegram), JGP to FWP, both Oct. 24, 1861.

36. JGP to CFA, Nov. 25, 1861, Adams MSS; FWP to JGP, Nov. 8, 1861, Feb. 4, July 9, 1862.

37. A. G. Browne, Jr., to F. W. Bird, Dec. 4, 1861, Bird MSS; C. E. Norton to JGP, Dec. 16, 1861; JGP, MS-J, Dec. 20, 1861; Catton, *Mr. Lincoln's Army*, pp. 72–73.

38. FWP to Sumner, Dec. 21, 1861, Jan. 6, 1862, Sumner MSS; JGP to Andrew (copy), Jan. 10, 1862; JGP to FWP, Jan. 11, 1862.

39. Andrew to JGP, Jan. 11, 1862; W. R. Lee to JGP, Apr. 29, 1862; FWP to Dana, Apr. 30, 1862, Dana MSS; FWP to JGP, Jan. 27, 1862; Phillips to JGP, Apr. 28, 1862; JGP, MS-J, May 2, 1862.

40. JGP to Trumbull, Apr. 30, 1862, Trumbull MSS; JGP to FWP, July 13, 1862; JGP to Anna Hallowell (draft), May 25, 1863.

41. JGP to MAP, Sep. 19, 1862.

42. JGP to JCP, Feb. 10, 1865.

43. JGP, MS-J, Nov. 2, 1862; Hallowell to JGP, Oct. 31, 1862.

44. JGP to C. G. Loring, Nov. 7, 1862, Loring MSS; JCP to JGP, Dec. 28, 1862.

45. MAP to JCP, May 17, 1862; JCP to MGP, Jan. 4, 1863.

46. JGP to JCP, Jan. 12, 1863.

47. JCP to MGP, May 18, 1863.

48. JGP, MS-J, Mar. 11, 26, Apr. 29, 1863; Recruiting Certificate, Nov. 22, 1864.

49. Parkes to JGP, Jan. 5, 1861; Mill to JGP, July 18, 1863.

50. JGP to Longfellow, May 14, 1861, Longfellow MSS; ARP to JCP, Dec. 6, 1861; D. N. Cooley to JGP, Aug. 20, 1864.

51. Hale to JGP, May 17, 1861; JGP to CFA, Mar. 5, 1863, Adams MSS.

52. JGP to WTP, Aug. 1, 1865.

53. JGP to British Unitarian Assn. (draft), Sep. 11, 1865; JGP, MS-J, Apr. 11–17, 1865.

XVI: The Celebrated New Englander

1. JGP, MS-J, July 1, 1865; JGP to JCP, July 1, 1865.

2. JCP to Crowninshield, May 4, 1865; JCP to JGP, Aug. 10, 1865.

3. Crowninshield to JGP, Oct. 2, 1865; JGP, MS-J, Dec. 31, 1865.

4. JGP to WTP, May 29, 1865; WTP to JGP, June 29, 1865.

5. MAP to WTP, July 29, 1865; JGP to WTP, Aug. 1, 1865.

6. WTP to JGP, Oct. 4, 14, 1865.

7. Seward to JGP, Nov. 6, 1865; JGP to WTP, Nov. 3, Dec. 6, 1865; WTP to JGP, Jan. 29, Feb. 7, 1866.

8. WTP to JGP, May 20, 1866.

9. HWP to JGP, June 28, Sep. 5, 1866; JGP to WTP, Sep. 27, 1866.

10. New York *Times*, Oct. 9, 1866; George Palfrey to JGP, Oct. 27, 1866.

11. MAP to JCP, July 6, 1868; JCP to ARP, June 18, 1868; JGP, MS-J, July 1, 7, 1868.

12. WTP to JGP, Sep. 30, 1858. The correspondence of family reconciliation is published in Frank Otto Gatell (ed.), "The Slave-holder and the Abolitionist; Binding Up a Family's Wounds," *The Journal of Southern History*, XXVII (August 1961), 368–391.

13. JGP to JCP, Dec. 7, 1863.

14. Chandler to JGP, Sep. 21, 1864; JGP to F. W. Bird (copy), Jan. 31, 1865; Bird to JGP, Feb. 2, 1865.

15. Amos Tuck to PMG (copy), May 22, 1865; JGP to CFA, May 27, 1865, Adams MSS.

16. Dennison to Sumner, June 29, 1865; JGP to CFA, Aug. 2, 1865, Adams MSS.

17. JGP to P. W. Chandler (copy), Apr. 25, 1867; *Boston Daily Advertiser*, Dec. 26, 1865; JGP to C. G. Loring, Dec. 28, 1865, Loring MSS; C. G. Loring to J. A. Andrew, Dec. 28, 1865, Andrew MSS; Fessenden to P. W. Chandler (copy), Dec. 29, 1865.

18. Sumner to JGP, Jan. 6, 1866; "Ex-Andersonville" to JGP, Sep. 26, 1866.

19. Burt to C. Deane, Apr. 10, 1866, Deane MSS; Boston *Evening Transcript*, Jan. 12, 1929.

20. Bird to Sumner, Apr. 13, 1867, Sumner MSS; Gardiner to JGP, Apr. 15, 1867.

21. Sumner to JGP, Apr. 14, 1867; Burt to JGP, Apr. 29, 1867; JGP, MS-J, June 18, 1869.

22. JGP to Longfellow, Mar. 6, 1868, Longfellow MSS; Wendell Phillips Garrison and Francis Jackson Garrison, *William Lloyd Garrison* (New York, 1889), IV, p. 230; JGP to W. H. Furness (draft), Dec. 17, 1866.

23. Henry Adams, *Education*, p. 29; JGP to T. Parsons, Oct. 8, 1867, Parsons MSS; Longfellow to Sumner, Dec. 8, 1867, Longfellow MSS.

24. JGP to W. H. Gardiner, Apr. 17, 1867, Gardiner MSS; JGP, MS-J, Jan. 26, 1868; JGP to CFA, June 25, 1866, Adams MSS.

25. JGP to R. C. Winthrop, Apr. 11, 1866, Winthrop MSS; C. Lowe to JGP, Feb. 1, 1867; JGP, MS-J, June 12, 1866.

26. *Ibid.*, May 2, Sep. 6, 1869, May 2, 1870.

27. Sumner to Howe, Mar. 26, 1868, Sumner MSS; JGP to Sumner, Apr. 11, 1868.

28. *Boston Daily Advertiser*, Jan. 2, 9, 25, Feb. 17, 26, 1869.

29. H. Adams to JGP, Feb. 19, 1869; JGP, MS-J, Mar. 5, 1869.

30. JGP to Sumner, Nov. 21, 1868; JGP to G. W. Julian, Feb. 8, 1869, Giddings-Julian MSS.

31. JGP to CFA, Aug. 2, 1869, Adams MSS; JGP to C. E. Norton, Nov. 7, 1870, C. Norton MSS.

32. JGP to F. B. Sanborn (draft), May 6, 1872; JGP to F. W. Bird, June 21, 1872, Bird MSS; JGP, MS-J, Nov. 5, 1872.

33. JGP, MS-J, June 28, 1868; JGP to W. H. Gardiner, Aug. 3, 1869, Gardiner MSS.

34. MAP to JCP, [March 1871]; JGP, MS-J, Oct. 4, 1871.

35. Ibid., Dec. 2, 1871; MAP to MGP, [1871]. For a deadly, fictional version of a New England widow and her daughters see Henry James' "Europe," a story based loosely on the Palfreys.

36. JGP to C. E. Norton, Apr. 5, 1855, C. Norton MSS; JGP, MS-J, Oct. 25, 1873.

37. JGP, Hist. of New England, I, 43.

38. S. H. Gay to W. C. Bryant, Sep. 6, 1877, Bryant-Godwin MSS.

39. JGP, Hist. of New England, II, 504n.

40. Ibid., p. 140.

41. Ibid., I, 43, 166, 181, 232; Longfellow to JGP, Dec. 28, 1864.

42. Hist. of New England, I, 274-278.

43. Ibid., I, 406-425, 472-512, II, 452-485. Recent historians have been more sympathetic to the Puritans in discussing the problem of security and obstreperous dissenters; for example, see Edwin S. Morgan, The Puritan Dilemma: The Story of John Winthrop (Boston, 1958), and Daniel J. Boorstin, The Americans: The Colonial Experience (New York, 1958).

44. John Wall to B. Mayer, Feb. 8, 1867, Mayer MSS; JGP, Hist. of New England, III, 109, IV, 484.

45. Ibid., II, 342, III, 100, IV, 229, 375, 469.

46. CFA, Jr., to JGP, Mar. 23, 1873; Henry Adams to JGP, Oct. 15, 1875, Harold Dean Cater (ed.), Henry Adams and his Friends (Boston, 1947), pp. 70-71. Palfrey started Henry Adams on his historical career, encouraging him to write an essay on John Smith and the Pocahontas legend; ibid., pp. 8-10, 14-15, 29-30. See also JGP to C. E. Norton, July 31, 1866, C. Norton MSS.

47. JGP, Hist. of New England, IV, 341-342, V, 488.

48. Ibid., III, viii; Boston Evening Transcript, Apr. 27, 1881.

49. JGP, MS-J, June 18, 1869.

50. Henry Adams, Education, p. 222.

51. Wilson to JGP, July 8, 1874.

52. CFA to JGP, Mar. 24, 1871, Adams MSS; JGP to Eloise Payne, Mar. 4, 1873, Payne MSS; JGP to W. H. Gardiner, Nov. 17, 1872, Mar. 18, 1873, Gardiner MSS.

53. JGP, MS-J, Dec. 3, 9, 1873; JGP to W. H. Gardiner, Jan. 3, 1874, Gardiner MSS.

54. H. W. Longfellow, MS-J, Aug. 10, 1877, Longfellow MSS; JGP, MS-J, Sep. 20, 22, 1877.

55. J. L. Sibley, MS-J, Apr. 27, 1880, HUA; JCP, Epilogue to JGP, MS-A, pp. 217-220.

56. FWP to W. H. Gardiner, Apr. 26, 1881, JGP to W. H. Gardiner, Nov. 17, 1872, both in Gardiner MSS.

57. Boston *Evening Transcript*, and *Boston Daily Advertiser*, both Apr. 27, 1881.

58. CFA, Jr., *Autobiography*, p. 100; JGP, MS-A, pp. 48-49.

Index